PIPER
A LEGEND ALOFT

Edward H. Phillips

 FLYING BOOKS INTERNATIONAL

1401 KINGSWOOD ROAD, EAGAN, MINNESOTA 55122-3811

PIPER — A Legend Aloft

By Edward H. Phillips

Published as part of the
"HISTORIC AIRCRAFT SERIES"
FLYING BOOKS INTERNATIONAL, Publishers & Wholesalers

1401 Kings Wood Rd., Eagan, MN 55122-3811
612/454-2493
James B. Horne, Publisher

On the front cover—Oil painting entitled "Solo Flight" by Douglas Nielson. Painting depicts young Jim Horne, owner of **Flying Books International**, on his first solo flight, Victory Airport, Brooklyn Center, MN, 1944.

Five significant Piper aircraft are depicted in gauche color sketches by reknowned aviation artist Josef Kotula, whose Model Airplane News covers, model kit box paintings and aviation scenes, were inspirational to buffs from the 1930's on.

On the frontispiece—An oil painting titled "CUB" by Douglas Nielson. The Cub in flight is superimposed over the loveable Piper Cub logo. Nielson was awarded an Honorable Mention at the 1992 EAA art competition.

The "**HISTORIC AIRCRAFT SERIES**" is published to document the careers and service of the men and machines that gave America wings. Other titles in this series from Flying Books International are:

Beechcraft, Pursuit of Perfection
by Edward H. Phillips

Cessna, A Master's Expression
by Edward H. Phillips

Travel Air, Wings Over the Prairie
by Edward H. Phillips

Wings of Cessna, Model 120 to the Citation III
by Edward H. Phillips

Speed, the Biography of Charles Holman
by Noel Allard

The 91 Before Lindbergh
by Peter Allen

DH-88: The Story of DeHavilland's Racing Comets
by David Ogilvy

Of Monocoupes and Men
by John Underwood

The Stinsons
by John Underwood

Aircraft Service Manual Reprints
Piper J-3 Cub
Aeronca 7AC Champ
Aeronca 11AC Chief
Taylorcraft BC-12D

Aircraft Flight Manual Reprints
F-51D Mustang
B-29 Superfortress

PIPER — A Legend Aloft

First published in 1993 by
Flying Books International,
Publishers & Wholesalers.
1401 Kings Wood Rd.,
Eagan, MN 55122 U.S.A.

© 1993 Flying Books International

Library of Congress Cataloging in Publication Data
90-81379
Phillips, Edward H.
PIPER
A Legend Aloft
A History of Piper Airplanes
ISBN 0-911139-14-1 Hardcover

Printed and bound in the United States of America
Art Director, Noel Allard
Layout, James B. Horne
Artists, Douglas Nielson
    Jo Kotula

FOREWORD

PIPER — A LEGEND ALOFT traces the genesis and evolution of the Piper Aircraft Corporation, its airplanes and their development from humble beginnings as the Taylor Brothers Aircraft Corporation in 1928, through the lean years of the Great Depression, the dark days of World War Two and onward into decades of expansion and growth.

The book is intended as a reference and historical guide for owners of Piper airplanes, and for those with an interest in how the company came to be one of the world's most prolific and successful manufacturers of general aviation aircraft. Each section of the publication is designed to present the development of Piper airplanes in a chronological format, beginning with the early Taylor brothers aircraft and proceeding through the Cheyenne series of turboprop business airplanes.

The author is indebted to the following people who helped make this book possible: A sincere, special thanks is due Piper aircraft historians Roger W. Peperell and Colin M. Smith, whose years of reseaching Piper history yielded much of the data on prototype Piper airplanes, constructor numbers and total aircraft produced; special thanks to Mal Holcomb, J. Earle Boyter, A. Stone Douglass, Charles M. Suma and Renee White of Piper Aircraft Corporation; Dennis Hoffman, Margaret Hoffman, Madelyn Blesh and former Piper company test pilot Clyde Smith, Sr., of Sentimental Journey and the Piper Aviation Museum in Lock Haven, Pennsylvania; Stephen E. Miller, who patiently reproduced hundreds of Piper photographs for the book; Christopher P. Fotos, who edited the text; Patricia Gangloff and Larry A. Richmond of the Bradford Area Public Library; Taylorcraft historians Chester L. Peek and Dr. James Hays; aero historians Peter M. Bowers and Joseph P. Juptner; former Piper engineers Grahame Gates and Fred E. Weick; Jim Horne and Cedric E. Galloway; John Zimmerman and the staff of Aviation Data in Wichita, Kansas; Vincent J. Berinati; Thomas Heitzman and Ted Koch, who provided a series of unique Piper photographs; Edward W. Stimpson and Shelly R. Snyder of the General Aviation Manufacturers Association who supplied additional production and shipment data about Piper aircraft; and the research library and photographic staff of the Smithsonian's National Air and Space Museum.

INTRODUCTION

Among American aircraft companies perhaps none is better known to the citizenry or more widely associated with private flying than Piper Aircraft Corporation. For decades the public has labeled any light airplane passing overhead as "a Piper Cub," testifying to the company's identity as a small aircraft builder.

The story of Piper's success, however, properly begins with the story of the Taylor brothers. The two energetic young men from Rochester, New York had their eyes fixed on the sky in the mid-years of that unforgettable decade known as the Roaring Twenties.

From 1925 to 1930 the talented Clarence Gilbert Taylor designed and built a series of attractive monoplanes featuring both open cockpits and enclosed cabins. In 1928 he bestowed upon his latest design the clever name "Chummy" to denote its two-place, side-by-side configuration.

When the expanding company moved to larger facilities at Bradford, Pennsylvania late in 1928, an enterprising businessman named William T. Piper, Sr., had become an investor-in-absentia and held stock in the infant company. Although the future of the Taylor Brothers Aircraft Corporation looked bright, the death of G.A. Taylor in 1928 and the financial holocaust that followed in the wake of the October, 1929 Wall Street debacle swiftly brought the tiny but successful company to the point of bankruptcy.

Into this desparate scene stepped Mr. Piper. In 1930 amidst a deepening Great Depression, he plunged into the uncertain and capricious aviation business by purchasing the assets of the defunct Taylor company.

Allied with C. Gilbert Taylor as chief engineer, Piper believed the newly formed Taylor Aircraft Company would survive the Depression if it built sturdy, economical and inexpensive airplanes designed for everyday flying from grass strips and cow pastures.

Fortunately, for pilots past, present and future, William T. Piper bravely gambled against the odds and won. His actions directly helped to engender a name that has become so famous and intimately associated with the name Piper.

It was the mating of Taylor's new, pedestrian two-place monoplane with the capricious but affordable Continental A-40 reciprocating engine that created the immortal Cub—an airplane that evolved to become the symbol of general aviation in the United States and the progenitor of future Piper and Taylor designs.

With C.G. Taylor's departure late in 1935, William Piper took control of the company and moved to Lock Haven, Pennsylvania, in spring, 1937. There it became Piper Aircraft Corporation in November of that year, and began its long sojourn to fame in American aeronautics.

The company weathered tough economic times through the late 1930s, and answered the call to arms during World War Two by providing thousands of Cubs to train fledgling pilots as well as large numbers of L-4 Grasshoppers for liaison and observation duties in every major theater of combat.

During the ensuing years of peace and prosperity, Piper returned to development of business and personal aircraft with famous names like Colt, Pacer and Tri-Pacer. In 1952 it unveiled the all-metal Apache twin-engine business airplane, followed over the years by the single-engine Comanche and the popular Cherokee family of light aircraft.

In the 56 years since 1937 Piper has built more than 127,000 airplanes, ranging from the ubiquitous J-3 Cub to the turboprop Cheyenne 400. The death of company founder and guiding light William T. Piper, Sr., on January 15, 1970, ushered in a dark era frought with hostile takeovers, mismanagement, and rising product liability costs.

Before Piper's death, however, the company's course already was being charted by powers outside of the Piper family. Chris Craft, famous for its boats, shared ruling power at Piper with rival corporation Bangor Punta in 1969 before that company obtained complete control in 1977.

Lear Siegler, in turn, took over Bangor Punta in 1984 and was itself acquired by Forstmann Little & Company in 1987, who in turn sold Piper Aircraft Corporation to Monroe Stuart Millar in May of that year. After only four years Millar was forced to place Piper Aircraft Corporation under the protection of Federal Bankruptcy laws and production slowed to a standstill.

Following a series of buyout attempts by foreign groups that failed to materialize, Piper Aircraft Corporation slowly began to emerge from Chapter 11 and set its course toward profitability in 1993.

The business courage and skill displayed more than half a century ago by William T. Piper, Sr., carried him to lasting fame and earned the company a well-deserved place in the annals of aviation history. Mr. Piper's most fitting epitaph is not found on a cemetery headstone, but upon the airplanes bearing his name. They have become a legend aloft.

William T. Piper

CHAPTER ONE
THE TAYLOR YEARS

Polio—a dreaded, deadly and debilitating disease that for centuries had inflicted terrible pain and anguish on the human race. As the 20th Century dawned not only was there no cure for polio, but no method of prevention against it.

When an 18-month-old toddler named Clarence Gilbert Taylor contracted the illness in 1900, it left the boy with a permanent paralysis in his left leg and foot. Indeed, fate had dealt Taylor a harsh blow. Yet, from that time forward, the polio that had struck him down in his youth also bred within him a fierce, unconquerable spirit of defiance and sheer determination to

Self-taught engineer and aviator Clarence Gilbert Taylor spent his adult life pursuing aviation dreams. The Taylor E-2 Cub and its successors helped preserve the American light airplane industry and promoted commercial aviation through the troubled years of the Great Depression. (Chester L. Peek via Duke Iden)

succeed that was to prove both a blessing and a curse throughout his life.

Born in Rochester, New York, on September 25, 1898, Clarence Gilbert was one of six children in the family of Arthur Taylor, a highly skilled tool and die maker and, perhaps most importantly, a natural, self-taught engineer. He was born in England and emigrated with his family to Hamilton, Ontario, Canada in 1885. He was apprenticed as a machinist at an early age, and moved to Rochester, New York in 1889 where he operated a machine shop that specialized in custom metalwork as well as building bicycles.

Throughout his son's childhood, Arthur Taylor patiently encouraged C.G.—as he became known to the family and eventually to virtually everyone—to be successful at whatever he chose to do despite his disability. In addition to being a spirited, determined individual, C.G. Taylor possessed a brilliant mind and a talent for things mechanical. At an early age he began mastering the operation of basic machine tools, and under the tutelage of his father gained a deep respect for craftsmanship.

A turning point in Taylor's life came in 1911, when the 13 year-old boy saw famed aviator Calbraith Perry Rodgers flying his Wright biplane dubbed the "Vin Fiz" in the first successful attempt to span the nation by air. After witnessing Rodgers flying slowly overhead, Clarence Gilbert Taylor became hopelessly infected with flying fever. Airplanes immediately

caught the youthful C.G.'s fancy and became his passion for the next 70 years.

From that day onward, he began a tumultuous struggle to build and sell rugged, affordable and dependable light airplanes—Taylorcrafts—that have since become the paragon of simplicity and proudly withstood the test of time.

Determined to construct and pilot his own flying machine, the teenage Taylor designed and fabricated what could be considered the first Taylorcraft during his years as a student at the West High School in Rochester. Using the small attic of the family home as his workshop, he built the craft in sections and lowered them to the ground for final assembly in the yard below.

Although C.G. Taylor had built his first airplane, he had no engine to power it. To make matters worse, World War One was raging in Europe and the availability of small powerplants for airplanes was almost nonexistent. Therefore, the airplane never flew.

That setback, however, did not dampen Taylor's enthusiasm for aviation and only further whetted his appetite for flight. He made several trips to Buffalo, New York and tried to get a ride aloft. Finally, he succeeded. During his junior year in high school, Taylor's persistence was rewarded with a brief flight in the front cockpit of a Curtiss JN-4 "Jenny" biplane.

Having experienced the unique thrill of flight, C.G. was certain that a career in aeronautics was his destiny. When he graduated from high school in 1917, C.G. had serious intentions of getting into the flying game somehow, somewhere, someday.

Taylor went to work that year for the Thomas Anderson Gun Company in Rochester, gaining valuable engineering and craftsmanship experience that would help in his quest to build airplanes. In 1918, he took employment with the Northeast Electric Company in the same city, working as an apprentice and gaining additional engineering experience.

With the help of their father, C.G. Taylor and his brother Gordon rebuilt and modified a two-place Curtiss JN-4 into a three-place configuration. In 1927 they flew the big biplane on barnstorming tours in the northern New York region. The brothers operated under the name "North Star Aerial Service Corporation." (Chester L. Peek)

Perched upon the JN-4's often cantankerous Curtiss OX-5 engine, C.G. Taylor makes adjustments to the powerplant during a barnstorming stop at Sodus, New York. Note vertical placement of water radiator and redesigned nose section. (Mitch Mayborn Collection via Tom Heitzman)

Northeast Electric later became famous as the Delco Appliance Co.

With the war to end all wars concluded and peace restored to the world, C.G. looked forward to making his aviation dreams come true. In 1920 he took the first step toward making those dreams become reality. He joined forces with his brother Gordon and their father in operating the Tool, Die and Specialty Co. in Rochester.

For the next five years, in his spare time C.G. Taylor studied aeronautics from books and continued to assimilate knowledge of machinery, design and production methods that would become invaluable in the years ahead. In addition to gaining knowledge and experience, Taylor also gained a wife and life-long companion when he married Josephine Woodward on March 31, 1920.

Both Clarence Gilbert and Gordon Taylor shared a common interest in aviation, with C.G. exhibiting

An early Taylor-designed aircraft was the "Loomis Special" monoplane delivered in August, 1926 to pilot Jack Loomis. The aircraft's cabin seated two passengers ahead of the open cockpit. Note assist step on right side of the fuselage and push-pull rod connected to the aileron. (Chester L. Peek via Robert Taylor)

a penchant for design and construction and Gordon a talent for public relations and salesmanship. February, 1926 would prove to be the true genesis of C.G. Taylor's aviation career. That year the brothers bought a war-surplus Curtiss JN-4 for $750 from Jack Loomis, a Binghamton, New York resident and barnstorming pilot.

He flew the airplane, with C.G. as a passenger and new student pilot, to Newark, New York where C.G. Taylor had moved from Rochester. Working in his father's machine shop that winter, Clarence Gilbert, Gordon and Arthur Taylor rebuilt the capricious JN-4 and incorporated their own innovations and improvements during the process.

Modifications included designing a metal main landing gear assembly and relocating the water coolant radiator above the 90 hp. Curtiss OX-5 engine. The fuselage was enlarged to accommodate three separate cockpits, the stagger of the double-bay wings was increased and the wing panels rerigged to move the airplane's center of gravity forward.

After completion in April, 1927 the airplane was trucked to Binghamton, assembled and test-flown by Loomis. Satisfied with Taylor's work on the modified JN-4, Loomis agreed to instruct Taylor in the rudiments of airmanship and the young man even-

The Loomis Special was powered by a 10-cylinder Anzani air-cooled, static radial engine rated at 110 hp. The obsolete Anzani was a capricious powerplant, but was inexpensive and easy to obtain during the late 1920s. (Chester L. Peek via Robert Taylor)

Arthur Taylor (center) stands next to the Loomis Special flanked by Loomis and another pilot on his right, with sons Clarence Gilbert and Gordon Taylor on his left. The airplane was damaged in August, 1927 but was rebuilt and flown using a 135 hp. Hallett static radial engine. (Chester L. Peek via Robert Taylor)

The prototype Arrowing A-2 was built by the Taylor Brothers Aircraft Manufacturing Company, located in Rochester, New York. Appropriately named the Chummy, Taylor's little monoplane seated two occupants side-by-side. Note shock cord suspension on main landing gear and absence of wheel brakes. (Mitch Mayborn collection via Tom Heitzman)

The Chummy was powered by a 90 hp., 10-cylinder Anzani static radial engine featuring spring-loaded, suction-operated intake valves. The exhaust valves were opened by cam-operated push rods and rocker arms. Note push-pull rod connected to the elevator and slack rudder control cable. (Peter M. Bowers collection) ▶

tually soloed the big biplane.

Thrilled by their success and full of renewed enthusiam for aviation, C.G. and Gordon formed the North Star Aerial Service Corporation, based in Rochester. During the summer they barnstormed in the Taylor "Jenny" around the northern New York region, sometimes earning up to $400 per day giving rides.

Impressed with what the Taylor brothers had done with the old JN-4, Jack Loomis wanted them to design and build a special, three- to four-place ship designed expressly for the still popular—and sometimes lucrative—barnstorming trade.

C.G. and Gordon tackled the job with gusto, and the custom-built monoplane was soon ready to fly. The airplane featured a strut-braced, parasol-wing configuration with a wide, open cockpit for the pilot and one passenger located aft of an enclosed cabin that seated two passengers.

Taylor used a Clark Y airfoil for the wing, which spanned nearly 40 feet. The welded steel tube fuselage had a length of 24 feet, and a small door on the left side allowed entry to the forward cabin. An Anzani 10-cylinder, static, air-cooled radial engine rated at 110 hp. powered the ship.

In spite of the sometimes whimsical powerplant and its lackluster horsepower, the new cabin monoplane performed well—a characteristic that would become inherent in all future Taylorcraft airplanes. The cabin biplane was sold in August, 1926 but was not placed on register until May, 1927. The ship was designated as constructor number 2 and was wrecked in August of that year.

Despite their initial successes, both C.G. and Gordon Taylor were unable to devote themselves full-time to their aviation interests. In 1927 C.G. left the family tool and die business and went to work as a designer for the Knowlton Paper Box and Machine

Company in Rochester.

In May, 1927 Taylor and millions of other Americans celebrated the success of Charles A. Lindbergh's epic flight from New York to Paris which precipitated a flying frenzy in the United States. Sensing that the once uncertain market for private airplanes had suddenly exploded with opportunity, in September, 1927 C.G. and Gordon formed the Taylor Brothers Aircraft Manufacturing Company, based in Rochester.

That fall C.G. began designing a two-place, high-wing monoplane powered by a cantankerous and obsolete 10-cylinder Anzani radial engine of 90 hp. Constructed during the winter of 1927-1928, the airplane featured a welded steel tube fuselage, wood wings and with spruce spars and was fabric-covered in accor-

Early in 1928 the Taylor Brothers Aircraft Corporation built a second airplane known as the Taylor A-2 Chummy, powered by a seven-cylinder Ryan Siemens-Halske SH-11 static radial engine rated at 96 hp. The airplane was displayed at the Detroit aircraft exhibition held in April, 1928 in Detroit, Michigan. (Peter M. Bowers collection)

4

During a demonstration flight at the Detroit show the second Chummy crashed, killing Gordon Taylor. Note the three-strut arrangement designed by C.G. Taylor to support the wing. The Chummy had a maximum speed of 105-110 mph. with the Ryan Siemens-Halske engine. (Chester L. Peek)

Photographed in 1931, the original Taylor Brothers Aircraft Corporation factory built at Bradford, Pennsylvania in 1929 to produce the Chummy is the large building at left. Smaller buildings at right were constructed to support production of the E-2 Cub. (Piper Aviation Museum)

dance with standard practice of the era. Completed in February, 1928 it was registered as X4203 and assigned constructor number 3.

True to its name, the Arrowing A-2 Chummy's cockpit seated two snugly in a side-by-side configuration. Maximum gross weight was 1,500 lb., with a maximum speed of 110 mph., a crusing speed of 100 mph. and a landing speed of 38 mph.

The market appeal and performance of the Chummy, coupled with the public's increasingly insatiable demand for small airplanes convinced the Taylors it was worthy of being produced in quantity. Therefore, in April, 1928 the company name was changed to Taylor Brothers Aircraft Corporation. A second aircraft was under construction, designated as the Taylor A-2 Chummy and assigned constructor number 4.

The two-place monoplane was completed in the spring of 1928 and displayed at the large Detroit air exposition that April. Powered by a Ryan-Siemens Halske SH-11 static, air-cooled radial engine rated at 96 hp., the sporty little Chummy created much interest at the show where it competed for attention amongst the Travel Airs, Cessnas, Stinsons and Wacos of the day.

Being the more gregarious of the two brothers, Gordon attended to sales promotion at the exhibition and made demonstration flights with the little monoplane. Unfortunately, on April 24 during a demonstration flight the Chummy crashed, killing Gordon Taylor.

Devastated, C.G. Taylor withdrew from aviation for a brief time to ponder the future and what it held for his career as well as the fledgling Taylor Brothers Aircraft Corporation. Deeply saddened at the loss of his brother and friend but determined to forge ahead, C.G. eventually returned to building airplanes. Based on success with the earlier A-2 Chummy, Taylor developed the improved B-2 Chummy in the summer of 1928.

He intended to sell the airplane with either a Ryan-Siemens Halske or a 90 hp. Kinner K-5 static, air-cooled radial engine. The Kinner eventually was selected to power production airplanes.

The sturdy, attractive B-2 Chummy monoplane had a wingspan of 34 feet, a length of 22 feet 6 inches and stood 7 feet 6 inches tall. With a gross weight of 1,643 lb., the airplane had a maximum speed of 110 mph. and cruised at 90 mph.

Powered by a Kinner K-5 engine, the prototype B-2 was completed in June, 1928, registered 7303 and assigned constructor number 7. A second B-2 was

registered X140E in November and was used only for static display. The improved Chummy sold for about $4,000—a relatively high price at that time for an aircraft in the entry-level, lightweight class.

It should be noted that in addition to the Chummy, Taylor also completed work on a special, four-place monoplane powered by a 180 hp. Hispano-Suiza engine. Fitted with EDO floats, the airplane reportedly was used during the Prohibition Era to fly loads of liquor across the border from Canada to the United States. A second, similar airplane, however, was not completed.

As the fateful year of 1929 began, C.G. Taylor was optimistic about the future as he prepared the tiny company to produce the Kinner-powered Chummy. The stock market was still flying high, and it seemed as though everyone wanted to invest money in the airplane business or learn to fly.

The first production B-2 Chummy, constructor number 9, registered X492, was completed in February. The small facilities at Rochester were rapidly becoming inadequate to support expanded production. Larger quarters were needed if C.G. were to meet the anticipated demand for his airplane.

To Taylor's rescue came the city of Bradford, Pennsylvania. Located near Pennsylvania's northern border with the State of New York, Bradford was a bustling oil and lumber town in the mid-1920s with aspirations to broaden its industrial base.

In the autumn of 1928, a group of men representing the Bradford Board of Commerce had visited the

The Kinner K-5 five-cylinder, air-cooled static radial engine powered the B-2 Taylor Chummy series and proved to be a reliable powerplant. Manufactured by the Kinner Airplane and Motor Corporation, Glendale, California, the K-5 developed 90 hp. at 1,810 rpm. or 110 hp. at 1,880 rpm., weighed 278 lb. and cost $1,800. (Smithsonian Institution, National Air and Space Museum Negative Number 93-2076)

The first prototype Taylor B-2 Chummy was built at Rochester, New York in June, 1928 and assigned constructor number 7. Registered 7303 the airplane was powered by a 90 hp. Kinner air-cooled, static radial engine. (Piper Aviation Museum)

Taylor facilities in Rochester to evaluate the company's potential. After inspecting the shops and discussing business with Taylor and other company officials, the men from Bradford were impressed with what they saw.

Bradford, however, was not the only city interested in luring Taylor to a new home. A group of businessmen from Utica, New York had considered making a similar offer to relocate Taylor to that city, but the lack of a suitable airport thwarted further efforts and the quest was terminated.

J.M. Brooder, a member of the investigating team from Bradford, said the under-capitalized corporation "possesses a good character" and that Taylor's bankers reported the company's fiscal responsibility was "first class" but added that "it has no money."

After returning to Bradford and discussing the matter, the Pennsylvania bankers and oil men were willing to provide Taylor with stock purchases worth $50,000 if he would relocate the company to Bradford. Another stipulation of the agreement was that Taylor would agree to use Bradford oil products in the new production airplanes.

When Taylor and his little band of workers received the formal offer in October, it seemed heaven-sent. Like many other budding airplane builders of the time, Taylor was long on talent but short on cash.

CERTIFYING THE TAYLOR B-2 CHUMMY

In May, 1929 C.G. Taylor spent more than a week in Washington, D.C., discussing design and construction details of his B-2 Chummy monoplane with aeronautical inspectors and engineers assigned to the Bureau of Air Commerce. For nearly a year prior to his Washington visit, Taylor had been carefully documenting stress analysis, construction and performance data on the Chummy in preparation for government approval.

Chiefly because of the company's limited financial resources and Taylor's desire to put the Chummy into production as soon as possible, he decided to obtain Group Two Approval. The Group Two certification method was less expensive and more expedient than enduring the more complex and costly Approved Type Certificate procedure.

Group Two Approval was awarded in memoran-

dum or letter form, and was often sought for modification in gross weight, engine type and major design changes made to a particular airplane. Although intentionally less stringent, the process was demanding and required inspections to ensure compliance with manufacturing processes as well as flight tests to assess an aircraft's structural integrity, airworthiness and handling characteristics.

Following initial review of the Chummy design in May, Bureau of Air Commerce officials authorized a series of flight evaluations prior to issuing final approval. Government inspectors already had flown the aircraft and the scheduled tests were completed by summer.

Taylor's little monoplane had met or exceeded all requirements for the issuance of a Group Two Approval and on August 27, 1929, the aircraft was formally granted Memorandum Number 2-114. Taylor received confirmation of the Memorandum via a telegram from Washington.

The approval applied only to the Taylor B-2 Chummy as a two-place, open cockpit land monoplane powered by a 90 hp. Kinner K-5 radial engine. Maximum gross weight was limited to 1,643 lb., and the approval was valid for constructor number 9 and above.

Taylor B-2 Chummy constructor number 9, registered C492 is illustrated after issuance of the Group Two approval. Constructor number 12 and constructor number 14 also were approved under the memorandum. (Mitch Mayborn collection via Tom Heitzman)

Following C.G.'s tentative acceptance, Andrew W. Legge, chairman of the stock committee, told the citizens of Bradford that the money had to be raised quickly in order to bring the company to town.

By October 26, $20,000 had been subscribed and several oil companies in the area were planning to invest as well. Officials of a local lumber company offered to trade building materials for the factory for remuneration in Taylor company stock. The majority of stock subscriptions had been sold by December.

H.M. Shaw, business manager for the Taylor Brothers Aircraft Corporation, said that about $17,000 from the sale of Taylor stock would be used to construct a factory building at the local Emery Airport. The facility would be 90 feet wide and 100 feet long, he said.

L.S. Bannister, who served as secretary and treasurer for the Taylor company, said of the 2,000 shares of common stock originally issued by the Taylor Brothers Aircraft Corporation in Rochester, 1,040 shares had been subscribed and were owned or controlled by Taylor, Shaw, Bannister and other company officials. The remainder were unsold.

In early November, Taylor had informed the Bradford Board of Commerce that he intended to move the company to Pennsylvania and planned to establish limited operations in temporary facilities until the factory was completed. Shaw projected that at least 100 Chummys would be built in the first year of operation at Bradford, with production eventually reaching one aircraft per day. He said the spacious new factory would be capable of producing 200 airplanes annually—a highly-optimistic projection.

Having a large manufacturing facility located directly on an established airport would make operations much easier for Taylor. In Rochester, airplanes were built and assembled, then dismantled and trucked about seven miles to the municipal airport where they were reassembled and test flown before delivery.

Among the businessmen who championed Taylor's move to Bradford was William H. Emery, a well-known pilot and Travel Air airplane distributor for the Eastern Unites States region. In February, 1929 the Board of Commerce paid Emery $1,000 for land "located on the cross-roads at the local airport on the southeast side of the old Erie (railroad) right-of-way, along the tracks adjacent to the old school house," according to the Bradford Era newspaper.

Blueprints for the factory were completed in early February and ground-breaking was scheduled for mid-month after contractor bids had been awarded. Of the $50,000 stock offering, less than $30,000 had been subscribed, the remainder being delayed until property was secured.

Although about $18,000 worth of Taylor stock remained to be sold, construction of the new factory was underway by March and cost about $20,000 to complete. Late in March, Taylor Brothers Aircraft Corporation officials sought and received approval from the Bradford Board of Commerce to incorporate under the laws of the State of Pennsylvania. Of the five men chosen to serve on the company's Board of Directors, three were Bradford citizens. Although the company had no permanent facilities, an office was located at the Option House in the city.

With incorporation assured and financing forthcoming, Taylor expected to begin manufacturing Chummys early in June. That month, however, Captain Richard Reid of Chicago announced that he intended to move the Taylor company to the Windy City.

Reid was a pilot who had flown during the recent Memorial Day aviation celebration held in Bradford. He also was president of the Universal Aeronautical Association of Illinois and of the Aeronautical Society of America. An optimistic Captain Reid promised to sell 50 Chummys per year in the Chicago area alone, and vowed to take delivery of the first three production airplanes himself.

To counter the Chicago threat, 50 prominent oil and businessmen met at the Hotel Emery in Bradford and launched a campaign to raise an additional $35,000 in stock to complete the company's financing and keep C.G. Taylor and the Chummy in Bradford. Among the three men representing the Board of Commerce at the meeting was one William T. Piper, Sr.

Although Reid's threat to move the Taylor Brothers Aircraft Corporation to Chicago proved impotent, it had galvanized the citizenry of Bradford to take action. Money was raised to help accelerate construction of the new factory.

In September, 1929 the small building adjacent to the local airport was nearing completion and production machinery was being installed. Only a few workers had been hired to build the Chummy, but plans called for hiring up to 12 additional employees. Taylor himself confidently predicted manufacture of at least 50 Chummys in the first year of production.

Unfortunately, friend and fellow aviator William Emery did not live to see C.G. Taylor's Chummy emerge from the Braford factory. In September, 1929 he was piloting a Travel Air monoplane in darkness and dense fog when the airplane crashed into a mountainside, killing Emery, his brother and two other passengers. He was only 20 miles from Bradford when the accident occurred.

Emery's untimely death, however, spared him the agony of the approaching Great Depression. Even as finishing touches were being put on the Taylor Brothers Aircraft Corporation factory that summer, the national economy was showing serious signs of instability.

Some businessmen—including those with money in aviation—were becoming increasingly uneasy. The shock waves of uncertainty were felt all the way from New York to Los Angeles as well as the small city of Bradford.

Most people, including Taylor, were too busy planning for the future to seriously consider the economic ramifications that could result from the wild fluctuations occurring with worrisome regularity on Wall Street. After all, it was the "Roarin' Twenties"!

The roar was about to cease in the months ahead, however, as a handful of company workers struggled to complete the first Bradford-built B-2 Chummy in the autumn of 1929. Sales were almost nonexistent, and some of the Bradford stockholders—now including William T. Piper—knew the Chummy's nearly $4,000 price tag was largely to blame. True to his stubborn nature, however, C.G. Taylor staunchly defended the airplane and its cost.

Members of the Bradford Board of Commerce were becoming impatient for a return on their investment. It had become obvious to the investors, and the citizens of Bradford, that the Taylor Brothers Aircraft Corporation was not the aeronautical bonanza they had hoped it would be.

As a member of the Taylor board of directors, Mr. Piper was well aware of the young company's problems and offered a partial solution. In August, 1929 the Board of Commerce and Piper reached an unique agreement.

Piper was given deed to the land with the stipulation that he would compensate the Board "if the property can be made to pay off said sum of $1,000," according to the agreement. He obtained a loan and bought the land and the factory, and agreed to allow Taylor to use the facility to manufacture airplanes until the company's financial health improved.

In addition, the agreement stipulated that if the Taylor Brothers company eventually repaid Piper for his investment or if Piper sold the land, he would pay the Board of Commerce the $1,000 they had originally paid W.H. Emery for the property.

Despite Mr. Piper's plans, stock subscriptions and a new factory, no production airplanes had been built in Bradford when that black day in October, 1929 dawned. Empires collapsed overnight, dreams were shattered and the sinister veil of the Great Depression settled over America like a plague.

When Wall Street crashed, so did prospects for Chummy sales. Taylor's hopes of selling 50 to 100 airplanes in the first year vanished into thin air. Clinging to his dreams despite overwhelming odds, in November Taylor was still struggling to build airplanes. Selling them would prove virtually impossible.

Despite the onset of the Great Depression, early in November the Bradford Board of Commerce voted unanimously "to make every effort to retain" the Taylor Brothers Aircraft Corporation "as a Bradford industry," Colonel A.D. Burns, president of the board, said.

Of the $50,000-worth of Taylor Brothers stock originally offered only $29,000 had been purchased by Bradford citizens and companies by November, 1929. Of that amount, $20,000 had been spent to build the factory, buy machinery and complete two airplanes.

Burns emphasized that "the Taylor company must have money to go on" and that the B-2 Chummy "was a worthy craft fully capable of exciting favorable attention." As a result of the meeting, special committees were formed and charged with selling the remaining stock to the local citizenry.

As the Bradford Board Of Commerce struggled to sell stock and keep their fledgling airplane company alive, C.G. Taylor was busy preparing his factory to produce the Chummy. Although the Kinner K-5 radial engine was standard on the B-2 series, Taylor replaced the optional and expensive Ryan-Siemens Halske radial with the inexpensive Brownbach Tiger static radial engine.

Sporting six-cylinders instead of the more conventional seven- or nine-cylinder configurations, the 90 hp. Brownbach powerplant was a product of the Light Manufacturing and Foundry Co., of Pottstown, Pennsylvania. Although Taylor offered the engine as an option for the B-2 Chummy, no evidence is known to exist that indicates the Brownbach Tiger was installed in a Chummy built by Taylor.

The Chummy was offered in two versions—the Trainer and the Sport. The two airplanes were described by Taylor sales literature as being identical in performance and specifications, and featured dual control sticks, adjustable stabilizer, detachable, swing-away engine mount and Fabrikoid leather upholstery. The Sport, however, also incorporated a cabin heater, wheel brakes, tail wheel, an airspeed indicator and a magnetic compass.

Prices in late 1929 for the Taylor B-2 Chummy Trainer equipped with the Kinner or Brownbach powerplants were $3,985 and $3,735 respectively. The Sport variant powered by the Kinner or Brownbach engine sold for $4,375 and $4,125 respectively.

During the autumn months Taylor had designed and built a special, modified Chummy for the Guggenheim Safe Aircraft Contest. Constructor number 7 B-2 Chummy was rebuilt as constructor number 10 and designated as the C-2 variant with a variable-incidence wing.

The Guggenheim event was held in December, 1929 at Mitchel Field on Long Island. Sponsored by the Daniel F. Guggenheim Fund, the contest offered the huge sum of $150,000 to the designer of the world's safest aircraft. Taylor hoped to clinch the prize but he faced overwhelming competition from more established aircraft companies that were prepared, both technically and financially, for the difficult challenge.

With his hopes flying high, Taylor had the C-2 Chummy flown to Long Island for the competition. Although the airplane successfully completed a series of preliminary trials, it was unable to meet a require-

After relocating to Bradford, Pennsylvania, Taylor modified B-2 Chummy constructor number 7 as the C-2 Chummy for the 1929 Guggenheim safe airplane competition. The aircraft was fitted with a variable incidence wing and was powered by a 90 hp. Kinner K-5 static radial engine. (Mitch Mayborn collection via Tom Heitzman)

Although the C-2 was competitive early in the Guggenheim challenge, it eventually was eliminated from the competition. Note drooped trailing edge of variable incidence wing. The ship was dismantled after returning to Bradford. (Mitch Mayborn collection via Tom Heitzman)

The final Taylor Chummy sold was photographed in front of the W. H. Emery Travel Air hangar at Bradford. Note refinements made to the aircraft compared with earlier Chummys, including deletion of third lift strut, installation of a one-piece windshield, and exhaust collector ring in front of the 90 hp. Kinner K-5 static radial engine. (Piper Aviation Museum)

ment to maintain steady flight at slow speed and was subsequently eliminated. The airplane was returned to Bradford and eventually dismantled.

Guggenheim officials selected the Curtiss Tanager as the safest airplane and winner of the grand prize. Speaking to the Bradford Board of Commerce early in December, C.G. Taylor lamented that the C-2 was unable to win the competition but said he "had several improvements in mind" that could be incorporated for future safe airplane contests.

Taylor Brothers Aircraft Corporation treasurer William T. Piper also addressed the meeting and praised Taylor and the Chummy for their efforts to win the prize. The board's disappointment that the C-2 was not victorious "was greatly allayed by the extrememly creditable showing made in the competition with more expensive ships manufactured by companies in business for many years," Piper said.

Unfortunately, by July, 1930 sales of outstanding stock had been poor, and the Bradford Board of Commerce was virtually impotent to help their struggling aircraft company remain in operation. With the private airplane market in shambles and no money forthcoming to capitalize the business, Taylor designed and built a small, primary training glider in an effort to stay solvent and wait for better times. Only one glider was built.

In 1930 C.G. Taylor designed an inexpensive single-seat glider in an effort to save the company from bankruptcy. Only one was built, but the glider helped establish William T. Piper and C.G. Taylor's concept for a lightweight, low-powered airplane that became the legendary Cub. (Piper Aviation Museum)

As C.G. Taylor quickly learned, the country was flooded with cheap gliders produced by Cessna Aircraft Company, Alexander Eaglerock and other builders in their own vain attempt to stay in the black. The powerless ships cost as little as $300, complete with launching apparatus.

By August, 1930 the end was near. After building six B-2 Chummys—three of them at Bradford—the Taylor Brothers Aircraft Corporation was on the verge of bankruptcy. All of the cash from the stock purchases was gone, and Taylor had obtained loans from a Bradford bank to help stave off the final collapse.

Mr. Piper, however, had other plans. Although he was not a pilot and harbored only a minor interest in aviation itself, Piper believed there was a market for light airplanes despite the Great Depression. He suggested to Taylor and the company board of directors that an inexpensive, simple aircraft should be designed to replace the high-priced Chummy.

In addition, Piper intended to sell the airplane primarily to operators of flying schools, not private buyers. It was a bold and novel concept. Discouraged but undaunted, Taylor took up the challenge and returned to his drawing board.

Because Piper had been using his oil money to help keep the factory doors open, he already had assumed the title and office of company treasurer. With liabilities outweighing assets, he realized that the most prudent option for the Taylor Brothers Aircraft Company was insolvency. Piper filed a petition for voluntary bankruptcy and when the assets were declared for sale, he bought them for less than $800.

The business was renamed Taylor Aircraft Company, with C.G. Taylor holding 50% interest and the title of president. Mr. Piper owned the other 50% and again declared himself treasurer.

Taylor was still in aviation, but he was disheartened. The onset of the Depression had dealt him the third in a series of hard blows—his polio affliction, the death of his brother and the loss of his airplane business. With Piper as his partner, Taylor knew he no longer was in direct control of his destiny.

Fortunately for thousands of future pilots around the world as well as the United States aviation industry itself, William T. Piper and C.G. Taylor took the risks of introducing a new airplane into a Depression market, and in so doing created one of the most enduring legends in aviation history.

CHAPTER TWO
BIRTH OF THE CUB

As the Great Depression tightened its merciless grip on America in 1930, the design genius of Clarence Gilbert Taylor and the business acumen of William Thomas Piper were combined to create the immortal Cub—the airplane that saved general aviation in America.

Both men had been raised to be members of America's hard-working blue collar class, and each had learned the virtues of hard labor as they grew to manhood. William T. Piper was born in Knapp Creek, New York, on January 8, 1881, to Thomas and Sarah Maltby Piper. His father was in the oil business—a profession young William would one day embrace for himself. At age 17 he enlisted in the United States Army to fight in the Spanish-American War of 1898, and saw limited action against the enemy. After his discharge from the service he attended Harvard University and was graduated in 1903 with a degree in mechanical engineering.

He worked in construction for nearly 12 years before teaming up with business associate Ralph Lloyd in 1915 to found the Dallas Oil Company in Bradford, Pennsylvania. William Piper was following in his father's footsteps at last, and airplanes were the farthest thing from his mind.

When America entered the World War in 1917, Piper was given the rank of captain in the Army Corps of Engineers but did not serve in Europe. By 1919, he was back in civilian life striving to make a living amongst Bradford's plethora of oil fields.

He and his wife, the former Marie van de Water, had five children including three boys who eventually played active roles in their father's aviation business; William, Jr., Thomas Francis and Howard. An astute businessman and stern father, Mr. Piper not only had the challenge of raising his three boys but also the monumental task of raising an airplane company from the depths of bankruptcy to profitability. Unfortunately, Mrs. Piper died in December, 1937.

In July, 1930 C.G. Taylor began designing what would become his most famous flying machine and one of the most important airplanes ever conceived and produced. The challenges to create an inexpensive, docile, and cheap-to-fly airplane in the midst of the Great Depression seemed insurmountable, but he was determined to succeed.

It was of paramount importance to Taylor and Piper that the new ship be as simple and spartan as possible, chiefly because production costs had to be kept to an absolute minimum to achieve a low price. Therefore, every detail of the aircraft's materials and construction were considered to be critical.

After deliberation and discussions with Piper, Taylor settled on a high-wing, two-place tandem seat configuration for the new aircraft. He would design the ship to have a maximum gross weight of about 800-900 lb. and a wing loading of less than 5 lb. per square foot to ensure benign, low-speed handling characteristics.

In its final configuration, the wing spanned 35 feet 2 inches. with a chord of 63 inches and used the USA-35B series airfoil section. Total wing area was 186 square feet. Spars were fabricated from spruce and aluminum alloy ribs gave shape to the wing surface.

The fuselage, horizontal and vertical stabilizers were constructed of welded steel tubing and a simple tail skid was employed. Using some materials once used to build the B-2 Chummy, Taylor, his father Arthur and company employee Kenneth Tibbets began building the prototype aircraft at Bradford in late July, and within a month the basic airframe structure had been completed.

Designated the Taylor E-2, the first airplane was

C.G. Taylor and pilot Rensselaer C. "Bud" Havens admire the first Taylor E-2 Cub, constructor number 11, registered 10547. The airplane is fitted with a 40 hp. French Salmson AD-9 air-cooled, static radial engine. Simple, rugged and affordable, the diminutive Cub became a legend. (Chester L. Peek)

Although the Salmson engine was not installed in production airplanes, it powered the prototype Taylor E-2 Cub during demonstration tours and development flight testing. (Piper Aviation Museum)

The Brownbach Tiger Kitten engine was an inverted inline, air-cooled, two-cylinder powerplant that developed 20 horsepower at 2,400 rpm. Displacement was 77 cubic inches and the engine weighed 80 lb. (Smithsonian Institution, National Air and Space Museum Negative Number 93-2074)

given constructor number 11 and was registered 10547. Taylor knew the airplane had to use a powerplant of low horsepower to achieve the economy of operation sought by Mr. Piper. There were only a few such engines available when the E-2 was prepared for its first flight in September, 1930.

Different versions of how the the E-2's first flight was made have circulated over the decades. C.G. Taylor, however, disagreed with most of the stories and in 1983 explained his version to Taylorcraft historian Chester L. Peek. According to Taylor, he had ordered a small, 40 hp. French Salmson AD-9 static radial to use on the first flight, but it had not been shipped from New York City when the little monoplane was ready to fly.

Prior to completing the aircraft George Kirkendall, a representative of the Light Manufacturing and Foundry Company in Pottstown, Pennsylvania, had talked with Taylor about mounting a diminutive Brownbach Tiger Kitten engine in the aircraft for its maiden flight. The little Tiger Kitten was a two-cylinder, air-cooled, inverted in-line engine that developed 20 brake horsepower at 2,400 rpm. Displacing a mere 77 cubic inches, the powerplant had eight moving parts, weighed only 80 lb. and featured a single carburetor and magneto.

Without Taylor's invitation or approval, Kirkendall flew a Tiger Kitten and propeller to Emery Airport and urged Taylor to install them on the E-2's engineless airframe. C.G. Taylor remained reluctant, primarily because he knew the engine was inadequate and that the airplane would not fly properly on such miniscule power. To make matters worse, the Emery Airport field elevation was more than 1,400 ft. above sea level, further depriving the Tiger Kitten of power.

The Salmson radial, however, was unavailable and considering the time and effort Kirkendall had expended to provide the Tiger Kitten, Taylor felt obligated to give him at least one opportunity to prove his mettle. An engine mount was fabricated and the powerplant installed. On September 12, 1930, Kirkendall was ready to fly. Taylor and some associates watched as the pilot and the anemic Tiger Kitten tried in vain to get the E-2 airborne.

During three or four attempted takeoffs, the airplane lifted off the ground less than one foot and covered only 10-15 feet before settling onto the cinder runway. Frustrated, Kirkendall taxied back to the hangar. The engine was removed, Taylor thanked him for his efforts and a dejected Mr. Kirkendall flew back to Pottstown.

According to Taylor, Kirkendall later claimed to have made the the first flight of the E-2 and that he derived the famed "Cub" name from the Tiger Kitten

engine. Taylor vehemently denied these claims. He said fellow employee Ted Weld coined the name Cub from the Tiger Kitten, not Kirkendall nor Gilbert Hadrel, another Taylor employee.

C.G. Taylor also adamantly maintained that Kirkendall was not a company employee, representative or test pilot for Taylor or William T. Piper, Sr., and that Kirkendall had no part in the design and construction of the first E-2 Cub, according to historian Peek. After the petite Salmson radial arrived and was installed, the true first flight of the airplane occurred late in September, 1930.

Although the Salmson was beautifully crafted and developed sufficient power, it cost too much, was built to metric standards and, unlike engines built in the United States, its crankshaft rotated counter-clockwise. Therefore, it was rejected as a production engine but powered the airplane for demonstration and test flying. As for the name Cub, Taylor and his associates liked the title and it was quickly adopted.

As news spread about Taylor's latest aerial flivver a large number of pilots became interested in flying the small monoplane. The E-2 Cub was hailed by local Bradford pilots as "the greatest little ship that ever left an airport," and was chosen to form the nucleus of several flying clubs that sprang up overnight around the Bradford area.

Early in October, 1930 company pilot Rensselaer C. Havens flew the prototype E-2 Cub on a demonstration tour to Warren, Pennsylvania. After putting the

Production E-2 Cubs were powered by 37 hp. Continental A-40-2 and A-40-3 engines featuring a single magneto. Ignition, cylinder head gasket and crankshaft failures plagued the A-40 initially, but Continental eventually resolved the engine's problems. E-2 Cub constructor number 31, registered NC12626 was photographed at the Taylor factory in Bradford, Pennsylvania on December 21, 1931. The E-2 sold for $1,325 in 1932. (Piper Aviation Museum)

Designed for the Great Depression market, Taylor's spartan E-2 Cub was affordable and easy to fly. The second E-2 built and the first 13 aircraft produced were licensed under Group Two Approval Number 2-358 before Approved Type Certificate Number A-455 was issued in November, 1931. Mary Alice Baab, office manager for the Taylor company, was photographed at the Bradford Airport with E-2 Cub registered NC14712. (Piper Aviation Museum)

The E-2 Cub's cabin enclosure was a popular option on early production airplanes, especially for cold-weather flying. In 1932 the enclosure was made standard equipment on the Cub. (Mitch Mayborn collection via Tom Heitzman)

ship through its paces at the new airport, he made an additional 32 flights with eager Cub admirers.

Mr. E.M. Farris, general manager and vice president of Warren Airways, was appointed a Cub dealer and placed an order with Havens for a production ship. Havens also conducted demonstration tours in Elmira, New York and other cities within the state. Before the Cub departed Bradford, Kenneth Tibbits, one of the original Taylor Aircraft Company employees, successfully soloed the Cub after receiving only 30 minutes of dual instruction.

Throughout most of October, the spunky little E-2 Cub and its Salmson engine were flown by nearly 500 pilots and potential customers as Havens demonstrated the ship in New York, Connecticut, Massachusetts and other east-coast states. At least nine orders were secured and three dealerships

established during the tour.

Although the little Salmson radial had proven itself reliable, an American-bred engine was a necessity if Cub sales were to be sustained. In their quest to find a suitable powerplant, early in 1931 Mr. Piper and C.G. Taylor made a trip to the Continental Aircraft Engine Company in Detroit, Michigan. Continental had developed the new, 37 hp. four-cylinder A-40 piston engine designed for the light airplane market, and it promised to be exactly what the Taylor Cub needed.

Continental was no stranger to the aircraft engine business. The A-70, seven-cylinder, air-cooled static radial engine of 165 hp. was a successful design. The engine had been fitted to a number of popular airplanes of the period, such as the rugged Waco

THE ENGINE THAT SAVED THE CUB

Without the Continental A-40 engine, the Cub would not have achieved its legendary fame or played such a pivotal role in preserving general aviation in the United States.

Although small piston engines had been built for aircraft after World War One, their designers found it impossible to compete against war-surplus powerplants such as the ubiquitous and plentiful 90 hp. Curtiss OX-5 engine. In addition, the air-cooled, static radial engine had dominated the powerplant market for commercial aircraft since the early 1920s.

Despite the Great Depression, officials of the Continental Aircraft Engine Company in Detroit, Michigan were convinced that a need existed for a small, inexpensive engine for the slowly expanding light airplane market. As a result, in 1930 they

authorized development of the four-cylinder, horizontally opposed A-40 piston powerplant.

Like the E-2 Cub, the A-40 engine was an unsophisticated design. The one-piece crankcase was manufactured from aluminum alloy to save weight, and the four-throw crankshaft was supported with only two main bearings—one at the front of the case and another at the rear. The center section of the crankshaft was not supported.

Displacing 115 cubic inches (1.9 liters), the engine featured four cast iron cylinders that were produced in pairs with integral cooling fins. Each set of cylinders were spanned by single, one-piece aluminum alloy L-type heads with one spark plug per cylinder. The cylinders had a 3½-inch bore and a 3¼-inch stroke.

The ignition system used a single Bendix Scintilla or Bosch magneto driven by the crankshaft and the camshaft drove the tachometer. An updraft carburetor was fitted beneath the crankcase. Developing 37 hp. at 2,500 rpm., the A-40 weighed 144 lb. and was intended to operate 200 hours between major overhauls.

Chiefly because of the inefficient, L-type cylinder heads, the engine's specific fuel consumption was relatively high at 0.7 pounds per horsepower per hour (0.318 kg) but total fuel consumption was an acceptable 2.8 gallons per hour. The engine was easy to start, ran smoothly and became more reliable after improvements were made to the crankshaft and cylinder head designs.

Continental's elementary A-40 engine was the first commercially successful, mass-produced horizontally-opposed piston engine in the United States. Most importantly, the A-40 saved C.G. Taylor's Cub from obscurity. (Smithsonian Institution, National Air And Space Museum Negative Number 93-2073)

biplanes and the graceful Verville cabin monoplanes.

The company's sales and engineering officials believed a vast market existed for a simple, reliable engine priced at the low end of the civil powerplant spectrum, and in 1930 design of the A-40 was initiated. Dynamometer tests began by mid-summer, and a prototype A-40 was installed in a Buhl Bull Pup monoplane that made its first flight in November. Continental was awarded an approved type certificate for the engine on May 19, 1931.

Returning home with an engine they had purchased, Taylor and Piper believed the little A-40 was the answer to their dilemma. The powerplant was installed in E-2 Cub constructor number 12, registered NC10594 and test-flown in April, 1931 by R. C. "Bud" Havens.

Despite Piper's high hopes for the little powerplant, during initial flight testing the A-40 Continental failed to live up to expectations. In the first 30 days, pilots Havens and Taylor experienced no fewer than 26 forced landings.

The engine was notoriously unreliable. The single magneto often failed. Valves burned and cylinder head gaskets blew with uncanny regularity. Worst of all, the crankshaft broke after about 100 hours of flying. Taylor and Piper were indignant. They had a good

airplane, but it was virtually useless without a reliable engine.

Despite its teething troubles, the Continental A-40 was exactly what the Cub needed. When E-2 production began, the first 14 airplanes were produced under Group Two Approval Number 2-358 in June, 1931 before the Department of Commerce granted the A-40-powered E-2 an approved type certificate on July 11. Early production airplanes were fitted with the 37 hp. version of the A-40 engine.

It should be noted that in addition to the Continental A-40, early Taylor sales literature for the E-2 Cub listed a 40 hp. version of the Brownbach Tiger Kitten engine as an alternate powerplant. No evidence is known to exist, however, to indicate that the more powerful Tiger Kitten variant was factory-installed on any Taylor Cub. A selling price of $1,295 was quoted for the Brownbach-equipped airplane.

The first production, Continental-powered airplane was constructor number 13, registered NC10784. Although the Cub was priced at only $1,325, sales were sluggish and only 21 airplanes were built in 1931. The Great Depression seemed determined to destroy Piper's plan for success, but fortunately the rugged, utilitarian, easy-to-fly Cub kept selling, albeit in small

The first E-2 Cub to be exported was constructor number 14, registered CF-ARA delivered in August, 1931 and flown to its home base at Ottawa, Canada. The E-2 was restricted to solo from the rear seat chiefly because of weight and balance requirements. (Chester L. Peek)

Taylor E-2 Cub constructor number 124, registered NC14385 was completed on October 12, 1934, and delivered to Camel City Flying Service, Winston-Salem, North Carolina. Powered by a Continental A-40-2 engine, the aircraft featured a red fuselage with silver striping and silver wings. (Mitch Mayborn collection via Tom Heitzman)

The Taylor Brothers Aircraft Corporation built 352 E-2, F-2 and H-2 Cubs. The final E-2 produced was constructor number 363, registered NC15931 completed in February, 1936. The E-2 Cub illustrated was constructor number 196, registered 15045. (Esposito via Peter M. Bowers)

A three-cylinder Aeromarine AR3-40 air-cooled, static radial engine was fitted to Taylor's little monoplane and approved in February, 1934 as the F-2 Cub. A float-equipped F-2S Cub, constructor number 115, registered X14729 is illustrated. Note aileron control cable and pulley on wing lift strut. (Piper Aviation Museum)

numbers. In terms of making Mr. Piper a profit in the aviation business, however, the Cub was not an overnight success. Only Piper's oil profits kept the Taylor Aircraft Company airborne.

Despite its slow start in the marketplace, the Cub's relatively low acquisition cost and economy of operation were the airplane's forte and became key reasons for its eventual success. The E-2 was miserly with a gallon of fuel, had acceptable if lackluster performance, and parts for both the airframe and powerplant were plentiful and inexpensive.

As William T. Piper had prophesied, flight school operators gradually realized that the lowly Cub was an irresistable bargain, and in 1932 began buying them in growing numbers for training fledgling aviators. In addition to Cubs delivered to customers in the United States, E-2 Cub constructor number 14 was the first airplane exported by the company. Completed in June, 1931 the aircraft was flown to Canada in August bearing the registration CF-ARA.

As Cub sales increased in 1932, so did improvements. The original, open cockpit was replaced by an enclosed structure and optional engines were available in an effort to boost business and provide an alternative to the Continental A-40.

The other engines included the 40 hp. Aeromarine AR3-40 static radial used in the Taylor F-2 Cub, which received its approved type certificate in February, 1934. F-2 constructor number 74, registered X13272, was built in December, 1933 and became the first production Cub to use the AR3-40 engine.

Taylor also experimented with an engine of his own design, but the powerplant was not used on production airplanes. A prototype engine was installed in E-2 Cub constructor number 149, registered NX-14756 and tested as the G-2 Cub.

The pilot of Taylor F-2 Cub constructor number 102, registered NC14346 straps into the aft seat in preparation for takeoff. The F-2 Cub sold for $895 without engine and propeller. Note shock cords on main landing gear. (Esposito via Peter M. Bowers)

Continuing his search for alternative engines, Taylor next installed a 35 hp. Szekely SR-3-35 three-cylinder radial engine on E-2 Cub constructor number 149, creating the Taylor H-2 Cub. Although it received an approved type certificate in May, 1935 the H-2 version was not produced.

By 1935 Continental had succeeded in resolving most of the A-40's chronic problems and the engines became increasingly dependable. In an effort to reduce costs, early powerplants used a single Bendix Scintilla or Bosch magneto driven directly from the crankshaft. In addition, a Stromberg carburetor was made standard equipment in 1932 and reduced the number of forced landings because of fuel flow anomalies.

Other improvements to the A-40 series included a redesigned front thrust bearing for the crankshaft and additional cylinder head studs. The A-40-2 and A-40-3 became the standard engines on Taylor E-2 Cubs. A total of 352 E-2, F-2 and H-2 Cubs were built from 1931 to 1936.

The last production E-2 was constructor number 363, registered NC15931, and completed in February, 1936. All of the E-2 Cub airplanes were produced at the Bradford factory.

In 1935 Cub sales had zoomed to more than 200 airplanes, but business and personal relations between the pragmatic Mr. Piper and the stubborn Mr. Taylor had plunged to new lows. Despite their individual talents, the two men were a mismatch and their tenuous partnership was rapidly approaching the breaking point.

To power the Taylor F-2 Cub, the Aeromarine AR3-40 engine was derated to 40 hp. from its normal 50 hp. rating. The engine weighed 140 lb. and cost $510 equipped with a single magneto. In the late 1930s it was renamed the Lenape Papoose. (Smithsonian Institution, National Air and Space Museum Negative Number 93-2072)

Candid photograph of Taylor F-2 Cub constructor number 100, registered 14344 powered by a 40 hp. Aeromarine AR3-40 static radial engine. The Taylor F-2 Cub sold for $1,495 fly-away-factory. (Mitch Mayborn collection via Tom Heitzman)

Taylor was becoming increasingly dissatisfied with Piper's handling of the business. Although the Cub was selling well, he had urged William Piper to consider building a side-by-side version, but to no avail. To the talented, visionary Taylor, such a rebuff was difficult to accept and constituted a personal affront.

To Piper's way of thinking, his theory about selling cheap airplanes to flight schools was working and there was no reason to change the status quo. Money was still scarce, and there was none to spare for development of a new Cub variant. Fortunately, Piper's oil profits helped keep the company solvent although production line workers were barely able to exist on the low wages Piper could afford to pay the dedicated little band of laborers.

Among those workers was young Walter C. Jamouneau, who had come to work for Taylor in January, 1933. Jamouneau was a pilot and a graduate of Rutgers University. He was not an aeronautical engineer, but had studied aeronautics diligently in college and was thoroughly familiar with the aerodynamic and technical aspects of airplanes. After several months on the job at no salary, Mr. Piper put young Jamouneau in an E-2 Cub factory demonstrator, paid him $15 per week and sent him off with orders to sell, sell sell!

Because he was part owner and the treasurer of a struggling airplane company, William T. Piper, Sr., believed it would be good for business if he learned to fly, and reasoned that becoming a pilot would be viewed as an endorsement of his own product. Therefore, he began taking lessons in a Cub and eventually earned his license.

During his many hours aloft in E-2s he came to appreciate the Cub's docile flying qualities and knew it was a good flying machine for the Depression market. By mid-1935, however, he was convinced that the Cub's angular lines needed some revision to improve the airplane's looks and further boost its sales appeal.

According to Taylor historian Chester Peek, Taylor conceded that some improvements could be made to the Cub, and in the fall of 1935 he had assigned Jamouneau to upgrade the airplane but added a strict caveat—to leave its basic configuration unaltered.

Unfortunately, the almost total lack of communication between company president Taylor and company treasurer Piper was a serious liability that complicated Jamouneau's task. Taylor had been absent from his factory office for several weeks that autumn because of an illness and was recovering at his home next to the Taylor facilities. He had a good view of the airport from his window vantage point and spent time each day watching the factory as well as airplanes tak-

Interior of Taylor factory showing fuselage welding and wing construction areas. Note E-2 Cubs undergoing final assembly in background. (Piper Aviation Museum)

ing off and landing.

One day in October, 1935 a different Cub was rolled out into the daylight. Taylor soon spotted the ship, with its graceful, rounded wingtips and rudder as well as a widened landing-gear tread. The aircraft had been converted from an existing E-2 Cub.

To Taylor, it was obvious that the modifications had been covertly made in his absence. For him, this was not only unacceptable but tantamount to rebellion as well as a direct challenge to his position as president and chief engineer. Confronting Mr. Piper on the matter soon thereafter, Taylor demanded to know who had authorized the changes. Piper attempted to explain that he had instructed Walter Jamouneau to proceed with incorporation of the wingtip and empennage changes the young engineer believed would improve the Cub's appearance.

C.G. Taylor's sensitive ego had been severely bruised, and Piper had grown tired of his partner's gruff personality, lack of cooperation and resistance to change. After an uneasy association that had lasted four years, the clash of wills between the two men had been forced to the forefront and they both knew it had to be resolved.

According to Taylor historian Peek, on December 7, 1935, Piper penned a terse note to production supervisor Kenneth Tibbits: "Mr. Taylor has been and still is physically unable to transact business and from now on I have taken complete charge of the shop and you will take orders from me only until instructed differently."

In what amounted to an uneasy ultimatum, Mr. Piper had taken command of the Taylor Aircraft Company and patiently awaited his partner's response. When C.G. Taylor did respond, it was obvious to both men that only one of them would emerge the victor.

To Piper the solution was a simple one. He offered to let Taylor buy his interest in the company, or Piper

The Taylor J-2 Cub was a refined version of the E-2 with rounded wing tips and empennage surfaces and an increased landing gear tread. Production began in October, 1935 and 1,207 were built. (Piper Aviation Museum)

The J-2 was powered by a 37 hp. Continental A-40-2, A-40-3 or 40 hp. A-40-4 engine equipped with a single magneto. Touted as "The New Cub" by Taylor, the J-2 cost $1,470. Airplane illustrated was constructor number 647, registered NC16632 photographed at Floyd Bennett Field in 1936. (Vincent J. Berinati)

As production rates increased, the J-2 Cub's price decreased to $1,270. Young engineer Walter C. Jamouneau refined the spartan E-2 into the more aesthetic and popular J-2 variant. (Piper Aviation Museum)

would buy Taylor's interest. But C.G. was unable to purchase Piper's share, and Piper lacked the cash to pay back Taylor's investment.

The issue was settled when Piper obtained credit at a Bradford bank and agreed to pay Taylor $250 per month for three years and to pay life insurance costs, according to Piper Aircraft Corporation's official version of the showdown. Taylor's version of the story, however, is different. He said Piper offered him $5,000 paid at $40 per week, and that if Taylor refused his offer Piper threatened to intentionally bankrupt the company.

Believing fate had dealt him yet another hard blow, Taylor realized he had no choice but to accept the terms. In December, 1935 he departed the company that bore his name and had nurtured his dreams. As for Walter Jamouneau, Piper appointed him chief engineer. The tall, lanky young man embarked on a long and distinguished career with the Taylor com-

pany and later the Piper Aircraft Corporation.

The airplane he had modified, in keeping with the letter sequence of Taylor designs, would have been designated as the I-2 Cub but that letter was not used. Instead, the attractive little ship was dubbed the J-2. Popular legend ascribes the J-2 designation to Jamouneau, but no evidence corroborating that contention is known to exist.

Still smarting from his firefight with Piper, C.G. Taylor was determined to design and build an airplane that was superior to the Cub. In early 1936, he designed the Taylorcraft "A" monoplane at Butler, Pennsylvania. Powered by a Continental Motors A-40-3 engine rated at 38 hp., the airplane sold for $1,495 and proved to be a tough competitor for the J-2 Cub.

In July he moved to Alliance, Ohio and began production in the vacated Alliance Aircraft Corporation facilities located there. A small number of key Piper workers had joined Taylor in his new endeavor, and more followed as the company began to grow.

Until his death in 1988, C.G. Taylor feared that history would deny him the recognition he so richly deserved as a gifted engineer and creator of the Taylor E-2 Cub. Fortunately, Taylor's place and that of his little monoplane are secure in the annals of American aviation history. Other than the Wright Brothers and their Flyer, no other person or airplane have so significantly influenced the future of flying as did Clarence Gilbert Taylor and his beloved Cub.

The Taylor factory at Bradford, Pennsylvania as it appeared in 1936. Before his departure in 1935, C.G. Taylor lived in the two-story building next to the main facility. J-2 Cubs are parked outside. The Taylor factory site eventually became home for the University of Pittsburg, Bradford Campus. (Piper Aviation Museum)

◄ *EDO Corporation flew a 1936 J-2 Cub, constructor number 700, registered X16395 to obtain certification for the J-2S variant that was fitted with Model 1070 floats. (Mitch Mayborn collection via Tom Heitzman)*

William T. Piper, Sr., poses with a J-2 Cub. A talented businessman, Mr. Piper learned to fly in Cubs and remained an active pilot well into his senior years. (Piper Aviation Museum)

Factory-fresh J-2 Cubs being loaded onto a Rock Island Line railroad boxcar for transport to their new owners. Note wings stacked inside the car. (Piper Aviation Museum)

The Everel Propeller Corporation tested its single-blade, wood design on a Taylor J-2 Cub and also used the aircraft to demonstrate the propeller to prospective buyers and airframe manufacturers. The Everel propeller was not popular and few J-2 Cubs were equipped with them. (Piper Aviation Museum)

Workers are shown in the Taylor factory fabricating metal wing ribs that were placed in carts for transport to the wing assembly department. (Piper Aviation Museum)

Clarence G. Taylor poses with a special, deluxe version Taylorcraft Model A monoplane built specifically for the National Aviation Show held in New York City in January, 1937. The E-2 Cub and the Taylorcraft earned C.G. Taylor everlasting fame as an aircraft designer. (Alliance Public Library)

In 1938, J-2 Cub constructor number 1718, registered N(X)19518 was fitted with an experimental five-cylinder, 60 hp. Angle static radial engine. Designed by Glenn D. Angle, formerly chief powerplant engineer at famed Wright Field, Dayton, Ohio, the engine was not produced. (Mitch Mayborn collection via Tom Heitzman)

Famed speed flier Frank M. Hawks poses with his Taylor J-2 Cub dubbed "Time Flits"—a humorous reference to the much larger and powerful "Time Flies" racer built in the late 1930s expressly for Hawks. (Piper Aviation Museum)

After his departure from the Taylor Aircraft Company late in 1935, C.G. Taylor designed the Taylorcraft Model A that became a competitor to the J-2 and J-3 Cub and later the Piper J-4 Cub Coupe. Taylor initially relocated to Butler, Pennsylvania to build the Model A but moved production to Alliance, Ohio in 1937. (Chester L. Peek)

CHAPTER THREE

LOCK HAVEN OR BUST!

By the time of C.G. Taylor's departure from the company in December, 1935 William T. Piper's Taylor Aircraft Company was on the verge of becoming a financial and aeronautical success. The company had completed the initial J-2 Cub, constructor number 500, registered X15951 in October, 1935. The J-2 received Approved Type Certificate A-595 on February 14, 1936, and the first production aircraft was constructor number 501, registered NC15956.

Piper's problems with Continental engines had decreased significantly as improvements to the powerplant's design were incorporated. To power the sporty J-2, the 37 hp. Continental A-40-3 was selected and in September, 1936 the 40 hp. A-40-4 version also was adopted to power the Cub. In addition to standardizing on Continental engines for the J-2, Mr. Piper chose an overall silver paint scheme for production aircraft accented by a variety of trim colors.

The factory also built seaplane versions of the J-2 designated J-2S, equipped with EDO Model 1070 floats. In addition, J-2 Cubs were fabricated at Bradford and shipped to Aircraft Associates in Long Beach, California for completion and sale. Aircraft Associates was a Taylor distributor for the West Coast.

These airplanes were officially known as "Western Cubs" and received Approved Type Certificate number A-620 in December, 1936. Twenty-two Western Cubs were built or assembled at Long Beach, including constructor number 899 through 902 and constructor number 1245 through 1262. The type certificate for the Western Cub expired on September 30, 1939.

Priced at $1,470 at the factory or a mere $1,035 without the engine and propeller, the J-2 could be bought for a downpayment of only $490 with a year to finance the balance. Later in 1936, the price was

reduced to $1,270 thanks to increased demand and more efficient production methods. In mid-1936, the J-2S version was approved for operation on EDO Model D-1070 floats. The seaplane sold for $1,895.

Within the tiny factory at Bradford there was reason for optimism and the immediate future, at least, looked bright in 1936. From selling only 21 E-2 Cubs in 1931, under the careful guidance and frugal fiscal policies of William T. Piper the company had sold more than 500 Cubs in 1936. But despite better times, money remained scarce.

Piper's eldest son, William Piper, Jr., had become secretary and assistant treasurer in 1937 and both men expected their aviation business to become profitable by the end of the year. To keep up with increasing demand for the Cub, the factory was building airplanes at the rate of eighteen per week and a second shift of workers kept the production line humming until late in the night.

Piper knew the already inadequate facilities at the Bradford airport would not be sufficient for the future, but he had no money to expand and no plans to move elsewhere. On the cold night of March 16-17, 1937, fate dealt Mr. Piper a hard blow. About 10:45 P.M the little factory caught fire and despite heroic efforts by about 20 workers and Central Fire Station firemen to extinguish the blaze, in less than two hours most of the buildings were destroyed.

The fire began in the paint shop where men were

After the devastating fire at Bradford, Pennsylvania in March, 1937, William T. Piper, Sr., resumed production of the J-2 Cub two months later in a vacant silk mill located at Lock Haven, Pennsylvania. Production of the classic J-3 series Cub began there late in 1937. (Piper Aviation Museum)

Fuselage welding area inside the Lock Haven factory. Cub sales soared to new heights from 1939 through 1941. (Piper Aviation Museum)

Prior to the beginning of World War Two Piper offered the J-3 Cub in three versions, including the attractive Cub Sport with wheel fairings. Piper sold the J-3 Cub Sport for $1,270 in 1938. Early production Cubs had a nine-gallon fuel tank. A 12-gallon tank became standard when engine horsepower increased. (Piper Aviation Museum)

brushing coats of highly flammable cellulose nitrate dope on the fuselage fabric of J-2 Cubs. An overheated furnace located adjacent to the shop was blamed for the ensuing conflagration, not sparks from a drill bit as some workers speculated, Ted V. Weld, president of the Taylor company, told the Bradford press.

Regardless of how the fire started, once ignited the dopes burned fast and furious. A few men frantically tried to remove cans of dope from the premises but were forced to evacuate the building as explosions rocked the factory.

When the fire department arrived, two hoses were employed to fight the growing blaze. They were unable to save the paint shop, welding room, wing and final assembly areas, and the sweeping flames forced firemen to abandon the original, main factory building that had housed the entire Taylor aircraft operation in 1930. Fortunately, William Piper had insured the main building, which he owned, for $14,000.

Taylor employees saved at least 15 airplanes from certain destruction and their heroic actions helped to save the company. Unfortunately, incomplete aircraft and one J-2 Cub ready for delivery as well as virtual-

Cabin of the Cub Sport was equipped with thickly-padded seats and upholstered sidewalls. Stabilizer trim control was adjacent to front seat. (Smithsonian Institution, National Air And Space Museum Negative Number 92-8009)

ly all of the raw materials needed to build more Cubs were lost. Perhaps worst of all, engineering drawings and prints also were damaged or totally consumed by the blaze.

At the time of the fire, the Taylor company employed about 165 workers who were producing 18 airplanes per week, and Mr. Piper had plans to boost that number to 25 per week. In addition, orders were on hand for at least 75 new ships, according to Ted Weld.

He estimated total losses at $200,000, including about $70,000 worth of raw materials and about $40,000 for the factory complex. Sadly, Weld informed William Piper about the fire. William T. Piper, Sr., who had been attending the Pacific Aircraft Show in Los Angeles, California, quickly returned to Bradford to assess the damage and the future of his airplane company.

The fire was an ill-timed, disastrous event for Piper and his company. He was on the verge of genuine financial success after five years of struggling to make the company profitable. Both Piper and his associates expected the demand for Cubs would continue to grow, but without a factory to produce them precious time and business opportunities would be lost. In addition, the annual onset of warmer flying weather was about to boost Cub sales further, and both distributors and customers would soon be clamoring for their nonexistent airplanes.

A search was begun to find temporary quarters in which to continue production, but the Bradford area offered no permanent solutions. Yet only one day after the fire, five employees were busy making aircraft parts from patterns and dies salvaged from the factory and hastily installed in a downtown workshop. To further help the recovery, Aircraft Associates in California built and shipped some new fuselages to the company in Bradford.

Most of the office equipment and files were saved from destruction. As a result, the sales, accounting and purchasing departments of the company quickly resumed operations in the McKean County Motor Club offices on Chestnut Street in Bradford, and at the Emery airport administration building.

By the end of March, a few J-2 Cubs had been built and were assembled in makeshift facilities at the airport. After an incredibly short time and thanks to the hard work of many employees, the Taylor Airplane Company was back in business, albeit temporarily.

The primary challenge facing William Piper was whether to rebuild at Bradford or seek a new location. Although a small number of Bradford citizens were willing to reinvest in the Taylor company and help it rebuild in the city, most businessmen of Bradford were not forthcoming in their civic or financial support of Piper and his airplane business.

Their negative attitude was understandable to Mr. Piper. Bradford was still dominated by the oil industry, which paid high wages. Conversely, the lowly Cub paid its makers only pennies and had proved less than popular with Bradford's citizenry as a source of employment and economic success.

When word spread that the Taylor buildings had burned, however, a large number of cities and states began wooing Piper their way. Among them was the town of Lock Haven, Pennsylvania. Situated along the West Branch of the flood-prone Susquehanna

Piper produced the Lycoming-powered J-3L series as an alternative to the Continental-powered J-3C Cub. The four-cylinder O-145 engine was available in 50 hp., 55 hp. and 65 hp. versions. Early J-3 Cubs featured plain, hinged-type ailerons. Improved, Frieze-type ailerons became standard in 1940. (Piper Aviation Museum)

River and surrounded by ancient, once heavily wooded mountains, Lock Haven had risen to prominence as a lumber town in the early 19th Century before reckless felling of timber had depleted the forests by the late 1880s.

Such irresponsible logging helped precipitate the onset of major floods in the region, and a disastrous flood in 1936 had severely impaired the city's economy. New businesses—including companies that built airplanes—were sincerely welcomed.

Jacob W. Miller, known to virtually everyone as "Jake," was a distributor for Taylor Cubs and operated a small flight service operation at Lock Haven. He succeeded in bringing together William Piper, Sr. and city officials to discuss relocating the Taylor company to Lock Haven.

Of particular interest to both parties was a large, empty building that had been operated in Lock Haven by the Susquehanna Silk Mills. The facility had been silenced by the Depression in 1932. Although not designed for aircraft manufacture, the mill did have a huge amount of space—about 50,000 square feet on the ground floor and nearly as much room in the upper level. The burned-out Bradford site was diminutive by comparison.

In September, 1938 Piper received government approval of the J-3L-50 Cub powered by a 50 hp. Lycoming O-145-A1 engine equipped with a single magneto. The J-3L-55 Cub was powered by a 55 hp. O-145-A2 engine. The J-3L-65 was the most ubiquitous of the J-3L-series, and was powered by 65 hp. O-145-B1 and -B3 powerplants. (Smithsonian Institution, National Air And Space Museum Negative Number 93-2079)

After a series of negotiations with its owners, a group of William T. Piper's savvy business associates obtained investor funding to purchase the facility for slightly more than $96,000. To further sweeten the deal, the City of Lock Haven agreed to pave a 2,800 foot-long runway located next to the mill.

The elder Piper was elated with both the price and the location, despite the fact that he had to share ownership of the company in order to resurrect it from the ashes and provide for its future. Production of the highly successful J-2 Cub series was resumed at Lock Haven in June, 1937 and the exodus of personnel and equipment from Bradford was completed during the summer.

The Taylor J-2 Cub had been a winner for Mr. Piper. As the end of that momentous year of 1937 drew near, however, William T. Piper was becoming as anxious to refine the J-2 as he had been two years earlier to improve Taylor's E-2 design.

Production of the spartan but reliable J-2 Cub continued at Lock Haven throughout the remainder of 1937 and into 1938 before the J-2 was superseded by the improved J-3 version. The last production J-2 Cub was constructor number 1975, registered NC20175. A total of 1,207 J-2 series were built from October, 1935 through May, 1938.

By autumn, 1937 company engineers were hard at work modifying a J-2 into the most classic of all light airplanes—the J-3 Cub. Assigned constructor number 2000 and registered NC20000, it was one of a number of prototypes that emerged from the Lock Haven factory in December. An earlier J-3 prototype had been completed in October.

The J-3 still retained the J-2's overall configuration, but was a more attractive, comfortable and capable airplane compared with its predecessor. The vertical stabilizer shape was revised and the rudder incorporated an aerodynamic balance ahead of the hinge line. The elevators were reshaped, a tailwheel replaced the simplistic skid found on earlier Taylor designs and the main landing gear incorporated hydraulic brakes.

In terms of pilot comfort, the J-3 sported a large, upholstered front seat with a wider, upholstered seat behind it. The instrument panel also was upgraded to include a magnetic compass and airspeed indicator in addition to a tachometer and engine instrumentation.

As for color, the basic paint scheme was bright yellow overall with a black trim stripe along the fuselage and the famous Cub logo on the vertical stabilizer. Three versions of the airplane were available: Cub, Cub Sport and the Cub Trainer.

An important factor in design of the J-3 was incorporation of Society of Automotive Engineers (SAE)

The Franklin 4AC-176-BA2 engine developed 65 hp. and equipped J-3F-65 Cubs. Note that the Franklin engine mounted horizontally, not radially as did the Continental powerplants. (Piper Aviation Museum)

X-4130 grade molybdenum steel tubing for the fuselage and engine mount structure. Stronger than the SAE 1025 grade steel used on the J-2 series, the 4130 tubing allowed Piper to certify the newest Cub with engines of increased horsepower.

To power the J-3 Cub series, Piper offered three different powerplants of various horsepower ratings:
1. The 40 hp. Continental Motors A-40-4 was fitted to the J-3C-40; the 50 hp. A-50-1, -3, -5, -7 and -8 was installed in the J-3C-50, and the 65 hp. A-65-1. -3, -7, -8 and -9 powered the J-3C-65.
2. The 40 hp. Franklin 4AC-150-S40 was installed in the J-3F; the 50 hp. 4AC-150-S50 was fitted to the J-3F-50; the 65 hp. 4AC-176 series were installed in the J-3F-65, and the 4AC-150-A and a small number of 4AC-171 engines were installed in the J-3F-60.
3. The Lycoming 50 hp. 0-145-A1 was used in the J-3L;

A J-3C-65 Cub registered NC38007 was the 7,000th Cub trainer produced by the company. Piper had built more than 10,000 J-3-series Cubs by the end of 1941, and produced 19,888 Cubs from 1937 to 1947. (Piper Aviation Museum)

J-3 Cub production at the Lock Haven facility continued until 1942 when commercial manufacture was terminated because of the war. Late in 1941 extruded, aluminum alloy wing spars replaced the J-3's wood spars. The J-3F illustrated was powered by a Franklin 4AC-150-series engine. (Piper Aviation Museum)

the 55 hp. O-145-A2 and 65 hp. O-145-B1 and -B2 also were fitted to the J-3L and J-3L-65 versions respectively.

The Department of Commerce issued approved type certificates for J-3C-50 and J-3F-50 in July, 1938, followed by certificates for the J-3L-50 in September and the J-3P in August. A small number of Cubs designated J-3P were equipped with the 50 hp., three-cylinder Lenape LM-3-50 static radial engine—a new name for the Aeromarine radial that had powered a small number of early production Taylor Cubs. One J-3P, constructor number 2595, registered NX21806 featured a wing equipped with trailing edge, slotted flaps. A second J-3P with slotted flaps was registered NX3352S.

By the autumn of 1937 William T. Piper, Sr., and his associates had a spacious factory complex in

The J-3F-50 Cub was powered by a Franklin 4AC-150 engine that developed 50 hp. at 2,300 rpm. The J-3F-50 illustrated is equipped with triangular rocker box covers and above-cylinder exhaust system common to the 4AC-150 50 hp. and 60 hp. powerplants. (Piper Aviation Museum)

After World War Two a small number of J-3 Cubs were converted to tricycle landing gear configuration. (Piper Aviation Museum)

In May, 1938 pilots Kenneth Kress and Glenn Englert flew a J-3P, constructor number 2080, registered NX20280 nonstop from Newark, New Jersey to Miami, Florida, and return in 63 hours, 54 minutes. The engine was a three-cylinder LM-3-50 Lenape Papoose air-cooled radial. (Piper Aviation Museum)

The float-equipped J-3C-65S was another popular version of the venerable Cub. Many flight schools such as Embry-Riddle used Cubs to teach pilots the art of seaplane operations. (Piper Aviation Museum)

The J-3C Cub illustrated was modified into an agricultural duster and operated in the Restricted Category. Note lack of rear cabin windows and aft seat replaced with a chemical hopper. Fuselage side reads "Jack Reynolds Airplane Crop Dusting." (Piper Aviation Museum)

which to build the J-3 Cub, but the company needed a large infusion of funding to prepare for future expansion and production demand. To get the money Piper desperately needed, however, would-be investors wanted some important changes: a new name for the company and a public stock offering. The first requirement was relatively simple; the second was not.

After some discussion among themselves, in November, 1937 company officials agreed to change the name to Piper Aircraft Corporation. Not only was C.G. Taylor gone, but also his name. The first Cub to bear the Piper name may have been J-2 constructor number 1937, registered NC20137, according to Piper historian Roger W. Peperell.

As for the stock offering, strict regulations put forth by the United States Government's new Securities and Exchange Commission made the transaction more difficult. The commission had been created after the debacle on Wall Street in October, 1929 as part of a series of safeguards designed to help prevent such disastrous events from occurring again.

Despite setbacks, delays and complicated behind-the-scenes negotiations, the investors, Piper officials and the Securities and Exchange Commission even-

tually reached agreement and in March, 1938 Piper Aircraft Corporation went public with a stock offering for $250,000. Additional stock offerings followed in later months as business momentum increased along with the number of stockholders.

Benefitting from the J-2's widespread market acceptance, the J-3 Cub further capitalized on that popularity and became known as the paragon of light airplanes. It had worthy challengers in the Aeronca Chief and C.G. Taylor's Taylorcraft, but the Cub's inherent qualities and William Piper's penchant for efficient production and low price kept the Cub ahead of its competition.

When introduced in early 1938, the J-3 Cub trainer version sold for $1,270 or a buyer could obtain financing after making a down payment of $425. The Cub Sport cost $1,395 and a J-3S on EDO D-1070, 54-1140, 1320 or 1400-series floats sold for $1,985. In addition to EDO, Piper also offered Heath, McKinley and Wollam floats.

As improved manufacturing methods evolved and production increased further, Piper lowered prices in 1939 to $1,249 for the Cub trainer, then to $1,098 and finally to only $995. The tremendous success of the J-2 and J-3 Cub airplanes vindicated Mr. Piper's belief that small aircraft were essentially destined to be trainers and nothing more. That philosophy had worked well for him, but in 1938 he began to realize that other aircraft, albeit in small numbers, could be added to the Piper product line without endangering the bread-and-butter Cub.

As a result, in May, 1938 the prototype J-4 Cub Coupe, constructor number 4-400, registered NX21599, made its first flight powered by an inverted

Piper introduced the side-by-side, two-place J-4 Cub Coupe in 1938, powered by Continental A-50-1 or A-50-3 engines. The airplane illustrated was Canadian CF-BOM, constructor number 4-1207 built in 1940. (Kenneth M. Molson via Joseph P. Juptner)

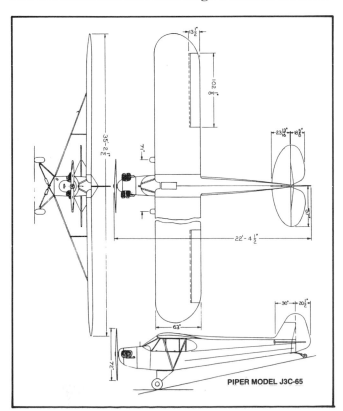

PIPER MODEL J3C-65

An aspiring aviatrix poses with a Piper J-4A Cub Coupe and its 65 hp. Continental A-65 engine. Note the above-cylinder exhaust system and open cowling with air scoops similar to those of the J-3C-65 Cub. (Piper Aviation Museum)

four-cylinder, 60 hp. Skymotor engine. Designed under the guidance of chief engineer Walter C. Jamouneau, the J-4 featured side-by-side seating for two in a cloth-covered cabin, a 105-lb. baggage capacity, internally sprung conventional landing gear and a larger, more complete instrument panel. A 50 hp. Continental A-50-1 or A-50-3 engine powered the initial J-4 series.

Priced at $1,995 at a time when the prewar United States economy had gathered renewed strength, the Cub Coupe was an instant success and spawned a series of new airplanes. Mr. Piper had quickly learned that there was more to the airplane business than trainers, and that meant more profits.

The original J-4 received its approved type certificate in October, 1938, and production began that month. The first airplane completed was constructor number 4-401, registered NC21835. The J-4A series was issued an approved type certificate in July, 1939

Instrument panel of a factory-fresh Cub Coupe shows twin control sticks, airspeed indicator and altimeter on left side, engine tachometer in center with magnetic compass directly above. Magneto switch is ahead of throttle, with fuel tank selector mounted below. Note pedals for heel-operated brakes. (Piper Aviation Museum)

and were powered by 65 hp. Continental Motors A-65-1, -3, -7, -8 and -9 engines.

Piper later offered the J-4B with a 60 hp. Franklin 4AC-171 engine that was approved by the Civil Aeronautics Authority in March, 1939 as well as the J-4E powered by a Continental A-75-9 and the J-4F with a 65 hp. Lycoming O-145-B2 powerplant. Approved type certificates for the J-4E and J-4F were granted to Piper in April, 1941 and March, 1940 respectively. In addition to the J-4E and J-4F versions, Piper J-4 constructor number 4-502 registered NC22881 was a J-4C powered by a Lenape radial engine.

Another J-4C was constructor number 4-468, built in January, 1939 with an LM-3-50 Lenape radial engine that was replaced by a Franklin 4AC-171 in March, 1939. The Lock Haven factory built 1,251 J-4 series airplanes before production ceased in December, 1941.

One experimental J-4 variant was designated J-4RX and was identified as constructor number RX-2, registered NX22941. Powered by a 75 hp. Continental A-75-8 engine, the aircraft was built specifically to test a tapered wing designed by Harrison R. Tucker at the behest of William K. Rose.

Tucker's wing boasted large trailing edge flaps as well as leading edge slats that were designed to increase lift. During flight tests, however, the wing failed to improve performance compared with the basic J-4 wing and the experiments were terminated.

Whereas the J-3 Cub and the J-4 Cub Coupe were two-place ships, the J-5 Cub Cruiser developed in the summer of 1939 was the company's first three-place airplane and paved the way for further product expan-

Piper built 1,251 of the J-4 Cub Coupe series from 1939 to December, 1941 when production was terminated. The J-4E illustrated, registered NC41227 was operated by the Civil Air Patrol when photographed in December, 1948 at Keene, New Hampshire. (Charles N. Trask via Joseph P. Juptner)

When J-4A production began in 1939 Piper offered an optional nine-gallon fuel tank located in the left wing root. Canadian-registered CF-KUU was a J-4A Cub Coupe built in 1940. (Kenneth Molson via Joseph P. Juptner)

Introduced in 1940, the J-5 Cub Cruiser essentially was a three-place version of the J-4 Cub Coupe. The second J-5 prototype, constructor number 5-2, registered NX26071 on right wing and NC26071 on the rudder, was powered by a four-cylinder, 75 hp. Continental A-75-8 engine. (Piper Aviation Museum)

Cabin of a J-4 Cub Coupe shows plush, upholstered seats and cluster of gauges on the instrument panel. (Piper Aviation Museum)

Piper received Civil Aeronautics Authority approval for the Lycoming-powered J-4F in March, 1940. The four-cylinder O-145-B2 engine was rated at 65 hp. and gave the Cub Coupe a maximum speed of 100 mph. The J-4F illustrated was registered NC35971. (Ralph Nortell via Joseph P. Juptner)

sion. Essentially a J-4 with the pilot seated ahead of the two rear seat passengers, the prototype J-5, constructor number 5-1 registered NX24573, first flew in August and the Cub Cruiser was granted an approved type certificate in April, 1940.

Because of its seating configuration, the airplane was especially popular with small flight schools and air taxi operators who used it for charter work as well as student flight training duties. Like its J-3 and J-4 siblings, the J-5 Cub Cruiser was approved for operation on skis and floats.

Powered by a 75 hp. Continental A-75-8 engine, the J-5A production version began deliveries in early 1940 and an estimated 510 to 513 airplanes were built that year. The J-5B, Lycoming-powered version was introduced in early in June, 1940 and featured a 75 hp., geared engine.

Although a geared, 75 hp. Lycoming GO-145-C2 powerplant was installed that summer, production of the J-5B variant was delayed until 1941. Some former J-5A airplanes were later retrofitted and approved in July, 1942 with the 80 hp. Continental A-80-8 or -9 engine and were designated J-5A-80.

Piper introduced the J-5C version of the popular Cub Cruiser in 1942. Equipped with a 100 hp. Lycom-

The J-5A Cub Cruiser was popular with air taxi operators and flight schools. Piper was awarded Approved Type Certificate Number 725 for the J-5 Cub Cruiser in April, 1940. (Ralph Nortell via Joseph P. Juptner)

Piper J-5A Cub Cruiser photographed at Oakland, California, in May, 1941 was equipped with wheel fairings and navigation lights. (Peter M. Bowers via Joseph P. Juptner)

Displaying United States and Mexican registry, a J-5A photographed in September, 1946 reveals numerous repairs to its fuselage fabric. Note Vultee BT-13 basic trainer in background. (Peter M. Bowers via Joseph P. Juptner)

William "Bill" Piper, Jr., poses with a J-5B early in 1941. The J-5B series were powered by geared Lycoming GO-145-62 engines rated at 75 hp. The J-5B Cub Cruiser cost $2,150. (Piper Aviation Museum)

ing O-235 engine, the first prototype aircraft was constructor number 1309, registered NX41333, and a second was constructor number 5-1385, registered NX41599, according to Roger W. Peperell and Colin M. Smith in their book Piper Aircraft And Their Forerunners.

Production began in 1942 but only about 35 J-5C airplanes were completed before the United States Government halted all civil aircraft manufacture because of the Second World War. During the war Piper engineers performed design work on a J-5D variant that was powered by a 125 hp. Lycoming O-290 engine, but company records do not indicate that any airplanes were built until 1946.

In October, 1945 one J-5C, constructor number 5-1601 was built and assigned registration NX41561. The aircraft served as a prototype for the PA-12 Super Cruiser introduced after the war. With a maximum speed of 95 mph., a range of 300 statute miles and priced at only $1,798 in 1940, the J-5 series found a ready market and 1,510 were built (including military HE-1/AE-1, YL-14/L-14 derivatives) before production was terminated in 1946.

By 1941 Piper Aircraft Corporation had been the world's largest producer of light aircraft for more than a year and sales continued to soar. As the company's success increased, so did research and development aimed at producing a complete line of Piper airplanes for America's ever-expanding light aircraft market.

Piper introduced the Lycoming-powered J-5B Cub Cruiser in 1941. Photographed at Keene, New Hampshire, in December, 1947 a J-5B registered NC38251 was equipped with Marston skis for winter flight operations. Marston skis featured hydraulic cylinders to position the skis during flight. (Charles N. Trask)

In-flight photograph of a J-5C registered NC33532, constructor number 5-1390. The J-5C had a cruising speed of 100 mph. and a range of more than 375 statute miles. (Piper Aviation Museum)

William T. Piper, Sr. expresses his approval of the J-5A Cub Cruiser. His doubts that a three-place Piper airplane would sell proved unfounded. (Piper Aviation Museum)

The J-5C was powered by a 100 hp. Lycoming O-235-C engine enclosed in a pressure-type cowling. The airplane illustrated was the second prototype, constructor number 5-1385, registered NX41599. (Piper Aviation Museum)

In 1940 the company had evaluated the Applegate Duck Amphibian designed by Raymond Applegate, a flying boat pilot who had served in World War One. Boasting an aluminum alloy hull and fuselage, the pusher amphibian was rebuilt by Piper engineers with wings from a Piper J-3 Cub and modified J-3 tail surfaces. Other sources indicate the aircraft was equipped with J-5 Cub Cruiser wings that were shortened one foot per panel.

The original Essex automobile engine was replaced at Lock Haven with a 60 hp. Lenape static radial powerplant. In its original configuration, the amphibian did not fly well and a 75 hp. Continental engine was fitted in an attempt to improve performance.

Piper engineers next installed a 130 hp. Franklin opposed powerplant and made additional modifications to the airplane, including relocating the landing gear ahead of the lift struts. The revised prototype was designated as the P-1 Cub Clipper and given constructor number P-1, registered NX27960.

During trials on the West Branch of the Susquehanna River the aircraft continued to perform poorly, chiefly because it was underpowered. The P-1 needed an engine in the 150-200 hp. class but no such engine was readily available. As a result, Piper terminated its agreement with Raymond Applegate and ceased further development of the Cub Clipper.

In addition to the abortive P-1, Piper built a number of experimental airplanes for research programs in the early 1940s before the outbreak of

In 1940 Piper experimented with the Applegate Duck Amphibian designed by Raymond Applegate, and renamed it the Cub Clipper. The original, Essex automobile powerplant had been replaced by a 60 hp. Lenape Papoose static radial engine when this photograph was taken. Note rubber-covered floats. (Smithsonian Institution, National Air And Space Museum Negative Number 93-2390)

Photographed at the Lock Haven factory, Cub Clipper registered NX17866 displays its Lycoming GO-145 engine and floats faired with fabric. Piper engineers also fitted a Continental A-75 engine to the aircraft. (Smithsonian Institution, National Air And Space Museum Negative Number 93-2391)

Piper modified the original airframe and installed a 130 hp. Franklin engine on a redesigned mount. Despite engineering improvements, flight tests of the Cub Clipper were unsatisfactory and the program was terminated. The second, modified prototype registered NX27960 is illustrated. Note triangular rear window. (Smithsonian Institution, National Air And Space Museum Negative Number 93-2389)

hostilities. A chief protagonist of such work was Howard "Pug" Piper, the youngest of William Piper's three sons.

Howard studied engineering in college and was constantly seeking new concepts for Piper aircraft. Although chief engineer Walter Jamouneau presided over a conservative engineering department, Pug was a Piper and his opinions were heard and often heeded.

Among the pre-war experimental designs underwritten by Howard Piper were the P-2 and the P-4. Designed in 1941, the P-2 prototype was a two-place, high-wing monoplane powered by a 60 hp. Franklin 4AC-171 engine enclosed in a full cowling. A 75 hp. Continental A-75-8 was later installed.

Given constructor number 0 and registered NX33281, the P-2 was similar to the J-3 but featured a cabin door like that of the J-5. The P-4 design was a four-place airplane that retained Piper's traditional high wing configuration and added a 120 hp. Lycoming 0-290 engine enclosed in a cowling. A sole prototype was built and assigned constructor number 1, registered NX38300.

Both the P-2 and the P-4 did not progress beyond the experimental stage chiefly because of the threat of war, but their virtues were later incorporated into the postwar PA-11 and PA-14 series airplanes. The beginning of World War Two in September, 1939 had little effect on Piper's burgeoning airplane business. It already had built thousands of aircraft and had plans to build thousands more as the decade of the 1940s arrived. The future looked exceptionally bright.

Events in China, Japan and the spreading hostilities in Europe had, by late 1940, begun to dim

The two-place Piper P-2 Cub was designed in 1941 and was powered by a 60 hp. Franklin 4AC-171 engine. Assigned constructor number 0 and registered NX33281, the experimental P-2 was not developed for production. Note fully-cowled engine and right-side cabin door. (Piper Aviation Museum)

The larger, four-place Piper P-4 Cub experimental aircraft made its debut in 1941 and featured a 120 hp. Lycoming O-290 engine. Assigned constructor number 1 and registered NX38300, the handsome P-4 was not produced. (Piper Aviation Museum)

hopes for peace. Public opinion increasingly held that the United States not only should help Great Britain survive, but more importantly should rapidly prepare herself for the horrors of yet another global war.

At Piper Aircraft Corporation, however, the threat of war seemed remote. Business was brisk and airplanes were selling almost as fast as the workers could build them. Profits, too, were on the rise. At that time, the company's output represented about 45% of all small airplane production in the United States.

After being relocated to Lock Haven in 1937, the Piper factory had built more than 8,000 airplanes and produced nearly 3,200 aircraft in 1941 alone. The payroll had escalated to 2,000 people and manufacturing facilities were being expanded to cope with anticipated further increases in production.

William T. Piper announced to stockholders in September, 1940 that the company had achieved sales of more than $3.2 million and showed a profit of $157,823 after taxes and depreciation. He and the

Piper team had earned every cent of it.

Piper was proud that the company had been able to succeed without resorting to government contracts for aircraft. He also believed, with equal fervor, that the venerable J-3 Cub could be a valuable asset to field commanders, particularly for directing artillery fire and performing liaison duties.

Although Piper viewed dependence upon government contracts with disdain, he was not opposed to selling aircraft to Uncle Sam. In February, 1935 he had instructed company sales manager Ted Weld to write the War Department regarding sales of E-2 Cubs as military primary trainers. The War Department's assistant secretary for aeronautics, however, refused Weld's offer of further discussions and a demonstration flight.

As 1941 began, light airplane manufacturers including Piper were still struggling to win an opportunity to prove to the United States military that small aircraft could be valuable—not as primary

In the summer and autumn of 1941, Piper, Taylorcraft and Aeronca provided commercial aircraft for use during war maneuvers conducted by the United States Army. Piper provided J-3C-65 Cubs that were painted flat olive drab for the war games. A wind-driven generator, shown mounted on the main landing gear of a J-3C-65 Cub, powered a communications radio. (U.S. Army Military History Institute via Mal Holcomb)

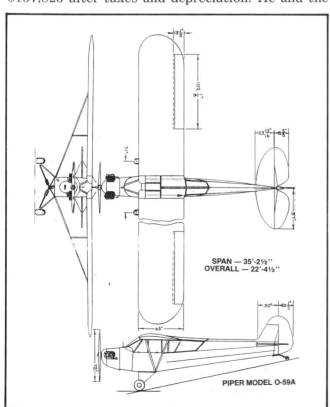

SPAN — 35'-2½"
OVERALL — 22'-4½"

PIPER MODEL O-59A

trainers but as alternatives to traditional observation aircraft and ground-based vehicles.

In 1940 the United States Army Air Corps was still under the direct control of the Army. The service had numerous types of observation aircraft in inventory such as the North American O-47, Curtis O-52 and some Stinson O-49 Vigilant ships.

Although well designed and ruggedly built, most of the army's observation aircraft were either too large, too fast or incapable of performing their intended role,

William T. Piper, Sr. (center, pointing with finger), flew Cubs and participated in the war games alongside his pilots. He championed the belief that small airplanes could provide valuable support for military units in combat. Note grasshopper symbol on fuselage. (Smithsonian Institution, National Air And Space Museum Negative Number 93-2383)

or could not operate properly without extensive ground service support. Perhaps worst of all, they cost taxpayers more than they were worth and did little to meet the needs of field commanders.

To Piper and officials of other light airplane companies, it seemed logical that their aircraft could do the job better—and at much less cost—if given the chance to prove it. He knew the Cubs, Aeroncas and Taylorcrafts were capable of performing observation duties, evacuating wounded personnel, ferrying soldiers to other locations, carrying messages and flying short-range patrol for ground troops.

It was obvious to Mr. Piper that if war came and light airplanes were not participants it could have an adverse effect on the industry as a whole, especially after the war ended. His competitors agreed, and the

big three—Piper, Aeronca and Taylorcraft—joined hands and finances in a united front aimed at getting small aircraft into combat.

Although they wisely hired skilled lobbyists such as John E.P. Morgan to preach their gospel in the halls of Congress and the War Department, tremendous obstacles barred the path to success. In addition to not having the money allotted for such aircraft, the military displayed little interest and some open hostility toward such a proposal.

After months of stating convincing arguments to military officers and employing expert lobbying tactics, the lightplane companies were smarting from repeated rejection by the United States Army and United States Navy. Their continued persistence paid off, however, and the little airplane builders finally got their chance.

In the summer of 1940, a Piper J-4 Cub Coupe was flown to Camp Beauregard, Louisiana, to direct artillery fire during ground maneuvers held by the Texas National Guard. Flying from dirt roads, the Cub Coupe did an impressive job as an airborne courier and spotter but the military remained unimpressed.

Responding to demands from senior army officers including General Adna R. Chaffee, who had spearheaded development of the army's armored divisions, the United States Army Air Corps bought six Stinson Voyager aircraft in 1940 and designated them YO-54. Despite their capabilities, little was done by air corps pilots and observers to evaluate the Voyager's potential.

In July, 1941 army maneuvers held at Fort Bliss, Texas proved exactly how valuable the small Piper and Aeronca ships were. Flown by company pilots from Piper, Aeronca and Taylorcraft, the lightplanes flitted about the battlegrounds performing mundane but important duties, easily flying into and out of rough landing strips that could not be used by the army's big liaison aircraft.

During the war games staged in 1941, the little aircraft were at first denigrated by officers and relegated to flying unimportant errands. Through persistence, however, the civilian lightplane pilots were able to demonstrate to the army how versatile their mounts truly were. Both Pug Piper and Tony Piper were

Throughout the war games, Cubs, Aeronca Defenders and Taylorcraft Tandems performed aerial reconnaissance, directed artillery barrages and troop movements, ferried personnel and supplies and accomplished a myriad of other duties. The Grasshoppers soon became indispensable to field commanders who realized their unique versatility. White crosses painted on the fuselages identified the aircraft as war game participants. (U.S. Army Military History Institute via Mal Holcomb)

Because the Cubs and other light airplanes participating in the maneuvers could virtually go anywhere the troops went, pilots found themselves eating, sleeping and living alongside their aircraft. The little airplanes were originally referred to as "Grasshoppers" by United States Army Major General Innis P. Swift, and the name stuck. (U.S. Army Military History Institute via Mal Holcomb)

A Piper J-3C-65 Cub refuels at a local gasoline station during war games as horse-mounted troops pass by and children flock around the airplane. Note civil registration visible on right, upper wing surface. (Smithsonian Institution, National Air And Space Musuem Negative Number 93-2387)

Two Piper Cubs await orders during military maneuvers. ➤ The small airplanes were easy to repair in the field using local materials, and replacement parts were inexpensive compared with the army observation aircraft. A Grasshopper's greatest asset was its ability to operate from dirt roads and unprepared fields with a minimum of logistical support. (U.S. Army Military History Institute via Mal Holcomb)

Piper YO-59 before delivery to the United States Army in 1941. (Piper Aviation Museum)

among the pilots who flew Cubs during the war maneuvers.

It was not long before the generals, war game judges and even lowly lieutenants began to realize that the Piper Cubs, Taylorcraft Tandems and Aeronca Defenders and Chiefs were capable of doing jobs no other vehicle in the army's limited—and mostly obsolete—inventory could perform. Flying low and slow and hedgehopping across the countryside, they quickly earned the nickname "Grasshoppers."

For its part in showing the military that it needed lightplanes, Piper had provided a small number of J-3- and J-4-series aircraft with pilots on loan to the army during the war games. Compared with their military counterparts, the Grasshoppers were a resounding success.

The lightplanes burned cheap and plentiful automotive fuel—the Stinson O-49 needed 100 octane aviation gasoline. The Cubs and Taylorcrafts could land virtually anywhere—the army's observation airplanes often needed prepared runways. The rough-and-ready Pipers and Aeroncas were repaired quickly and easily in the field with existing materials—the army's aircraft often had to be trucked back to repair depots. Perhaps best of all, one small, two-seat J-3 Cub cost less than the propeller of a three-seat North American O-47!

Convinced that the aerial Grasshoppers were worthy of military use, in September, 1941 the United States Army Air Forces bought four Cubs that were designated as YO-59s as well as another 40 airplanes designated O-59 that were delivered in November. Both Taylorcraft and Aeronca also had received aircraft orders respectively for YO-57 and YO-58 aircraft.

By the end of 1941, army tank and troop commanders as well as the general staff had been convinced that they needed light airplanes on the field of battle. But who would control them, the air forces or the army ground forces? In June, 1942 the issue was settled: the War Department established an aviation section within the army and the American lightplane became an important part of the nation's military inventory.

The humble Cubs had proven themselves in the field and unknowingly had begun one of the most interesting chapters in the airplane's hallowed history. William T. Piper, Sr., had won his battle to prove that the army needed small airplanes and that Piper Aircraft Corporation was prepared to produce them.

During the months of innocent mock combat that grossly misrepresented how the ongoing world war was actually being fought, the little Grasshoppers had done well and proved their worth. As the fateful year of 1941 unfolded, the Japanese and their Nazi allies were plotting to bring war to America's doorstep—a war that would change the course of modern history and plunge Mr. Piper's Cub into its baptism of fire.

CHAPTER FOUR

PIPER GOES TO WAR

The surprise attack by the Imperial Japanese Navy against Pearl Harbor, Territory of Hawaii, on December 7, 1941, found the United States military machine relatively weak and virtually unable to take the offensive. Its air arms, both on land and at sea, were particularly impotent after two decades of neglect, political indifference and chronic underfunding. The situation was exacerbated by Congressional and War Department ignorance coupled with a fervent national desire to maintain international isolationism.

Although Uncle Sam severely lacked aircraft to fight the war, fortunately a large pool of civilian pilots did exist thanks largely to President Franklin D. Roosevelt's foresight in launching the Civilian Pilot Training Program (CPTP). Inaugurated early in 1939, thousands of collegiate men and women—including those attending at least nine black colleges and four women's universities—earned their wings in light airplanes. About 75% of the airplanes used nationwide to teach the fledgling aviators were Piper Cubs.

Administered by the Civil Aeronautics Authority in Washington, D.C., the CPT program's goal was to have 20,000 college students each year earn a private pilot license. By 1940, 10,000 people had learned to fly under the guidance of CPT instructors and by January 1, 1941, more than 63,000 students had become certificated pilots.

Once licensed, many of the pilots entered a second tier of training that included flight instruction in

During World War Two Piper L-4 aircraft were used to train prospective combat glider pilots. With the L-4's engine shut down, student pilots made initial approaches from 1,000 feet altitude and gradually increased to 5,000 feet as their skill improved. (Mal Holcomb)

Beechcraft Model 17 biplanes, Waco biplanes and Stinson monoplanes. Airplanes such as the Beechcraft were equipped with up to 400 hp. air-cooled, static radial engines, constant-speed propellers and retractable landing gear.

The advanced training later proved invaluable to America's war effort. Some of the conflict's greatest aces and combat pilots first took flight in a CPT Piper Cub, Taylorcraft or Aeronca, including P-38 Lightning pilot Richard I. Bong, the highest scoring United States ace with 40 victories; United States Marine Corps pilot Joe Foss, who flew his Grumman F4F Wildcat so bravely at Guadalcanal, and many other airmen and airwomen too numerous to mention.

Soon after the debacle at Pearl Harbor, civilian flying was severely curtailed but production of commercial airplanes continued into 1942. During those months Piper had amassed hundreds of unsold J-3 Cubs at Lock Haven, but had no buyers. Fortunately, Brazil bought many of the J-3F-65 Cubs and the United States Navy acquired 230 J-3C-65 aircraft and designated them NE-1.

Prior to receiving military orders for light airplanes, Piper already had begun efforts to transform the J-3 Cub into a flying machine better suited to its new military mission. In January, 1942 J-3C-65 constructor number 8175, registered NX41555 was modified to install additional windows above and to the sides of the rear seat observer to improve visibility. The change was commonly referred to as the "greenhouse" cabin, according to Roger W. Peperell and Colin M. Smith in their book titled Piper Aircraft and Their Forerunners.

In February Piper received United States Army

Held in check by chocks, an L-4A dubbed "Elizabeth" prepares for takeoff from the flight deck of the aircraft carrier U.S.S. Ranger on November 9, 1942, during the Allied invasion of North Africa. The pilot is Captain Ford E. Allcorn. Note United States insignia with yellow outer circle applied specifically for the invasion. (Piper Aviation Museum)

United States Army sergeant Frank Perkins poses with his L-4A named "Super Snooper." (Piper Aviation Museum)

Air Forces (USAAF) orders for 948 airplanes, the first of thousands built for the war against Axis aggression. Designated O-59A, the aircraft featured the greenhouse cabin modification. Powered by Continental O-170-3 engines (military designation for the A-65-8), these airplanes initially were designated L-4 but were redesignated L-4A during the production run. The predecessor YO-59 and O-59 ships became the L-4 variant. Piper began delivering L-4A aircraft in February, 1942.

Legendary stories about the Cub in combat have emerged over the years since World War Two. The United States Army's initial use of Piper L-4s came during the invasion of North Africa in November, 1942 when the aircraft were assigned primarily to direct artillery fire against the entrenched German and Italian troops.

Launched from the flight deck of the aircraft carrier U.S.S. Ranger, the three Cubs and their pilots were greeted by a wall of gunfire from American ground troops at the beachhead as they attempted to fly inland. Flying to their destination air strip, one L-4 was damaged first by United States gunners and then shot down by the Vichy French. The other two Cubs were subjected to a hail of ground- and anti-aircraft fire as well, and their pilots were forced to land short of their goal.

It was an inauspicious beginning for the Grasshoppers, and the Army had much to learn regarding how to use them effectively, including notifying troops that friendly aircraft would be flying overhead. In a more successful use of Cubs during the North African campaign, in March, 1943 L-4 pilots discovered elements of Field Marshal Erwin Rommel's famed Afrika Corps preparing a major armored attack

against Allied positions near El Guetter.

As the German 10th Panzer Division rolled toward its target, the Grasshoppers radioed coordinates to artillery units and directed a massive bombardment of the hapless Germans, blunting the assault and leaving the swirling desert sands littered with dead soldiers, dead tanks and dead Nazi hopes. In the heat of battle, the diminutive Grasshoppers had helped achieve an important Allied victory.

Among United States Army generals who regularly used Grasshoppers for transportation and liaison missions were Lt. Gen. Mark Clark, who flew in L-4s during preparation for the invasion of Italy, and Lt. Gen. George S. Patton, Jr. Patton himself was a pilot and had flown his personal Stinson Voyager during

A flock of United States Army L-4-series aircraft were photographed on their European airfield in 1944. Invasion stripes have been removed from the upper half of the fuselage and the upper surface of the wing panels, indicating that the photograph was taken after the June 6, 1944 assault on Hitler's "Fortress Europe". Note fuel containers, camouflage netting and dirt revetments. (Piper Aviation Museum)

The United States Army Air Forces operated L-4 aircraft in the remote China-Burma-India Theater as well as in Europe and the Pacific. Photograph shows maintenance personnel performing repairs to an L-4's 65 hp. Continental engine amidst crude, jungle conditions. (Piper Aviation Museum)

Using a street in Naples, Italy for a runway, Lt. General Mark W. Clark and his pilot Major John T. Walker prepare to take off in an L-4A named "Eleanor II". Clark advocated and supported use of light aircraft such as the L-4 in combat operations. (Piper Aviation Museum)

32

During the Allied invasion of Sicily in 1943, L-4 liaison aircraft were launched from a specially-built runway 270 feet long and 16 feet wide constructed aboard a United States Navy Landing Ship-Tank (LST). (Piper Aviation Museum)

The victor and the vanquished. An L-4 assigned to the Army's First Cavalry Division in Japan takes off over damaged Nakajima Ki-84 fighters in October, 1945. Fast and maneuverable, the Ki-84 was one of Japan's best fighters of the war. (Piper Aviation Museum)

A civilian J-3C-65 Cub based in Japan after the war was housed in a reinforced concrete hangar. During the closing months of World War Two, the camouflaged structure had been used by the Japanese to protect fighter aircraft flown in defense of the home islands. (Piper Aviation Museum)

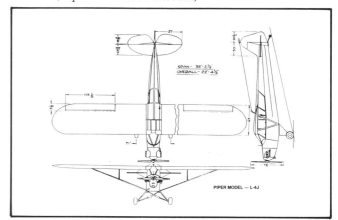

the prewar maneuvers and flew in small airplanes throughout the war.

General Dwight D. Eisenhower, also a pilot, used Cubs and other small aircraft like airborne Jeeps, greatly increasing his mobility on the battlefield. Lt. General Omar Bradley also flew in L-4s during the war. In the 1943 campaign to capture Sicily—which became the Allied springboard to the conquest of Italy—short, narrow flight decks were built on United States Navy Landing Ship-Tank vessels. The lightweight Cubs were airborne in 50 yards with a headwind and proceeded to fly inland where they helped direct artillery barrages against the enemy.

During the landings at Anzio, Italy, L-4s directed not only Army Howitzers but the big guns of the United States Navy's capital ships as they pounded the beachhead and associated targets. Missions of medical evacuation and airlifting of food, ammunition and life-giving whole blood were flown by the Grasshoppers both in the European and South Pacific

theaters of operations.

In the Pacific war, both the army and navy made good use of Cubs to assist ground troops. Piper L-4s often were among the first airplanes to land on islands recently won from the determined Japanese, who had vowed to die in their defense and not surrender. Cubs flown by the United States Marine Corps ferried food and blood plasma to small units fighting in the dense jungles that typified the South Pacific island groups.

General Douglas MacArthur eventually came to appreciate the capabilities not only of airpower itself, but the value of small airplanes in combat. The navy's LSTs carried many Grasshoppers to the islands where they were unloaded sans wings, quickly reassembled within a few hours and made ready for a myriad of missions.

When MacArthur returned to the Philippines in 1944, Piper Cubs were there as well. Some of the first airstrips hacked out of the jungle on Leyte were used by Cubs. On Okinawa, L-4s were launched and

Instrument panel of a United States Army Air Forces L-4. Placards read "Rear Seat For Solo Flying" and "Service Ceiling 11,950 ft." Yellow arc on airspeed indicator was set at 90 mph., redline at 120 mph. (Smithsonian Institution, National Air And Space Museum Negative Number 82-7962)

In addition to land operation, L-4-series aircraft were equipped with floats and flown from lakes and rivers. The L-4B illustrated was serving with the United States Army's 32nd Corps Artillery in January, 1945, flying from Lake Mott near Fort Bragg, North Carolina. (Piper Aviation Museum)

In 1942 Piper began delivering TG-8 training gliders to the United States Army Air Forces. The TG-8 essentially was an engineless J-3 Cub with an extended canopy and redesigned landing gear. (Mal Holcomb)

Piper built 253 TG-8 gliders. The aircraft were used to train pilots who later flew Waco CG-4A troop-carrying gliders in the famed D-Day invasion of Europe and the ill-fated Operation Market Garden. After the war many of the TG-8 gliders were converted to J-3 Cub configuration. (Mal Holcomb)

recovered from LSTs using the ingenious Brodie Device—a system designed by Army Captain Jeff Brodie that allowed an L-4 to be launched and retrieved on a cable suspended between supports. The Brodie Device was especially useful when landing fields were not available for L-4 aircraft.

Piper L-4s and other Grasshoppers were flown extensively in support of artillery and troops fighting in the India and Burma Theater of Operations. They were used to help survey the famous Ledo Road across northern Burma that joined with the equally famous Burma Road that ran from Lashio to Kunming, providing a critical supply line to Allied and Chinese Nationalist forces fighting the entrenched Japanese.

Although most Cubs flew unarmed during the war, various weapons were adapted to the airplane's rugged airframe and used with some success against the enemy. Installations included army bazookas mounted on the lift struts as well as small rockets that were capable of destroying small tanks, trucks and wreaking havoc on infantry columns. For operations against ground troops and machine gun nests, hand grenades mounted in wing racks were released and armed via a cable in the cockpit.

Regardless of where and how the little Grasshoppers were employed by Allied Forces, they proved their worth time and time again. Field commanders,

generals and United States Navy officers were quick to give the humble aircraft their share of credit for many of the hard-won victories in the European and Pacific campaigns.

William T. Piper, Sr., and other lightplane company officials could be proud of what their airplanes had done to help win the war. Their belief in what the Cubs, Taylorcrafts and Aeroncas could achieve, coupled with their tenacity to prove it had fully vindicated their faith. For its part in the war effort, Piper produced more than 5,600 light airplanes for the military, mostly Cubs in olive drab L-4 guise.

In addition to performing gallantly as artillery spotters and forward observation platforms in every major theater of war, the versatile J-3 Cub also underwent transformation from powered airplane to unpowered glider. Designated as the TG-8, Piper built 253 training gliders specifically to teach glider pilots how to fly the large, box-like Waco CG-4A troop and cargo carrying glider, of which more than 13,900 were built during the war.

Aerial view of the Piper factory early in World War Two shows L-4 liaison airplanes parked outside. Note flood-prone West Branch of the Susquehanna River and the railroad that transported raw materials to the Piper facilities. (Piper Aviation Museum)

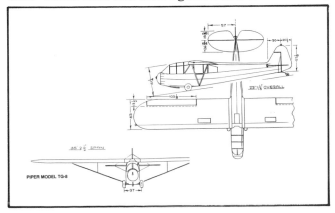

34

The ambulatory HE-1 (later redesignated AE-1) were built for the United States Navy. Based on the J-5C Cub Cruiser, the aircraft featured a turtledeck that hinged forward to accommodate a single litter in the cabin. (Piper Aviation Museum)

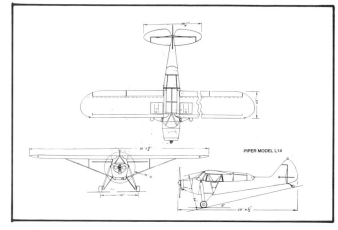

In addition to the Cub, Aeronca Defenders and Taylorcraft Tandems were modified into training gliders during the war. Essentially light airplanes without engines, the TG-8 and its Aeronca TG-5 and Taylorcraft TG-6 companions had an extended cockpit section in place of the powerplant.

Operated as part of the War Training Service, which replaced the pre-war Civilian Pilot Training Program in 1942, the glider training course took six months to complete. Students received three months of combat training and technical instruction on gliders and spent one month with Taylorcraft L-2, Aeronca L-3 and Piper L-4 ships learning to fly, including how to make power-off landings from as high as 5,000 feet.

After mastering the challenging task of making consistent, intentional forced landings in a confined area, the pilots transitioned to the TG-5, TG-6 or Piper TG-8 training gliders for additional instruction. Formation tows behind Douglas C-47 transports were an important part of the curriculum, since the C-47 would also be towing the combat gliders during offensive operations.

Another view of the same L-14 photographed in 1986 in Alaska. The plexiglass panels had been eliminated and a new turtledeck fabricated to blend smoothly with the fuselage. The engine cowling also had been modified from the original design. Note deflected wing flaps. (Noel Allard collection)

An L-14 registered NC69255 was photographed in October, 1947 in Pennsylvania. The clear plexiglass panels in the aft cockpit were painted. The YL-14 and L-14 aircraft were powered by 125 hp. Lycoming O-290-C engines. (Peter M. Bowers)

The sixth month was spent flying the Waco CG-3A advanced trainer, which gave pilots their first experience with a full-scale, heavy troop glider before graduating to the combat-ready CG-4A.

Assigned constructor number G-1 to G-253, the first 26 Piper TG-8 aircraft were constructed in 1942 and the remainder in 1943. The first TG-8 was under construction as a J-3 (constructor number 9102) before it was modified with the extended canopy. Although most of the TG-8s were used by the United States Army, the United States Navy acquired three aircraft for flight trials under the designation XLNP-1.

Although elementary in design and inexpensive to build, the most important feature of the little gliders was their availability at a time when America needed thousands of silent aircraft and brave pilots to fly them. In addition to the crucial D-Day invasion of Europe and the ill-fated Allied Operation Market Garden in 1944, the Waco CG-4A also was used for troop and supply sorties against the Japanese in the

India and Burma Theater of Operations. None of the TG-series training gliders were engaged in combat operations.

Although Piper's J-3 Cub was the primary airplane built by the company for the war effort, there were other members of the Piper aircraft family that did their part for victory. Like its J-3 brother, the side-by-side J-4 Cub Coupe also went to war but in significantly fewer numbers. Fifteen Cub Coupes were impressed into military service, with 14 aircraft designated as L-4E and one as a C-83B.

Another wartime aircraft was the J-5 Cub Cruiser. The United States Navy purchased 100 military ambulance versions of the J-5C designated HE-1 that were built between November, 1942 and June, 1943. Piper built the experimental J-5CA in May, 1942 as a two-place ambulatory aircraft that served as the prototype HE-1. The airplane was registered NX41551 and assigned constructor number 5-1386.

To accomodate a single stretcher, the HE-1's aft turtledeck was hinged to rotate upward and forward, allowing the patient to be easily loaded aboard. With the advent of helicopters, the HE-1 designation was changed to AE-1 to avoid confusion between the two types of aircraft and their missions.

Early in the war Piper designed a military observation version of the J-5 Cub Cruiser that was intended to be the company's next-generation liaison airplane. Designated J-5CO, the original airplane was registered NX41552 and assigned constructor number 5-1387 in 1942. A second airplane was built in 1944 to become the prototype L-4X registered NX33529, constructor number 5-3001. The airplane was powered by a Lycoming O-290A rated at 125 hp.

A third airplane, registered NX33534 and assigned constructor number 5-3002 was built in 1945 and designated as the L-14 prototype powered by a 125 hp. Lycoming O-290C. The J-5CO, L-4X and L-14 featured increased window area to improve pilot and observer visibility both vertically and horizontally. The L-14s were the first production Piper airplanes to incorporate trailing edge wing flaps.

The two YL-14 prototypes and three additional YL-14 ships (constructor numbers 5-3003--5-3005) were delivered to the United States Army in the spring and summer of 1945. Although 850 aircraft were to be produced, most of the order was cancelled in August, 1945.

Before cancellation of the army contract nine airplanes were under construction. Because Piper had obtained an approved type certificate from the United States Civil Aeronautics Authority for the L-14, these ships were sold in 1946 to civilian buyers but retained their military designation.

Like the J-3 and J-4, the J-5 was pressed into military service during the war. Forty-five J-5A airplanes were redesignated L-4F and were operated by the United States Army. Forty-one J-5B versions were designated L-4G, and four J-5A Cub Cruisers intended for evaluation as C-83 light cargo transports instead were designated as L-4F.

Although the L-4 series airplanes were the most common Piper product to participate in the war, the company did develop other interesting, if abortive, designs. In 1942 the PT-1 low-wing trainer was built

(Left to right): William T. Piper, Sr., Walter Jamouneau, PT-1 designer Dave Long, and George Hemphill pose with the prototype airplane. (Piper Aviation Museum)

Powered by a six-cylinder, 130 hp. Franklin 6AC-298-D3 engine, the PT-1 featured a retractable landing gear system and was capable of aerobatic maneuvers. Photograph shows Piper experimental test pilot Clyde Smith, Sr., flying the prototype airplane. (Piper Aviation Museum)

The two-place, tandem-seat Piper PT-1 first flew in 1942. It was developed chiefly as a multi-role trainer aircraft for flight schools administering the Civilian Pilot Training Program. (Piper Aviation Museum)

Photographed high above the Pennsylvania countryside, the PT-1's wooden wing and plain-type, trailing edge flaps are evident. Tailwheel was fixed. (Piper Aviation Museum)

and flown. Intended as a multi-mission airplane for the wartime Civilian Pilot Training Program (CPTP), the PT-1 was designed by Piper engineer David Long under the supervision of chief engineer Walter Jamouneau. Pulaski Broward and George Hemphill assisted Long in developing the aircraft.

David Long had operated a CPTP school in addition to his job at Piper, and he incorporated many of the suggestions made by other CPTP operators regarding a new trainer. He designed the PT-1 to perform primary flight instruction, advanced training and instrument flight training, as well as to be capable of performing basic aerobatic maneuvers.

The prototype was assigned constructor number 1 and registered NX4300. The two-place ship was powered by a Franklin 6AC-298-D3 piston engine rated at 130 hp. Long's airplane featured a Warren truss-type, welded steel tube fuselage with an integral nose-over structure between the cockpits.

The full cantilever wood wings used box-type spruce spars, and each panel was bolted to the center section outboard of the main landing gear. The wings were sheathed with 3/32-inch mahogany plywood covered by fabric. In addition, the wings were built to have 6 degrees of dihedral and sufficient washout at the tips for acceptable stall recovery characteristics. Each wing featured a two-to-one taper ratio and incorporated trailing edge flaps.

A USA-35B15 airfoil section was used for the root of the wing, with the USA 35B10 section at the tip. The airfoil possessed good lift characteristics, allowed a relatively high cruising speed and exhibited benign handling during stall and spin recovery.

Wing area was 164 square feet, with a loading of 12.2 lb. per square foot. Two stainless steel wing tanks located in the center section held 40 gallons of fuel. The full-cantilever horizontal stabilizer and the vertical stabilizer were wood with plywood covering. The rudder, elevators, ailerons and flaps also were of wood and fabric construction.

A large, sectioned canopy covered the student pilot and the instructor and permitted excellent visibility. Sliding windows were incorporated into each side, and the cockpit was entered by first sliding the left window down and opening the upper section.

In another first for Piper, a conventional, retractable landing gear system was used but the tailwheel was fixed. The landing gear was manually operated and featured visual indicators in each cockpit as well as an aural gear warning system.

The PT-1 incorporated a number of safety features for its intended role as a CPTP trainer, including a wide landing gear tread of 100 inches to improve taxi, takeoff and landing control, adjustable rudder pedals with military-type toe-operated brakes and vertically adjustable seats. The airplane could be soloed from either the front or rear cockpit. Despite good performance, safety features, multi-mission capabilities and the use of non-strategic materials in its construction, the PT-1 failed to win a contract for Piper and only one was built.

Another of Piper's wartime endeavors was the Glomb project. In 1942 the United States Navy was developing a pilotless gliding bomb that would be towed to its target by a Grumman F4F Wildcat fighter flying at speeds approaching 300 mph.

Once the objective was sighted, the controlling aircraft would release the glide bomb and direct the aircraft to the target using radio control. The bomb featured a crude television camera in the nose section that transmitted an image back to the controlling pilot.

Packed with two tons of high explosives, the Glomb—an acronym for gliding bomb—seemed like an ideal weapon for the Pacific war. Designed to be expendable and save human lives, the project was doomed to oblivion. The technologies and time required to bring the Glomb to an acceptable level of reliability delayed development and eventually precluded its use in combat.

Piper was selected along with Pratt-Read and the Taylor Aircraft Company to manufacture the advanced weapons. Only three XLBE-1 aircraft were built by Pratt-Read. Taylor produced 25 LBT-1 versions. Piper built at least one LBP-1 Glomb, but it is uncertain if additional glide bombs were produced.

Perhaps the most interesting project undertaken by Piper during the war years involved a series of flight tests to determine what modifications were needed to improve the speed of its most famous airplane, the J-3 Cub. A standard J-3C-65 was procured from the factory to complete the high-speed experiments that began in December, 1944. During the program 31 flights were conducted to evaluate the effect of aerodynamic modifications made to the test airplane.

Piper had contracted to build 100 LBP-1 gliding bombs in 1942, but none were manufactured by the company. Known as the Glomb, the pilotless aircraft was designed to be towed behind a Grumman F4F Wildcat fighter, released near the enemy and guided to its target by remote control. (Piper Aviation Museum)

In 1944 Piper conducted flight tests of a modified J-3C-65 Cub, constructor number 9110, registered NX42111, designated as the P-5 and also known as the J-3X and Cantilever Cub. The chief change was deletion of wing lift struts, but the aircraft's empennage surfaces and landing gear also were modified for drag reduction. (Piper Aviation Museum)

The PWA-1 Skycoupe was designed during World War Two in preparation for the post-war light airplane market. Powered by a 113 hp. Franklin engine, the twin-boom Skycoupe was a two-place, side-by-side aircraft that was not developed for production. (Piper Aviation Museum)

Photograph of the Skycoupe's instrument panel reflects ▶ Piper's attempt to duplicate an automotive-type interior. (Piper Aviation Musuem)

Chief among these changes was installation of a full-cantilever wing spanning 30 feet, fitted with NACA leading edge slots and plain flaps. The new wing had an area of 150 square feet compared with 178 square feet for the original J-3 wing, which spanned 35 feet 3 inches. The slots were eventually covered because they provided no performance improvement.

When equipped with the strutless wing, the airplane became known unofficially as the Cantilever Cub and was designated both as the J-3X and the P-5. It was assigned constructor number 9110 and registered NX42111. Without the added drag of lift and jury struts, the J-3X achieved a maximum speed of 111 mph., compared with a maximum speed of 83 mph. for a standard production J-3C-65 Cub.

Although the clipped wing provided higher speeds, the "increased induced drag caused by the smaller wing largely nullified this gain. The net result was a bigger increase in the landing speed than in top speed," according to the Piper J-3X flight test report.

Other changes were made to the J-3X:
1. The landing gear shock struts were replaced with ½ inch diameter streamlined rods, and the trailing edge of the landing gear vees were faired to a knife-edge.
2. The trailing edges of the wing and empennage surfaces were faired to a knife-edge with balsa wood and fabric tape.
3. A J-5C engine cowling faired into the fuselage was installed.
4. J-4 Cub Coupe horizontal stabilizer fillets were added.
5. Aileron and flap gaps were sealed with fabric.
6. The tailwheel and spring were replaced with a streamlined wood block.
7. Empennage surface gaps were sealed with fabric.
8. The turtledeck was rounded from the 30% chord point of the wing to the vertical stabilizer.
9. Wing tips were faired to a knife-edge with reshaped wood-tip bows and fabric.
10. Fabric on the landing gear vees was removed and and each strut faired.
11. A Roby controllable-pitch propeller was installed

for some tests, but only increased speed to 110 mph. from 109 mph.

In evaluating the program results, Piper engineers concluded that eliminating the lift struts produced the most significant speed increase, followed by streamlining the landing gear and eliminating the wing leading edge slots. Clyde Smith, Sr., a Piper test pilot who joined the company in December, 1941 said the cantilever-wing J-3X "was fast but had to be flown carefully" since the wing essentially was no stronger than that of the J-3.

After each modification was completed in the experimental shop, Smith was among the pilots who flew the airplane over a measured, one-mile course at least six times in each direction—and in smooth air—to obtain accurate data. Although the tests provided useful drag information, none of the modifications were incorporated into production J-3 airplanes.

As the war moved toward its climax in 1945, Piper officials already had begun planning for the post-war era. One of the first airplanes built was the PWA-1, or Post War Airplane that was named the Skycoupe. Designed in 1943, the PWA-1's unconventional configuration was a bold thrust for Piper.

The all-metal, low-wing Skycoupe featured twin booms similar to those used on the Lockheed P-38 Lightning, and a pusher engine. The tear drop-shaped cabin had left- and right-side entry doors and room for two occupants seated side-by-side. Generous window area provided good visibility.

The wing loading was 12.2 lb. per square foot with a power loading of 14.1 lb. per horsepower. Useful load was 501 lb. and the airplane had a maximum fuel capacity of 27 gallons. Only one prototype was built, constructor number 1, registered NX4500, which underwent a limited flight test program. Powered by a Franklin 4ACG-199-H3 powerplant rated at 113 hp.,

the PWA-1's maximum speed was about 110 mph. at a maximum gross weight of 1,597 lb.

Little is known about the Skycoupe's short existence except that it was not produced. From a safety and ground handling standpoint, however, the airplane had some innovative features including a fixed, tricycle landing gear that made taxiing, takeoff and landing easier for the pilot, and a propeller that was shielded by the twin booms.

After the war ended, future business projections made by virtually all United States light aircraft manufacturers were highly optimistic. Much of the reason for that attitude centered on the anticipated wave of flying mania predicted to sweep the country when peace returned.

Piper, like its larger competitors Beech Aircraft Corporation and the Cessna Aircraft Company, was preparing a fresh batch of airplane designs that it hoped would bring it success in the post-war marketplace. Cessna president Dwane L. Wallace was about to unleash the two-place Model 120 and Model 140 aircraft, and Walter H. Beech's engineers had developed the four-place Model 35 Bonanza that was

The experimental department crew that developed the PA-6 engine installation included (left to right): Wilford Kling, Clarence Monks, Paul Supold, Warren Finch, George Wrye and George Eldred. (Piper Aviation Museum)

The PA-6 Sky Sedan was a four-place, high-performance airplane with retractable landing gear. The aircraft illustrated was constructor number 6-01, registered NX580. (Smithsonian Institution, National Air And Space Museum Negative Number 93-2388)

◀ *Piper experimental test pilot Clyde Smith, Sr., prepares to board the prototype Sky Sedan for a test flight. Powered by a 165 hp. Continental engine, the PA-6 had a maximum speed of 160 mph. (Piper Aviation Museum)*

destined to become a classic general aviation design.

William T. Piper, Sr., was looking ahead to the future as well. In 1944 company engineers were hard at work developing the modern Sky Sedan and the diminutive Skycycle for the light airplane market. The prototype Sky Sedan, constructor number 6-01, registered NX580 was a hybrid airplane technologically when it appeared in 1945. The airframe was of mixed all-metal and fabric-covered construction and the vee-shaped windshield of the prototype sported "airliner-type windshield wipers," which Piper literature hailed as a first for personal aircraft.

The four-place Sky Sedan retained a conventional landing gear configuration with a fixed, full swiveling tailwheel. The landing gear was retractable and electrically operated. The Sky Sedan's potential competitor, the Beechcraft Model 35 Bonanza, had a tricycle-gear arrangement.

A manually-operated, crank-down emergency landing gear extension system also was provided on the Sky Sedan. Dual control wheels were standard fit. Gyroscopic flight instruments and a metal adjustable pitch propeller were planned as optional equipment. A Sensenich fixed-pitch, wood propeller was standard.

Powered by a six-cylinder, 165 hp. Continental E-165 engine, the original Sky Sedan prototype was superseded in 1947 by a second prototype identified as the PA-6. Featuring a one-piece windshield and other minor refinements, the revised aircraft was assigned constructor number 6-1 and registered NC4000M.

Projected to sell for less than $4,000, the sleek aircraft had a maximum speed of more than 160 mph., a projected cruise speed of 140 mph. and a landing speed of 49 mph. with flaps extended. Carrying 40 gallons of fuel, the Sky Sedan was calculated to have a cruising range of 620 statute miles.

Maximum gross weight was 2,400 lb. with a wing span of 34 feet 8 inches., length of 25 feet 5.5 inches and a height of 7 feet 3 inches. A maximum of 100 lb. of baggage could be carried under the rear seat. It is interesting to note that the PA-6 reflected much of the same design philosophy as the four-place Cessna

Another of Piper's abortive designs for the post-war market was the diminutive, single-seat Cub Cycle. Renamed Skycycle, the second prototype illustrated made its first flight in January, 1945 powered by a 37 hp. Continental A-40 engine. (Piper Aviation Museum)

P-370 "Family Car of the Air" project that was conceived in 1944 and cancelled in 1945.

Cessna's aircraft closely resembled the PA-6 in both design and performance, and had the P-370 design entered production it would have likely competed spinner-to-spinner with Piper's modern Sky Sedan. Unfortunately, Piper management shelved the PA-6 and the design languished, never to be resurrected. Howard "Pug" Piper, who championed the fight to put the Sky Sedan into production in 1947, would later lament that had the PA-6 been produced it may have helped Piper avoid the financial plight it suffered in the late 1940s.

Another airplane that failed to achieve production after the war was the Cub Cycle. The epitome of simplicity, the Cub Cycle boasted a fuselage made from a droppable fuel tank carried on Vought F4U Corsair-series fighters. Piper had produced these tanks by the thousands during the war.

Intended for one person, the tiny prototype was assigned constructor number 1, registered NX47Y, and first flew in August, 1944 powered by a two-cylinder Franklin air-cooled, horizontally opposed engine. Further refinement led to installation of a 37 hp. Continental A-40-3 and the aircraft was first flown with the new powerplant in September. The mid-wing ship featured a fixed, conventional landing gear with a tailwheel, and the wings were covered with fabric.

Unhappy with the original Cub Cycle's perfor-

The Skycycle's cockpit was covered by a hinged canopy. Note Cub-type fuel quantity indicator, and massive fillets between wing root and fuselage boom to streamline airflow. Piper abandoned the Skycycle in favor of more orthodox designs. (Piper Aviation Museum)

mance, Piper engineers revised the design into the improved Skycycle. Given constructor number 2 but retaining the original prototype's NX47Y registration as well as the 37 hp. Continental engine, the second ship first flew in January, 1945.

After giving the second prototype constructor number 8-01 and identifying it as the PA-8, engineers installed a 55 hp. Lycoming O-145-A2 engine in an effort to further improve performance. Only fragments of data are known about the airplane's short career, but maximum speed was about 120 mph. with a cruise

Small size of the pugnacious Skycycle was evident compared with a Douglas C-47 transport parked at the Lock Haven airport. (Piper Aviation Museum)

After World War Two ended, Piper resumed production of the J-3 Cub. Registered NC87700, the J-3C-65 illustrated was the 1,000th Cub delivered after V-J Day. (Piper Aviation Museum)

Pug Piper championed the fight to put the PA-6 Sky Sedan into production, but lost. He was a visionary who was not afraid to try new concepts in small aircraft design. If the PA-6 had been produced it would have been a worthy competitor to the Beechcraft Model 35 Bonanza. (Piper Aviation Museum)

speed of 95 mph. The Skycycle had a maximum gross weight of 630 lb., wingspan was a mere 20 feet and length only 15 feet 8 inches. Unfortunately, the diminutive Skycycle was plagued by unacceptable handling characteristics and William T. Piper, Sr., cancelled the program.

When the second atom bomb dropped on Japan ended World War Two in August, 1945, the management team at Piper Aircraft Corporation was restless to resume full-scale production of commercial light airplanes. In September, the company completed its fiscal year with sales of $7,700,000 and the escalating backlog of civilian orders approached $11 million.

Piper needed a large amount of cash to restart postwar production of its high-wing airplanes. There was no money to spare for the certification and tooling costs required to bring to fruition aircraft such as the modern PA-6 Sky Sedan and the innovative PA-7 Skycoupe. Simple economics forced management to abandon both designs.

Despite the promise of record sales and profits, Mr. Piper, his sons and the entire company were ill-prepared financially to meet customer demand and to deal with the rough years that lay ahead. World War Two was over, but Piper's fight to survive was about to begin.

Piper built a small number of commercial J-3C-65 Cub Specials during the war years, including NX33527, constructor number 2361A. (Piper Aviation Museum)

CHAPTER FIVE

SEASONS OF CHANGE

After five years of bloodshed, incalculable destruction and holocaust, the war had ended in victory for the Allied nations. During those terrible years, the airplane had come of age as a lethal weapon and had helped bring the Axis empires to their knees.

Many officials within America's light aircraft industry hoped that thousands of bomber and fighter pilots would be eager to swap their B-17s and Mustangs for Pipers and Cessnas. To help returning service personnel win their wings, Congress was prepared to approve a new GI bill that would provide financial assistance to men and women who wanted to learn to fly. Almost overnight, such legislation would spawn hundreds of new flight schools that would in turn need thousands of new airplanes.

For America's light airplane industry in 1945, such possibilities boggled the mind and conjured up fanciful visions of overflowing corporate coffers. There was, however, a problem: supply. When the United States Government finally began releasing stocks of strategic materials to a myriad of industries for postwar production, Piper and other aircraft manufacturers found themselves pitted against the likes of General Motors, Ford, Boeing and Douglas in a bidding war for their share of the steel, aluminum alloy, wood, rubber and chemical stocks that were available.

The result caught William T. Piper, Sr., and his company unprepared to deal with the situation. He needed to buy large amounts of materials in order to produce record numbers of airplanes, but industrial suppliers, well aware that when wartime contracts evaporated so would their profits, demanded that he order huge quantities or none at all.

The aircraft suppliers were equally adamant. The Continental Aircraft Engine Company, for example, wanted each lightplane manufacturer to buy hundreds or thousands of engines. The reason was strictly economic. Like many other large companies, Continental had to compete for materials it needed and as a result was reluctant to accept anything less than bulk orders for its products.

Mr. Piper had no choice. The company complied with suppliers' demands and soon filled the Lock Haven factory with everything from propellers to tailwheels. It was a tremendous—and dangerous—gamble. If demand materialized as many in the aviation industry predicted it would, then thousands of new airplanes would be built. If not, as some prophets of doom believed, Piper and other manufacturers would be in serious, if not catastrophic financial trouble.

In calendar year 1945 Piper sold 1,802 aircraft. Much to William T. Piper's relief, it became obvious early in 1946 that the anticipated postwar demand for small aircraft would rapidly become a reality. Soon the Lock Haven factory was buzzing with three shifts of workers building airplanes six days a week.

Piper was flooded with orders for aircraft, primarily the J-3 Cub series. The company had more than 50 United States distributors and more than 1,300 dealers clamoring for their share of new ships. Reflecting the market's pent-up desire, Piper built a record 6,432 Cubs during the calendar year.

When Piper completed its fiscal year in September, 1946, the company had sold a total of 7,782 airplanes and accumulated more than $11 million in sales. Despite that great achievement, the balance sheet showed a net loss of more than $26,000. Although he

Introduced in 1947, the Piper PA-11 Cub Special was an upgraded version of the legendary J-3 Cub. The engine was fully enclosed and the fuselage-mounted fuel tank was relocated to the left wing. The PA-11 was approved for solo flight from the front seat. (Piper Aviation Museum)

42

In 1949 Piper built 105 military versions of the PA-11 designated L-18B. The airplanes were produced under contract to the United States Air Force under provisions of the Mutual Defense Assistance Pact for service with Turkish armed forces. (Piper Aviation Museum)

Interior of a 1948 Cub Special. Additional legroom was provided by moving the rear seat aft. Engine ignition, fuel selector, cabin heat and elevator trim controls were accessible to either occupant. Forward visibility was improved by installation of a new instrument panel and engine cowling. (Piper Aviation Museum)

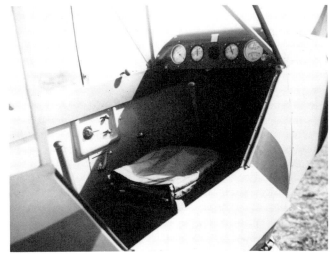

did not realize it until too late, Mr. Piper's airplane prices were too low.

The year 1946 had brought other problems as well, though of a different nature. In May, heavy, persistent rainfall had swollen the West Branch of the Susquehanna River, eventually covering the floor of the Piper factory with as much as eight feet of water.

In addition to the damage done inside to unfinished airplanes, components and tooling, some new aircraft huddled together for delivery were submerged and had to be rebuilt or scrapped. Throughout the year orders for new airplanes kept pouring into Lock Haven. With demand still climbing and production still falling short, Piper and his staff of three sons ordered more and more materials, hired additional workers and urged the engineering department to create more and more new models.

One of the many creations of chief engineer Walter Jamouneau and his staff in 1946 was the PA-11 Cub Special—one of several new postwar Piper airplanes to roll off the assembly lines. It was essentially a J-3 Cub with an upgraded interior, fuel tank relocated to the left wing and a full cowling around the Continen-

tal A-65-8 powerplant.

The prototype aircraft was constructor number 11-1, registered NC91913 and completed in March, 1946. Two additional airplanes were built that year for testing, and production of the 65 hp. Cub Special began in March, 1947. A more powerful version using a 90 hp. Continental Motors C-90-8 was offered in 1948.

Piper produced the PA-11 under the J-3 Cub's approved type certificate, and 1,541 aircraft were manufactured from 1947 to 1949 including 105 L-18B aircraft purchased in 1949 by the United States Air Force and shipped to Turkey. In terms of performance, the 65 hp. PA-11 was faster than the J-3 with a maximum speed of 100 mph. and a cruise speed of 87 mph. The 90 hp. version cruised at 100 mph. Max-

Piper developed the PA-11 into the workhorse PA-18 Super Cub, which replaced the Cub Special on Lock Haven production lines in 1949. The photograph illustrates a PA-11 factory demonstrator aircraft, fitted with spray equipment for agricultural operations. (Piper Aviation Museum)

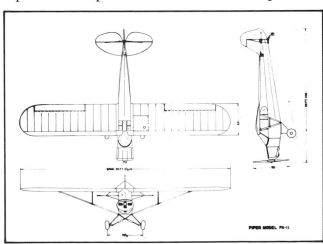

imum gross weight for both versions was 1,220 lb.

Other developments included the three-place PA-12 Super Cruiser, an upgraded derivative of the 1942 J-5C Super Cruiser. The PA-12 had two fuel tanks—one in each wing—and sported a new interior and minor airframe refinements to improve appearance. Powered by a Lycoming O-235-C rated at 100 hp., the prototype was J-5C constructor number 5-1601, registered NX41561. It first flew in October, 1945.

The prototype airplane was later redesignated as the first PA-12, constructor number 12-1. A 108 hp. Lycoming O-235-C1 engine replaced the 100 hp. version after production began early in 1946. Piper offered the Super Cruiser in two versions, Utility Category or Normal Category. The former had a gross weight limited to 1,550 lb. and the latter to 1,750 lb.

Attesting to the PA-12's stamina, two modified PA-12 Super Cruisers were flown around the world in 1947. Registered NX2365M and NX3671M, the two ships were flown by Clifford V. Evans and George Truman respectively. The globe-girdling flights began in August at Teterboro, New Jersey, and ended at Van Nuys, California, in November. Both airplanes were capable of carrying up to 138 gallons of fuel that provided a range of nearly 2,400 statute miles.

A PA-12 licensed in the Utility Category cost $2,995 initially, rising to $3,205 without options in 1947. Licensed in the Normal Category, a PA-12 cost $3,295, increasing to $3,495 in 1948, the last year of production. Piper produced 3,758 Super Cruisers.

Early in 1947, the nation's thirst for small airplanes continued unabated. The Lock Haven factory was producing up to 30 ships per day but still fell short of demand. To augment the Pennsylvania facility, in the summer of 1946 Piper had established a second factory and assembly facility at Ponca City, Oklahoma.

The new operation quickly began building J-3 Cubs,

The three-place PA-12 Super Cruiser first flew in October, 1945 with Piper test pilot Clyde R. Smith, Sr., at the controls. Based chiefly on the J-5C Cub Cruiser, the PA-12 entered production in 1946 and was powered by 100 hp. and later 108 hp. Lycoming O-235 engines. (American Aviation Historical Society via Joseph P. Juptner)

PA-11 Cub Specials and PA-12 Super Cruisers in an effort to keep dealers and their impatient customers happy. From summer, 1946 until manufacture ceased in spring, 1948 the Ponca City site produced 1,190 J-3 Cubs. A total of 325 Cub Specials were built there, as well as 236 PA-12 airplanes. In March, 1947 the PA-11 had replaced the J-3 on the Ponca City production line.

With two facilities operating at maximum capacity, Piper was making a profit and the market was showing no indications of slackening the pace. Business was brisk as 1946 faded into history and the fateful year of 1947 took its place.

In general, the aviation optimists of 1945 had proven correct—the light airplane industry had more business than it could cope with and anticipated a bright future. Multitudes of flight schools had opened for business, many operated by ex-pilots who traded their Mustangs and Corsairs for Cubs and Cessnas.

For 18 months manufacturers had supplied thousands of small aircraft to such flying schools, and the private flier who wanted to pilot his or her own ship for business and pleasure had created a new, lucrative market. But like their optimistic counterparts, the prophets of doom also had their say.

As early as 1946 many had warned that bitter—not better—days were ahead. "Woe to those who overproduce, woe to those who build airplanes with reckless abandon, for there shall be wailing and gnashing of teeth across the land when the days of famine arrive," they cried to inattentive ears.

The PA-12S was approved for operation on EDO as well as other types of floats. Piper built 3,760 Super Cruisers before ending production in 1948. Super Cruisers were produced at Lock Haven and Ponca City, Oklahoma facilities.(Piper Aviation Museum)

PA-12 registered NC7848H photographed when it was equipped with large, low-pressure tires for operations on unimproved airfields. The low-pressure tires were more effective than the Whittaker tandem gear arrangement. (Peter M. Bowers collection)

William T. Piper, Sr., poses with a PA-15 registered NC4164H. The rugged Vagabond was powered by a Lycoming O-145 engine rated at 65 hp., and had a wingspan of 29 feet 3 inches. (Piper Aviation Museum)

In March, 1947 their prophecies suddenly came true. Seemingly overnight, the light airplane market collapsed in a catastrophic event that exceeded the Great Depression in its swiftness and ferocity. Alas, there was great wailing and gnashing of teeth in the lightplane bastions of Wichita, Kansas, Alliance, Ohio and Lock Haven, Pennsylvania.

What had happened? The quintessential villain was overproduction and excess supply, but complacency also contributed to the disaster. Piper as well as other builders had lost touch with the postwar market's changing ideas of what a small airplane should be. The Taylorcrafts, Aeroncas and Pipers of 1947 were essentially warmed-over versions of 1940 aircraft. They were dull, lacked performance and above all, comfort. The chieftains of industry had failed to ascertain that airplanes designed in 1940 would not sell in 1947.

In addition, dealers, in an effort to make a sale had contracted for airplanes with two or three manufacturers. Whoever delivered first won the day. Flight schools had bought more airplanes than they actually needed and to make matters worse, the United States Government had been selling war-surplus airplanes—up to 35,000 of them—at incredibly low prices.

In short, the market was inundated with airplanes it did not want and could not use. There were many victims of the lightplane debacle, including the legendary Taylorcraft company. By the end of March, 1947 Piper was selling only a few airplanes per week, not hundreds. That summer, a stockpile of unsold airplanes began building up at the factory including large numbers of PA-11 and PA-12 ships.

The final J-3 Cub had been built at Ponca City in March, ending a production run of 19,888 airplanes in the United States. An additional 150 were built in

First of the short-wing family of Piper airplanes, the PA-15 Vagabond was a spartan, inexpensive two-place ship designed specifically to help return Piper Aircraft Corporation to profitability. The basic airplane sold for $1,990 fly-away-factory early in 1948. (Piper Aviation Museum)

Canada after the war and designated as the J-3 Prospector. Including military and Canadian airplanes, more than 20,200 J-3-series Cubs were manufactured.

With sales virtually nonexistent and unpaid bills accumulating rapidly, Mr. Piper faced a serious situation. He had huge amounts of materials on hand to build airplanes that nobody wanted. The company's net operating loss reached more than $560,000 that year and suppliers demanded payment for their goods. Worst of all, perhaps, were the company's New York financiers who accused the Piper clan of mismanaging the business.

Reluctantly and at the behest of Wall Street, in April Piper initiated pay reductions that soon were followed by massive layoffs and other cost-cutting measures. Employment plummeted from 2,600 people to a few hundred workers.

Despite these unpopular actions, the situation continued to deteriorate. The New York bankers still were not satisfied that enough was being done. In June, they appointed a financial wizard named William C. Shriver to take control of the company and attempt to preserve it.

Shriver promptly banished Mr. Piper to exile in a nearby hangar office. The Ponca City, Oklahoma facility was closed and the entire work force furloughed. In September, Shriver instructed Walter Jamouneau and his engineering staff to design a spartan, economical two-place airplane that could be built from existing stockpiles of material and, more impor-

Piper's Vagabond cruised at 92 mph. and was approved for a maximum gross weight of 1,100 lb. The Lock Haven factory built 387 Vagabonds before production was terminated in 1949. (Piper Aviation Museum)

Known as the Vagabond Trainer, the PA-17 was an improved, two-place version of the PA-15 powered by a 65 hp. Continental A-65-8 powerplant. The airplane cost $2,195 in 1948. (Smithsonian Institution, National Air and Space Museum Negative Number 80-17087)

A PA-17 Vagabond Trainer converted to tricycle landing gear configuration. The installation was similar to that used for the PA-22 Tri-Pacer. (Peter M. Bowers) ▶

tantly, put Piper on the road to fiscal recovery.

Six weeks later a short-coupled, high-wing, side-by-side aircraft emerged from the factory. Designated the PA-15 Vagabond, the pedestrian ship was powered by a 65 hp. Lycoming O-145-B2 engine and the wing span was six feet shorter than the J-3 and PA-11. The Vagabond was the first of the famed short-wing Pipers.

Featuring a rigid, conventional landing gear without shock cords, the PA-15 had a maximum gross weight of 1,100 lb. and a cruise speed of 90-95 mph. The wings used spruce spars with aluminum alloy ribs but later production aircraft had aluminum alloy spars. Both the fuselage and wings were covered with fabric.

The prototype was constructor number 15-1, registered NC5000H, that was completed in December, 1947. The Vagabond received its approved type certificate in July, 1948 and 387 airplanes were produced. Priced at $1,990 "fly-away factory," the PA-15 proved to be a simple but adequate performer and was the right airplane at the right time for Piper. It probably saved the company from bankruptcy, but from a technology standpoint the Vagabond was obsolete before it was built.

An upgraded version known as the PA-17 Vagabond or Vagabond Trainer was introduced in May, 1948 and sold for $2,195. The PA-17 sported a shock

The PA-14's wings featured metal spars and slotted flaps. A fixed-pitch, wood propeller was standard but an optional, two-position Koppers Aeromatic propeller was available. PA-14 N5179H, constructor number 14-497 illustrated was equipped with a Koppers propeller. (American Aviation Historical Society via Joseph P. Juptner)

cord suspension for the main landing gear and dual control sticks were standard equipment.

Instead of the Lycoming engine of the PA-15, the Vagabond Trainer was powered by the ubiquitous 65 hp. Continental A-65-8 engine. Performance was virtually identical to the PA-15. Piper built 214 PA-17s before production was terminated.

By 1948 the light airplane customer was tiring of two-place ships with cramped, noisy cabins and 65 hp. engines. The competition already was producing four-place aircraft with success and market acceptance was on the rise. To answer the challenge, Piper responded with the PA-14 Family Cruiser, essentially a four-place version of the highly successful PA-12.

First flown in March, 1947 the prototype was constructor number 14-1, registered NC2658M. The airplane had a redesigned fuselage that was five inches wider in the forward cabin to give additional room for the front seat occupant.

Continuing its use of the more powerful Lycoming series of piston engines, Piper selected the 115 hp. O-235-C1 for the PA-14. Priced at $3,825 when introduced in May, 1948 the Family Cruiser had a maximum speed of more than 120 mph. and a cruise speed of 110 mph. In keeping with Piper's tradition of value, it was one of the most inexpensive four-place ships on the market.

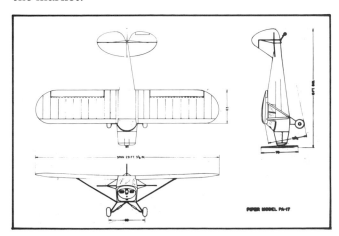

Powered by a 115 hp. Lycoming O-235 engine, the PA-14 cruised at 110 mph. and could fly 500 statute miles on 35 gallons of fuel. Only 238 Family Cruisers were built. In 1948 the airplane's base price was $3,825. The PA-14 illustrated, registered N5103H was photographed at Boeing Field in 1949. (Peter M. Bowers collection)

Piper PA-14 Family Cruiser fitted with the Whittaker tandem landing gear system developed in 1949 by Art Whittaker, in Portland, Oregon. (Peter M. Bowers collection) ►

Piper included slotted, trailing edge flaps on the wings that were virtually identical to flaps used on the postwar L-14. Like the Super Cruiser, the Family Cruiser's wing spars and rib structure were aluminum alloy and fabric-covered. Two tanks in the wings held 35 gallons of fuel that provided a zero-wind range of 500 statute miles.

Unfortunately for Piper, the PA-14 was introduced after the lightplane market had all but collapsed. Only 238 Family Cruisers were built from May, 1948 to September, 1949. In addition to the PA-14, Piper had another four-place airplane in its stable by December, 1948. Before his departure from Piper late that year, William Shriver had acquired the Stinson Division of the Consolidated-Vultee Corporation despite strong objection from William T. Piper, Sr.

As a result of Shriver's actions, Piper Aircraft Corporation became the owner of not only the Stinson name and tooling but also acquired 200 unsold

Interior of a PA-14. To create the Family Cruiser from the PA-12 Super Cruiser, Piper engineers widened the forward cabin five inches to accommodate a fourth occupant. (Piper Aviation Museum)

Voyager 108-3 and Station Wagon-series airplanes as well. From a historic standpoint it is important to note that drawings for the proposed Twin Stinson, which would later become the prototype Piper PA-23 Apache, were included in the acquisition.

The Voyager and Station Wagon airplanes were marketed briefly as the Piper-Stinson, and about 325 aircraft were eventually sold. Of those, 125 aircraft may have been assembled in 1949 and 1950 from remaining parts inventories. Although a well-built and popular airplane, the Stinson was unwelcome at Piper and was quickly brushed aside.

Following Shriver's departure, a hard-fought battle ensued for control of the company between the Piper family and the New York bankers. Piper Aircraft Corporation was selling airplanes once again, and the financial picture had improved significantly. The Wall Street wizards, however, seemed to sense an opportunity to push Mr. Piper out of the company and reap the profits for themselves.

But it was not to be. More than a year later in January, 1950 William T. Piper, Sr., managed to regain control of the company after shrewd political maneuvering with the help of loyal employees and friends. Frustrated by Piper's tenacity and increas-

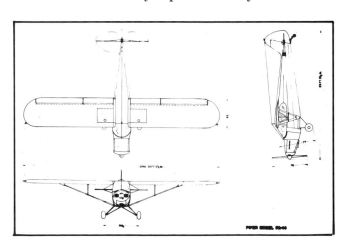

In December, 1948 Piper acquired the assets of the Stinson Division of the Vultee Aircraft Corporation that included Stinson 108-3 Voyager and Station Wagon airplanes. Unfortunately, the Stinson became a competitor to Piper's PA-14. (Piper Aircraft Museum)

◄ *Instrument panel of a Stinson 108 Voyager. Note similarity of control wheels with those of the PA-20 Pacer and PA-22 Tri-Pacer. (Piper Aviation Museum)*

number 16-1.

In terms of performance the Clipper was slightly faster than the Vagabond, with a maximum speed of 125 mph. and a cruise speed of 112 mph. Maximum gross weight was 1,650 lb. and the ship could fly 600 statute miles. Confident that the Clipper was a more sophisticated and therefore more appealing airplane than its predecessor, Piper began producing the PA-16 early in 1949.

After building 736 aircraft, the company redesigned the successful Clipper into the PA-20 Pacer which entered production in January, 1950. Unlike the Clipper, the Pacer had wing flaps and two wing fuel tanks as standard equipment. The empennage was slightly revised, the main landing gear was widened to improve ground handling and the cabin interior was upgraded to improve comfort and appearance.

Completed in July, 1949 constructor number 20-01 served as the Pacer prototype and was registered N7000K. A second prototype, constructor number 20-1, registered N7100K was built and completed in October. The fourth in a series of short-wing Piper aircraft, the PA-20 prototypes were powered initially by 115 hp. Lycoming O-235-C1 engines. Production airplanes were equipped with Lycoming O-290-D engines rated at 125 hp. The 115 hp. Lycoming engine was optional.

A fixed-pitch wood propeller was standard and a controllable-pitch metal propeller was optional. Piper offered the more powerful 135 hp. Lycoming O-290-D2 engine in mid-1952 until Pacer production ended in September, 1954 after 1,120 PA-20s had been

ingly occupied with other financial temptations, the bankers retreated into the shadows.

During the more than two years of turmoil that was behind him, the elder Piper had taken the time to think about what he had done wrong and how best to restructure the company for the decades ahead. He realized that to survive the business would have to be run more efficiently and professionally than in the past—the last thing he wanted was another duel with the financiers from Wall Street. William Piper knew his sons were up to the task, and in April, 1950 he named Thomas Francis "Tony" Piper as the company's new vice president and general manager.

Amidst the two years of infighting that had nearly destroyed the company, Piper engineers were working on improved and new aircraft. In January, 1948 the first PA-16 Clipper was completed. Sporting four seats, the Clipper was an upgraded version of the two-place Vagabond and featured shock cord suspension for the landing gear and dual controls as standard equipment.

The single fuel tank was relocated from the forward fuselage to the left wing, and a 115 hp. Lycoming O-235-C1 powerplant was installed. Constructor number 16-01, registered NC4000H, was the prototype that later was redesignated as constructor

Introduced in 1950, the PA-20 Pacer was a refined version of the PA-16 Clipper with dual, wing-mounted fuel tanks, wing flaps, increased landing gear tread and a redesigned empennage. The Pacer illustrated was constructor number 20-813, registered N1579A. (Piper Aviation Museum)

Photograph of a PA-20 cabin shows functional layout of engine and flight instruments in center panel, flanked on both sides by avionics. (Piper Aviation Museum)

48

Powered by a 125 hp. Lycoming O-290-D engine, the Pacer 125 had a maximum speed of 135 mph. and cruised at 125 mph. PA-20 registered N7730K was photographed flying near Lock Haven, Pennsylvania. (Piper Aviation Museum)

◄ *The PA-16 Clipper was a four-place, upgraded version of the PA-15 Vagabond. Dual controls and shock cord suspension were standard equipment. The airplane was powered by a 115 hp. Lycoming O-235 engine. The PA-16 illustrated, registered N5203H was an early production Clipper. (Piper Aviation Museum)*

built.

The four-place Pacer was a successful airplane chiefly because it combined increased horsepower and performance with a more comfortable cabin than that of the PA-16. Piper was giving the customer more for the money, and the market responded favorably.

Although the legendary J-3 Cub had vanished from

A PA-20 Pacer visits an oil drilling site early in the 1950s. Initial production airplanes were powered by a 125 hp. Lycoming O-290 engine, but a 115 hp. version of the O-290 also was available. In 1952 a 135 hp. engine was optional. (Piper Aviation Museum)

the production lines in 1947, Piper engineers developed the equally famous PA-18 Super Cub in 1949. Like the Cub before it, the PA-18 proved to be a highly successful aircraft. The Super Cub enjoyed one of the longest production runs of any Piper airplane, and underwent numerous engine changes and airframe modifications during its lifetime.

Replacing the PA-11 Cub Special in November, 1949 early production PA-18 airplanes were powered by the 90 hp. Continental C-90-8F and C-90-12F engine and lacked flaps but had a larger rudder than the PA-11. A single fuel tank mounted in the left wing was standard equipment with a second tank being optional. Known as the Super Cub 95, the ships were destined to serve flight schools and flying clubs as economical, rugged trainers and cross-country aircraft.

In 1950 the PA-18 powered by a 100 hp. Lycoming O-235-C1 engine was offered in addition to the original 90 hp. PA-18 version. Later that year, the 100 hp. Super Cub was superseded by the 125 hp. PA-18, which featured a Lycoming O-290-D engine.

Flaps were fitted to the wings. The second fuel tank was a popular option as was the metal, controllable-pitch propeller for the 135 hp. Lycoming O-290-D2 powerplant. Dual, wing-mounted fuel tanks were made standard equipment in 1952.

As horsepower increased, so did performance. Maximum speed varied from 112 mph. for the 90 hp. Super Cub to 127 mph. for the 135 hp. PA-18. The Super Cub's wingspan and length remained unchanged until the advent of the 135 hp. PA-18-135, when span was decreased to 35 feet 2.5 inches instead of 35 feet 4 inches for the previous airplanes. Maximum gross weight remained at 1,500 lb.

Piper continued to refine the PA-18 series throughout the late 1950s. The PA-18-105 Special was built specifically for the Civil Air Patrol beginning in September, 1952 and ending in March, 1953. This version also was known as the PA-18T. These airplanes did not have flaps and special seats were installed to accommodate parachutes.

Customers quickly found new ways to use the versatile Super Cub, but clamored for more horsepower. In August, 1954 the first 150 hp. Lycoming O-320-powered PA-18-150 variant made its first flight. The aircraft was constructor number 18-3771, registered N1656P.

In 1952 and 1953 the Civil Air Patrol took delivery of PA-18-105 Super Cubs designated as the PA-18-105 Special. Powered by 108 hp. Lycoming O-235 engines, the airplanes were used primarily for flight training duties but lacked wing flaps. (Piper Aviation Museum)

Production of the popular 150 hp. Super Cub began in October of that year. Fitted with Lycoming O-320-A2A and later -A2B engines, the PA-18-150 became Piper's workhorse airplane and remained essentially unchanged until production was terminated in 1993.

A popular variant was the PA-18A, designed as an low-cost agricultural application aircraft. Offered in a sprayer, duster or combination configuration, the PA-18A featured a 110-gallon hopper that was loaded through a door aft of the wing. To make room for the chemical hopper, the rear seat and accompanying flight controls were deleted from the airplane.

A small, wind-driven fan turned dual agitators in the hopper and forced the chemicals into a six-foot wide venturi spreader mounted under the fuselage. Much of the development work on the agricultural application option was accomplished with the help of aeronautical engineer Fred E. Weick, a man who later

Aviatrix Anna Louise Branger set an altitude record of 26,800 feet in April, 1951 flying a PA-18-95 Super Cub. (Piper Aviation Museum)

Like its ancestor the J-3 Cub, the PA-18 Super Cub also became a legend with wings. Designed as a utility airplane, the Super Cub initially was equipped with a 90 hp. Continental engine when it was introduced in 1949. The PA-18-105 illustrated was equipped with Whittaker tandem landing gear for rough field operations, manually-operated wing flaps and a 100 hp. Lycoming O-235 engine. (Piper Aviation Museum)

The United States Department of the Interior's Fish and Wildlife Service operated a Super Cub 125 equipped with a spray dispersal system. Note chemical tank in aft seat position. The airplane was licensed in the Restricted Category for spray operations. (Piper Aviation Museum)

would become a prominent figure at Piper.

Because of the inherent dangers of operating low-flying agricultural aircraft, Piper included wire cutters on the leading edge of the landing gear struts and heavy-duty seat belt and shoulder harnesses for the pilot. In addition, the metal panels installed on the bottom of the fuselage could be removed for cleaning and inspection of the welded steel truss structure. Piper was granted approval by the Civil Aeronautics Authority to operate the PA-18-A at a maximum gross weight of 2,070 lb. Piper eventually delivered 2,650 PA-18A agricultural aircraft.

Intertwined with commercial PA-18 production were numerous military airplanes bought by the United States Army and United States Air Force for use by American and selected foreign forces, including those of the North Atlantic Treaty Organization. One variant was designated as the L-18C that did not have wing flaps and featured greenhouse cabin glazing reminiscent of the World War Two L-4 series.

First produced in 1950, these aircraft were powered by 95 hp. Continental C-90-8F engines. A total of 832 were built in several batches, including 67 in 1950, 380 in 1951, 163 in 1952, 183 in 1953; and 39 in 1954, the last year of L-18C production.

From 1952 to 1957, the United States armed forces bought additional military versions of the Super Cub. Two YL-21 and 150 L-21A aircraft were powered by the 125 hp. Lycoming O-290-11 engine. From 1952 to 1957, 584 L-21B airplanes were built featuring the 135 h.p. Lycoming O-290-D2 powerplant.

Two more L-21B were delivered in 1962 and completed production of the series. All YL-21 and L-21 airplanes had wing flaps. In addition to these military PA-18s, in 1949 and 1950 Piper built three Super Cubs designated as PA-19 before company management decided that all commercial and military Super Cubs would carry the PA-18 designation.

Piper was not, however, without stiff competition for such military contracts, nor was Howard "Pug" Piper beyond some professional chicanery to help the company win an order. According to a friend of Pug's who was present during the telling of the tale, during the 1950s Piper was competing against the famed Lockheed Aircraft Company for a lightplane military contract.

Lockheed's representative Carl Friend was flying

Cabin and instrument panel of a PA-18-125 Super Cub at Lock Haven. Note location of Lear navigation radio, heel brakes and flap control handle. (Piper Aviation Museum)

Piper received FAA approval of the Lycoming O-320-powered PA-18-150 in October, 1954. The 150 hp. engine became the Super Cub's standard powerplant. Piper built 10,222 Super Cubs before production was suspended in 1982. (Piper Aviation Museum)

Under Monroe Stuart Millar's ownership in the late 1980s Piper resumed limited production of the PA-18-150, but new Piper management terminated Super Cub production after 1993. Super Cub N6691A illustrated was built in 1990. (Piper Aircraft Corporation) ▶

its "Little Dipper" aircraft during the fly-off competition held at Fort Bragg. He was doing well against competing aircraft, including Piper's Super Cub, flown by Pug Piper himself. When the day's flying stopped for the night, Friend went to sleep confident that on the morrow the Little Dipper would win the final phase of the trials—off-airport operations—and secure a lucrative contract for Lockheed.

When he arrived at the field the next morning, however, the ground had turned to a quagmire although no rain had fallen overnight. Despite his valiant efforts, Carl Friend could not get the Lockheed ship airborne as it sank to its axles in mud.

Next, it was Pug Piper's turn. He wheeled the Super Cub onto the field and promptly took off without incident, thanks to the airplane's large, low-pressure tires that prevented it from getting mired in the muck. As a result, Lockheed was disqualified and Piper was declared the winner. Flabergasted at the outcome, Carl Friend asked Pug Piper how he knew the field would be muddy and that low-pressure tires would be required. Piper answered with a twinkle in his eye, "You would be surprised what a company of volunteer firemen will do for a keg of beer!" Pug Piper had an excellent sense of humor that even his competitors could not criticize.

Over the decades since the first PA-18 was delivered, the airplane has earned a reputation for ver-

satility, reliability and operating efficiency. It enjoyed virtually no competition throughout its production life and Super Cubs were likely to be flying well into the 21st Century.

In August, 1981 Piper sold all marketing rights for the PA-18 series to Wes-Tex Aircraft in Lubbock, Texas, along with 15 airplanes that had been built that year but not sold. Production tooling and the PA-18 approved type certificate were retained by Piper.

Because most PA-18s flew in a utility role, Piper intentionally kept the standard airplane's frills to a minimum. Beginning in 1971 the company offered a deluxe version that increased cabin embellishments. In keeping with its workhorse image, the Super Cub was approved for operation on EDO floats, Federal

In addition to the commercial PA-18, Piper also built military versions of the Super Cub. The YL-21 illustrated was constructor number 18-750, Army serial number 51-6496 was one of two PA-18-135 aircraft provided to the United States Army for evaluation. (Piper Aviation Museum)

The service test YL-21 aircraft were followed by orders for 150 L-21A versions with 125 hp. Lycoming O-290 engines. L-21A constructor number 18-860, United States Army serial number 51-15695 is illustrated. (Piper Aviation Museum)

◄ Rear, oblique view of L-21A 51-15695. The airplane was photographed at the Lock Haven factory. (Piper Aviation Museum)

skis and low-pressure, balloon-type tires.

After building 10,222 PA-18s in five basic versions over a period of 33 years, Piper terminated production in November, 1982. The final Super Cub built at Lock Haven was constructor number 18-8309025, registered N91293.

After Monroe Stuart Millar bought Piper Aircraft Corporation in May, 1987 he revived the Super Cub and resumed production of the PA-18-150 version. The airplane was available from the factory ready to fly away, or could be built from kits. To reduce costs, the kits were offered with and without an engine and propeller for $35,395 and $24,195 respectively. The kit concept was innovative but failed. Piper employees built one airplane, constructor number 1809033, from a kit before the program was cancelled.

Most customers chose the factory-built version

Jacob Willard Miller played a key role in bringing William T. Piper and his airplane company to Lock Haven in 1937. He also helped formulate and direct the company's sales and marketing strategies for the Apache and subsequent airplanes produced in the 1950s and 1960s. (Piper Aviation Museum)

that cost $45,995 in 1989. During 1988 and 1989 a total of 52 PA-18-150 airplanes were built. Six Super Cubs were built in 1990, zero in 1991 and one PA-18 was delivered in 1992. Another two Super Cubs built in the 1992 model year were delivered in January, 1993, according to Piper officials.

Another 19 PA-18-150 Super Cubs were scheduled to be built in 1993 for Piper distributor Muncie Aviation located in Muncie, Indiana. These airplanes would be sold by Muncie to retail customers and Piper officials had no plans to resume Super Cub production.

As the decade of the 1940s drew to close, Piper management realized that many new pilots as well as student aviators were less than enthusiastic about learning their trade in conventional-gear, or tailwheel, airplanes. Regardless of who built them, tailwheel aircraft were viewed by many pilots as harder to taxi and more difficult to handle on the ground—especially in a crosswind—and provided a challenge during takeoff and landing that many would-be fliers disliked.

Having become more sensitive to how its products were perceived by those who bought and used them, Piper management reasoned correctly that a tricycle-gear airplane would be much easier to master. To meet the need without developing a totally new aircraft, Piper engineers used the conventional-gear PA-20 Pacer as the basis for creating the successful tricycle-gear PA-22 Tri-Pacer. Chief changes to the Pacer design centered on relocating the main gear farther aft and redesigning the engine mount structure to accommodate the nose gear.

Referred to in Piper Tri-Pacer sales literature as the "hydrasorb tricycle landing gear," the new configuration "automatically makes the airplane roll straight on takeoff" and "eliminates the need for quick, corrective rudder work." In addition, the nose gear tire was the same size as the main gear tires and aided ground operation on soft or unimproved fields.

To make flying the airplane easier, the aileron and rudder controls were interconnected and allowed pilots "to fly with wheel alone or feet alone" when

The Tri-Pacer was accepted with enthusiasm by Piper customers. Early production airplanes were powered by 125 hp. Lycoming O-290 engines. The nose gear tire was the same size as main gear tires to improve rough field operations. (Piper Aviation Museum)

The PA-22 Tri-Pacer was developed in 1950 and featured a ▶ tricycle nose gear arrangement designed to make taxi, takeoff and landing operations easier for pilots. The prototype airplane, constructor number 22-1, registered N7700K is illustrated. J. W. Miller is the pilot. Note Pacer 125 nameplate on the cowling. (Piper Aviation Museum)

making turns, according to the sales literature. Such encouraging words helped to sell airplanes.

The Tri-Pacer prototype was constructor number 22-1, registered N7700K, and was completed at Lock Haven in May, 1950. It was powered by a Lycoming O-290-D engine rated at 125 hp. A second prototype, constructor number 22-2, registered N7777K was completed in November before production began in December, 1950. The PA-20 was built at Lock Haven along with the PA-22 until Pacer production was terminated in September, 1954.

Selling in large numbers from its introduction, the Tri-Pacer proved to be a docile, easy-to-fly airplane that was readily accepted by student pilots and ex-

Instrument panel of a late-model Tri-Pacer featured flight instruments that were placed in front of the pilot, with avionics in the center and engine instrumentation on the right side of the panel. (Piper Aviation Museum)

perienced flyers alike. During nearly 14 years of manufacture, the PA-22 was built in three versions— the standard Tri-Pacer, the Carribean and later the two-place Colt.

A total of 9,490 airplanes were produced including 12 PA-22-150 Tri-Pacers manufactured for the French army in 1963. These were used primarily for observation and liaison duties in Chad and the Malagasy Republic. The new fleet of 12 ships replaced 11 Tri-Pacers operated by the French since 1958.

Initial production airplanes sported the 125 hp. Lycoming powerplant which was replaced in June, 1952 by the 135 hp. Lycoming O-290-D2 variant beginning with constructor number 22-534, registered N1962A. In autumn, 1954 horsepower was increased with introduction of the 150 hp. Lycoming O-320-A2B-powered PA-22-150 followed in September, 1957 by the PA-22-160 version powered by a 160 hp. O-320-B Lycoming engine.

In its 160 hp. configuration, the Tri-Pacer possessed good performance that satisfied most buyers. With a maximum gross weight of 2,000 lb., the PA-22-160 had a maximum speed of 141 mph. and cruised at 134 mph. Range with 36 gallons of fuel was a respectable 536 statute miles. An optional fuel tank holding eight gallons boosted capacity to 44 gallons and increased range to 655 statute miles.

It is interesting to note that Piper's installation of a nose gear on the Tri-Pacer helped convince a conservative Dwane L. Wallace, president of Cessna Aircraft Company, that tricycle-gear airplanes would sell. In the face of Tri-Pacer competition in the early 1950s, Wallace watched sales of the all-metal, four-place

54

TRI-PACER

RUGGED NOSE WHEEL

No "stubbing your toe" with the Tri-Pacer. Over 4000 landings and 3000 miles of gruelling taxiing—much of it on a special rough obstacle course—went into testing the Tri-Pacer's nose wheel, which is same size as main wheels. This testing is the equivalent of more than 15 years of normal use.

now THE FAMOUS PIPER PACER
WITH TRICYCLE GEAR FOR FLYING EASE

Here's the biggest news in private flying since the first Cub flew 20 years ago. Piper, leading builder of business, farm and personal planes, now brings you the sensational new Tri-Pacer, which makes flying so simple an eight-year-old girl learned to take off and land in six short lessons!

Yes, here's the Piper Pacer, famous for its speed, range, comfort and ecomomy, now available with a rugged tricycle landing gear which makes flying easier for everyone.

Steerable nose wheel makes ground-landing easier than steering a car. Interconnected rudder and ailerons let you fly with wheel alone or feet alone! Yet you have fully operating rudder, aileron and elevator when you want them.

You get all this in addition to the proven features of the Piper Pacer, which make it the largest selling four passenger plane built today...separate front and rear doors, nonflammable, longer lasting Duraclad finish, roomy cabin with added sound proofing...and over 120 mph cruising speed. Write for brochure. Dept. G-2.

UTILITY with ECONOMY

For business and farm, the Tri-Pacer is as useful as it is easy to fly. It will carry four people two miles a minute at less cost than for bus fare, or, with rear seat removed, it can carry a quarter-ton of cargo, easily loaded through convenient rear door.

PIPER
AIRCRAFT CORP.
LOCK HAVEN, PA., U.S.A.

MODEL PA-20 *The Pacer is available, too, with regular landing gear. In both Pacers you get the wonderful solid big airplane feel which makes long flights comfortable and pleasant. Be sure to fly the new 1951 Pacers and see for yourself why more people buy Piper than any other business or personal plane.*

1951 advertisement hailing the qualities of the Tri-Pacer and Pacer. (Piper Aviation Museum)

The Colt was popular with flying clubs as well as private pilots. Piper built 9,490 Tri-Pacers and Colts before production was terminated in March, 1964. 1961 PA-22-108 Colt constructor number 22-8001, registered N4501Z is illustrated. (Piper Aviation Museum)

In 1958 Piper replaced the PA-22-150 Tri-Pacer with the less expensive, utilitarian PA-22-150 Carribean. In 1960 the Tri-Pacer was replaced by the new, all-metal PA-28 Cherokee. (Piper Aviation Museum) ▶

Cessna 170 slowly dwindle until it was equipped with a nose gear in 1956 and reintroduced as the ubiquitous, stunningly successful Model 172 and 172 Skyhawk. More than 35,000 commercial and military versions of the Model 172 had been built by 1985.

With sales of the 160 hp. Tri-Pacer outpacing those of the 150 hp. version, Piper developed the PA-22-150 Carribean as a low-cost, no-frills aircraft aimed specifically at airport operators and flight schools. The Carribean began replacing the standard PA-22-150 on Lock Haven production lines in late 1958. Performance was virtually identical to that of the Tri-Pacer.

A final variant of the PA-22 series was the PA-22-108 Colt. Designed primarily for the flight training role the Colt featured only two seats, wing flaps were deleted and the airplane was powered by the economical Lycoming O-235-C1B engine of 108 hp. A single fuel tank was mounted in the wing. Piper completed the first Colt, constructor number 22-8000, registered N4500Z, in September, 1960.

Because the company did not have an all-metal, two-place trainer in production when the new PA-28 Cherokee was introduced in 1960, Piper kept the PA-22-108 Colt in production at Lock Haven into the early years of the decade.

Despite its low price and proven reliability, however, it was difficult for the Colt to compete with the all-metal, equally inexpensive Cessna 150-series aircraft which eventually dominated the trainer market in the United States.

By the mid-1960s the PA-28-140 Cherokee replaced the Colt as Piper's chief training airplane. Without fanfare, the final production PA-22-108 Colt rolled off the assembly lines on March 26, 1964. The airplane was constructor number 22-9848, registered N5974Z.

Until the early 1950s, Piper was known universally as the company that built the J-3 Cub and marketed a host of similar airplanes burdened with 1930s technology. One man in particular, Pug Piper, knew it was time to leave the Cub legacy behind and

The PA-22 series were approved for operations on floats, and were frequently flown with the rear seat removed to accommodate bulk cargo. (Piper Aviation Museum)

With the advent of the Cherokee in 1960, Piper developed the two-place PA-22-108 Colt to serve as an interim flight trainer until the Cherokee 140 was introduced in 1964. The Colt lacked the wing flaps and rear cabin windows of the Tri-Pacer, and was powered by a 108 hp. Lycoming O-235 engine. The Colt illustrated was equipped with optional wheel fairings. (Piper Aviation Museum)

Piper's first twin-engine design was the PA-23 Apache, developed in 1952 and 1953. The prototype, constructor number 23-01, registered N1953A first flew in mid-1952 at Lock Haven. Note retractable landing gear and twin vertical stabilizers, similarity of cabin windows with those of the Stinson 108 Voyager. (Piper Aviation Museum)

◄ *Photographed in 1953, the twin-engine, pusher Bauman Brigadier airframe was suspended above the prototype PA-23 Apache in a hangar at Lock Haven. In 1949 Piper management had proposed building a tractor version of the Brigadier (note new engine mount), but the plan proved too costly and was abandoned in favor of the PA-23 design. (Piper Aviation Museum)*

It must be explained here that of William Piper's three sons, Pug Piper was chiefly responsible for introducing modern aircraft designs into Piper's product line. As one engineer who worked closely with Pug aptly put it, "He was always willing to give a concept a try, no matter where it came from." He would "pursue promising concepts" but if they failed "he immediately stopped working on them and looked at other concepts instead."

Although Pug was not an engineer, he was eventually appointed vice president of engineering for the company. "His forte was developing the conceptual specification and then seeing that it was carried

develop new, modern all-metal airplanes.

Howard Piper's brother Tony Piper had become vice president and general manager of the company in April, 1950, although William T. Piper, Sr., still made the final decisions on new products. Both Pug and Tony agreed that Piper needed to introduce a new generation of airplanes, but how?-by building a twin-engine airplane, Pug insisted.

Thomas Francis Piper viewed the PA-23 Apache project as an essential step in moving the company away from its image as a manufacturer of small, unsophisticated light airplanes such as the J-3 Cub and Tri-Pacer. (Piper Aviation Museum)

Walter C. Jamouneau joined the Taylor Aircraft Company in January, 1933. A graduate of Rugters University, he supervised development of the PA-23 Apache and eventually became a senior official with Piper Aircraft Corporation. (Piper Aviation Museum)

through to a flying aircraft. He knew what had to be done and saw to it that it got done," the engineer said.

Without Pug Piper's insistence that the company progress from steel tube and fabric to all-metal construction, the Apache may never have left the drawing board. The market for light airplanes was growing by leaps and bounds in the early 1950s. A strong United States economy was fueling expansion in virtually every industry, including transportation and its important general aviation segment.

Thousands of pilots and companies were using small aircraft for business as well as private flying, and along with the increase in utilization came the growing desire for multi-engine reliability and redundancy. The lack of—and demand for—a low-priced, economical light twin-engine airplane in the early 1950s was a chief reason for Piper's decision to develop the PA-23 Apache.

The first impetus to build a multi-engine Piper airplane had come in 1949 when the company purchased the pusher-engined, prototype Bauman B250 Brigadier. The airplane was not developed chiefly because the task of redesigning the Brigadier from a pusher to a tractor configuration was impractical and too costly.

Piper was not alone in its quest for a small, multi-engine airplane. West of the Mississippi River in Kansas, Cessna Aircraft Company president Dwane L. Wallace already had his engineers working on the sleek Model 310 twin, and Beech Aircraft flew its Model 50 Twin Bonanza prototype in November, 1949.

Unlike Beech and Cessna which had built thousands of twin-engine airplanes in World War Two, Piper's Walter Jamouneau and his staff had no experience in designing or producing such aircraft.

A number of different two-engine concepts were discussed at the Lock Haven factory, but after additional study a new four-place, low-wing design proved to be the most logical configuration and was selected for development. Powered by two 125 hp. engines, the aircraft would be capable of single-engine flight at 5,000 feet and would possess speed and range comparable to existing single-engine airplanes.

In the summer of 1952 an engineering proof-of-concept aircraft, constructor number 23-01, registered N1953A, was completed and prepared for its maiden flight. In its original configuration, Piper's first light twin was a mixture of the old and new and reflected the company's inexperience with technologically sophisticated airplanes.

The prototype Apache was powered by 125 hp. Lycoming O-290 engines that later were replaced by 150 hp. O-320 powerplants. (Piper Aviation Museum)

PA-23 Apache constructor number 23-2, registered N1000P was one of two pre-production airplanes completed by Piper for certification by the Civil Aeronautics Authority. Jacob W. Miller is at the controls. (Piper Aviation Museum)

The fuselage was constructed of welded steel tubing with fabric covering, and the empennage sported twin vertical stabilizers similar to those installed on the Beech Model 18. Full cantilever wings were mounted low on the fuselage and were built from aluminum alloy except for the outer panels. In addition, the airplane featured a retractable, tricycle landing gear.

The USA-35B airfoil section was selected for the wings, which boasted 187 square feet of area and spanned 35 feet. During flight tests the area was increased to 204 square feet and the span increased to 37 feet to reduce wing loading.

Two Lycoming O-290-D engines each rated at 125 hp. powered the airplane when it took to the skies above Lock Haven on March 4, 1952, only 14 months after the project was initiated, according to a report prepared by chief engineer Walter Jamouneau. Early flight testing revealed that the engineering prototype PA-23 was underpowered and exhibited relatively high rudder forces and yawing moment under single-engine conditions.

To correct this problem, in only two days another bay two feet long was spliced into the 22.8-foot-long tubular fuselage. The lengthened fuselage increased the moment arm and improved significantly the aircraft's single-engine handling qualities.

During the initial flight test program, the twin tail arrangement was replaced by a single vertical stabilizer design borrowed from the stillborn PA-6 Sky Sedan. In addition to simplifying production, the single tail and rudder configuration improved the Apache's appearance without sacrificing directional stability during flight with one engine inoperative.

Although engine cooling was satisfactory under normal, two-engine flight conditions, with one engine inoperative cooling proved inadequate. After experimenting with various unsuccessful cowling modifications, Walter Jamouneau decided to employ exhaust ejector tube cooling to resolve the issue.

After initial flight testing, Piper engineers modified the prototype PA-23 with a conventional empennage borrowed from the still-born PA-6 Sky Sedan. The aft fuselage was redesigned to accommodate the assembly. Apache N1953A is illustrated with the new empennage, but before feathering propellers were fitted. (Piper Aviation Museum)

Further testing dictated the need for feathering propellers, and two-blade Hartzell units were installed on the prototype along with Lycoming O-320 engines, each rated at 150 hp. Single-engine and two-engine climb rate as well as cruise speeds were improved with the new engines and propellers.

Another problem encountered early in the Apache's flight test program was premature stalling of the wing, and vibrations near the root section coupled with vibrations at low speed in the landing configuration. The engineers studied the problem but found no immediate explanation.

In an attempt to remedy these flaws, a variety of methods were tried, such as slots, external slats, trailing edge fillets and minor modifications to the airfoil itself. None of these fixes were completely satisfactory.

Determined to find an answer, Piper conducted wind tunnel tests with a PA-23 model at Pennsylvania State University. The tunnel experiments disclosed that airflow was being disrupted over the upper surface of the inboard wing by flow around the fuselage and nacelle.

The tufted model displayed a strong vortex aft of the nacelle and a weaker vortex adjacent to the fuselage. By moving the nacelle outboard, the vortex was diminished and airflow improved across the inboard wing surface. The nacelle, however, could not be positioned farther outboard primarily because it would adversely affect single-engine yawing moment and degrade control.

Finally, small fillets were added to the inboard wing leading edge causing a gradual airflow transition from the wing to the nacelle and fuselage. Although not an ideal solution, the fillets worked.

As the prototype's flight test program continued into 1953, a major redesign of the Apache from the cabin aft was initiated to upgrade the twin-engine ship into a truly marketable airplane.

The welded, chromoly steel tube structure in the cabin was retained but the entire fuselage was converted to aluminum alloy construction. On July 29, 1953, the PA-23 Apache production prototype made its first flight. Assigned constructor number 23-1 and registered N23P, the airplane flew well and accumulated more than 300 hours of certification flight

testing by the Civil Aeronautics Authority (CAA) before the Type Certificate was granted on January 29, 1954.

Piper had initiated production of the Apache in December, 1953 and began delivering airplanes soon after the type certificate was issued. With a price tag of $32,500, however, the Apache was not welcomed by many Piper dealers unaccustomed to such a huge sum of money for a Lock Haven airplane. Despite reluctant salespeople and a seemingly high price, the PA-23 sold itself—once again it was the right airplane at the right time for Piper.

In the PA-23 Apache, Piper Aircraft Corporation had succeeded in designing a comfortable four-place, high-performance twin-engine airplane that provided a cruise speed of up to 170 mph. and a range of more than 700 statute miles. Pilots liked the Apache and quickly learned that its relatively low wing loading helped make it easy to fly. The four-cylinder Lycomings with their thrifty fuel consumption and 800-hour time between overhaul (TBO) made the Apache economical to operate.

In keeping with Piper's reputation as the industry's price and value leader, the Apache was the least expensive light twin-engine aircraft on the market. It was significantly slower than Cessna's Model 310, which cost $49,000 and cruised at more than 200 mph., and less spacious than the $70,000 Beechcraft Model 50 Twin Bonanza—a larger airplane that carried five persons and also cruised above the magic 200-mph. mark.

As autumn, 1954 arrived Apache sales had climbed higher than Piper management had anticipated and the factory was struggling to meet demand. Production had reached one airplane per day in September, and 59 had been sold by the end of the month.

By December the company was feverishly trying to get ahead of still-growing demand but had fallen nearly 200 airplanes behind by Christmas. Eventually, production increases were able to cope with demand. The Apache was a hallmark airplane for Piper. It was affordable, had good twin-engine performance and set the pace for other manufacturers to follow. In summary, the PA-23 was a multi-engine airplane for the masses.

With the PA-23 Apache, Piper had left the Cub era far behind and entered the modern world of all-metal airplanes. In the years ahead the company would introduce the PA-24 Comanche and the PA-28 Cherokee, two airplanes that would carry the fortunes of Piper Aircraft Corporation to new heights.

CHAPTER SIX

TRIBAL EXPANSION

The decades of the 1950s and 1960s were a time of tremendous growth for the general aviation industry. As for Piper Aircraft Corporation, the company experienced unprecedented expansion during these years as it became one of the world's premier builders of light aircraft.

With PA-23 Apache sales accelerating in the mid-1950s, Piper embarked on a program designed to improve its first lightweight, twin-engine airplane. Horsepower, performance and comfort were upgraded with each version, and strong sales reflected the Apache's ongoing popularity.

For the 1955, 1956 and 1957 model years the B model, C model and D model Apaches respectively featured a maximum gross weight of 3,500 lb. and a maximum speed of of 180 mph. Powered by 150 hp. Lycoming engines, the airplanes had a fuel capacity of 72 gallons with 108-gallon capacity optional by installation of two 18 gallon tanks near the wingtips. The extra fuel boosted range to 1,260 statute miles from 840 statute miles at economy cruise power settings.

Available in Standard, Custom or Super Custom configurations, the PA-23 could be equipped with a Narco Omnigator VHF transceiver and navigation radio, a Narco Simplexer VHF receiver and Lear ADF-12 automatic direction finder. Normally, Piper did not install any avionic equipment in the Standard version.

Dual controls for pilot and co-pilot were standard, and a Southwind heater rated at 20,000 BTUs provided cabin heat. Fuel for the heater was drawn from the wing tanks. A fifth passenger seat mounted in the aft cabin was made standard in 1955, but the berth provided only limited space and comfort for most adults.

Standard color combinations included Daytona White and Dakota Black with Pasadena Rose, Cadillac Red or Key West Blue trim colors. The 150 hp. Lycoming engines initially had an 800-hour time between overhaul that later was increased to 1,200 hours, and the powerplants drove hydraulically operated constant-speed, full-feathering propellers.

The first major change in the PA-23 lineage came in 1958 with introduction of the E model PA-23-160 Apache. The installation of 160 hp. Lycoming O-320-B engines complimented a maximum gross weight increase to 3,800 lb. from the 150 hp. version's 3,500 lb. limit.

Although overall performance was similar to previous Apaches, the higher gross weight reduced two-engine service ceiling to 17,000 feet and rate of climb to 1,260 feet per minute. Takeoff and landing distance also were increased slightly.

An additional cabin side window was added beginning with the 1960 G model Apache to provide a better exterior field of view for the fifth-seat passenger. The PA-23 series was well received by flying businessmen. They liked its economical operation as well as the airplane's performance.

One owner and pilot of an Apache said, "I use a 65 per cent power setting and speed seems to true out at about 170 mph. at any altitude. Fuel consumption varies from 18 to 19 gallons per hour." Another happy owner commented that "The Apache is the simplest, safest and most easily operated aircraft a pilot could wish to fly." Piper continued to produce

Equipped with 150 hp. engines and constant-speed, full-feathering propellers, the PA-23 Apache cruised at 160 mph. and could carry four people in comfort. The airplane illustrated was registered N2000P, constructor number 23-229 and served as the production prototype for the 1956 Apache. (Piper Aviation Museum)

60

In March, 1955 Howard Piper and his brother William Piper, Jr., flew an Apache named "The Spirit of Pretoria" to South Africa for delivery. (Piper Aviation Museum)

◄ *Instrument panel of an early PA-23-150 Apache. Note same size, shape and color of handles on throttle, mixture and propeller controls; landing gear and flap handles and emergency gear extension hand pump below throttle quadrant. (Piper Aviation Museum)*

airplanes were identified publicly using the PA-23 designation.

With its additional power, the Aztec had a maximum speed of 215 mph. and cruised at 205 mph. Maximum gross weight increased to 4,800 lb. and two-engine service ceiling was 22,500 feet. A batch of 20 new Aztecs was delivered to the United States Navy in 1960 for transportation duties. These aircraft were designated UO-1.

In 1961 the Aztec B and the new Apache 235 variant were developed. The Aztec B was the first version to feature a lengthened nose section that included a second baggage compartment. A total of 300 lb. could be stowed in both compartments.

the Apache until January, 1962 when manufacture was terminated after 2,047 airplanes had been built since 1954.

Despite their satisfaction with the Apache, many owners wanted more power, more speed and more useful load. Piper management realized that the airplane had matured to the point where a major upgrade was justified. As a result, in 1958 the company designed a much-improved airplane designated the PA-23-250 Aztec. Principal changes included 250 hp. Lycoming O-540-A1D5 engines, a larger, swept vertical stabilizer and installation of a stabilator.

The prototype Aztec was constructor number 27-1, registered N4250P. Production for the 1960 model year began late in 1959 after the Federal Aviation Administration (FAA) issued the Aztec's type certificate. Piper allocated the PA-27 designation to the Aztec series for production reference only—all

The F model Apache built in 1959 featured 160 hp. Lycoming O-320 engines first installed in the 1958 Apache, and an improved autopilot system. The airplane illustrated was constructor number 23-1426, registered N3454P. (Piper Aviation Museum)

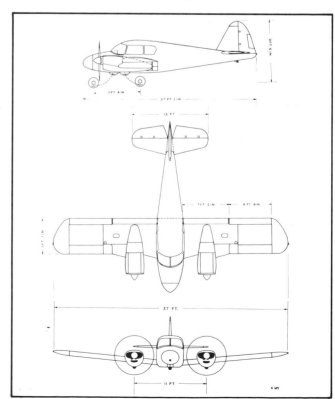

For the 1960 model year Piper added a third cabin window to create the G model Apache. The windows provided improved visibility for the fifth seat passenger. 1960 Apache registered N4374P, constructor number 23-1880 is illustrated. (Piper Aviation Museum)

Instrument panel of a G model Apache shows center-mounted avionics and Piper Altimatic autopilot installation. Note that throttle, mixture and propeller controls are color-coded. (Piper Aviation Museum)

Introduced in November, 1962 during the 22nd Annual Piper International Sales Conference held in West Palm Beach, Florida, the standard-equipped version of the Aztec B sold for $52,990 including full IFR instrumentation but without avionics. Fitted with the Super Custom option, the airplane cost $58,460 and the Autoflite version was priced at $59,260.

The cabin was capable of seating six occupants and the instrument panel was redesigned. Useful load decreased from 2,025 lb. to 1,900 lb. Piper's Apache 235 essentially was a reduced-power, lower cost version of the PA-23-250 Aztec, with 235 hp. Lycoming O-540-B1A5 powerplants instead of 250 hp. engines.

Although only 118 were produced, the Apache 235 offered a 191 mph. cruise speed, a range of nearly 1,000 statute miles with fuel reserves and a hefty useful load of 2,065 lb. The Apache 235 was built alongside the Aztec until June, 1966 when production was terminated.

As with the earlier Apache, Piper implemented a series of design and systems improvements to the Aztec during its production life. The Aztec C was introduced in 1964, and sported longer, redesigned cowlings for its fuel-injected 250 hp. Lycoming IO-540-C4B5 engines or optional turbocharged TIO-540-C1A powerplants that were each rated at 250 hp. and featured AiResearch turbochargers.

In addition, the Aztec C had a redesigned exhaust system that eliminated the augmentor-type tubes used on earlier aircraft. In late 1967, Lycoming improved the TIO-540 by adding long-reach spark plugs,

strengthened cylinder heads and crankcase as well as 1200-series Bendix magnetos.

These improvements allowed the Turbo Aztec C to use a new "Turbo Cruise" setting of 2,400 propeller rpm. and 28.5 in. Hg. manifold pressure from sea level up to 24,000 feet. As a result, maximum cruise speed increased to 250 mph. at Flight Level 240.

A new landing gear door system fully enclosed all three tires when the gear was retracted, and useful load was boosted to 2,267 lb. Maximum gross weight increased to 5,200 lb.

It is interesting to note that in 1961 Piper management wanted to replace traditional paints used on the Apache, Aztec and Comanche airplanes with a new coating that was designed to better withstand harsh environmental conditions, retain its gloss and reduce owner maintenance.

Developed for Piper by E.I. duPont de Nemours and Company, Inc., the new paint was known as Lucite High Gloss, an acrylic lacquer that was originally created for the automotive industry. Unlike older finishes, the new paint dried to a full luster without buffing.

To evaluate the coating, Lucite-painted panels were subjected to three years of laboratory tests by Du-Pont as well as extensive on-site experiments at Lock Haven and at the new factory at Vero Beach, Florida.

Satisfied with these tests, Piper painted 10 1961 Comanches with the Lucite High Gloss paint. The airplanes were bought by retail customers who based them at airports across the United States in an effort to expose the paint to various climatic conditions.

DuPont inspected the airplanes at three-month intervals and found that the owners were enthusiastic

Piper introduced the PA-23-250 Aztec in 1959. Although similar to the Apache, the Aztec featured a new empennage assembly that incorporated a stabilator and swept vertical stabilizer. Six-cylinder Lycoming O-540 engines powered the six-place airplane. Base price was $49,500. (Piper Aviation Museum)

Constructor number 27-1, registered N4250P was the prototype Aztec built in 1958 at the Lock Haven factory. Deliveries of production Aztecs began in 1959. (Piper Aviation Museum)

PA-23-250 Aztec instrument panel fitted with Piper Autocontrol autopilot system. (Piper Aviation Museum)

Piper delivered 20 Aztecs to the United States Navy in 1960. The aircraft were designated UO-1 by the military service. (Piper Aviation Museum)

about the paint. Piper was satisfied that the new finish was acceptable and began applying the Lucite paint to all Apaches, Aztecs and Comanches beginning with the 1962 model year.

By the mid-1960s, Piper Aircraft Corporation was dominating the Unites States general aviation industry. In January, 1964 Piper had delivered its 60,000th airplane, a Twin Comanche registered N60000, and an official proclaimed that the company had "produced more aircraft, civil or military, than any other aircraft manufacturer in the world."

Production at the Lock Haven and Vero Beach factories had reached 60 airplanes per week and gross sales for 1964 were $46 million—a 21% increase over 1963 sales of $38 million. In April, 1965 the company set a record by delivering 422 airplanes and sold $7,195,470 worth of new aircraft, breaking the previous record set only a month before when 400 new Pipers were delivered and sales totaled $7,038,846.

Aztec sales were flying as high as the airplane. To meet steadily growing demand, production was increased in the spring of 1965 to 40 airplanes per month from 30 per month. In addition, the assembly area at Lock Haven was doubled in size to help meet the new production schedule.

At the end of 1965, the Aztec was the best-selling twin-engine airplane in the United States. Piper delivered 365 of the popular PA-23-250 that year com-

Aerial view of the Piper factory at Lock Haven in the early 1960s. Aztec, Apache, Comanche and Pawnee aircraft are parked on the field. (Piper Aviation Museum)

pared with 315 Aztecs in 1964.

To better appreciate how well Piper's twin-engine product line was selling at that time, in the first seven months of fiscal year 1965 deliveries of 454 Aztec and Twin Comanche aircraft accounted for nearly 50% of all four- and six-place twin-engine light airplanes sold. The combined output of Beech, Cessna and Aero Commander amounted to 459 airplanes.

In addition to domestic sales many of the airplanes were being exported to European, South American and African nations as well as other countries. The Argentine army bought six Aztec C aircraft late in 1964 to supplement a fleet of five Apaches and PA-11 Cub Special observation aircraft already in service, and a small fleet of Aztecs were operating in Kenya transporting big game hunters to and from their safari base camps.

Financially, the Aztec was doing more than its share to increase Piper's profits. In 1964 the company claimed nearly 50% of the light aircraft market overall and had gross sales of $54,378,377. A total of 716 twin-engine airplanes were sold by Piper that year.

From 1954 to the end of 1964 more than 4,000 Piper twin-engine airplanes had been built, including 2,204 Apaches, 97 Apache 235s, 483 Aztecs, 520 Aztec B, 234 Aztec C and 672 Twin Comanches. The powerful and popular Aztec changed little over the next few years until the Aztec D was introduced in 1968 followed by the 1970 Aztec E. The D model's instrument panel was new with flight instruments arranged in the

Early in 1961 pilot Max Conrad circled the world in Aztec N4544P, constructor number 27-49. He completed the flight in eight days, 18 hours, 36 minutes and averaged 123.2 mph. Note wing and empennage deicers, words New Frontiers and Let's Fly. (Piper Aviation Museum)

To increase the Aztec's sales appeal, in 1962 Piper began delivering the upgraded PA-23-250 Aztec B that featured a longer nose section and six-seat cabin. (Piper Aircraft Corporation)

industry-standard "T" configuration.

Electrical switches and many controls were relocated to reduce pilot workload and avionics were mounted in the center of the instrument panel. The chief change for the E model was a nose section one foot longer than that of the Aztec D. The new nose tapered to a point and provided more baggage capacity.

In 1968 Melridge Aviation Company, a Piper dealer in Vancouver, Washington, and the Jobmaster Company of Seattle developed the Nomad version of the Aztec C and Aztec D that were certified for operation on EDO Model 679-4930 floats. Approved under a Supplemental Type Certificate by the FAA, the Nomad modification included a left-side cabin door for convenience of the pilot.

Equipped with floats the airplane cruised at 160 mph. and carried 120 gallons of fuel. One-engine service ceiling at the 5,200-lb. maximum gross weight limit was more than 4,000 feet. Useful load was 1,800 lb.

By the mid-1970s, the Aztec had evolved into a highly refined airplane. The PA-23-250 had developed a faithful following of owners and operators worldwide who appreciated the aircraft's rugged construction, reliability and operating economics.

The final variant produced was the Aztec F, introduced in the 1976 model year. Horsepower remained the same as the Aztec E, and turbocharging continued to be a popular option with many operators. As part of a program to improve handling characteristics, the flight control and flap systems were interconnected and the stabilator was reconfigured to a rectangular shape with extended mass balance weights at each tip.

The fuel system was redesigned for improved operation and optional wing tip tanks could be fitted. Maximum speed of the turbocharged Aztec F was 248 mph. and two-engine service ceiling was 24,000 feet.

Unquestionably, the Aztec was one of Piper Aircraft Corporation's most successful airplanes. The company had built 4,929 Aztecs when production stopped in November, 1981. Combined with the Apache, nearly 7,000 twin-engine aircraft had been manufactured over a period of 27 years.

In the wake of the Apache's success, Piper management decided to proceed with development of a single-engine airplane that would complement the PA-23 and provide the company with a second strong foothold in the marketplace. Dubbed the PA-24 Comanche, the four-place ship embodied many of the complex systems pioneered by Piper on the Apache and later used on the Aztec such as an all-metal, low-wing

The Apache 235 mated the Aztec's airframe with 235 hp. Lycoming O-540 engines. Unlike the six-place Aztec, the Apache 235 was limited to four or five seats. Base price was $44,990 in 1962. The prototype Apache 235 was constructor number 27-460, registered N4914P. (Piper Aviation Museum)

The Aztec C illustrated, registered N6185Y was used by Melridge Aviation located in Vancouver, Washington, to obtain certification of the PA-23-250 Nomad on EDO Model 4930 floats. A left-side cabin door was fitted as part of the approval. Kits were made available to convert aircraft in the field. (Piper Aviation Museum)

In 1965 Piper upgraded the Aztec B to the Aztec C configuration. Fuel-injected Lycoming IO-540 or turbocharged TIO-540 powerplants were available, enclosed in sleek "Tiger Shark" cowlings. When retracted, the landing gear were completely covered by fiberglass doors that were hydraulically operated. Aztec C N5427Y, constructor number 27-2505 was the first production airplane. (Piper Aviation Museum)

The Aztec D was introduced for the 1968 model year. Constructor number 27-3636, registered N6496Y was a turbocharged Aztec D. (Piper Aviation Museum)

Piper's 1971 Aztec E featured a lengthened, redesigned nose section and improved avionics. Aztec E registered N54202 is illustrated, equipped with optional wing and empennage deicers, weather radar and windshield hot plate. (Piper Aircraft Corporation)

◄ *The Aztec F was introduced in 1976. It incorporated a new, larger horizontal stabilizer with extended tips. Optional wing tip fuel tanks also were available. (Piper Aircraft Corporation)*

design, retractable landing gear, a swept vertical stabilizer and a stabilator. In addition, the wing utilized limited natural laminar flow to help achieve cruise performance.

The Comanche was intended to be a low-price competitor to the more expensive Beechcraft Model 35 Bonanza that was dominating the high performance, single-engine market in 1955. By the time of the Comanche's development in 1956, Beech already had delivered several thousand Bonanzas and was selling the G35 version for $21,990. As for Cessna, its fastest single-engine airplane was the new Model 182 Skylane, developed almost concurrently with the Comanche.

With its 225 hp. engine the G35 Bonanza cruised at

The experimental, PA-41P pressurized Aztec powered by 270 hp. Lycoming TIO-540 engines first flew in 1974 but was not developed. Note semi-oval cabin windows, ice shields on nose section and large NACA duct on engine cowling. Upon completion of the test program, PA-41P registered N9941P, constructor number 41P-1 was donated to the Mississippi State University. (Mal Holcomb)

a fast 170 mph. The fixed-gear 182 managed a respectable cruise speed of 150 mph. with its 230 hp. Continental engine. It should be noted that Cessna's retractable-gear Model 210—a worthy competitor to both the Bonanza and the Comanche—did not make its first flight until 1957.

Completed in June, 1956 the prototype Comanche was constructor number 24-1, registered N2024P, powered by a Lycoming O-360-A1A engine of 180 hp.

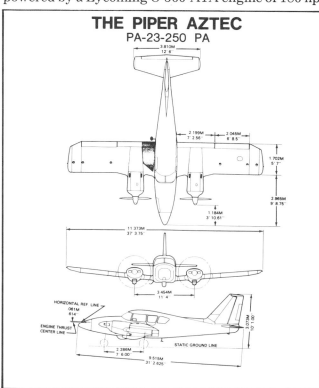

THE PIPER AZTEC
PA-23-250 PA

The prototype PA-24 Comanche was constructor number 24-1, registered N2024P. Built in 1956, it was powered by a 180 hp. Lycoming O-360 engine equipped with a constant-speed propeller. Note experimental trailing beam landing gear that was not incorporated on production Comanches. (Piper Aviation Museum)

Piper also built a second prototype Comanche, constructor number 24-2 registered N6000D. Designed to compete against the Beechcraft Model 35 Bonanza and Cessna Model 210, the Comanche had a cruise speed of 160 mph. and a range of more than 900 statute miles at a 75% power setting. (Piper Aviation Museum)

and fitted with a constant-speed propeller. Flight tests showed a maximum speed of 167 mph. and a cruise speed of 160 mph. Range with standard 50-gallon fuel tanks was 750 statute miles at sea level or 920 statute miles at optimum altitude.

Piper commenced production of the 180 hp. PA-24 Comanche in October, 1957, for the 1958 model year. Priced at $14,500, the airplane was a resounding success and sales soared. Many loyal Piper customers gladly forsook their obsolete, slow and cramped-cabin Tri-Pacers for the sleek, fast and spacious Comanche.

Less than six months after introduction of the PA-24-180, Piper unleashed the PA-24-250 powered by a 250 hp. Lycoming O-540-A1A5 engine. With the additional 70 hp. the Comanche's cruise speed climbed to 181 mph. and maximum speed was increased to 190 mph.

In 1962 a fuel-injected IO-540-C engine rated at 250 hp. was offered as an option to the carburetor-equipped O-540 series engine. The first production

Three-view of PA-24 Comanche 260. (Smithsonian Institution, National Air And Space Museum Negative Number 93-2379)

airplane to be fitted with the new IO-540 powerplant was constructor number 24-3025, registered N7968P. Because of its more powerful engine, the base price of the PA-24-250 increased to $17,900.

With the PA-24's speed, efficiency and reputation for reliability it was soon in demand for long-distance, globe-girdling flights that set world records. In June, 1959 famed pilot Max Conrad flew PA-24-250 constructor number 24-695, registered N110 LF from Casablanca to Los Angeles. The letters LF stood for "Let's Fly."

He flew the 7,668 miles non-stop at an average speed of 130.9 mph. Flight time was 58 hours, 38 minutes. In November of that year, Conrad flew a 180 hp. Comanche from Casablanca to El Paso, Texas— a distance of 6,967 miles. Both flights were sanctioned and recognized as records by the Federation Aeronautique Internationale (FAI).

Piper received good publicity from such flights, which underscored the PA-24's efficiency. It is interesting to note that in 1959 Piper estimated the total hourly operating cost of a 180 hp. Comanche to

1960 Comanche instrument panel was equipped with Piper's AutoFlite autopilot option. Note landing gear control handle at upper, right center of panel, and manual flap control lever below propeller control. (Piper Aviation Museum)

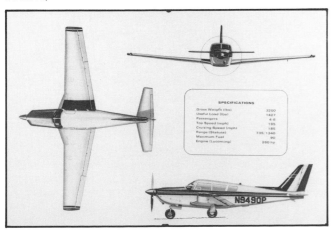

British aviatrix Sheila Scott stands on the wing of her 1966 PA-24-260 Comanche B registered G-ATOY, and dubbed "Myth Too" by Miss Scott. Max Conrad's Comanche 250 N110LF is in the background. The two airplanes, Miss Scott and Conrad already had accomplished eight trans-oceanic crossings and eight world speed and distance records when this photograph was taken at Lock Haven in 1968. (Piper Aviation Museum)

By the early 1960s the Comanche had established itself as a sales leader in the competitive single-engine, high performance aircraft market. A 1962 PA-24-180 Comanche registered N7623P is illustrated. (Piper Aviation Museum)

A 250 hp. Lycoming O-540 engine powered the PA-24-250, which was introduced in 1958. The Comanche 250 illustrated was photographed at the Beech Aircraft Corporation factory in Wichita, Kansas where it was evaluated by Beech engineering and marketing personnel. (Mal Holcomb)

◄ *In 1959 Max Conrad flew Comanche 250 constructor number 24-695, registered N110LF from Casablanca to Los Angeles, California in 58.6 hours. (Piper Aviation Museum)*

be a mere $10.62 if the airplane was flown 400 hours per year. That figure decreased to $8.50 based on flying 1,000 hours per year, which few, if any, Comanche owners achieved.

In Standard equipment configuration the PA-24-180 sold for $16,445 in October, 1960. Three other optional versions, the Custom, Super Custom and Autoflite, were priced at $18,236, $19,256 and $20,056 respectively. A 90-gallon fuel system was standard for the Super Custom and Autoflite models. Lock Haven produced 822 Comanches in the 1960 model year, with the 250-hp. version proving more popular than the PA-24-180.

Piper had a winner in the Comanche. Its speed, utility, large baggage compartment and overall efficiency endeared it to many pilots and in 1961, the PA-24 emerged as the best-selling airplane in its class for the fourth consecutive year.

According to Piper officials the Comanche captured 39.39% of its market in 1961, compared with 29.38% for the Beechcraft Bonanza and the low-price Debonair, and 19.26% for Mooney. Cessna, with its high-wing Model 210, ranked fourth with 11.52% of the market.

Despite the excellent sales success and good performance of the Comanche 250, in 1961 Piper developed what would become three years later the world's

Interior of 1962 Comanche 180 registered N7623P shows redesigned instrument panel, upgraded upholstery and carpeting compared with earlier Comanches. (Piper Aviation Museum)

The Comanche's optional Palm Beach interior featured leather fabrics available in red, blue, green, brown or gray colors. (Piper Aviation Museum)

In 1963 the Comanche 250 sported a new, three-tone paint design. Optional fuel tanks increased capacity to 90 gallons and boosted zero-wind range to more than 1,600 statute miles at economy cruise power settings. (Piper Aviation Museum)

fastest production single-engine, piston-powered light airplane—the PA-24-400 Comanche. Although officially known as the PA-26, production airplanes were identified as PA-24-400 by Piper.

Essentially a standard Comanche airframe fitted with an eight-cylinder, 400 hp. Lycoming IO-720-A1A engine and a three-blade propeller, the PA-24-400 entered production in August, 1964. Only 148 were built before Piper ended production in November.

Although fast with a maximum speed of 223 mph. and a cruise speed of 213 mph., the Comanche 400 was more than the market wanted. The engine was expensive to operate, primarily because it burned much more fuel per hour than the Comanche 250's powerplant.

Unfortunately, the IO-720 was more costly to maintain and hot-starting the engine occasionally proved difficult and frustrating for owners. In later years, prices for PA-24-400s remained depresssed. Piper did build an experimental, 300 hp. Comanche in 1967 designated as the PA-24-300 but it was an engineering aircraft and served only as a test airframe for the engine.

To further improve the Comanche, in 1964 Lycoming introduced the 260 hp. O-540-E4A5 engine that became the PA-24-260 variant when the latest version of the Comanche entered production in September of that year. In contrast to the 260 hp. Comanche, sales of the economical, 180 hp. PA-24 were waning by 1964 because most pilots preferred the higher horsepower engines and the increased performance they provided. As a result, the 180 hp. engine was discontinued after

Piper unveiled the PA-24-260 Comanche for the 1965 model year. A 260 hp. Lycoming O-540 engine was installed and flight-tested in N8383P, constructor number 24-3642 to obtain certification. In addition to increased horsepower, the Comanche 260 featured an improved, single-fork main landing gear strut. (Piper Aviation Museum)

the 1964 model year.

The first major upgrade to the PA-24 series was the 1966 Comanche B, which featured a lengthened cabin to accomodate optional fifth and sixth passenger seats. A third cabin side window was provided, more soundproofing material was added to the cabin and seat contours were redesigned for more comfort.

Baggage capacity was increased 50 lb. to 250 lb. in the aft seat area, and a higher useful load of 1,372 lb. allowed the airplane to carry four 170-lb. adults, 250 lb. of baggage and 60 gallons of fuel. Along with the boost in useful load, maximum gross weight was raised to 3,100 lb. from the Comanche's 2,900 lb. limit. The Comanche B's base price was $23,990, and Piper manufactured 359 airplanes in the 1966 model year.

In 1966 celebrated British aviatrix Sheila Scott flew a Comanche B around the world in 33 days, flying 29,055 miles and establishing a women's speed record for circling the globe. She also established 12 intercity speed records during the trip.

After eight years of production, more than 4,000 Comanches had been built at Lock Haven and the PA-24 had carved a special niche for itself in the competitive high-performance, single-engine market. The final variant of the venerable Comanche series was the PA-24-260 Comanche C which had a base price of

A minor upgrade to the PA-24 series occurred in 1966 when Piper added a third cabin window and redesigned the interior to accommodate a fifth and sixth seat. Maximum gross weight increased 200 lb. to 3,100 lb. Comanche B prototype registered N8794P, constructor number 24-4247 is illustrated. (Piper Aircraft Corporation)

Produced only during the 1964 model year, the PA-24-400 Comanche 400 was powered by a 400 hp. Lycoming IO-720 engine driving a three-blade, constant-speed propeller. At a 65% power setting the airplane cruised at a true airspeed of 213 mph. (Piper Aviation Museum)

The 1969 Comanche C featured a new "Tiger Shark" cowling to enclose the Lycoming IO-540 engine. A new interior was installed and throttle, mixture and propeller controls were grouped together in a "SportsPower" quadrant. Maximum gross weight increased to 3,200 lb. When production ended in 1972, Piper had manufactured 4,717 Comanches. (Piper Aviation Museum)

$27,500. Introduced on June 2, 1968, and produced for the 1969 model year the airplane featured a 100-lb. higher maximum gross weight of 3,200 lb., a new instrument panel with center-stack avionics, rocker switches and a quadrant-type grouping of throttle, mixture and propeller controls.

The chief exterior change was a new engine cowling dubbed by Piper the "Tiger Shark nose." Similar to that used on the PA-30 Twin Comanche, the extended nose was created to enclose the propeller shaft that had been extended six inches forward, primarily to reduce cabin noise and vibration.

Time between overhaul (TBO) of the fuel-injected Lycoming IO-540-E4A5 engine was increased to 1,800 hours, as were the engines in Piper's naturally aspirated, single- and twin-engine airplanes and the Turbo Aztec in 1969. The airplane's standard 60 gallon fuel capacity could be increased to 90 gallons by installation of dual auxiliary fuel tanks. With standard tanks, the Comanche C had a maximum range of 870 statute miles; with the auxiliary tanks range increased to 1,340 statute miles.

Along with improvements in external appearance and interior layout, the Comanche C also boasted improved performance compared with its older siblings. Maximum speed increased to 195 mph., with an optimum cruise speed of 185 mph. occurring at an altitude of 6,300 feet.

After manufacturing 4,717 Comanche-series airplanes, Piper management let the floodwaters of the Susquehanna River and its West Branch tributary bring an end to PA-24 production in June, 1972. That month only 28 Comanches had been built before disaster struck. Hurricane Agnes had caused the river and its estuaries to engulf parts of Lock Haven itself as well as the Piper factory, and most of the Comanche tooling and other production equipment were damaged or destroyed. Worst of all, however, was the loss of many airplanes worth millions of dollars. It was the most severe flood in Lock Haven's history up to that time.

Success with the PA-24 series led Piper to develop the PA-30 Twin Comanche in 1962 as a fuel-efficient, lightweight twin-engine airplane that was faster than the Comanche but more economical to own and operate than the PA-23 Aztec. Using the PA-24 airframe for its basis, the Twin Comanche was designed to carry four people more than 1,000 statute miles at speeds approaching 195 mph.

The 400 hp., eight-cylinder Lycoming IO-720 engine was the most powerful horizontally opposed powerplant installed in the single-engine PA-24 Comanche series. (Smithsonian Institution, National Air And Space Museum Negative Number 93-2080)

Hailed by Piper officials as "The fastest single-engine aircraft in production," the Comanche 400 had a maximum speed of 223 mph. and boasted a three-blade Hartzell propeller with a diameter of 77 inches. Despite high performance and a base price of $28,750, only 148 airplanes were built. (Piper Aviation Museum)

William T. "Bill" Piper, Jr., possessed the friendly personality of his famous father. He eventually became president and chief executive officer of Piper Aircraft Corporation. (Piper Aviation Museum)

In 1962 Pug Piper hired engineer Edward Swearingen to transform a PA-24 Comanche registered N5808P into the prototype PA-30 Twin Comanche. Photographed at Swearingen's San Antonio, Texas facility, the PA-30 prototype awaits its first flight. (Edward Swearingen)

The two 160 hp. Lycoming IO-320 engines that powered the prototype PA-30 were housed in sleek nacelles and cowlings. The PA-30 first flew in November, 1962 at San Antonio, Texas. Piper completed FAA certification at Lock Haven. (Edward Swearingen)

The PA-30 was the brainchild of Pug Piper. In the late 1950s he had conceived the idea of a next-generation airplane based on the Comanche but equipped with two engines. When his concept was presented to the company's engineering staff, however, it met with some skepticism. In addition, they had a high workload designing the Aztec and other current and future Piper projects.

Howard Piper continued to ponder his idea. In 1962, he was relating his plans for the new airplane with none other than William P. Lear of Learjet fame. Lear was in the midst of establishing a factory in Wichita, Kansas to build his Model 23 Learjet business aircraft, and when Piper lamented that he wanted to build the PA-30 but was uncertain if the engineering staff could accept the added workload, the indefatigable Lear had a solution.

He told Piper about a young, talented aeronautical engineer named Edward J. Swearingen who could design and build Pug Piper's PA-30. Swearingen had worked for Lear earlier in his career and in February, 1959, had started his own aircraft modification business in San Antonio, Texas.

Acting on Bill Lear's recommendation, Piper went to San Antonio and met with Swearingen. As a result of that meeting, Swearingen was given the initial task of performing minor aerodynamic drag reduction on the PA-23 Apache.

Howard Piper told Swearingen about his plans to build a small, twin-engine airplane using as much ex-

isting Comanche tooling as was possible. He authorized Swearingen to submit several proposals for the new aircraft, ranging from a conventional, twin-engine design like the Aztec to a three-engine layout or one with two engines mounted in the nose driving a single propeller.

At a board of directors meeting in Lock Haven a few weeks later, Ed Swearingen submitted his proposal for a conventional, twin-engine airplane. Although the other two designs promised increased safety during single-engine flight and intrigued Pug Piper, Swearingen defended his choice: "People talk about safety and buy speed," he told the officials.

Pug Piper was convinced, but explained to the Texas engineer that production airplanes had to cost no more than $35,000. With that goal in mind, Swearingen set about designing the prototype Twin Comanche early in 1962. A PA-24 airframe constructor number 24-888, registered N5808P, provided to Swearingen was transformed into the prototype twin-engine PA-30.

Although the Twin Comanche shared the Comanche's laminar flow wing, the leading edge aluminum alloy skins were thicker and the wing root ribs were strengthened. To cope with increased gross weights, a larger, heavier main and rear spar were used.

The vertical stabilizer was six inches taller and had 1.4 square feet of additional area compared with the empennage of the PA-24, and the stabilator was larger. Where the Comanche's engine had been, a sleek, tapered nose section was installed that provided maintenance access to key systems components.

Although work progressed rapidly, some serious technical obstacles had to be overcome. The 160 hp.

Instrument panel of Twin Comanche registered N7002Y is configured with Piper's "Executive 222" avionic option that included dual 360-channel Narco Mark 12 VHF transceivers, Motorola ADF, AltiMatic autopilot and VOR and ILS receivers. Throttle, mixture and propeller controls had distinct shapes for identification by touch as mandated by the Federal Aviation Administration. (Piper Aviation Museum)

In-flight photograph of Twin Comanche constructor number 30-2, registered N7001Y. Introduced in May, 1963 the PA-30 had a base price of $33,900. (Piper Aviation Museum)

Photograph of 300 hp. Lycoming engine installation in Twin Comanche N7000Y. (Edward Swearingen)

Lycoming engines selected to power the PA-30 were enclosed in thin, streamlined nacelles designed for low drag. To achieve good ram pressure recovery at the cooling inlets Swearingen wanted to install a six-inch extension on the engine's crankshaft, thereby moving the propeller farther forward, away from the cowling.

Lycoming engineers disagreed with Swearingen's idea and forbade such modifications, according to Swearingen. Frustrated but confident his idea would work, he fabricated the crankshaft extensions and installed them on the engines. The PA-30 prototype made its first flight in November, 1962 with Ed Swearingen at the controls. During initial tests Swearingen was delighted to learn that the crankshaft extensions worked well but was unhappy about vibrations that made the instrument panel and wingtips a blur at cruise power settings.

After instrumenting the airframe and conducting further flights, he discovered that the fuselage sides and the wings were vibrating at one-half the vibratory frequency of the engines. Swearingen believed the problem could be cured most easily by reducing

In 1966 Piper introduced the improved Twin Comanche B that featured a third cabin window and six-place seating. A turbocharged version was available, powered by 160 hp. Lycoming TIO-360 engines. Wing tip fuel tanks were standard equipment on turbocharged airplanes. The PA-30 illustrated, constructor number 30-853, registered N7750Y was the Twin Comanche B prototype. (Piper Aviation Museum)

engine-induced vibrations.

As was the practice at that time, the Lycomings were suspended in their mounts by hard rubber discs. The discs transmitted power impulses from the four-cylinder engines directly into the airframe instead of absorbing them. A superior method of mounting the engines had to be found.

To resolve the problem, Swearingen consulted the Lord Corporation in Erie, Pennsylvania. Lord specialized in designing mount systems for aerospace applications, including piston engines. They developed an innovative system that would suspend the powerplant but used elastomeric compounds within each mount to absorb motions of the engine. Several different configurations were tried before an optimum design was chosen.

The vibration problem was solved. Realizing that they had a unique product, Lord began marketing the system as the "Dynafocal" mount. Piper, Beech, Cessna and other aircraft manufacturers quickly applied the product to their airplanes.

Another problem that Swearingen had to contend with on the prototype airplane was the engine's troublesome fuel injection system. Designed by the AC Delco Division of General Motors Corporation, the installation often failed to work properly, leaving Swearingen with "one engine dead and the other one running badly" as he returned from many of his test flights, he said.

Fortunately, Lycoming rejected the AC Delco system and selected a Bendix fuel injection installation for production engines. Swearingen continued to develop and flight test the prototype PA-30 before Piper accepted the aircraft and completed certification early in 1963.

In terms of performance, the PA-30 met or exceeded all of Swearingen and Piper's design goals. In terms of expenditures, the Twin Comanche development program had cost Pug Piper a mere $60,000 and Swearingen beat the airplane's mandated $35,000 price by $1,100.

Following FAA approval, Piper formally introduced the Twin Comanche in May, 1963 for the 1963 model year and initial deliveries began that summer. Lock Haven workers produced 142 PA-30s in 1963. Adhering to Piper's tradition of providing the most value for the dollar, the Twin Comanche cost $33,900

The Twin Comanche C entered production in 1968. Minor improvements included an upgraded interior and redesigned instrument panel. The prototype Twin Comanche C, registered N8568Y, constructor number 30-1717 is illustrated. Piper built 2,001 Twin Comanches before production ended late in 1969. (Piper Aviation Museum)

for the Custom version, making it the lowest-priced general aviation twin-engine airplane available at that time.

Piper also offered Executive, Sportsman and Professional equipment groups, which differed primarily in the sophistication of the avionic suites installed, including the 90- and 360-channel versions of the famous Narco Mk 12 VHF transceiver. Two 160 hp. Lycoming IO-320-B engines powered the aircraft. The small powerplants had a combined fuel consumption of only 15.2 gallons per hour at a 65% power setting and 17.2 gallons per hour at 75% power.

The propeller shaft extensions developed by Swearingen moved the blades six inches forward to help reduce cabin noise, and required a large spinner to cover the hub mechanism. The spinner blended gracefully with the streamlined "Tiger Shark" cowlings.

At its maximum gross weight of 3,600 lb., the PA-30 had a cruise speed of 194 mph. at an altitude of 8,000 feet and a maximum speed of 205 mph. at sea level. Two 30 gallon and two 15 gallon fuel tanks in the wings provided 90 gallons of fuel, with 84 gallons useable.

Piper outfitted the four-place cabin with a plush Palm Beach interior similar to that of the single-engine Comanche. Vinyl fabrics were standard on the Custom, and leather was standard for the optional Sportsman 300 upgrade. For improved passenger comfort, the heating and ventilation systems were redesigned from those used in the Comanche to provide increased mass flow into the cabin. Two-engine service ceiling was 18,600 feet and the single-engine ceiling was 5,800 feet at maximum gross weight.

To convince potential buyers of the airplane's frugality with a gallon of aviation gasoline, Piper claimed that if a Twin Comanche was flown 300 hours per year the direct operating costs would be 10.2 cents per mile—only 1.5 cents higher than the Comanche 250. The PA-30's miserly fuel consumption prompted famed long-distance flier Max Conrad to make another of his record flights in 1964. The 61-year old airman piloted Twin Comanche N7003Y nonstop from Capetown, South Africa to St. Petersburg, Florida in December. Average speed was 138.52 mph.

He took off from Capetown on December 24 and flew the the great circle distance of 7,868 miles in 56.8 hours, landing in Florida December 26 with 30 gallons of fuel remaining. His flight established a world record for Class 4 aircraft. On takeoff the aircraft had weighed 6,614 lb.—nearly 2,500 lb. above the 3,600-lb. maximum weight approved for the airplane. A total of 720

gallons of fuel were carried in 13 separate tanks including a specially-designed 40 gallon tank built into Conrad's seat.

It is interesting to note that soon after the original Twin Comanche entered service, Pug Piper had directed Swearingen to redesign the PA-30's main landing gear to improve landing characteristics. Swearingen had intentionally placed the wing's trailing edge low to the ground because Piper had specified that passengers be able to step directly onto the wingwalk without the aid of a step. He designed the airplane to meet that criteria, but some pilots complained that during the flare the nose tire could strike the runway before the main gear with its short stuts.

As a result, a set of experimental shock struts with longer strut travel were installed on a production airplane and obviated the need for an excessive nose-high attitude on landing. The new struts, however, were not incorporated into production Twin Comanches but were used on the experimental PA-33 pressurized Comanche, according to Edward Swearingen.

Piper built 901 Twin Comanche's from model year 1963 to 1965 before introducing the improved Twin Comanche B and the new turbocharged Twin Comanche B for the 1966 model year. The most salient change was the addition of a third window on each side of the fuselage that was part of the PA-30's expanded, optional six-place cabin with quickly removeable fifth and sixth seats. Baggage allowance was increased to 250 lb.

Wing tip fuel tanks became available for the first time, and increased total capacity to 120 gallons from 90 gallons with 114 gallons useable. With the tanks installed, maximum gross weight was raised 125 lb. to 3,725 lb. The turbocharged version cruised at 223 mph. at an altitude of 24,000 feet with an approved operating altitude of 30,000 feet. Single-engine ceiling was 19,000 feet and the airplane had a range of 1,460 statute miles at higher altitudes.

Fitted with Lycoming TIO-320-C1A powerplants each rated at 160 hp., the Turbo Twin Comanche had a built-in oxygen system and wingtip tanks as standard equipment. The engines were approved for a time between overhaul of 1,200 hours—same as the naturally aspirated Twin Comanche.

With a base price of $34,900 for the PA-30 and $45,680 for the turbocharged version, the airplanes sold well and the Turbo Twin Comanche quickly attracted its own group of admirers. The 1,000th Twin Comanche—and the 4,781st Piper twin built at Lock Haven—rolled off the assembly line in 1966 and was delivered to the Harlan Manufacturing Company of Harlan, Iowa. The milestone was reached by Piper only two and one-half years after the company had delivered the first production PA-30.

In the first 11 months of 1966, Piper sold 411 Twin Comanches and 412 Aztecs and led the general aviation industry as the largest manufacturer of twin-engine airplanes. Sales continued strong until the United States economy began to slow in the late 1960s. As the number of sales dwindled, so did Twin Comanche production. For example, in model year 1966 the company produced 521 Twin Comanche B and Turbo Twin Comanche B airplanes, and manufactured an additional 257 in 1967. The next year only 65 were built.

Despite a slack national economy, Piper introduced the Twin Comanche C for the 1969 model year. Essentially the same as its predecessor on the outside, the inside had been improved significantly. A new instrument panel featured rocker-type electrical switches and the magneto and starter switches were relocated to the left sidewall.

In addition, the interior and seats were made more comfortable and the selection of fabrics and colors were expanded. And, for the first time in the Twin Comanche, Piper offered to paint the exterior one color overall if the customer desired.

To simplify power management a new system was devised by Lycoming and Piper that was similar to that used earlier on the Aztec D. Four cruise settings were recommended for both the naturally aspirated or turbocharged Twin Comanche C.

The settings allowed higher cruise speeds thanks to special modifications made to the 160 hp. Lycoming engines. These included Inconel valves, stronger cylinder heads, long-reach spark plugs, a stronger crankcase, hybrid camshaft and Bendix 1200-series

In 1970 Piper replaced the PA-30 Twin Comanche series with the improved PA-39 Twin Comanche C/R. The PA-39 was powered by two 160 hp. Lycoming IO-320 or turbocharged TIO-320 engines. The right powerplant's propeller rotated counter-clockwise to improve single-engine safety. Piper produced 155 PA-39 aircraft. (Piper Aviation Museum)

As part of an experimental program, in the mid-1960s Swearingen installed two 300 hp. Lycoming IO-540 engines in PA-30 constructor number 30-1, registered N7000Y. Unofficially known as the PA-30-300, the airplane was reconverted to standard PA-30 configuration after Pug Piper cancelled the project. (Edward Swearingen)

magnetos as well as improved lubrication.

With the Turbo C's engines set to 28 in. Hg. manifold pressure and 2,400 propeller rpm., cruise speed increased 19 mph. at an altitude of 12,000 feet. At 24,000 feet, cruise speed was 240 mph. Priced at $39,900 for the non-turbocharged airplane, the Twin Comanche C was phased out of production in November, 1969 after 256 airplanes had been built. Lock Haven had manufactured 2,001 PA-30s since 1963.

Before PA-30 production ceased, Piper had experimented with more powerful versions of the Twin Comanche that were not produced. One involved installation of 200 hp. engines in a Twin Comanche B in 1967. The other project was done by Edward Swearingen, who at the behest of Pug Piper fitted two, 300 hp. Lycoming IO-540 engines to PA-30 registered N7000Y. Possessing a spectacular power-to-weight ratio, the airplane "almost cruised at 200 mph. on one engine alone," Swearingen said.

Reminiscing about one test flight in the ultra-powerful Twin Comanche, Swearingen recalled that he came upon a prototype, high-speed Mooney that was undergoing development in nearby Kerrville, Texas. The Mooney had a reputation as a fast, single-engine airplane.

Stalking the unwary pilot, Swearingen shut down one of the Twin Comanche's engines and flew by the Mooney and its astonished occupants. To prove that he had not overtaken the airplane out of a dive, Swearingen flew a wide circle around the Mooney and pass-

ed it once again. Despite its phenomenal performance, the fire-breathing "PA-30-300" did not impress Pug Piper and the airplane was converted back to a standard Twin Comanche, much to the disappointment of Edward Swearingen.

To replace the PA-30, in 1970 Piper began production of the PA-39 Twin Comanche C/R—the letters C/R stood for Counter-Rotating propellers. The chief difference between the two airplanes was the PA-39's right engine and propeller that rotated counterclockwise compared with a clockwise rotation for the left engine.

To make the right-side powerplant turn in the opposite direction, Lycoming simply reversed the rotation of specific gears and other components within the engine and changed the firing order. The counter-rotating propellers improved flight characteristics under single-engine conditions by moving the thrust vector of the right engine inboard. Therefore, regardless of which engine failed the airplane would react the same, with neither powerplant being critical from a piloting standpoint.

Other benefits included symmetrical downwash on the empennage surfaces and elimination of trim changes as airspeed increased or decreased. To improve stall characteristics, Piper mounted small, triangular strips on the wing leading edge. At high angles of attack, the strips induced airflow separation along the inboard wing sections first, allowing the outboard wing to retain lift deeper into the stall.

Powered by Textron Lycoming IO-320-B1A and left-rotation LIO-320-B1A engines each rated at 160 hp., the PA-39 superseded the PA-30 on the Lock Haven production line early in 1970. Initial customer deliveries were made in April. Only 155 PA-39s were built, the last being completed in May, 1972. Piper management decided to terminate production following the disastrous flood that occurred in June of that year.

Although the PA-30 Twin Comanche already was in development by 1962, Pug Piper had begun contemplating a six-place airplane equipped with three engines—a configuration similar to that of the famous Ford Trimotor transport of the 1920s. Like the famed "Tin Goose," Piper's airplane would have fixed landing gear and fixed-pitch propellers to help reduce costs and simplify manufacture.

Designated the PA-32-3M and registered N9999W, the aircraft was "a quick rebuild of the original prototype Cherokee Six and was a non-conformity aircraft," according to Grahame Gates, a retired Piper engineer assigned to work on the project. The

The three-engine PA-32-3M Cherokee Six first flew in May, 1965 and evolved into the PA-34 Twin Six. (Grahame Gates)

airplane's wings were fitted with two 115 hp. Lycoming O-235 powerplants in pseudo-Twin Comanche nacelles in addition to the 250 hp. Lycoming engine installed in the nose section.

The fuel tanks were removed from the wings and new structure was added to support the 115 hp. powerplants. Tanks installed in the wingtip area provided fuel for the two smaller engines, and a PA-25 Pawnee fuel tank mounted in a steel-tube cradle in the aft cabin section fed the larger Lycoming.

The airplane made is first flight as a three-engine ship in May, 1965 but the anemic 115 hp. engines did not provide adequate power when the center powerplant was made inoperative. The wing engines were replaced with 150 hp. units and testing was resumed.

Further flights showed that although the three-engine concept had merit from a safety standpoint, the fixed-pitch propellers could not be feathered if an engine was shut down. The blades created too much drag and seriously compromised single-engine handling characteristics.

Although constant-speed, full-feathering propellers would improve single-engine performance, they also would significantly increase cost and complexity and would defeat the original goal of building an inexpensive, safe, lightweight three-engine aircraft. Frustrated by these setbacks, Piper engineers abandoned the three-engine configuration of the PA-32-3M and transformed the six-place design into the PA-34 Twin Six. Still equipped with a fixed, tricycle landing gear, the Twin Six prototype, constructor number

Piper's Twin Six initially flew with fixed landing gear and was powered by two 180 hp. Lycoming O-360 engines. (Grahame Gates)

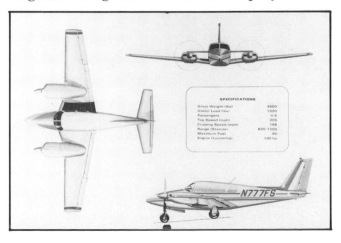

SPECIFICATIONS	
Gross Weight (lbs)	3600
Useful Load (lbs)	1230
Passengers	4-6
Top Speed (mph)	205
Cruising Speed (mph)	198
Range (Statute)	830-1200
Maximum Fuel	90
Engine (Lycoming)	180 hp

The first production PA-34-200 Seneca was constructor number 34-7250001, registered N1021U built in 1971. Production airplanes were powered by 200 hp. Lycoming IO-360 engines with constant-speed propellers. The right engine's propeller rotated counter-clockwise. (Mal Holcomb)

◄ In the 1975 model year Piper introduced the PA-34-200T Seneca II. Powered by turbocharged, 200 hp. Teledyne Continental L/TSIO-360 engines, the Seneca II offered significant performance improvements compared with the original Seneca. (Piper Aircraft Corporation)

1,500-lb. useful load was less than some operators desired.

Piper was well aware of these shortcomings and took action to resolve them. To improve useful load, the Seneca's maximum gross weight was increased 200 lb. to 4,200 lb. for 1973 production airplanes, and 1974 models received an additional cabin window with

Three-view of PA-34-200T Seneca II. (Smithsonian Institution, National Air And Space Museum Negative Number 93-2370)

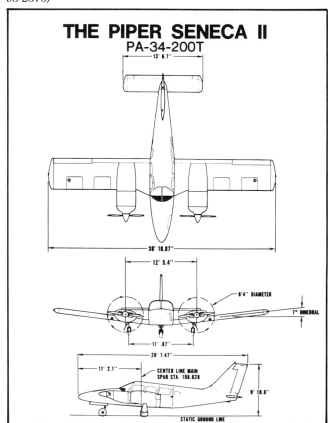

34-E1, registered N3401K, first flew in April, 1967 and was powered by two 180 hp. Lycoming O-360 engines driving constant-speed propellers.

The conventional, twin-engine configuration worked well, and a second prototype was fitted with a larger empennage and a electro-hydraulic retractable landing gear system similar to that installed in the PA-28R Arrow. Piper's Twin Six needed more power, however, and a pair of 200 hp. Lycoming IO-360-A1A and left-rotation LIO-360-A1A engines were installed in a third prototype that first flew in October, 1969. Like the PA-39, the PA-34 featured counter-rotating propellers with the right engine turning counterclockwise.

In preparation for production, Piper marketeers redesignated the Twin Six as the Seneca. FAA certification was granted in the summer of 1971 and initial deliveries for the 1972 model year began in September from the Vero Beach factory.

Although it did not sport three engines as originally envisioned by Pug Piper, the PA-34-200 Seneca was a lightweight twin-engine airplane capable of carrying six people, or hundreds of pounds of cargo with the seats removed. Accepted by the marketplace with the same enthusiasm it had shown for the rugged PA-32 Cherokee Six five years earlier, the Seneca provided air taxi and charter operators with an affordable and economical multi-engine transport.

In the first year of production 360 airplanes were built, followed in 1973 and the 1974 model year by 353 and 220 PA-34s respectively. Despite its solid success, the initial Senecas had their drawbacks. Pilots complained about the airplane's lethargic handling characteristics, and like virtually every other piston-powered twin-engine airplane the Seneca exhibited marginal performance under one-engine inoperative flight conditions. In addition, the PA-34-200's rounded corners on each side of the fuselage as well as optional wing and empennage deicers.

To further upgrade the Seneca, in the 1975 model year Piper introduced the turbocharged PA-34-200T Seneca II powered by Teledyne Continental Motors TSIO-360-E and left-rotation LTSIO-360-E powerplants, each rated at 200 hp.

Chief modifications to improve handling characteristics included balanced ailerons, a larger stabilator and a redesigned rudder antiservo tab for improved yaw control with one-engine inoperative. Maximum gross weight was increased to 4,570 lb. and additional wing fuel tanks were optional, boosting capacity to 123 gallons of useable fuel. These improvements silenced most objections from PA-34 owners and operators.

With its turbocharged engines, the Seneca II could climb to an altitude of 25,000 feet and cruise at 191 knots at a 75% power setting. Piper produced 326 Seneca IIs in the 1975 model year. Only minor changes were made to the airplane until 1981, including a redesigned instrument panel, revised interior, optional club seating arrangement and more durable main gear wheel brakes and tires that shortened landing distance.

Manufacture of the much-improved PA-34-220T Seneca III began at Vero Beach in late 1980 with deliveries commencing in January, 1981. Although the semi-tapered wing of the PA-28-151 Warrior was tested on a prototype Seneca III, it was rejected and the traditional, rectangular wing planform was retained.

The most salient technical change was installation of Teledyne Continental Motors TSIO-360-KB2A and left-rotation LTSIO-360-KB2A engines driving three-blade Hartzell propellers. A one-piece windshield further improved the Seneca's appearance and a new interior and instrument panel layout were included to complete the upgrade.

Although many Senecas were used in air taxi operations, some were employed as multi-engine trainers by fixed-base operators and flight schools until Piper introduced the PA-44 Seminole in the late 1970s.

Workers at Vero Beach built 4,354 PA-34-200, PA-34-200T and PA-34-220T Senecas from 1972 through the 1987 model year. Because of the severe downturn that struck the United States general avia-

The Seneca III featured 220 hp. Teledyne Continental L/TSIO-360 engines, three-blade, counter-rotating propellers and a one-piece windshield. (Piper Aircraft Corporation)

tion industry throughout the 1980s, PA-34-220T production rates sharply declined from 276 airplanes in 1981 to only 39 in 1987.

When Monroe Stuart Millar bought Piper Aircraft Corporation in May, 1987 the Seneca III remained in production. Piper built 56 Senecas that year, 56 in 1988 and 44 in 1989. Forty-eight Seneca IIIs were manufactured in 1990, followed by 13 in 1991 and another 13 in 1992. Additional PA-34-220T aircraft were scheduled to be built in 1993. The basic equipped price was $419,400.

After bankruptcy proceedings were initiated in July, 1991 Piper slowly resumed limited Seneca assembly operations in August. One Seneca III was completed and the first two of nine Seneca IIIs were delivered to British Aerospace in April, 1992. These aircraft were used as advanced trainers at the British Aerospace and Ansett Flying College located in Tamworth, New South Wales, Australia.

In addition to building thousands of airplanes in the 1960s, Piper Aircraft Corporation also built a new factory in sunny Florida. The facilities at Lock Haven

Aeronautical engineer Fred E. Weick poses with the AG-3 agricultural aircraft he designed at Texas A & M University, College Station, Texas. The airplane was powered by a 135 hp. Lycoming engine and formed the basis for Piper's PA-25 Pawnee. (Piper Aviation Museum)

One of two pre-production Pawnees, constructor number 25-2, registered N9101D was photographed at Piper's research and development center in Vero Beach, Florida. (Piper Aviation Museum)

◄ The initial five PA-25 Pawnees produced by Piper taxi away from the Lock Haven ramp enroute to their new owners. In the foreground is the first production airplane, Pawnee N6000Z, constructor number 25-3. (Piper Aviation Museum)

Howard Piper believed a market existed for a rugged, economical, agricultural airplane to replace the modified, surplus World War Two Boeing-Stearman biplanes and other makeshift aircraft that were being widely used for spraying and dusting operations.

In 1953 Piper Aircraft Corporation sponsored Weick's development of a second-generation agricultural aircraft known as the AG-3 at Texas A&M. Under terms of the agreement, the airplane's design and construction would adhere as closely as possible to that used in the PA-18 and PA-22 in order to keep development and manufacturing costs to a minimum.

Smaller and intentionally less sophisticated than the AG-1, the AG-3 was powered by a 135 hp. Lycoming engine driving a fixed-pitch propeller. The ship featured a fabric-covered, welded steel tube fuselage, semi-cantilever fabric-covered wings with wide-span ailerons, short-span flaps and conventional landing gear.

Weick selected the US-35B airfoil section for the AG-3 chiefly because of its high lift and good low-speed capabilities—important characteristics for an agricultural airplane that would carry a heavy load and fly at slow speeds. A chemical hopper holding 800 lb. was installed ahead of the pilot—not behind the cockpit as had been done with the PA-18A—and the pilot's seat was located high in the cockpit to afford maximum visibility directly forward and during turns.

Based on the design and flight testing of the AG-3, Howard Piper was satisfied with what Weick and his staff had created. As a result, in April, 1957 Weick went to work for Piper at the Vero Beach development center.

Weick's first job was to prepare the AG-3 for production and transform it into a Piper airplane. By 1959 the AG-3 design had evolved into the PA-25 Pawnee prototype, constructor number 25-01, powered by a 150 hp. Lycoming O-320-A1A engine. The airplane featured a fiberglass and plastic hopper that would hold up to 20 cubic feet of dry chemicals such as dust and fertilizer or 150 gallons of liquid

were incapable of handling the demand for airplanes, and Mr. Piper and his sons sought new ground in the Sunshine State.

Vero Beach, a small, quiet town with 9,000 residents on the eastern coast was selected, although the city of Venice, Florida also had been seriously considered. The people of Venice, however, objected to having an airplane factory near their city.

Although a production facility was not built at Vero Beach until 1959-1960, in October, 1957 a small engineering building was completed on the former United States Navy base that served as the city's airport. Known as the Piper Aircraft Development Center, the building and its group of about 25 engineers and technicians were headed by a talented aeronautical engineer named Fred E. Weick. The center's mission was to develop new airplanes, produce experimental prototypes and flight test the aircraft.

The Piper clan already was familiar with Weick's abilities as an engineer and designer before he joined the company. Weick had performed engineering work for Mr. Piper when he helped design the dust and spray system distribution apparatus for the PA-18A Super Cub in 1953, and the four Pipers held Weick's talents in high regard.

Howard Piper was chiefly responsible for hiring Weick away from his previous position at Texas A&M University in College Station, Texas. During his tenure at the institution, Weick and a small team of assistants had, at the behest of the CAA, designed and built the revolutionary, all-metal AG-1 experimental agricultural aircraft at the school's Aircraft Research Center during 1950-1951.

The Pawnee 235 made its debut in 1962, powered by a 235 hp. Lycoming O-540 engine. (Piper Aviation Museum)

A large, rolled aluminum pad was mounted above the Panwee's instrument panel to help minimize head injury to the pilot if the airplane crashed. Chemical hopper was mounted forward of the control stick. (Piper Aviation Museum)

chemical agent.

By placing the hopper directly on the Pawnee's center of gravity, Weick minimized the need for the pilot to readjust pitch trim depending whether the hopper was full or empty. In addition, a fiberglass fuel tank was located in the fuselage ahead of the pilot.

Although two pre-production airplanes were built at Vero Beach, no factory existed there yet and the Pawnee was manufactured at Lock Haven beginning in May, 1959. The first production airplane was constructor number 25-3, registered N6000Z. Piper Aircraft Corporation delivered the first five production PA-25 aircraft to Wes-Tex Aircraft Sales in Lubbock, Texas, in July, 1959.

Initial production Pawnees sold for $8,995, but that price did not include spray- or dust-dispensing systems. A spray system, comprised of lateral booms and spray nozzles that fitted under the wing trailing edge, was optional and cost $675. Eventually, Piper developed a spreader-type dusting system that could be quickly interchanged with the spray installation.

With its 150 hp. engine, the PA-25 had a maximum speed of 113 mph. and a stall speed of only 45 mph. Maximum gross weight was 2,300 lb. with a useful load of 1,080 lb. Because of the highly corrosive nature of many chemicals used for pest control and fertilizing, corrosion proofing and stainless steel control cables were standard and the inboard ends of the wing spars were coated with epoxy-base paint.

Operator response to the Pawnee was excellent. The airplanes sold well in the United States and were

soon being exported to foreign countries. Not long after the Pawnee entered service, however, Piper received two major complaints about the airplane that required correction.

First, to satisfy FAA certification requirements Weick had designed the PA-25's wing to provide a strong aerodynamic buffet prior to the stall, obviating a warning horn or light. Although some pilots appreciated Weick's attempt to simplify the airplane, most disliked the nagging buffet because they often made turns over the fields at speeds perilously close to stall.

To fix the problem the wing leading edges adjacent to the fuselage were modified to smooth airflow. Piper was forced, however, to add a stall warning light to meet federal regulations. The second problem centered on horsepower. Weick and his staff had designed the PA-25 to use a 150 hp. engine primarily to reduce costs without compromising performance.

Piper Pawnee 235 registered OH-PIG was used by a Piper dealer in Helsinki, Finland to fertilize forests situated around Lake Kyyjarvi, which also served as a frozen, snow-covered runway for the Pawnee. (Piper Aviation Museum)

The 800 lb.-capacity hopper was included to provide a large load-carrying capability and therefore improve efficiency, but it was restricted to only 150 gallons of liquid.

As a result, agricultural operators quickly discovered they could fill the hopper with dry chemicals without exceeding 800 lb., but could exceed the 800-lb. weight limit with liquid chemicals before filling the hopper. To cost-conscious aerial applicators, not being able to fill the hopper with fluid was unproductive and reduced profits. Conversely, filling the hopper was illegal and reduced the Pawnee's performance with only 150 hp. available.

The solution was more horsepower. In spring, 1962 Piper strengthened the Pawnee airframe to take additional stress imposed by a more robust powerplant and installed a 235 hp. Lycoming O-540-B2B5 engine in PA-25 constructor number 25-02, registered N74829.

With added power and a higher gross weight of 2,900 lb., the PA-25-235's 20-cu. foot hopper could be loaded to 1,200 lb., and operators enthusiastically accepted the new version. Virtually identical to the previous 150 hp. Pawnee, the 235 hp. airplane featured a fiberglass and plastic nose bowl that withstood in-service abuse better than the original aluminum alloy unit.

Other improvements included a second set of jury struts between the main lift struts and the wing, double bracing wires between the empennage surfaces, and a four-leaf tailwheel spring. In addition, the landing gear was lengthened three inches to accommodate a new propeller with a diameter of 84 inches.

The PA-25-235 also featured removable panels on the sides and bottom of the fuselage, providing access to clean the airframe structure. Piper began building

A major upgrade program led to development of the Pawnee C, which entered production in 1967. Key improvements included removeable fuselage panels and turtledeck, burst-resistant polyurethane fuel tank and raising the cockpit 10 inches. N4437Y was constructor number 25-4068 and served as the Pawnee C production prototype. (Piper Aviation Museum)

the PA-25-235 alongside the PA-25-150 in March, 1962. Within a few months demand for the more powerful Pawnee had banished the 150 hp. version from the Lock Haven production lines after 730 airplanes had been produced since 1959.

After building nearly 2,000 Pawnees by 1964, Piper incorporated recommendations from operators and pilots to create the Pawnee B introduced for the 1965 model year. Although the Pawnee B version retained the 235 hp. Lycoming O-540-B2B5 engine, the instrument panel was reconfigured to mount the stall warning light and spray pressure gauge within the pilot's field of vision, and an optional turn and slip indicator could be installed directly in front of the pilot.

A larger hopper with 21 cubic feet of volume was made standard but still held only 150 gallons of liquid chemical. The tank was covered by a removable access door fitted with an improved gasket that reduced fluid leakage onto the windshield and fuselage.

The dust venturi was mounted three inches lower than in previous Pawnees, placing it in an area of strong ram air to improve dispersal of solid chemicals. The distributor was widened to provide an additional 5 feet to 10 feet of swath coverage.

For liquid chemicals, the spray booms were relocated farther aft of the wing trailing edge to improve dispersal characteristics. Gross weight and useful load for the PA-25-235B were the same as for the previous Pawnee. More than 1,100 of the "B" version were built through 1965 and 1966.

Some Pawnees, especially those exported to third-world nations, were earning their keep under extremely rough conditions. One airplane operated in Tunja, Colombia, South America, flew regularly from a 4,300 foot airstrip 9,000 feet above sea level.

To clear high mountain peaks surrounding the base of operations, the Pawnee B had to climb as high as 13,000 feet. Spraying also was done in nearby valleys at an altitude of 8,500 feet. Another Pawnee exported to Helsinki, Finland was fitted with skis in the winter and flown from a frozen lake to fertilize forests in the Lake Kyyjarvi region.

Piper Pawnees were operated worldwide and 5,167 were manufactured before production was terminated in 1981. (Piper Aviation Museum)

Until 1966 the tremendous success of the Pawnee program allowed Piper to dominate the market for new production agricultural aircraft, but that dominance was soon threatened by its chief rival the Cessna Aircraft Company. Like the Piper family, as early as 1951 Cessna president Dwane L. Wallace had been well aware of Fred Weick's AG-1 project and had his engineers carefully study the growing need for modern agricultural aircraft.

In 1953, Cessna engineers modified a Model 305 military liaison aircraft into the Model 325 equipped with wing-mounted spray booms and a small hopper located behind the pilot where the observer's seat had been. The aft windows were eliminated and an air-driven pump to disperse liquid chemical was mounted between the heavy-duty main landing gear stuts.

Only four prototypes were built—two in 1953 and another two in 1956. Cessna cancelled the program primarily because the airplane was not marketable in its modified form. One airplane, however, was used in the mid-1960s for spray operations by Servicio Aereo Cantu S.A. in Santiago Veraguas, Republic of Panama.

By 1963 Cessna had learned valuable lessons from Piper's Pawnee program and was ready to launch a larger, all-metal airplane designated the Model 188 Agwagon. Like Piper before them, Cessna officials had talked with many agricultural aircraft operators and studied their needs and recommendations—including the desire for an airplane that was larger and more capable than the Pawnee.

First flown in February, 1965 the Agwagon closely followed Weick's Pawnee design but had a maximum gross weight of 3,800 lb. for operation in the Restricted Category. Introduced in 1966, the Model 188 featured a welded cockpit structure of 4130 chrome molybdenum steel tubing from the firewall to the cockpit, and a semi-monocoque aluminum alloy aft fuselage and empennage.

To keep their development costs to a minimum, Cessna engineers used wings from the Model 185 as well as the horizontal and vertical stabilizers, elevators and tailcone from the Model 180. The wing panels were attached to welded steel tube stub exten-

sions that were integral with the fuselage structure.

Like Piper's Pawnee B, Cessna's Agwagon featured access panels that covered key fuselage sections and could be removed for field maintenance and cleaning. The fiberglass hopper held 1,200 lb. and could be loaded from the top or from an optional side-loading system.

Priced at $15,998 for the Model 188 with a 230 hp. Teledyne Continental Motors O-470-R engine, the Agwagon cost more than the Pawnee B but presented a serious challenge to Piper's market share. In addition, Cessna offered the Model A188 powered by a 285 hp. Continental IO-520-D engine, and had a maximum gross weight of 4,000 lb. when operated in the Restricted Category.

In response to Cessna's Agwagon, in 1967 Piper unveiled the much-improved Pawnee C. Changes included a new fuel tank, higher capacity cockpit ventilation system, air-oleo shock struts that replaced the shock cord suspension used on previous Pawnees, and a new pilot seat.

An air-intake duct was incorporated into the overhead canopy section which was similar to that used on the Agwagon. Ram air from the duct was routed aft into the rear fuselage area and provided a positive pressure to help keep dirt and chemicals from entering the structure.

To speed the pilot's escape in case of an accident, the cockpit's two side window panels could be jettisoned by pulling "T" handles on the instrument panel. A burst-resistant polyurethane fuel tank was installed and a bulkhead aft of the tank prevented spilled fuel from entering the cockpit. To improve pilot comfort, a new seat was designed with a back cushion that was adjustable up, down, forward and aft.

The turtledeck cover over the fuselage spine as well as two large panels on each side of the forward fuselage section were designed for quick removal and easy access for cleaning and maintenance. Like the Pawnee B, the Pawnee C was available with an op-

The PA-36 Pawnee Brave was a larger, more capable agricultural airplane developed by Piper in the late 1960s. The prototype registered N36PA, constructor number 36-E1, is illustrated. A Teledyne Continental Motors 285 hp., 6-285 Tiara engine powered production aircraft from 1973 to 1976. (Piper Aviation Museum)

tional side-loading "Quick-Fill" inlet for chemicals.

Piper used Pawnee constructor number 25-4068, registered N4437Y, as a test aircraft for the modifications, and following FAA approval the PA-25-235C entered production in January, 1967. In November, 1967 Piper offered an optional, more powerful engine for the Pawnee C to compete with Cessna's 285 hp. A188 Agwagon version. A 260 hp. Lycoming O-540-E and optional constant-speed propeller could be fitted to the Pawnee, creating the PA-25-260C.

A large batch of Pawnee 235C and 260C airplanes were either damaged, destroyed or dismantled after the devastating flood on June 23, 1972, caused by Hurricane Agnes.

The flood almost ruined Piper, but as the decade of the 1970s progressed the Pawnee maintained its grasp on a significant share of the entry-level agricultural airplane market despite escalating competition from Cessna. Pawnees were operating around the world performing a myriad of missions to help people protect their land, animals and crops.

Some of the airplane's many roles included seeding and fertilizing fields, annihilating hordes of disease-carrying mosquitoes and their larvae, restocking lakes and rivers with fish, reseeding burned-out forests and deicing roads with salt compounds. In short, the Pawnee had been a blessing to humanity, nature and Piper's balance sheet.

Both the PA-25-235C and -260C remained in production until 1973 when the Pawnee D appeared. Similar to its predecessors, the PA-25-235D and PA-25-260D versions had fuel tanks relocated to the wings from the forward fuselage section and featured a new fuel system pioneered on the PA-36 Brave.

During initial design of the PA-25 in 1957, Fred Weick had opted to install the Pawnee's fuel tank in the fuselage chiefly because it simplified maintenance requirements and reduced costs both to Piper and Pawnee operators. By locating the tank ahead of the cockpit, fuel could flow by gravity to the engine's carburetor. If the tanks were placed in the wings, fuel pumps and additional plumbing would have been necessary.

Weick was well aware that aircraft accident and

safety experts believed the wing location would decrease the fire hazard for the pilot in the event of a crash, but studies indicated that post-crash fires occurred at about the same rate for airplanes with fuel tanks in the wings as for those with fuel tanks in the fuselage. As a result, the Pawnee's fuel tank remained ahead of the cockpit until advent of the "D" variant.

As good as the Pawnee was, Fred Weick knew a better airplane was needed to meet the changing nature of the agricultural application business in the 1970s. What Piper needed was a larger airplane that could match Cessna's Agwagon and Agtruck series, which had captured an increasing share of the market. He and a few selected staff engineers studied new concepts for several years before Piper management approved the program.

In 1967 work on the new Pawnee II, later renamed PA-36 Pawnee Brave, began in earnest at the Vero Beach development facility. Larger than the PA-25, the Brave had an all-metal, full-cantilever, low wing spanning 39 feet with an area of 225 square feet compared with 183 square feet for the Pawnee.

The wing used a NACA 63-618 airfoil section and featured fiberglass and plastic leading edges that could easily be repaired or replaced when damaged. A 30 cubic-foot hopper was standard fit and held up to 225 gallons. A larger 38 cubic foot, 275 gallon hopper was optional.

Although the Brave's wing was all-metal, the fuselage was a welded steel tube structure. Similar to that used in the PA-25, the tubing was covered with fiberglass and plastic-molded panels on the top and bottom, and removable, aluminum alloy panels on the sides that permitted quick, easy access for maintenance and cleaning. The entire fuselage was corrosion-proofed.

Bowing to customer preference, Piper put the gasoline tanks in the wings but incorporated a simplified fuel system that used gravity-feed from the tanks to a one-gallon header tank in the bottom of the fuselage. Fuel flowed from the tank through a single selector valve, strainers and two fuel boost pumps. Each bladder-type wing tank held 45 gallons.

To power the Brave, Weick had planned to use the reliable 235 hp. or 260 hp. Lycoming O-540 engine that had proven itself in years of service. The airplane's 3,900 lb. to 4,400 lb. maximum gross weight

A 1973 Pawnee Brave is illustrated with its Continental Tiara engine. Note access to structure afforded by removable panels. Production ended in 1983 after Piper had built 938 Pawnee Braves. (Piper Aviation Museum)

in the Restricted Category coupled with the larger hopper, however, dictated use of a more powerful engine.

Continental had been developing a series of piston engines that derived relatively high power from a small cubic inch displacement, but mounted the propeller on an extension of the camshaft that turned at one-half engine speed. The reduction in rpm. significantly improved propeller efficiency and reduced noise.

Designated "Tiara" by Teledyne Continental Motors, the 6-cylinder, 285 hp. version seemed to be the logical choice for the PA-36. Piper management favored using the unconventional engine, but Weick was reluctant. He had serious misgivings about mating an entirely new airframe with an entirely new—and unproven—powerplant, but eventually he was overruled. Therefore, Piper became the first United States general aviation aircraft manufacturer to use the powerplant in a production airplane.

The prototype Brave was constructor number 36-E1, registered N36PA. The airplane made its first flight in December, 1969 powered by a 260 hp. Lycoming O-540 engine. The Tiara 6-285 engine also flew in the prototype and performed well, with a significant reduction in noise level.

Built at the Vero Beach factory, the Brave entered initial production in spring, 1973 equipped with the Tiara 6-285 engine. Piper had planned to offer both the 285 hp. version and the 320 hp. 6-320 powerplant, but only 285 hp. engines were installed.

Favorably accepted initially by operators in the field, the Pawnee Brave soon encountered problems with its Tiara engine. Crankshaft failures began to occur with regularity. Despite modifications by Continental to correct the anomaly, the engine was quickly branded as risky and unreliable.

As a result, by 1975-1976 Tiara sales plummeted as did deliveries of the Brave. With customer faith in the Tiara shattered, Continental was forced to halt production of the engine. It became obvious that Piper had to reengine the airplane if production was to continue, and in 1977 the Brave was produced with a 300 hp. Textron Lycoming IO-540-K1G5 engine and a conversion kit was offered to operators choosing to retrofit the Lycoming in place of the Continental engine.

Because the Lycoming was heavier than the Tiara 6-285, performance suffered but the airplane slowly regained its place in the market and sales crept upward by 1978 when it was renamed the Brave 300. A more powerful, 375 hp. Textron Lycoming IO-720-D1CD engine was fitted to the PA-36 in 1977 and the combination was FAA-approved as the Brave 375. The first production airplane left the Lock Haven factory in February, 1978.

By 1981, Piper and other manufacturers in the general aviation business were beginning to feel the effects of a large-scale slowdown in the industry. Sales fell dramatically, ushering in the longest and most severe downturn since the debacle of 1947.

Facing mounting financial losses throughout the product line as well as internal, corporate problems in 1981 Piper management sold the marketing rights for the Brave 300 and Brave 375 to an agricultural aircraft organization in Lubbock, Texas. In addition, 19 1981 model year Brave 300 and 17 1981 model year Brave 375 airplanes were included in the sale.

Compared with the 5,167 PA-25 series airplanes produced by Piper from 1959 through 1981, the company built only 938 PA-36 airplanes. Production was split between Vero Beach for the 1973-1974 model years and Lock Haven for the 1975-1983 model years.

Production of the Brave 300 was terminated in June, 1981 followed by the Brave 375 in January, 1983. The final Pawnee 235 was built at Lock Haven in March, 1981. In retrospect, Piper dominated the small airplane, agricultural segment of the industry from 1960 to 1966. The company failed, however, to aggressively market the tough, versatile Pawnee as actively as it did other Piper airplanes.

When Cessna entered the market in 1966, they sold the Agwagon and its later descendants with the same vigor used to sell the popular Model 172 Skyhawk and the Model 150 trainers. The Wichita, Kansas-based company constantly upgraded and improved its product line and created an entire family of agricultural airplanes. Unfortunately, Piper chose to maintain the status quo and then responded too late with the Pawnee Brave.

Piper has the distinction of being a pioneer in the entry-level, agricultural airplane business and paved the way for Cessna and other manufacturers to follow. Thanks to Fred Weick, the pugnacious little AG-3 and Piper's foresight to take risks in a new market, the Pawnee became an indispensable ally in man's perpetual struggle to feed the masses and survive.

CHAPTER SEVEN

DAWN OF THE CHEROKEE

By 1960 Piper Aircraft Corporation had completed only half of its transition from the bygone era of steel tube and fabric technologies to the modern world of all-metal airplanes. Piper's chief competitors, Beech Aircraft Corporation and Cessna Aircraft Company, had been producing the all-metal Model 35 Bonanza and Model 170 lightplanes since 1947 and 1949 respectively.

Although the company had taken a major step forward when it introduced the popular PA-23 Apache, Piper had neglected the entry-level PA-22 Tri-Pacer, whose welded steel tube structure remained clothed in cotton. The chief reason for management's reluctance to replace the aging Tri-Pacer was essentially an economic one—it cost less to build than an all-metal aircraft and was selling well. In 1957, however, Thomas "Tony" Piper and his visionary brother Pug Piper knew the time had come to modernize the low end of the product line and replace the increasingly obsolescent PA-22.

Piper's need to develop an aluminum airplane had been acknowledged some years before. As early as 1952 company officials had discussed purchasing a four-place Mooney design that eventually became the Mark 20, but designer Al Mooney refused to sell.

After considering and rejecting the two-place Ercoupe and the sporty Thorpe Sky Scooter, the Piper clan decided it would design its own new, modern four-place airplane. In 1953 aeronautical engineer Fred E.

The PA-28 Cherokee propelled Piper Aircraft Corporation's entry-level, single-engine product line into the modern era of light airplanes. An experimental PA-28, constructor number 28-01, registered N9315R was built in 1959 and first flew in January, 1960 powered by 150 hp. Lycoming O-320 engine. (Piper Aviation Museum)

Weick was asked by Piper to conduct a cost study to determine if building an airplane from aluminum alloy was economically feasible when compared to the Tri-Pacer's tube and fabric construction.

For his comparison, Weick used cost data provided by Cessna for its four-place Model 170. He concluded that it was costing Piper eight per cent more to manufacture the Tri-Pacer than Cessna was spending to produce the Model 170. Production of the PA-22, however, continued unabated although Weick's study had planted the seeds of change in the minds of Tony and Pug Piper.

Three years later in 1956, Piper Aircraft Corporation was ready to leave the aging PA-22 behind and create the all-metal PA-28. While Weick was still employed at Texas A&M College he and Pug Piper established the airplane's overall design. The airplane would feature a low wing of constant chord from the root to the tip, and control surfaces with beaded skins to simplify production and reduce manufacturing costs.

The ship would be powered by a 150 hp. engine with a fixed-pitch propeller. To ease ground handling and crosswind operations, a tricycle landing gear was chosen with a tread of 10 feet between the main gear tires. Keenly aware that one restriction of the Tri-Pacer design was its small cabin, Pug Piper wanted a wider interior but the width was not to exceed 42 inches.

Weick preferred a wider width to increase comfort, but Piper did not want the PA-28's cabin to be as wide as that of the more expensive PA-24 Comanche that was about to enter production at Lock Haven. The Comanche's cabin was 44 inches wide.

In January, 1957 the company contracted with air-

Instrument panel of PA-28-160 Cherokee registered N5001W shows Tri-Pacer type control wheels and lack of toe-operated brakes on pilot's rudder pedals. Later production airplanes featured new control wheels and toe-operated brakes. (Piper Aviation Museum)

In-flight photograph of the production prototype PA-28-160, constructor number 28-03, registered N2800W. Piper initially offered the Cherokee with 150 hp. and 160 hp. engines. (Piper Aviation Museum)

craft designer John Thorpe to conduct a preliminary study on the PA-28. He completed the work in the spring of that year, but the Piper development center at Vero Beach was busy designing the PA-25 Pawnee and the PA-28 was temporarily shelved until September, 1957.

Fred Weick had joined the Piper staff at Vero Beach in April, 1957 and in September he assigned engineer Karl H. Bergey to the PA-28 project. In his autobiography Weick described Bergey as an "exceptionally competent designer." The two men worked well together and made rapid progress designing the new airplane.

Using Thorpe's report and input from Pug Piper, Weick and Bergey designed a simple, all-metal airplane that was easy to fly, easy to maintain, was light and reasonably fast and could be built for less than the Tri-Pacer. Piper named it the Cherokee.

In terms of engineering largess, Piper's Cherokee was the epitome of simplicity. The aircraft's basic structure had less than 50% of the parts and significantly fewer assemblies and rivets than the all-metal PA-24 Comanche.

To strengthen the cabin floor, which also formed the bottom skin of the airplane, a series of longitudinal stiffeners was riveted in place and provided the necessary rigidity. The fuselage configuration was kept simple as well, and the sheet metal covering the semi-moncoque structure required only bending to fit properly.

Borrowing proven technologies from the PA-25 Pawnee and other Piper airplanes, parts such as the nose cowl, wing, rudder and stabilator tips were fabricated from fiberglass and plastic to ease manufacturing work and expense.

The airfoil chosen by Weick and Bergey for the wing was the NACA 65-415 section that had its maximum thickness near the mid-chord point. The wing's depth allowed for a single main spar, and the I-beam type spar of each panel was attached to the fuselage by bolts through box beam joints. Wingspan was 30 feet, and the mechanically operated flaps and cable-controlled ailerons had beaded skins to reduce weight and production costs.

Like the Ercoupe Weick had designed before World War Two, the Cherokee's fuel tanks formed a part of the wing leading edge and were attached via flanges ahead of the main spar. Each metal tank held 25 gallons and were retained by machine screws. The

tanks were relatively easy to remove, repair, reinstall or replace.

The empennage was conventional with beaded metal skins on the vertical stabilizer and rudder to save weight and eliminate internal structure. To further reduce weight, size and complexity, the airplane featured a stabilator that combined the functions of a horizontal stabilizer and elevator into one unit.

Originally developed at NASA's Langley Research Center during World War Two, the stabilator was developed for the Cherokee by John Thorpe, who had used the device on his experimental aircraft designs. With the Cherokee program well into the final design stages by 1959, an experimental prototype PA-28 assigned constructor number 28-01, registered N9315R, was built and made its first flight on January 10, 1960. Pug Piper had the airplane he wanted, but he needed an approved type certificate from the FAA before production could commence.

To obtain it, Weick and his staff at the development center embarked on a grueling schedule designed to certify the Cherokee no later than February 1, 1961. After nearly 10 months of hard work, Weick and his engineers were awarded a type certificate for the Piper PA-28-160 on October 31, 1960.

Although the experimental prototype was powered by a 150 hp. Lycoming O-320-A2A, production aircraft would be powered by 160 hp. Lycoming O-320-D2A engines. A 150 hp. version was available but did not receive FAA approval until June, 1961.

In addition to the busy Lock Haven factory in Pennsylvania, in 1960 construction workers completed Piper's new manufacturing facility at Vero Beach, Florida. Built specifically to produce the PA-28 Cherokee, the factory was dedicated in January, 1961. Production began soon thereafter and initial deliveries were made in May.

Priced at less than $11,000 for the 150 hp. version, the Cherokee was an immense success for Piper Aircraft Corporation. Sales skyrocketed almost from the day the airplane was introduced, and the Vero Beach factory had to boost the production rate several times during the year to keep pace with escalating demand.

By the end of 1961 Piper had delivered 286 Cherokees, the majority of them equipped for instrument flight operations. Of these, 145 airplanes were equipped with the AutoFlite option featuring Piper's AutoControl automatic pilot and VHF radio and

For the 1963 model year Piper introduced the 180 hp. PA-28-180 Cherokee B. Constructor number 28-524, registered N5447W served as a production prototype. (Piper Aviation Museum)

navigation equipment. Another 104 were built to Super Custom configuration and 27 Custom Cherokees rolled off the assembly line. Only 10 Standard PA-28s were completed.

Welcomed by Piper dealers and distributors worldwide as a replacement for the Tri-Pacer and the two-place Colt trainer, Cherokees were exported to Latin American nations, England, France, West Germany, Italy, New Zealand, Australia and South Africa. In South America, PA-28s were delivered to owners in Argentina, Chile, Uruguay, Guatemala, Nicaragua, and El Salvador, and Peru, Brazil, Colombia and Venezuela.

Piper had reached a production rate of four airplanes per day in March, 1962, and that month delivered the 500th Cherokee to Mr. and Mrs. Herman Sundermann of Huntington, Indiana. The Cherokee's success was watched with envy by Beech Aircraft Corporation, which did not offer airplanes smaller than the Model 35 Bonanza and had long ignored the entry-level and training aircraft market.

In 1960, however, company president Olive Ann Beech authorized development of the four-place Model 23 Musketeer to compete with Piper's Cherokee. An all-metal airplane with an airfoil section similar to that of the PA-28, the Musketeer used bonded honeycomb construction technologies developed during Beech's subcontract work building control surfaces for the United States Air Force's Convair F-106 jet fighter.

Powered by a 160 hp. Lycoming engine, the prototype Model 23 made its first flight on October 23, 1961. Similar to the PA-28 in overall configuration but slightly larger and heavier, the Musketeer featured a stabilator and fixed, tricycle trailing beam-type landing gear.

Beech began deliveries of the Musketeer in October, 1962, for the 1963 model year, and the airplane sold for $13,300 with a single VHF radio and complete instrument flying equipment. A total of 553 airplanes were built in the first year of manufacture.

Meeting the Musketeer challenge head-on, Piper officials claimed that the popular Cherokee was "being very closely duplicated by another major aircraft manufacturer" but they emphasized that the PA-28 already had a two-year headstart on the competition.

Piper had nothing to fear, as in the years ahead the Cherokee would consistently outsell the Musketeer and its successor, the 180 hp. Sundowner.

In the wake of the PA-28's early success Piper upgraded the original design to create the Cherokee B in the autumn of 1962, in preparation for the 1963 model year. Aware that both dealers and customers wanted more performance and, therefore, more power in their Cherokees, Piper used a standard PA-28 airframe as a testbed for the Lycoming O-360-A2A 180-hp. version in late 1961 and received FAA approval for the PA-28-180B in August, 1962. With the addition of the new engine the Cherokee was available with 150 hp., 160 hp. or 180 hp. powerplants.

Chief design changes incorporated into the Cherokee B included new Dynafocal-type engine supports, which coupled with a redesigned mount reduced vibration and noise transmitted to the cabin. A new muffler and revised carburetor heat arrangement was used and additional soundproofing was added to the fuselage and interior. Improved airflow through the nose cowl provided better engine cooling and decreased drag, and a 35-ampere alternator replaced the generator used on previous aircraft.

Piper officials claimed the Cherokee B was the first production light airplane to use an alternator. The unit was developed for Piper by the Chrysler Corporation, who pioneered the use of alternators on automobiles in the early 1960s. The airplane's alternator was rotated by a rubber belt driven by the Lycoming engine's starter ring gear.

In addition to providing adequate current flow at low idle rpm., the alternator allowed use of a 25 ampere-hour battery that was smaller and weighed less than the 33 ampere-hour batteries used with the obsolete generator system. Piper engineers calculated that the new battery and alternator system weighed 10.6 lb. less than the previous generator installation.

Other improvements also were added to the Cherokee B. Baggage allowance was boosted from 100 lb. to 125 lb., rubber pads were added to the rudder pedals, the right-side cabin entry door was reinforced and featured a new, improved latch, and improved ducting provided more cooling air to the avionic equipment.

In terms of performance, the three Cherokees offered a range of speeds and useful load that suited most buyers. The PA-28-150 had a maximum speed of

In January, 1963 Piper delivered its 1,000th Cherokee, a PA-28-180 to Walter Bergmann, president of Chicago-based Ponte, Inc. Bergmann is second from left, shaking hands with James Miller, Piper Metal Products Manager. M.L. Blume, Vero Beach Plant Manager is at far left, with Stanley Davis, Piper dealer from Lake Village, Indiana, at far right. (Piper Aviation Museum)

To strengthen its position in the single-engine, fixed-gear segment of the general aviation market, in 1964 Piper developed the PA-28-180 Cherokee C. Major changes included an upgraded instrument panel and a new fiberglass engine cowling that reduced drag and improved powerplant cooling. (Piper Aviation Museum)

139 mph. and could fly 570 statute miles with standard fuel, or 790 miles without reserves. Useful load was 945 lb. with a maximum gross weight of 2,150 lb.

At 950 lb., the PA-28-160's useful load was only slightly above that of its 150 hp. sibling as was the airplane's gross weight of 2,200 lb. With 48 gallons of fuel, the 160 hp. Cherokee could fly 730 statute miles at 75% power setting or 810 miles at an economy cruise power setting of 55%.

For the PA-28-180B, the extra horsepower provided a maximum speed of 150 mph. but range was reduced to 695 statute miles at a 75% power setting. The useful load was a generous 1,175 lb.—a 200-lb. increase compared with the 160 hp. version and 250 lb. more than the 150 hp. airplane.

At a gross weight of 2,400 lb., the Cherokee 180B could accommodate four 170-lb. adults, 48 gallons of useable fuel and 175 lb. of baggage. To provide an additional 3 mph., Piper included fiberglass "Dynaflair" speed fairings as part of the PA-28-180B's standard equipment. They were optional on the other two versions.

Many of the early Cherokees were equipped with avionic equipment designed and manufactured by the Piper Electronics Division located at Vero Beach. Led by Peter Robeck, the division's first design was the AutoNav radio compass, which provided homing capability on low-frequency and standard broadcast stations.

By the summer of 1962 the division had created the PTR-1 transceiver radio and the companion O-1 omni navigation indicator. The PTR-1 was a 27-channel transmitter with 25 crystals and could tune from 108 MHz to 128 MHz. The minimum transmitter power was a mere 1.5 watts. Cost of the unit was $400 and the O-1 indicator cost an additional $200.

Piper offered all three of the Cherokee Bs with four levels of optional equipment: Standard, Custom, Super Custom and AutoFlite. Base price for the Standard PA-28-150B was $10,990 increasing to $13,990 for the AutoFlite variant, which included the Piper AutoControl system capable of holding headings and making turns.

The PA-28-160B cost $11,500 in Standard guise and $14,500 equipped with AutoFlite options, and the PA-28-180B sold for $12,900 or $15,900 with

AutoControl installed. Piper offered a float option for two versions of the Cherokee B. When equipped with EDO Model 89-2000 floats, the designation was changed to PA-28S.

FAA certification for the PA-28S-160B was received in February, 1963 with approval for the 180 hp. airplane following in May. Piper did not certify the 150 hp. Cherokee B on floats, chiefly because owners preferred the higher horsepower engines when operating from water. When fitted with floats, the PA-28S-160 cruised at 117 mph. at 7,000 ft. at a 75% power setting and had a maximum speed of 126 mph.

In addition to the float version of the Cherokee B, Piper also obtained FAA approval for the float-equipped PA-22-108 Colt, which had remained in production at the Lock Haven factory after the Cherokee was introduced. The airplane was fitted with Pee-Kay Model 1800 floats and the certification work was accomplished by Pee-Kay Aircraft products at International Falls, Minnesota. The floats weighed 102 lb.

The Cherokee had begun to establish itself as a leader in the light, single-engine market by the end of 1962, and Piper Aircraft Corporation profits were climbing almost as fast as the airplanes it sold. By the end of the first quarter of fiscal year 1963 in December, gross sales had risen to $8,278,160 compared with $6,900,838 for the same period one year earlier. Net income per share of stock was 42 cents—up from only nine cents in the first fiscal quarter of 1962.

In January, 1963 workers at Vero Beach reached a

Piper obtained FAA certification in 1962 for the PA-28S-160 equipped with Model 89-2000 floats manufactured by the EDO Corporation. (Piper Aviation Museum)

significant milestone by completing the 1,000th Cherokee, a PA-28-180B assigned constructor number 28-1000 and appropriately registered N1000P. Painted Daytona White with Monterey Maroon trim, the airplane was delivered to Ponte', Inc., a cosmetic company headquartered in Chicago, Illinois.

Although primarily intended for business or private flying, the Cherokee was capable of competing in air races. In July, 1964 a PA-28-160 flown by Mary Ann Noah and co-pilot Mary Aikens won the prestigious Powder Puff Derby by having the best score over the 2,573-mile route from Fresno, California, to Atlantic City, New Jersey. Seven of the first 10 places were captured by pilots flying Piper airplanes.

Less than two years after introducing the Cherokee B, Piper unveiled the Cherokee C which made its debut in the autumn of 1964 for the 1965 model year. The "C" version continued to be offered with a choice of 150 hp., 160 hp. or 180 hp. Lycoming engines and incorporated a number of improvements.

Among the most salient changes was a new, two-piece fiberglass engine cowling developed for the PA-28-235. Dual latches on each side secured the two halves together, and the top half could be easily and quickly removed to inspect the engine.

A different exhaust system was installed that featured two mufflers mounted transversely under the front section of the powerplant, with dual stacks enclosed in an integral, streamlined fairing located farther forward than in previous Cherokees. The new exhaust installation slightly reduced cabin noise.

Piper completed a new factory at the Vero Beach, Florida airport in 1960 that was designed specifically to produce the new Cherokee. (Piper Aviation Museum)

Sorensen Aircraft in Minnesota obtained a Supplemental Type Certificate for installation of a spray tank and dispersal system for the PA-28 Cherokee. Cherokee N7028W, constructor number 28-712 was used to obtain approval in 1964. (Piper Aviation Museum)

Fuel line diameter was increased and routing from the two wing tanks was changed to improve starting under high temperature conditions. The fuel gascolator drain and electric fuel boost pump were shrouded in an air box that was cooled by outside ram air to reduce undesirable fuel vaporization.

The Cherokee C was the first of the PA-28 series to have flight and navigation instruments located on the left side of the instrument panel. The new arrangment allowed room for a centerline stack of three radios with a fourth mounted in the right side of the panel next to the engine instruments.

In addition, the baggage compartment weight limit was raised to 200 lb. Designated the PA-28S when equipped with EDO Model 2000 floats, the Cherokee C also was approved for operation on skis for winter flights.

Piper built the 3,000th Cherokee in November, 1964 and after four and one-half years of production Piper built its 5,000th Cherokee, a PA-32 Cherokee Six sold to Texas businessman Houston L. McCann in late 1965. Flushed with success, Piper management scheduled the manufacture of 3,000 more PA-28-series airplanes in 1966.

With an eye toward the agricultural market, Piper worked with the Sorensen Aircraft Company of Worthington, Minnesota, in 1964 to modify a Cherokee 180 for spray operations. Offered in kit form for $945, the modification included a fiberglass tank with a capacity of 110 gallons of liquid that mounted under the fuselage between the wings. The boom assemblies each featured 17 nozzles and were mounted under the wings. With the spray system installed, the Cherokee was approved for operation in the Restricted Category.

Fed by a flying frenzy unheard of since the halcyon days of Charles A. Lindbergh, Piper sales jumped 27% in 1965 as it rode the crest of a "third wave" of enthusiasm that was "far ahead of anything we've ever seen before" for general aviation, J. Willard Miller, a long-time employee and director of marketing for Piper, said. In addition to growing domestic demand, export sales were on the rise and accounted for more than 20% of Piper's production.

To keep up with demand the company's manufacturing sites had to be expanded. A 41,000-square foot area was added to the Lock Haven factory to boost PA-23 Aztec production along with a 38,000-square foot paint building. Piper also launched a program to hire 1,000 new employees.

At Vero Beach a 48,000-square foot area was added to the Cherokee production facilities in March, 1966 followed by another 52,000-square foot enlargement soon thereafter, bringing total floor space to 385,000 square feet. By 1965 the Vero Beach factory employed more than 900 workers compared with only 300 in 1961 when Cherokee production began.

Although a strong national economy formed the foundation for much of the sales success that Piper was having in the mid-1960s, credit also must be given to the company's innovative $5 introductory flight program. Launched in 1962, the popular and successful campaign had not only introduced thousands to flying but also bore fruit in terms of product loyalty.

In the early 1960s there were about 60,000 student pilots in training for their private license, and many of them had received their first flight or dual instruction in a Piper airplane. Of those students who became certificated pilots many of them later bought Cherokees, moved up to Comanches and then purchased twin-engine Aztecs.

In May, 1966 Piper launched a similar "Fun To Fly" program that gave fledglings an opportunity to pilot a Cherokee, and it still cost only $5. By that time the flying fever sweeping across America had induced more than 120,000 new student pilots to sign up for lessons at more than 800 flight schools nationwide.

To train all these would-be aviators, Piper dealers sold flight schools the PA-28-140—a two-place version of the venerable 150 hp. Cherokee. Developed in 1963, the Cherokee 140 was Piper's belated answer to Cessna's two-place Model 150 which first flew in 1957 and had entered production in 1959.

Cessna marketing and management officials were impressed by what Piper had accomplished with its introductory flight program, and in 1963 Cessna essentially copied the idea and created its own version. In 1971 the company began to establish a chain of more than 1,100 Cessna Pilot Centers worldwide to reinforce the flight training and product loyalty theme.

Certified by the FAA in February, 1964, initial production Cherokee 140s were powered by a derated Lycoming O-320-A2A developing 140 hp. at 2,450 rpm. The 140 hp. version was soon superseded, however, by the 150 hp. O-320-A2B engine. With a maximum gross weight of 1,950 lb., the Cherokee 140 could fly 780 statute miles without VFR fuel reserves. The airplane was built in Custom, Executive and Sportsman configurations, differing primarily in the type and sophistication of avionic equipment.

When PA-28-140 production began in March, 1964 Cessna already had a firm grip on the two-place trainer market and was strengthening its hold. Piper's primary concern, however, was not to outsell Cessna but to supply Piper flight training facilities with a more modern trainer than the PA-22-108 Colt.

Priced at $8,500 fly-away-factory at Vero Beach, the PA-28-140 represented more airplane for the dollar compared with Cessna's 150D, which sold for about $8,800 and was powered by a 100 hp. Continental 0-200A engine. Both airplanes were good trainers, had gentle flight characteristics and proved to be highly reliable aircraft.

Demand for the all-metal, four-place PA-28-160 steadily increased after Piper introduced the Cherokee in 1961. By 1962 the Vero Beach facility was building airplanes at the rate of four per day. (Piper Aviation Museum)

In the first year of manufacture Piper built 655 Cherokee 140s and Cessna built 686 Model 150Ds in 1964. The two airplanes continued to battle each other over the years, with Piper producing 10,089 140s compared with 23,839 Cessna Model 150s, including 1,070 Aerobat acrobatic versions and European 150s built by Cessna's French affiliate, Reims Aviation.

Piper terminated manufacture of the 140 in 1977 and Cessna ceased 150 production in the 1978 model year. In 1978 both Cessna and Piper introduced new airplanes for the trainer market. Cessna unveiled the upgraded, Lycoming-powered Model 152 that continued to be built into the 1986 model year, and Piper introduced the all-new, two-place PA-38 Tomahawk trainer.

In addition to United States operators of the Cherokee 140 such as Purdue University and Embry-Riddle Aeronautical Institute, a large number of

The 1968 Cherokee D featured a new instrument panel with SportsPower console, third cabin window originally incorporated in the Piper Cherokee Arrow and a longer propeller spinner. A 1969 Cherokee 180D is illustrated. (Piper Aircraft Corporation)

The 1968 Cherokee D instrument panel placed engine gauges in front of the pilot. Note new control wheels and the SportsPower throttle quadrant. (Piper Aircraft Corporation)

airplanes were exported to foreign flight schools and flying clubs. The Honda Flying Club, based at its airport in Saitama Prefecture in suburban Tokyo, Japan purchased three 140s and a PA-22-108 Colt to form the club in 1965. In Oxford, England the Oxford Air Training School placed its first Cherokee 140 into service in July, 1964 and added two more airplanes in January, 1965.

In addition to the two-place Cherokee 140 Piper had added the Cherokee 140-4 to the product line. The addition of an aft seat essentially transformed the PA-28-140 into a standard PA-28-150 Cherokee. The aircraft was powered by a 150 hp. Lycoming O-320-A2A engine. In June the FAA issued its approval and the PA-28-140-4 entered production for the 1966 model year.

Popular, easy and fun to fly, the hard-working 140 underwent a series of improvements through the years. The 140B was built in 1969 and sold for $9,600 in the Custom configuration. That year Piper offered deluxe four-place seating for the 140B with availability of the new Cruiser option package. Powerplant controls were grouped in a quadrant-type "SportsPower" configuration similar to that used in the retractable-gear Cherokee Arrow.

The 140B was followed in 1970 by the 140C, featuring an upgraded interior and a redesigned instrument panel. The 1971 140D remained essentially unchanged, but the 1972 140E's interior was revamped and the four-place variant was renamed the Cherokee Cruiser. In 1973 the 140F boasted a padded instrument panel glare shield and more comfortable seats similar to those installed on the larger Cherokees.

Piper continued to upgrade the Cherokee 180 in the early 1970s. The 1972 Cherokee 180G illustrated featured a redesigned instrument panel but retained the short fuselage of the earlier PA-28-180 series. (Piper Aviation Museum)

Piper improved the Cruiser version in 1975 by installing vertically adjustable front seats and in 1977 upgraded the interior with new seats, redesigned the instrument panel, improved the cabin ventilation system and added a more durable latching mechanism for the cabin door. The base price for a 1977 Cherokee Cruiser was $17,170.

Despite these enhancements the number of Cherokee 140s being built continued to decline through 1977, the final year of manufacture when 290 airplanes were built. From 1964 to 1977 a total of 10,089 PA-28-140s were produced and all were built at the Vero Beach, Florida facilities.

To further promote the business of learning to fly, in 1968 Piper introduced another flight training innovation—the Piper Flite Center. More than 420 dealers in the United States and Canada initially participated in the unique program which offered student pilots a structured training curriculum, including use of audio-visual techniques to supplement traditional ground school classes. By the mid-1970s, the number of Flite Centers had grown to about 500.

To complement the Flite Center training concept, in 1970 the engineers at Vero Beach created the low-cost, two-place Flite Liner trainer. Based on the PA-28-140, the Flite Liner was strictly a no-frills flying machine and lacked the aft seat and cabin embellishments found in the upscale Cherokees.

The initial batch of airplanes were delivered in March, 1971 and production continued until 1975. Powered by a 150 hp. Lycoming O-320-E3D engine, the Flite Liner's performance was essentially identical to the PA-28-140B through PA-28-140F series, but useful load was decreased to 845 lb.

The tremendous learn-to-fly boom that began in the mid-1960s was beginning to wane by the mid-1970s. Inflation and an economic recession that struck the nation in the early years of the decade further degraded the numbers of new aircraft, and production rates of the PA-28-140 series began to decline. The peak years were 1966, 1967 and 1969, when 1,193, 1,533 and 1,332 airplanes respectively were built.

By the late 1960s the stunning success of the PA-28 series airplanes coupled with escalating sales of the company's twin-engine aircraft product line had put an unprecedented amount of black ink on Piper's balance sheet. At the end of fiscal year 1968 on

Three-view of PA-28-180 Challenger. Introduced in 1973, the Challenger featured a lengthened fuselage, increased wingspan and a larger stabilator compared with its Cherokee 180G predecessor. (Smithsonian Institution, National Air And Space Museum Negative Number 93-2381)

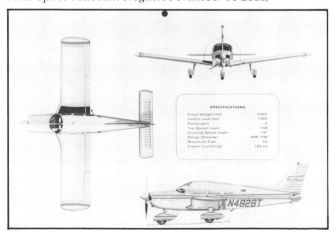

The Challenger was replaced by the PA-28-180 Archer for the 1974 model year. Cabin windows had rounded corners and the nose wheel steering system was improved. The Archer was replaced in 1975 by the Archer II fitted with a semi-tapered wing. (Piper Aircraft Corporation)

In 1964 Piper replaced the aging PA-22-108 Colt with the all-metal, two-place PA-28-140 as its primary flight training airplane. The prototype Cherokee 140, constructor number 28-20000, registered N6000W is illustrated with optional wheel fairings. (Piper Aviation Museum)

September 30, gross sales stood at $96,724,000 and represented a 20% increase compared with fiscal year 1967.

In 1969 sales rose to $106 million and Piper common stock was netting $2.36 per share. Happy with the company's financial success, company management kept improving its growing number of airplane products.

During the years when flight training was a high priority at Piper, the company did not neglect its popular four-place Cherokee family. In 1967, the next-generation Cherokee D was introduced for the 1968 model year and cost $13,900 for the standard-equipped airplane.

Externally, the PA-28-180D differed from its predecessors by having a third cabin window that was originally developed for the Cherokee Arrow. For power, only the 180 hp. Lycoming engine was available as Piper had terminated production of the 150 hp. and 160 hp. Cherokees after the 1967 model year.

Like the PA-28-180C, the engine was housed in a two-piece cowling, but the propeller installation featured a longer spinner. The new instrument panel was replete with modern, rocker-type switches and a "SportsPower" console that grouped throttle and mixture controls together was made standard equipment. Replacement of the long-lived, overhead stabilator pitch trim crank with a floor-mounted trim wheel and "T" flight instrument grouping were among the most obvious changes.

In a throwback to the PA-28-150 Cherokee of 1961, in 1966 Piper offered the PA-28-140 with four seats and a 150 hp. Lycoming O-320 engine. The name was changed to Cherokee Cruiser in 1972. N5373T was a 1973 Cherokee Cruiser, constructor number 28-7225318. (Piper Aviation Museum)

Customers liked the Cherokee D's styling and the new interior, and Vero Beach built 902 airplanes in 1968 followed by an additional 320 Cherokee Ds in 1969. As it had done in the past with the other Cherokees, Piper improved the airplane each year.

In 1970 new overhead fresh air vents were installed in the cabin headliner and in 1971 separate bucket-type seats replaced the bench-type seat in the aft cabin section. Only 260 airplanes were built in 1970, 234 were produced in 1971 and 318 Cherokee 180G were manufactured in 1972.

As part of its ongoing product improvement program, Piper had an experimental, upgraded 180 hp. Cherokee flying in 1971. Registered N4273T and assigned constructor number 28-E10, the first prototype was followed in 1972 by a second example registered N4373T and designated as constructor number 28-E13.

When the FAA granted its approval in May, the 1973 Cherokee 180 was renamed the Cherokee Challenger and was powered by a Textron Lycoming O-360-A3A engine rated at 180 hp. That year, air conditioning was optional, new seats were installed and the instrument panel glare shield was padded. The Custom version of the Challenger sold for $16,990.

As part of a program to provide commonality among the single-engine Cherokee series, the Challenger and its descendants incorporated structural changes made to the retractable-gear Arrow II. The fuselage was five inches longer, wingspan increased by two feet (a feature of the more powerful Cherokee 235), a larger stabilator was fitted to pro-

The 1971 Cherokee 140D incorporated minor airframe and cabin improvements. Constructor number 28-26737, registered N6001U was developed as a production prototype. (Piper Aviation Museum)

Piper introduced the PA-28-140 Cherokee Flite Liner in 1971 as a low-cost, two-place trainer for the company's learn-to-fly Flite Centers. The aircraft illustrated was the production prototype, registered N140FL. Piper built 10,089 Cherokee 140-series airplanes before production ended in 1977. (Piper Aviation Museum)

◄ *To expand its Cherokee product line, in 1963 Piper unveiled the PA-28-235. Powered by a 235 hp., six-cylinder Lycoming O-540 engine, a standard Cherokee 235 could carry four people, full fuel and 200 lb. of baggage. Base price was $15,900. The prototype airplane was N2800W that also had served as the Cherokee 180 prototype. (Piper Aviation Museum)*

vide increased pitch authority and gross weight was increased by 50 lb. Piper built 601 Challengers in 1973.

Additional changes were made in the 1974 model year when the Challenger was renamed the PA-28-180 Cherokee Archer. Powered by a 180 hp. Textron Lycoming O-360-A4A engine with a time between overhaul of 2,000 hours, the airplane had a base price of $17,990 and featured an improved nose wheel steering system as well as slightly restyled cabin windows and interior trim escutcheons.

Piper built 279 Archers in 1974 and 259 in 1975 when production of the Cherokee 180 series was discontinued in favor of the improved PA-28-181 Archer II. The Archer and Archer II were approved for operation on EDO Model 2000 floats.

In reflecting on the original PA-28 Cherokee's production run of 14 years, it can be stated that the airplane was one of the most popular four-place light aircraft produced by any general aviation aircraft manufacturer. The airframe's basic design was carefully planned and well executed and was constantly upgraded. The aircraft's ability to accept growth and higher horsepower were important factors in its success.

The Cherokee 180 series survived in a tough marketplace chiefly because they were reliable airplanes with good overall performance—in short, they were hard to beat. Beechcraft's 180 hp. Model 23 Sundowner was more expensive, slower and more difficult to land; Cessna's sleek Model 177 Cardinal and the more powerful Model R172K Hawk XP failed to outsell their Model 172 Skyhawk sibling and never posed a serious threat to the PA-28-180 Cherokee. The Gulfstream and later American General Aircraft Tiger, although fast and sporting a sliding canopy, failed to challenge the Cherokee's market dominance.

Whereas the Cherokee 180 eventually outlived Cessna's Cardinal, the more powerful PA-28-235 Cherokee entered the marketplace long after the popular and successful Cessna 182 Skylane. Introduced in August, 1963 the Cherokee 235 was designed primarily to fill a product gap between the Cherokee B and the retractable-gear PA-24 Comanche. It also would compete in the mid-price, single-engine market against the venerable Cessna 182.

Cessna had developed the Model 182 in 1956 from the rough-and-ready Model 180, but had wisely replaced the 180's tailwheel with a steerable nose gear. First flown in September, 1955 the four-place 182 was powered by a 230 hp. Continental O-470-L engine, had a maximum speed of 160 mph. and sold for $13,750. Cessna began production in January, 1956 and built 844 airplanes that year.

A resounding success, the airplane had evolved into the Model 182F by 1963 when Piper management decided to enter the upper echelon, four-place market with the Cherokee 235. It is interesting to note that when the PA-28-235 was introduced, Cessna already had built more than 6,000 182s and would build thousands more before production ended in 1986.

As for the Cherokee 235, the more powerful Lycoming O-540-B2B5 engine burned more fuel and was heavier than the smaller Lycomings used in the Cherokee B. To provide adequate fuel capacity and reasonable range, one additional fuel tank holding 17 gallons was installed in each wingtip. Wing span was increased 24 inches to 32 feet and wing area augmented by 10 square feet to accommodate the change.

A four-position fuel selector valve was mounted on the floor ahead of the flap control handle. With its maximum fuel capacity of 84 gallons, the Cherokee 235 could fly 991 nautical miles or more than 1,000 statute miles at a 55% power setting.

To enclose the big, six-cylinder Lycoming engine Piper developed a new two-piece fiberglass cowling

Early production Cherokee 235 instrument panel. (Piper Aviation Museum)

The Cherokee 235 featured a useful load higher than the empty weight of a standard airplane, and combined high performance with affordability. (Piper Aviation Museum)

that later was installed on the 180 hp. Cherokee C. To safely handle the 235's extra power and higher weight, Piper engineers strengthened the airframe structure by incorporating heavier spars and thicker aluminum alloy skin in the wings and other assemblies.

The PA-28-235 had a maximum gross weight of 2,900 lb. and a hefty 1,490-lb. useful load that was greater than the airplane's empty weight of 1,410 lb. From a weight and balance standpoint, a standard Cherokee 235 could accept a full panel of gyroscopic flight instruments, avionics and Piper's AutoControl flight control system, four 170-lb. adults, full fuel and 200 lb. of baggage without exceeding maximum gross weight.

Carrying that load the airplane could take off at sea level, climb at 825 feet per minute and fly at a maximum speed of 166 mph. In addition, the airplane possessed excellent short-field performance that soon endeared it to many pilots.

At maximum gross weight, Piper's husky Cherokee 235 was capable of taking off in only 800 feet at sea level with 25 degrees flap deflection, and required only 1,360 feet to clear a 50-foot obstacle. At a reduced weight of 2,400 lb., takeoff distance decreased to 600 feet and 1,040 feet were required to clear the 50-foot obstacle. Landing distance was 550 feet at that weight, or 1,060 feet over a 50-foot obstacle.

As standard features, the PA-28-235 was equipped with Dynaflair speed fairings and a two-tone Palm Beach exterior color scheme was applied over a Daytona White base color. To improve interior space and legroom, the rear cabin seat was relocated two inches farther aft compared with rear seats in the

The 1968 Cherokee 235C featured a third cabin window, new instrument panel with SportsPower console and an upgraded cabin interior. Base price was $16,900. Constructor number 28-11040, registered N9352W is illustrated. (Piper Aircraft Corporation)

Cherokee B.

Priced at $15,900 for the 1964 model year, the Cherokee 235 entered production at Vero Beach in the spring of 1963 and FAA certification was obtained in July. Piper built 585 airplanes in 1964 as many Cherokee pilots—and some former Cessna 182 pilots—enthusiastically accepted the bullish PA-28-235. In the 1965 model year 135 Cherokee 235s were produced.

For the 1966 model year Piper upgraded the airplane into the Cherokee 235B without increasing the price from 1964 levels. A two-blade, constant-speed propeller was optional and frequently ordered primarily because the airplane's excellent performance was compromised with the standard McCauley fixed-pitch unit.

A lengthened propeller spinner made from fiberglass was another change made to the airplane for 1966. The electrical system used a heavy-duty 60 ampere alternator that was belt-driven via the engine's starter ring gear. Chief improvements included new engine mounts and a shock-mounted cowling that reduced vibration and cabin noise; additional insulating material applied to the firewall; and an enlarged instrument panel to accommodate three radios in a stack with a fourth radio installed in the right side of the panel.

Of major concern to Piper was the high noise level in the original 235's cabin. Customers were unhappy about the unacceptable sound levels that became increasingly annoying on long cross-country flights. To make the 235B more tranquil inside, a team of Piper engineers led by Fred E. Weick stripped the entire interior out of a Cherokee 235 prototype airplane and in-

1970 Cherokee 235D, registered N9446W was constructor number 28-11165. The PA-28-235D's maximum speed was 166 mph. (Piper Aviation Museum)

92

1971 Cherokee 235E photographed at Vero Beach, Florida. (Piper Aviation Museum)

Piper's 1972 Cherokee 235F incorporated an improved interior and revised instrument panel. N5125S was the production prototype Cherokee 235F. (Piper Aviation Museum)

stalled audio equipment designed to measure noise levels during takeoff, cruise and landing.

Different types of sound proofing materials were evaluated and five sources of noise were identified: the side windows, windshield, engine mounts, the cabin itself and the wing. To reduce noise, double-pane side windows were developed and mounted in a special sound-dampening plastic compound that significantly lowered the sound level. Because a double-pane windshield was impractical, the two-piece plexiglas pieces were mounted in a thermoplastic compound instead of directly to the aluminum structure, further reducing noise.

Double-thickness soundproofing materials were applied to the cabin sidewalls and behind the instrument panel, and silicon-based damping spacers and a separate dampener were installed within the Dynafocal engine mount assemblies.

To their surprise, Weick and his crew discovered that much of the noise thought to be caused by the propeller slipstream interaction with the cowling was actually being generated from under the wing between the main landing gear struts.

By applying a special, lightweight plastic sound dampening material to the inside of the lower wing skins between the struts, most of the slipstream noise was eliminated. The method also was adopted to other

In 1974 Piper introduced the PA-28-235 Cherokee Pathfinder to replace the Cherokee Charger built for the 1973 model year. The Pathfinder was the final Cherokee 235 variant produced with the rectangular planform wing. (Piper Aircraft Corporation)

Piper airplanes.

Like its predecessor, the 235B was available in Custom, Super Custom and AutoFlite configurations. Although the airplane retained the hand-operated brake lever, for 1965 Piper made toe-operated brakes on the left set of rudder pedals standard with right-side brakes optional. Ground handling was improved by installation of a lengthened steering arm on the nose gear, reducing pedal forces required to make a turn.

Baggage area was increased five cubic feet to 24 cubic feet and a hatshelf for lightweight articles was molded integrally with the fiberglass bulkhead at the rear of the cabin. An improved electric fuel boost pump also was fitted.

Despite these improvements, sales declined and Vero Beach manufactured 121 235Bs in 1966. Another improvement program was initiated to boost the airplane's appeal and in 1967 the Cherokee C made its debut for the 1968 model year.

Following similar changes made to the Cherokee D and other single-engine Pipers, the 235C featured a third cabin window on each side of the fuselage, and the throttle, mixture and optional propeller controls were grouped into a "SportsPower" quadrant mounted on the lower subpanel structure.

Internally lighted, rocker-type electrical switches replaced the toggle-type switches used on previous airplanes and flight instruments were grouped in the standard "T" arrangement. The cabin was restyled and a double blanket fiberglass mat covered the entire interior structure. The 1968 235C had a base price of $16,900, and 187 airplanes were produced during the

PA-32 Cherokee Six prototype constructor number 32-01, registered N9999W made its first flight in 1963. (Piper Aviation Museum)

model year.

No major changes were made to the 1970 Cherokee 235D, 1971 235E and 1972 235F versions, but in the 1973 model year the name was changed to "Charger" and the fuselage was lengthened five inches. In addition to the longer fuselage, a larger stabilator of increased span was installed to provide adequate pitch authority, and the cabin door was widened for easier entry and egress.

Inside the cabin the seats were upgraded and the instrument panel glareshield was padded. The airplane's gross weight increased 100 lb. to 3,000 lb. Powered by a Textron Lycoming O-540-B4B5 engine rated at 235 hp., the Charger's base price was $24,390 when deliveries began in the summer of 1972.

During the years 1969 to 1973, Cherokee 235 production plunged to new lows. Only 29 were built in 1969, 78 in 1970, 28 in 1971 and a mere 23 in 1972 as a weak economy plagued the United States.

In what seemed to be a game of musical names, Piper again changed the 235's moniker to "Pathfinder" in 1974. Essentially identical to the Charger, the 1974 model featured rounded corners for the cabin windows and improved nose wheel steering. The 1975 version had vertically adjustable front seats and additional sound proofing was optional.

Production of the PA-28-235 Pathfinder continued until 1977 when it was terminated in favor of the new Dakota with its semi-tapered wing. Piper manufactured 109 Pathfinders in 1974, 135 in 1975, 181 in 1976 and 89 in 1977. In its basic configuration, the airplane cost $24,390 in 1974, rising to $35,060 in 1977. A total of 2,119 Cherokee 235s with the original, constant-chord wing were produced at Vero Beach.

In May, 1965 Piper Aircraft Corporation unveiled the newest member of its growing family of fixed-gear

airplanes—the six-place PA-32-260 Cherokee Six. Piper's big Six essentially was a new airframe and not a stretched version of the PA-28-235.

The aircraft featured a fuselage that was four feet longer and a cabin that was seven inches wider than those of its Cherokee siblings. The cavernous interior stretched 12 feet 9 inches from the firewall to the aft bulkhead.

Inside, the cabin seated six people in comfort and the rear four seats could be removed quickly for loading of outsized cargo, baggage, ambulance litters or mail. A second, larger cabin door measuring 34 inches high and 37 inches wide was mounted on the left side of the fuselage.

Without the aft seats installed, the rear cabin pro-

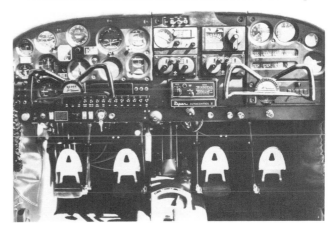

Cherokee Six instrument panel spanned a cabin seven inches wider than that of the smaller Cherokee airplanes, allowing installation of two separate stacks of avionic equipment. (Piper Aviation Museum)

The third Cherokee Six prototype N3200W was powered by a 260 hp. Lycoming O-540 engine. Designed with a useful load of 1,760 lb., a standard PA-32-260 could carry six people, full fuel and 200 lb. of baggage. (Mal Holcomb)

Piper certified the Cherokee Six 260 and 300 for operation on EDO Model 3430 floats, designated as the PA-32S-260 and PA-32S-300. Both versions received special corrosion preventive treatment and strengthened structure. (Piper Aviation Museum)

In 1969 Piper began delivering the improved Cherokee Six B that featured a new instrument panel with SportsPower console. The aircraft illustrated is Cherokee 300B registered N4169R, constructor number 32-40566. (Piper Aircraft Corporation)

vided 90 cubic feet of space or 110 cubic feet if the right front seat also was removed. In this configuration, the airplane could carry more than 1,300 lb. of cargo, the pilot and 50 gallons of fuel.

To help balance the longer fuselage, an 18-inch extension was inserted between the firewall and the cabin and served as a forward baggage compartment with eight cubic feet of volume. The compartment was limited to 100 lb. As an added feature, Piper provided four suitcases specifically made to fit the forward compartment and engraved the airplane's registration number on them. Additional baggage space was located behind the aft seats, and also was limited to 100 lb.

Wings and empennage were borrowed from the Cherokee 235 design and a 250 hp. Lycoming O-540 engine was installed in the prototype Cherokee Six, constructor number 32-01, registered N9999W, that first flew in December, 1963. A second and third prototype Cherokee Six were built in 1964 and the third ship was powered with the 260 hp. Lycoming O-540-E engine that was selected for production airplanes.

Following FAA certification in November, 1965 deliveries began later that year from the Vero Beach factory. With a maximum gross weight of 3,400 lb., the PA-32-260 had a useful load of 1,760 lb. if the standard fixed-pitch propeller was installed, or 1,735 lb. if the optional constant-speed propeller was chosen by the customer.

Available in Custom, Executive or Sportsman configurations, the Cherokee Six was priced at $18,500

Cherokee Six 300C registered N8939N was constructor number 32-40741, developed as the PA-32-300C production prototype. (Piper Aviation Museum)

for the Custom variant and had a maximum speed of 166 mph. at gross weight with the constant-speed propeller installed. Piper's AutoFlite wing leveler system was made standard equipment on all three option groups.

In its first year of production, Piper's PA-32-260 outsold Cessna's six-seat Model U206 Super Skywagon, with 317 airplanes built compared with 162 U206 aircraft. The Super Skywagon was a tough competitor, and had been available since 1963 as the Model 205 that evolved into the 206 series.

Powered by a 285 hp. Continental IO-520-A engine, the versatile U206 featured double doors for loading and was approved for operations on floats and skis. The airplane accommodated a 300-lb. external cargo pack, and could be fitted with a spray system for agricultural work or a special aerial ambulance kit.

Beech Aircraft Corporation's only single-engine, six-seat airplane was the 212 mph. S35 Bonanza built in 1965, although the Bonanza was not in the same class with the Cherokee Six because of its retractable landing gear. It was not until 1968 that Beech introduced the six-seat Model 36 Bonanza.

To make the hot-selling Cherokee Six more attractive to buyers, in 1967 Piper offered a 300-hp. Lycoming engine option and a seventh cabin seat option. The additional seat was much smaller than the others and was sandwiched between the two center row seats. In addition, the 1967 model had an optional, smaller auxiliary door adjacent to the rear door to improve loading of large, bulky items.

Many customers, particularly air taxi and charter operators, opted for the 300 hp. Lycoming IO-540-K

Two additional cabin windows were added to the 1974 Cherokee Six, and production of the Cherokee Six 260 version was terminated after the 1978 model year. A 1977 PA-32-300 is illustrated. (Piper Aircraft Corporation)

powerplant that was fuel-injected for improved fuel metering. A constant-speed propeller was standard equipment with the more powerful engine and the combination provided a cruising speed of 168 mph. The Cherokee Six 260 sold for $18,500 and the Cherokee Six 300—which eventually became more popular—was priced at $21,500.

Realizing that a utility airplane such as the Cherokee Six was a natural for operations on water, Piper certified the 300 hp. version for EDO Model 3430 floats as the PA-32S-300—the "S" indicating application of zinc chromate corrosion proofing treatment for the entire airframe and stainless steel control cables. FAA approval was secured in February, 1967.

Although less popular than floats, skis were fitted by some operators who wanted the flexibility of changing to skis in the winter season. In 1969, the FluiDyne company developed and won FAA approval for a Supplemental Type Certificate to install skis on the 260 hp. and 300 hp. airplanes.

Beginning with the 1969 model year, Piper added letter suffixes to the designations for both versions of the Cherokee Six. The 260B and 300B built that year had the instrument panels moved forward slightly and the six seats were moved inboard one inch to provide more shoulder room.

Like its smaller Cherokee sisters, the 1969 Cherokee Six had its flight instruments arranged in the standard "T" configuration and smaller, three-inch pictorial-type gyroscopic instruments were installed. Plastic-coated "Rams horn" control wheels with large hand grips afforded a better view of the panel. Throttle, mixture and propeller controls were grouped together in a "SportsPower" console.

Rocker-type electrical switches were grouped in a new panel mounted beneath the left front window instead of on the instrument subpanel. Base prices for the 1969 Cherokee Six B were $21,900 and $24,900 for the 260 hp. and 300 hp. versions respectively.

Production of the 1969 260B and 300B totaled 84 and 212 aircraft respectively as the 300 hp. version began to dominate sales. Most pilots and operators preferred the extra 40 hp. and the price differential between the two engines was not a deterrent.

By 1970 production of the 260 hp. Six had slowed as dramatically as that of the 300 hp. Six had escalated. Piper built 47 260C and 124 300C Cherokee Sixes in 1970, 23 260D and 168 300D airplanes in 1971 and 45 260E and 137 300E were built in 1972.

The popularity of the Cherokee Six continued well into the 1970s. Pilots liked the dependable, load-hauling Six and the airplane had carved a significant niche for itself in the overcrowded, highly competitive single-engine, fixed-gear marketplace. If there was any complaint about the Six, it centered primarily on the 300 hp. version and its seemingly insatiable appetite for fuel at high power settings.

In terms of handling, the Cherokee Six was easy to fly. It possessed the same benign flight characteristics found in the PA-28 series airplanes, although the aileron and stabilator forces were heavier because the aircraft weighed significantly more than the smaller Cherokees.

The thick, constant-chord wing gave more than adequate aerodynamic warning of an impending stall, and the stall itself was gentle whether the airplane was being flown solo or loaded to maximum takeoff weight. In summary, the Six was a pilot's airplane that earned its keep, and sales proved it.

No major changes were made to the PA-32 design during the 1970 through 1972 model years. In 1970 Piper engineers experimented with a 285 hp. Teledyne Continental Motors Tiara 6-285 engine as a potential powerplant. The engine was flown in a Cherokee Six 260C airframe but was not adopted for production aircraft.

In 1973 the Cherokee Six was upgraded slightly. The instrument panel featured a padded glareshield similar to that fitted on other Cherokee airplanes and improved cabin seats were installed. To simplify designations, the letter suffix was eliminated and the airplanes were known as the Cherokee Six 260 or Cherokee Six 300.

An additional cabin window was added to each side of the fuselage for the 1974 model year, and a thicker windshield was fitted in an effort to reduce noise levels. In addition, vertically adjustable front seats were made standard and the Cherokee Six series received the same improved nose wheel steering mechanism installed on the other Cherokees. The PA-32-300 cost $32,390 in 1974, and the company built 51 PA-32-260 and 170 PA-32-300 airplanes during that model year.

After building the Cherokee Six 260 for 13 years, Piper terminated production in the 1978 model year when only eight airplanes were built. Peak production for the Cherokee Six 260 occurred in 1966 when 534 airplanes were manufactured.

Production of the 300 hp. version reached its zenith in 1967 when 293 airplanes were built. For the 1978 model year Piper eliminated the name Cherokee and the aircraft was redesignated the Six 300 with a base price of $52,030. Improvements made to production airplanes focused on airframe drag reduction, chiefly through installation of new aerodynamic wheel fairings that increased speed 6 knots and slightly improved range. Club seating also was offered for the first time. Piper terminated manufacture of the PA-32-300 in 1979 when 290 airplanes were built.

In 1976 the Cherokee Six and its rectangular planform wing were modified to accept a hydraulically operated, retractable landing gear system similar to that installed in the PA-34 Seneca II and PA-28R Arrow II series. The new version was named the PA-32R-300 Cherokee Lance and a prototype first flew in August, 1974 powered by a Textron Lycoming IO-540-KIA5 engine rated at 300 hp.

Production commenced in late 1975 for the 1976 model year and 525 airplanes were manufactured, followed by 548 in model year 1977 and 68 in 1978.

Developed by Piper in the mid-1970s, the retractable-gear PA-32R-300 Cherokee Lance was a logical upgrade for the popular Cherokee Six series. (Piper Aircraft Corporation)

96

For the 1978 model year Piper introduced the PA-32RT-300 Lance II fitted with a T-tail empennage and 300 hp. Lycoming IO-540 engine. (Piper Aircraft Corporation)

The 1975 Lance cost $49,990 with standard equipment.

Piper installed a T-tail empennage on a prototype aircraft in 1976 to create the PA-32RT-300 Lance II. The purpose of the T-tail was to place the stabilator in clear, freestream air to reduce cabin noise and to decrease the size and weight of the stabilator.

Following FAA approval of the PA-32RT-300 in April, 1977 Vero Beach began production and deliveries were underway by early 1978. A 300 hp. Lycoming IO-540-K1G5 powered the Lance II, and 285 airplanes were produced during the model year. Another 105 airplanes were manufactured in 1979 before production of the Lance II was terminated that year.

Aesthetically, the T-tail looked good but some pilots disliked the airplane's handling characteristics. The chief complaint centered on excessively long takeoff rolls, but pilots who took the time to familiarize themselves with the Lance II grew fond of the airplane and gradually accepted its idiosyncrasies.

The Cherokee Lance became simply the "Lance" when Piper eliminated the Cherokee name. For the 1978 model year, the company offered a turbocharged version of the Lance II designated PA-32RT-300T Turbo Lance II, powered by a 300 hp. Textron Lycoming TIO-540-S1AD engine.

Initial deliveries began early in 1978. The PA-32RT-300T was built only in the 1978 and 1979 model years when 415 airplanes were produced, chief-

The Piper PA-28R-180 Arrow was one of the company's most successful airplanes. Introduced in 1967, the Arrow combined the PA-28-180's airframe with a retractable landing gear system to create an economical, high-performance single-engine airplane with a base price less than $17,000. N9995W was constructor number 28R-30003, the third prototype Arrow built. (Piper Aviation Museum)

Piper experimented with the PA-32-300M in 1968 as a potential weapons platform for military counter-insurgency operations. Each wing had hard points for ordnance. Constructor number 32-21, registered N3218W served as the development airplane. (Piper Aviation Museum)

ly because Piper was developing the next-generation PA-32-301 Saratoga series to replace the Lance II.

Perhaps the most unusual Cherokee Six developed by Piper was constructor number 32-21, registered N3218W. The airplane was modified in 1968 into the PA-32-300M by the experimental department as a testbed aircraft for military counter-insurgency (COIN) operations.

The wing had four hardpoints for carrying ordnance and other weaponry. The project was cancelled, however, and no PA-32-300M airplanes were produced. It is interesting to note that in 1965, Beech Aircraft Corporation developed its own series of military airplanes based on the Bonanza.

These included the Model D33 derived from the S35 but equipped with a conventional empennage that was later refined into the Model PD249 of the early 1970s. Like Piper, Beech did not produce the COIN airplanes.

Since its introduction, the PA-28 Cherokee series had been a fixed-gear family of airplanes and Piper Aircraft Corporation management was more than pleased with the success of their product line. By 1966 the company needed a step-up airplane to fill the gap between the Cherokee 235 and the Comanche as well as to compete against the lightweight, four-place Mooney M20C Mark 21 series of private aircraft.

In June, 1967 Piper had its answer in the retractable-gear PA-28R-180 Cherokee Arrow. The

Powered by a 200 hp. Lycoming IO-360 engine, the Arrow 200 was developed in 1968 and outsold its 180 hp. sibling. Piper ended production of the PA-28R-180 in 1971. The Arrow's automatic landing gear extension system was an innovative safety feature. A 1970 Arrow 200 registered N2864R is illustrated. (Piper Aircraft Corporation)

four-place airplane was destined to attain un-precedented popularity—so great that it was a factor in Piper's decision not to restart production of the PA-24 Comanche after the 1972 floods that devastated the Lock Haven factory.

Based largely on the PA-28-180 Cherokee, the Arrow's most salient feature was its retractable, tricycle landing gear that was electrically-controlled and hydraulically operated via a reversible, motor-driven powerpack installed beneath the aft seat.

The most innovative feature of the Arrow, however, was its automatic landing gear system championed by none other than Pug Piper. Designed by engineers Fred E. Weick and Gilbert Trimmer, the system was the epitome of simplicity—and it worked.

If the aircraft was approaching to land and airspeed fell below 110 mph. with the gear retracted, a pressure-sensing switch exposed to the propeller slipstream allowed the gear to free-fall into the down-and-locked position. During climbout at full throttle and with airspeed above 85 mph., the sensing switch would allow the gear to be retracted. A small lever located in the console between the front seats permitted the pilot to override the automatic gear-down system when necessary, such as during stall practice.

A fuel-injected, 180 hp. Textron Lycoming IO-360-B1E engine with a 1,500-hour time between overhaul powered the Arrow, and a two-blade, constant-speed propeller was standard equipment. Three prototypes were built for the FAA flight test program and made their first flights in 1966. FAA certification was completed in June, 1967 and initial customer deliveries began from the Vero Beach factory later in the year.

With a maximum gross weight of 2,500 lb. the PA-28R-180 Arrow could climb 875 feet per minute at sea level and cruise 162 mph. at a 75% power setting. As with other Cherokees, two wing tanks held 50 gallons of fuel and the Arrow could fly 995 statute miles at a 55% power setting.

The cabin was similar to those of other aircraft in the PA-28 series, and the throttle, mixture and propeller controls were grouped into a "Sportspower" quadrant. Rocker-type electrical switches were standard, along with left-side toe brakes and the familiar hand brake and parking brake lever.

Priced at $16,900, the Arrow was a benchmark airplane for Piper. Sales literally took off, and 351 Arrows were built in 1967 followed by 736 in the 1968 model year. The Arrow was chosen as "Plane of the Year" by Plane and Pilot Magazine in 1968 and in less than two years the PA-28R had become the best-

The Arrow B was similar to the Arrow 200 but incorporated swing-away sun visors, an improved gust lock and baggage door lock. Arrow B registered N5020S, constructor number 28R-35753 was photographed at Vero Beach, Florida. (Piper Aircraft Corporation)

selling lightweight, retractable-gear airplane on the market.

Piper offered an optional 200 hp. Lycoming IO-360-C1C engine in 1969, and the more powerful PA-28R-200 quickly dominated the assembly line. With 200 hp., maximum speed increased to 176 mph. and the company produced 392 aircraft in the 1969 model year. The 200 hp. Arrow's base price climbed only slightly to $18,500, and the 180 hp. Arrow's price increased to $17,500.

A minor upgrade of the Arrow program came in the 1970 model year when 20 PA-28R-180B and 220 PA-28R-200B airplanes were produced. Swing-away sun visors, a larger cabin radio speaker and flush-type door handles were among the improvements. In addition, six-way adjustable front bucket seats were optional and the microphone was relocated to the center of the instrument panel.

Only 13 180 hp. Arrow Bs were built in 1971 when that version was phased out of production, bringing the total of PA-28R-180 airplanes built to 1,283. Another, more comprehensive upgrade was accomplished for the 1972 model year.

Designated the Arrow II, the fuselage was lengthened five inches aft of the front seats to provide more interior space and a wider cabin door was incorporated. A redesigned interior was developed and "PiperAire" air conditioning was optional.

The stabilator was enlarged to compensate for the

Three-view of Arrow II. (Smithsonian Institution, National Air And Space Museum Negative Number 93-2382)

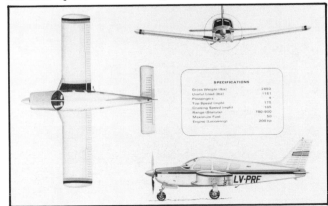

longer fuselage and maximum gross weight increased 50 lb. to 2,650 lb. compared with the Arrow B's 2,600 lb. limit. New fiberglass wingtips were fitted, adding 26 inches to the overall span of the wing.

All of these improvements raised the base price to $23,500 but the Arrow II continued its tight grip on sales in the entry-level, single-engine, retractable-gear market with 320 airplanes manufactured in the 1972 model year. Workers at Vero Beach found it difficult to keep up with demand, and following FAA certification in December, 1971 initial customer deliveries of the Arrow II began early in 1972.

In the next four model years Piper did not make significant changes to the Arrow II series. For the 1973 model year, a padded glareshield was added above the instrument panel and the cabin windows featured rounded corners compared with square corners found on the earlier Arrows.

When the Cherokee name was eliminated, the PA-28R-200 II was designated the Arrow II. Production totaled 466 aircraft in 1973, 320 in 1974, 383 in 1975 and 545 in the 1976 model year when manufacture of Arrows with the constant-chord wing was terminated in favor of the new Arrow III with its semi-

In 1972 Piper began delivering the PA-28R-200 Arrow II, featuring a longer fuselage, larger stabilator and increased maximum gross weight. Piper terminated production of the Arrow II after the 1977 model year in favor of the PA-28R-201 Arrow III with a semi-tapered wing planform. A 1975 Arrow II is illustrated. (Piper Aircraft Corporation)

tapered wing planform.

In less than two decades, Pug Piper, John Thorpe and Fred Weick's little PA-28 Cherokee had evolved into a complete family of modern, all-metal airplanes whose price, performance and reliability proved difficult to match, and virtually impossible to surpass.

Largely because of the Cherokee's success, by the late 1970s Piper Aircraft Corporation had increased significantly its share of the United States general aviation market. The airplanes of Lock Haven and Vero Beach were as modern as any built by competitors and were typically less expensive than their Cessna, Beech and Mooney counterparts.

Like the famous J-3 Cub before it, the PA-28 Cherokee had become an aviation icon in its own right—a simple, rugged design that had withstood not only the test of time, but would survive the tumultuous years ahead.

CHAPTER EIGHT

TAKEOVERS AND TAPERWINGS

As the decade of the 1960s drew to a close, Piper Aircraft Corporation had achieved worldwide success with its diverse product line of single- and twin-engine airplanes. The company had three factories and thousands of employees working full-time to produce the Cherokee series, Aztec, Twin Comanche and Comanche, and had advanced aircraft undergoing flight tests as well as new airplanes on the drawing board.

Piper stock was trading on Wall Street for as high as $72 in mid-1968, but fell to about $50 by the end of the year because of a slowing national economy. Prospects for the future, however, looked bright and management was optimistic about higher profits and earnings in the years ahead.

But success often breeds distress, and on January, 23, 1969, Piper Aircraft Corporation president William T. Piper, Jr., received an earfull of the latter during a telephone call. The man to whom he was listening was Herbert J. Siegel, president of the famous Chris Craft boat manufacturing company. Unfortunately, Siegel was not talking about buying an airplane. Instead, and much to William Piper, Jr.'s distress, Siegel stated that Chris Craft was planning to take control of Piper Aircraft Corporation.

Before making his fateful telephone call, Siegel already had orchestrated the purchase of 200,500 shares of Piper stock and by early February Chris Craft had acquired more than 545,000 shares. It needed an additional 300,000 shares to obtain a 51% majority and assume control of the aircraft manufacturer.

The junior William Piper was shaken by the unexpected turn of events. He took the Chris Craft threat seriously and aided by his aging father, two brothers and other corporate officials hastily tried to form an alliance with Long Island's Grumman Aircraft Company to ward off Chris Craft's hostile takeover attempt.

Upon learning about the proposed merger of Grumman and Piper, Siegel and Chris Craft lawyers acted swiftly and filed suit against the two companies. Although the coalition looked promising, the Piper-Grumman deal eventually was torpedoed not by pending legal action but by New York Stock Exchange officials, who disagreed with certain provisions of the agreement.

Confident that the takeover was proceeding smoothly, Siegel submitted a tender for more shares. In a counter action, Piper moved to dilute the stock's value by seeking yet another alliance, this time with the United States Concrete Pipe Company. In addition, he intended for Piper to acquire Southply, Incorporated, a building materials company that specialized in exterior-grade plywood products.

Unfortunately, the proposed agreement and acquisition failed after being vetoed by the Stock Exchange Board of Governors in April, 1969. Still determined to resist Chris Craft's attack, in May the Pipers arranged for Bangor Punta, a diversified holdings company based in Greenwich, Connecticut, to purchase more than 500,000 shares of the family's stock in Piper Aircraft Corporation thereby denying Chris Craft control of the company.

Eventually, Bangor Punta acquired a 51% stake in the company but Chris Craft continued the fight for a majority position. The end result of all the bloodletting was that by August, the Piper family had lost control of their company to the two dueling corporations.

It was a sad time for William T. Piper, Sr. He not only suffered the loss of his company to non-aviation entities, but he had lost his health as well and on January 15, 1970, he died at the age of 89.

Both William Piper, Jr., and Pug Piper soldiered on with the company until 1973 when they were forced to leave. "Pug" Piper moved to Wichita, Kansas and in 1980 founded Piper Advanced Technology, Inc. He died of cancer in 1981. Tony Piper had left the company in 1960 and later resigned from Piper's Board of Directors to manage family properties in Texas.

As for the unsettled dispute between Chris Craft and Bangor Punta for ultimate control of Piper Aircraft Corporation, the drama continued long after the Piper family had faded from the scene.

In an attempt to win control, Chris Craft lost an initial lawsuit against Bangor Punta in the Pennsylvania Courts but won on appeal. Bangor Punta appealed the decision to the Pennsylvania Supreme Court and lost. Finally, the case was presented to the United States Supreme Court, which upheld the original state court's ruling in favor of Bangor Punta.

As a result of the Court's decision, by 1977 Bangor Punta was firmly in control of Piper's destiny. Remaining Chris Craft personnel were purged from the board of directors and Bangor Punta officials took the reins. They managed the company until December, 1983 when Bangor Punta itself was swallowed up by Lear-Siegler Corporation, a large aerospace con-

The shape and size of the 1974 PA-28-151 Cherokee Warrior's semi-tapered wing planform is evident when compared with the PA-28-140's rectangular design. The new wing possessed improved low-speed, stall and crosswind control characteristics. (Piper Aircraft Corporation)

In 1977 Piper introduced the improved PA-28-161 Warrior II. The chief change was installation of a 160 hp. Textron Lycoming O-320 engine. The Warrior II illustrated was constructor number 28-7716002, registered N1190H. (Piper Aviation Museum)

Piper increased the maximum gross weight and useful load of the 1983 Warrior II. A 1987 Warrior II is illustrated. (Piper Aircraft Corporation)

glomerate based in Santa Monica, California.

With general aviation sales and production declining to record lows in the early 1980s, Lear-Siegler made significant changes to keep black ink on the balance sheet. Both the Lock Haven, Pennsylvania, and Lakeland, Florida, factories were closed and all operations were moved to the Vero Beach facilities.

As product liability costs soared in the mid-1980s, Piper sales and production went into a tailspin. The General Aviation Manufacturers Association (GAMA), which represented Piper and other United States light aircraft builders and the vendors who supported them, saw industry-wide aircraft production plummet to only 2,691 airplanes in 1983 from a high more than 17,000 aircraft in 1979.

Piper was not the only company adversely affected by the worsening situation. In 1986, Cessna had ceased production of its single-engine, piston-powered airplanes, and by 1982 Beechcraft had abandoned the trainer and small four-place airplane market altogether. Only the Bonanza series remained in production.

By 1990, United States light aircraft deliveries had fallen to record lows not experienced since the postwar decline of 1947, and in 1992 economic recession and other factors reduced deliveries to only 899 airplanes—the lowest in the industry's recorded history.

Battered by poor sales and faced with a bleak business outlook, in 1987 Lear-Siegler itself was ripe

In 1992 Piper Aircraft Corporation delivered 85 new airplanes, including 28 Warrior IIs. (Piper Aircraft Corporation)

for takeover and was acquired by the investment firm of Forstmann Little & Company, which in turn sold Piper to private businessman and entrepreneur Monroe Stuart Millar in May of that year.

All of the corporate and managerial infighting and changes in ownership that occurred at Piper during the troubled years of the 1970s and 1980s, however, did not prevent the company from improving its family of single-engine airplanes.

Gone were the PA-28 Cherokees that had given the company such a firm grip on much of the market in the 1960s. In their place an upgraded, new breed of Piper airplanes began to appear in the early 1970s.

First to make its debut was the PA-28-151 Cherokee Warrior—essentially an improved, more modern prodigy of the trusty Cherokee. The Warrior was a four-place, fixed-landing gear design that incorporated the longer fuselage of the PA-28-180 Challenger as well as its larger stabilator. The most important change, however, was a new wing.

Instead of the stubby, constant-chord wing that had served the Cherokee so well, Piper engineers had developed a new, more efficient design with a tapered outboard section. Piper exalted the wing's virtues. These included a higher aspect ratio that provided more lift per square foot without an increase in area from that of the older wing, and more docile stall characteristics thanks to an outer wing section that retained lift after the untapered, inboard sections had stalled.

Larger ailerons provided improved roll control at low speeds and in the stall, and the wing and aileron combination made the Warrior easier to handle in a strong crosswind. Powered by a 150 hp. Lycoming O-320-E2D engine turning a fixed-pitch propeller, the Warrior was intended to be a direct competitor against Cessna's ubiquitous Model 172 Skyhawk—another one of the most popular and prolific general aviation airplanes manufactured.

The prototype Warrior was constructor number 28-E10, registered N4273T, and was joined by the first production airplane constructor number 28-7415001 during the FAA flight test certification program. The Warrior received its type certificate from the FAA in August, 1973.

Introduced for the 1974 model year, the PA-28-151 was priced at $14,990 and 703 airplanes were produced in the first year of manufacture. Compared with the 1974 Cessna 172M, the Warrior had a slightly higher useful load and benefitted from having a cabin that provided more than four inches additional shoulder room that was lacking in the venerable Skyhawk.

The 172M also was powered by a 150 hp. Textron Lycoming O-320 engine, and the upgraded Skyhawk version preferred by most buyers had a maximum gross weight of 2,300 lb. as opposed to the Warrior's 2,325-lb. gross weight limit. In general, the airplanes were well matched in performance but the Warrior's cabin was more comfortable.

Piper built 449 PA-28-151s in 1975, 435 in 1976 and 314 during the 1977 model year when the 150 hp. Warrior was replaced by the 160 hp. PA-28-161 Warrior II, powered by a Lycoming O-320-D2G engine designed to operate on 100 octane, low-lead content aviation fuel. Along with the Warrior II's improvements came a higher price tag of $20,820 for the standard airplane.

Further improvements incorporated into the 1978 PA-28-161 centered on drag reduction. New speed fairings for the landing gear boosted cruise speed seven knots and a redesigned propeller spinner was fitted. Workers at the Vero Beach facilities produced 680 Warrior IIs in 1978 and 598 in 1979 as sales continued at a strong pace.

When the decade of the 1980s arrived, however, it brought with it an avalanche of product liability claims against small airplane manufacturers. Like its competitors, Piper had to pay higher and higher premiums to obtain liability insurance and therefore was forced to raise prices on its products to cover these escalating costs.

Warrior production declined to 373 airplanes in 1980, slid to 322 the next year, fell by nearly 100 units to 226 Warriors in 1982 and slipped to 109 aircraft in 1983. That year, the airplane's maximum gross weight was increased by more than 100 lb.

Although Piper lawyers fought and won many product liability cases, it cost the company millions of dollars for litigation and consequently aircraft prices were forced to new highs. As a result, sales and production of all Piper single-engine airplanes—not only the Warrior II—continued a slow but steady retreat.

In 1985 the Warrior II's base price was $46,240 and 99 airplanes were produced. A mere eight aircraft were built in 1986. Twenty-seven were built in 1987, 38 in 1988 and 19 in the 1989 model year when the Warrior II's base price increased to $67,900.

Only five aircraft were produced in 1990 and no Warrior IIs were manufactured in 1991. When additional cash became available to the company in 1992, Piper completed and delivered 28 Warrior IIs after resuming limited production activity, according to the General Aviation Manufacturers Association. For the 1993 model year, the Warrior II had a basic equipped list price of $128,800.

To stimulate the dormant trainer market, in 1987 Monroe Stuart Millar announced Piper would offer flight schools and fixed-base operators a two-place version of the popular Warrior II designed for the flight training role. Designated the PA-28-161 Cadet, the airplane was a no-frills flying machine with the interior stripped of its embellishments. To further reduce cost, the third cabin window and the aft seat were deleted. Powered by a Textron Lycoming O-320-D3G engine rated at 160 hp., performance was similar to that of the Warrior II.

As Millar had hoped, his promotion campaign to sell the trainer prompted flight training establishments to order Cadets by the hundreds.

Piper owner Monroe Stuart Millar introduced the PA-28-161 Cadet in 1987 as a low-cost primary and instrument trainer. Based on the Warrior II, the two-place Cadet lacked a third cabin window and aft seat. The Cadet illustrated was operated by FlightSafety International at its Vero Beach Flight Academy in Florida. (Dan Moore and FlightSafety International)

Piper had cash deposits for more than 400 airplanes by late 1987. With production underway, 39 Cadets were produced in the 1988 model year, followed by 268 in 1989 and 20 in 1990. Zero Cadets were built in 1991 as cash flow woes crippled the company's ability to produce the trainer.

In the 1989 model year the base price of a PA-28-161 Cadet had increased to $57,495 for the VFR version and $66,495 for the instrument trainer variant. In view of the serious financial troubles that were gripping Piper by the throat in 1990, Cadet prices were too low.

With vendors demanding their money and with Piper having none to give, Cadet production had slowed to a trickle by the end of 1991. The PA-28-161 Cadet was not produced in 1992 as Piper reduced its product line to 10 different airplanes. The Warrior II was among those that remained in production and preserved Piper's ability to build Cadets in the future.

In 1974 the Warrior had been the first Piper airplane to use the new semi-tapered wing, and by 1979 the wing had been fitted to all single-engine aircraft produced by the company. The PA-28-180 Archer received the new wing in 1975 and was transformed into the PA-28-181 Archer II.

The upgraded Archer II had a maximum gross weight of 2,550 lb.—100 lb. more than the original Archer—and was powered by a Textron Lycoming O-360-A4M engine rated at 180 hp. Maximum speed

In 1975 the PA-28-180 Archer inherited the Warrior's semi-tapered wing and became the PA-28-181 Archer II. (Piper Aircraft Corporation)

The Archer II had a cruise speed of 144 mph. and could fly more than 770 statute miles at a 75% power setting. A 1982 Archer II is illustrated. (Piper Aircraft Corporation)

was 151 mph. and range with the standard 50 gallons of useable fuel was 905 statute miles at 55% economy power setting, or 774 miles at 75% power.

In March, 1975 the prototype Archer II made its first flight and the FAA approved the design in July. The first production airplane was constructor number 28-7690002, registered N4319X, and was built at Vero Beach.

Pilot reaction to the Archer II was positive. They liked the gentle stall behavior of the airplane as well as the slightly higher cruise speed compared with their older Cherokee mounts. In addition, the ability to load a standard airplane with full fuel, four adults and maximum baggage without exceeding weight limitations was another important plus.

The 1976 Archer II cost $23,980 in standard configuration and eager customers bought 476 airplanes in the first year of manufacture. Vero Beach employees built 607 Archers IIs in 1977, and these airplanes shared improvements found on other Piper aircraft including more comfortable seats, a redesigned instrument panel, an improved entry door latch mechanism and a more efficient cabin ventilation system.

As with the Warrior II, the Cherokee name was deleted in the 1979 model year and the PA-28-181 was designated the Archer II. The new speed fairings used on other Piper fixed-gear, single-engine airplanes also were available on the Archer II.

Prices increased from $34,010 in 1980, when optional velour-type interiors became available in the

Piper upgraded the Archer II with minor improvements during the late 1970s and throughout the 1980s. A 1984 Archer II is illustrated, equipped with streamlined wheel fairings developed by Piper in the late 1970s. The fairings slightly increased maximum speed and range. (Piper Aircraft Corporation)

Archer II, to $75,450 in 1987 when 25 airplanes were delivered. The base price was reduced slightly in 1989 to $73,300, and Piper built 51 of the popular Archer II in 1988 and 50 in 1989, followed by seven in 1990 before production was halted.

Since manufacture of the Archer II began in 1975, Piper had built more than 3,400 of the four-place airplanes. When limited production resumed in 1992, 20 Archer IIs were delivered that year. The basic equipped list price of a 1993 PA-28-181 was $135,500.

Next in line to receive the semi-tapered wing was the former PA-28-235 Pathfinder which was transformed into the PA-28-236 Dakota beginning in the 1979 model year. Powered by a Textron Lycoming O-540-J3A5D engine rated at 235 hp., the Dakota was capable of cruising at 166 knots and could fly 748 nautical miles at a 75% power setting.

A standard Dakota could accommodate 72 gallons of fuel, four adults and 200 lb. of baggage without exceeding the 3,000-lb. maximum gross weight limitation. Useful load for a standard Dakota was a hefty 1,390 lb. Deliveries for the 1979 model year began from the Vero Beach factory in the summer of 1978 after FAA certification was obtained in June.

New speed fairings for the landing gear were optional and in 1980 velour fabrics were optional as well. A total of 335 Dakotas were built in the first year of manufacture and the airplane had a base price of $39,910.

Despite the Dakota's sterling performance and load-lifting virtues, production slowed to 151 airplanes in 1980 and progressively declined thereafter. Piper built 96 Dakotas in model year 1981, 45 in 1982, 25 in 1983, 31 in 1984 and 20 in the 1985 model year.

Only 12 PA-28-236 Dakotas left the production line in 1986, 12 were manufactured in 1987, six in 1988 and 10 in 1989 when the base price escalated to $103,900. Only one Dakota was built in 1990 and zero were built in 1991. Piper had completed and delivered two Dakotas by the end of 1992 and planned to build additional Dakotas in 1993. In the model years 1964 through 1992, Piper Aircraft Corporation had built more than 2,800 PA-28-235 Cherokee 235 and PA-28-236 Dakota-series airplanes.

It is interesting to note that from model year 1964 when the Cherokee 235 was introduced through model year 1974 when the improved Pathfinder made its debut, the base price of the airplane rose to $24,390 from $15,900. By contrast, in the model years from 1979 to 1987 the base price of a PA-28-236 Dakota had risen to $106,920 from $39,910. Basic equipped list price for a 1993 Dakota was $148,800.

These increases far exceeded the rate of inflation in the United States during that time period and were caused primarily by product liability insurance costs, according to Piper officials. Unfortunately, in 1993 the consumer was paying Piper more than $148,000 for an airplane that offered little additional benefit to the user than that of a $40,000, 1979 Dakota.

As a companion aircraft to the Dakota, Piper engineers developed the turbocharged PA-28-201T Turbo Dakota. The aircraft retained the PA-28-236's semi-tapered wing mated to an Archer II fuselage, but was fitted with a 200 hp. Teledyne Continental Motors TSIO-360-FB engine.

Introduced in the 1979 model year at a base price of $41,980, the Turbo Dakota had a service ceiling of 20,000 feet compared with 17,500 feet for the naturally-aspirated Dakota. A redesigned cowling enclosed the six-cylinder engine, and also housed the landing and taxi light.

Sales of the Turbo Dakota were slow and only 91 were built, all in the 1979 model year before production was terminated in mid-summer. A number of reasons may account for the airplane's lack of popularity. First, the turbocharging improved service ceiling by less than 4,000 feet. Second, the 200 hp. Continental engine had a time between overhaul of only 1,400 hours compared with 2,000 hours for the Dakota's Lycoming O-540 powerplant. Third, the performance differential between the two airplanes was not significant enough to entice a large number of buyers to choose the turbocharged version.

The fifth member of the original Cherokee line to be equipped with the semi-tapered wing was the PA-32-300 Cherokee Six. Already having distinguished itself as a versatile, workhorse airplane of many talents, the Cherokee Six would improve its reputation as an easy-to-fly, six-place airplane with the addition of the new wing and other important upgrades.

Three-view of PA-28-236 Dakota. (Smithsonian Institution, National Air and Space Museum Negative Number 93-2358)

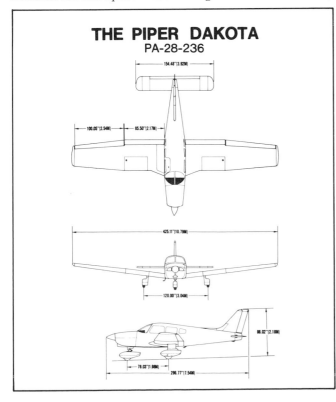

THE PIPER DAKOTA
PA-28-236

In 1978 the PA-28-235 Cherokee Pathfinder was transformed into the PA-28-236 Dakota with a semi-tapered wing. A 235 hp. Textron Lycoming O-540 engine powered the Dakota to a maximum speed of 148 kt. (Piper Aircraft Corporation)

Designated as the PA-32-301 Saratoga in its new configuration, the airplane's wing span was four feet wider than that of the Warrior II and the maximum gross weight was boosted 200 lb. to 3,615 lb. Other than the wing, the most salient change made to the Saratoga was the return of a conventional empennage in place of the T-tail configuration used on the earlier Lance II.

The first of two prototype Saratogas flew in November, 1978. A Textron Lycoming IO-540-K1G5 engine rated at 300 hp. was the standard powerplant but Piper also developed the PA-32-301T Turbo Saratoga in parallel with the naturally aspirated version. The -301T was powered by a 300 hp. Textron Lycoming TIO-540-S1AD engine, and both the turbocharged and non-turbocharged powerplants were equipped with a three-blade, constant-speed propeller.

The Dakota could accommodate four occupants and 80 gallons of fuel. The 1986 Dakota illustrated was photographed flying along the Florida coastline. (Mal Holcomb)

Piper developed a turbocharged version of the Dakota designated the PA-28-201T. Production was limited to the 1979 model year. The Turbo Dakota had a service ceiling of 20,000 feet and a cruise speed of 156 kt. (Piper Aircraft Corporation)

104

Like its four-place siblings, the six-place PA-32-300 Cherokee Six also received a semi-tapered wing to become the PA-32-301 Saratoga in 1979. Wingspan was increased four feet to 36 feet 5 inches. Deliveries began in the 1980 model year. (Piper Aircraft Corporation)

Production began at Vero Beach early in 1980 after the FAA certified the Saratoga and Turbo Saratoga in January. Base prices were $66,700 for the PA-32-301 and $74,900 for the PA-32-301T.

Piper built 335 Saratogas from model year 1980 to 1987, with 106 being built the first year before production declined to 26 airplanes in the 1986 model year. The Turbo Saratoga fared worse, with only 111 airplanes produced from 1980 until production was terminated in model year 1984, when two were manufactured.

In continuous production for 21 years, the Cherokee Six and Saratoga-series of fixed-gear, six-place aircraft were built in large numbers by Piper at its Vero Beach facilities. Piper built 29 Saratogas in the 1987 model year, 11 in 1988, 16 in 1989 when the base price increased to $133,300, 18 in 1990 and 10 in 1991. No Saratogas were produced or delivered in 1992.

The PA-32R-301 Saratoga SP, or Special Performance version was in development during the summer of 1978. Essentially a Lance II with a semi-tapered wing of increased span and a conventional empennage, the Saratoga SP could carry 102 gallons of fuel compared with 98 gallons for the Lance II.

As it had done with the Lance series, Piper co-developed a turbocharged version designated the PA-32R-301T Turbo Saratoga SP along with the naturally aspirated Saratoga SP. Both airplanes were powered by Textron Lycoming engines, with the standard SP using a 300 hp. IO-540-K1G5D and the turbocharged airplane the TIO-540-S1AD version rated at 300 hp.

Although a two-blade Hartzell propeller was standard fit on the Saratoga SP with a three-blade unit op-

The PA-32-301T Turbo Saratoga was introduced in 1980. A turbocharged, 300 hp. Textron Lycoming TIO-540 engine was enclosed in a new cowling. Note small fairing on nose gear strut. (Piper Aircraft Corporation)

A 200 hp. Teledyne Continental Motors TSIO-360-FB engine powered the PA-28-201T Turbo Dakota. (Teledyne Continental Motors)

tional, the Turbo Saratoga SP was factory-equipped with a Hartzell three-blade, constant-speed propeller. Piper began producing the PA-32R-301 and PA-32R-301T in late 1979 and initial deliveries to customers commenced early in 1980, when Vero Beach built 139 Saratoga SPs and 121 Turbo Saratoga SPs.

As with the other single-engine Pipers produced in the ill-fated 1980s, production of both the PA-32R-301 and PA-32R-301T declined rapidly after 1981. During eight years of manufacture, the prices of both airplanes soared while production rates stalled.

Whereas the 1980 Turbo Saratoga SP cost $88,400, the 1987 Turbo Saratoga SP sold for $179,820. Although the Saratoga SP and Turbo Saratoga SP remained in production in 1988, only 11 non-turbocharged PA-32R-301s were delivered and the turbocharged SP was not built that year. In 1989, 15 Saratoga SPs were produced followed by three in 1990 and zero in 1991. Four were delivered in 1992.

In February, 1993 Piper disclosed plans to begin deliveries in May of an upgraded version of the

Three-view of PA-28-201T Turbo Dakota. (Smithsonian Institution, National Air and Space Museum Negative Number 93-2359)

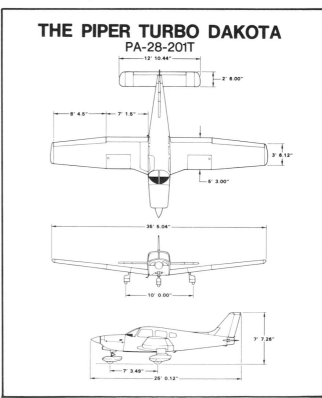

PA-32R-301 Saratoga. Designated the Saratoga II HP, the aircraft featured a redesigned engine cowling, three-blade Hartzell propeller, shades for the cabin windows and a new interior with restyled control wheels.

Other standard changes included a digital ammeter, exhaust gas temperature gauge, engine hour recorder, lighted rocker-type electrical switches on the pilot's instrument panel, heavy-duty brake system, wingtip recognition lights, super soundproofing and leather seats. Base price of the Saratoga II HP was $309,800.00 for constructor numbers 3213043 through 3213067.

Because of its immense success with the PA-28 Cherokee series and its descendants, virtually all of Piper's design efforts during the 1960s and 1970s had centered on four- and six-place, high-performance airplanes such as the Cherokee Arrow and the Saratoga. Little interest was shown in building two-place trainers for the flight training industry. Cessna had upgraded its Model 150 into the Lycoming-powered Model 152 in 1977, and Beechcraft's Model 77 Skipper had made its debut in 1979, intended primarily for instructing Aero Club members at Beechcraft facilities.

It should be noted that Pug Piper worked for Beech Aircraft Corporation in the late 1970s and helped develop the Model 77 Skipper as well as the twin-engine Model 76 Duchess. An engineer who worked closely with him during development of the Skipper said Pug wanted to install and flight-test a flaperon system on the engineering prototype aircraft instead of conventional ailerons and flaps. The engineer studied the concept and informed Pug Piper it would not work.

Undaunted, Pug insisted that the system be installed and tested. It was, and the test pilots reported un-

Piper delivered 19 PA-32-301 Saratogas in calendar year 1990 and 14 in 1991. No Saratogas were delivered in 1992. (Piper Aircraft Corporation)

satisfactory handling characteristics. Howard Piper, however, refused to believe them. After flying the airplane for 15 minutes he landed and insisted the flaperons be removed immediately and conventional controls installed. Pug Piper knew when he was wrong.

As for Piper Aircraft Corporation, the company had not marketed a two-seat trainer since the PA-22-108 Colt which had been replaced by the all-metal Cherokee 140 in 1964. In 1972 Piper was ready to reenter the trainer market and spent much time and effort discussing with flight schools and flight instructors what characteristics a new trainer should possess.

Armed with a plethora of data and opinions, the Vero Beach engineers went to work and by 1973 an experimental airplane had been completed. The low-wing aircraft featured a bulbous cockpit enclosure similar to that of the Beechcraft Skipper, and featured twin entry doors.

A trailing-beam type main landing gear and standard nose gear were employed in the design, along

Three-view of PA-32-301T Turbo Saratoga. (Smithsonian Institution, National Air and Space Museum Negative Number 93-2367)

Three-view of PA-32R-301T Turbo Saratoga SP. (Smithsonian Institution, National Air and Space Museum Negative Number 93-2369)

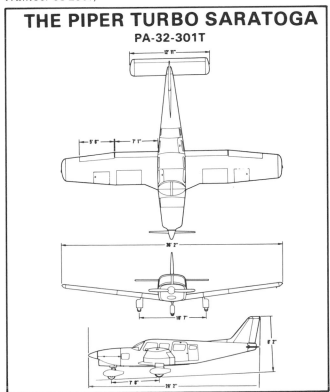

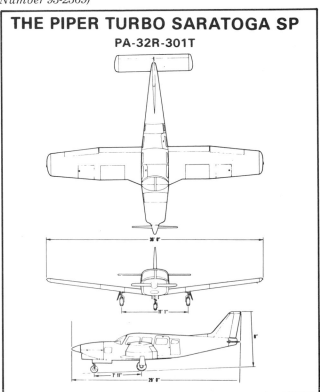

Piper co-developed the turbocharged PA-32R-301T Turbo Saratoga SP simultaneously with the Saratoga SP. Production of the turbocharged version ended in calendar year 1987. The PA-32R-301T illustrated is equipped with pneumatic wing and empennage deicers that were certified for production airplanes. (Piper Aircraft Corporation)

The first of two Saratoga II HP prototypes, constructor number 32R-321029, registered N777TH was fitted with the axisymmetric inlet cowl developed at Mississippi State University. The aircraft also featured an improved Hartzell three-blade propeller, aileron and flap gap seals and new fairings to reduce drag. (Mal Holcomb and Piper Aircraft Corporation)

with a conventional empennage configuration. A 100 hp. Teledyne Continental O-200A engine powered the aircraft. The constant-chord wing was based on the GA(W)-1 advanced airfoil.

First flown in August, 1973 the experimental airplane served as the foundation for a PA-38 prototype constructor number 38-7738001, registered N38PA. In keeping with its practice of naming aircraft after American Indian themes, the new trainer was dubbed the "Tomahawk."

A T-tail empennage was fitted and the engine was changed to a Textron Lycoming O-235-L2C rated at 112 hp. The airplane was approved for spins but its stall characteristics were not as benign as those of the Cessna 152, Beechcraft Skipper or the docile Cherokee 140. In general, the Tomahawk was easy to fly and relatively forgiving of fledgling pilots.

Like that of the Skipper, the Tomahawk's T-tail provided superior spin recovery capability—an important consideration for a basic trainer that would be used to teach spins to students and flight instructor applicants. The cabin and instrument panel were well-designed, and the wide track of the main landing gear helped make directional control easier during taxi, takeoff and landing.

The FAA granted certification for the PA-38-112 in March, 1978 and Piper began producing the Tomahawk at its Lock Haven facility. Initial customer deliveries occurred in April. Welcomed by the Piper dealers and Flite Centers it was designed to serve, the Tomahawk was priced at $15,820. The air-

Front view of the axisymmetric inlet cowling installed on the first prototype Saratoga II HP. The second prototype airplane, constructor number 32R-321042, registered N9197X, was fitted with restyled cabin windows and made its first flight on March 27, 1993, piloted by Dave Schwartz, Piper chief engineering test pilot. (Mal Holcomb and Piper Aircraft Corporation)

craft provided a much more comfortable cockpit than that of the Colt, but the noise level was too high. Fortunately, most Tomahawks were equipped with headset and intercom systems for communication between the instructor and student. In addition, visibility through the large windows was excellent—an important aid against mid-air collisions.

Unfortunately, the PA-38's initial entry into service was plagued by a series of airworthiness directives against the airframe that proved to be expensive for Tomahawk owners and operators alike. These included modifying clearance between the leading edge of the rudder and vertical stabilizer trailing edge; replacement of missing rivets in the aft main spar attach fitting; inspection and possible replacement of loose bolts in the empennage assembly; replacement of the engine mount before 1,000 hours time in service to preclude failure of the nose gear and inspection and repair of flanges on the aileron balance weights. Additional directives were issued against the Lycoming engine.

Despite its shortcomings, the Tomahawk was rolling off the Lock Haven assembly line at the rate of eight airplanes per day in 1978 and 1979, when 823 and 1,179 airplanes respectively were built. To correct the original PA-38's teething troubles, Piper revamped the airplane into the Tomahawk II for the 1981 model year. The airplane cost $22,090 and featured an improved interior, additional sound proofing materials to reduce noise and an exterior color scheme revised to distinguish the Tomahawk II from its predecessor.

After Piper dealers and other flight schools received their new Tomahawk IIs in 1981, the production rates slowed dramatically. In 1982 production of the PA-38 was terminated chiefly because demand had evaporated. Although Beech, Cessna and Piper officials did not yet realize it, the general aviation industry was entering the worst era in its history. Lock Haven built 173 PA-38-112 Tomahawk IIs in 1981 and 122 in 1982. Combined with the other three years of production a total of 2,519 airplanes were manufactured.

As it had done with its other single-engine airplanes, Piper began development in 1975 of an upgraded PA-28R Arrow with the new semi-tapered wing. Designated as the PA-28R-201 III, the airplane had an increased useable fuel capacity of 72 gallons and was powered by a Textron Lycoming

The PA-38 Tomahawk was a new basic trainer designed to replace PA-28-140 Cherokee aircraft. Deliveries began in 1978 from the Lock Haven, Pennsylvania factory. A 112 hp. Textron Lycoming O-235 engine powered the PA-38. The Tomahawk illustrated was registered N382PT, and was one of the first three production airplanes. (Piper Aircraft Corporation)

IO-360-C1C6 engine rated at 200 hp. Maximum gross weight increased by 100 lb. to 2,750 lb. compared with the previous Arrow II.

Performance, however, was essentially the same as the PA-28R-200 II, with a cruise speed of 122 knots at a 55% power setting. Piper began production of the 1977 Arrow III at Vero Beach and the company built 176 airplanes in the first year of production. Base price of the Arrow III was $37,850.

Built concurrently with the Arrow III was the PA-28R-201T that was fitted with a turbocharged, 200 hp. Teledyne Continental TSIO-360-F engine and featured a conventional empennage arrangement. To reduce costs, Piper and Continental selected a fixed-wastegate turbocharging system for the Turbo Arrow. Although simple in design and operation, the fixed-wastegate made the engine sensitive to rapid throttle movements and increased the possibility of overboosting the powerplant.

Maximum gross weight was increased by 250 lb. to 2,900 lb. Vero Beach workers produced 426 Turbo Arrow IIIs in the 1977 model year and the airplane sold for $41,800 in standard configuration. Piper was not alone in the competitive turbocharged market. Rockwell International had introduced its Commander 112TC with a 210 hp. turbocharged Textron Lycoming engine in 1976. Mooney had unveiled the new turbocharged 231 and Cessna joined the fray in

1979 with the TR182, a turbocharged, retractable gear version of the Model 182 Skylane.

Of these airplanes, Piper's Turbo Arrow proved to be the best seller. Cessna built about 1,400 R182s, Mooney built 890 231s and Rockwell was a distant fourth with slightly more than 300 112TC and 112TCA versions produced.

In the late 1970s sales were brisk for the new family of Arrows, and Piper continued to refine the Arrow III into the improved Arrow IV that entered production in 1978 for the 1979 model year. Two versions were developed. The PA-28RT-201 was powered by a naturally aspirated Textron Lycoming IO-360-C1C6 engine rated at 200 hp., and the PA-28RT-201T was powered by a 200 hp. turbocharged Teledyne Continental TSIO-360-FB engine.

Both the Arrow IV and Turbo Arrow IV had a fuselage 14 inches longer than that of the Arrow III. Base prices for the standard Arrow IV and Turbo Arrow IV were $44,510 and $49,150 respectively.

Production began at a strong pace with 265 Arrow IV and 309 Turbo Arrow IV built in 1979. By 1982 the devastating sales downturn began to harm the general aviation industry. Piper, Beech, Cessna and Mooney all experienced a marked decline in sales of single-engine, piston-powered aircraft.

Piper built only 26 Arrow IVs in 1982 before management decided to terminate production of the non-turbocharged version that year. The Turbo Arrow IV soldiered on despite troubled times, but the number built from 1982 until 1986 rapidly dwindled.

Fifty-one airplanes were manufactured in 1983, 32 in 1984, 15 in 1985 and 36 in the 1987 model year when the airplane's base price increased to $124,400. When Monroe Stuart Millar acquired Piper Aircraft Cor-

Although possessing good handling characteristics and approval for spin training, first-generation Tomahawks were plagued by a multitude of airworthiness directives issued by the FAA. Visibility from the cabin was superior to previous general aviation trainers. (Piper Aircraft Corporation)

In 1980 the improved Tomahawk II was unveiled with upgraded systems and additional sound-proofing. Deliveries began from Lock Haven in 1981. Tomahawk production ended in 1982 after 2,519 airplanes had been built. (Piper Aircraft Corporation)

The PA-28R-201 Arrow III featured a semi-tapered wing and a conventional empennage, as illustrated on the second prototype airplane, constructor number 28R-7737002, registered N3895F. (Piper Aviation Museum)

A turbocharged version of the Arrow III designated PA-28R-201T was developed in 1976. N4949F was the first production airplane. (Piper Aviation Museum)

poration in May, 1987 only the PA-28RT-201T Turbo Arrow IV remained in production. The company built only two Turbo Arrow IVs in 1988, 12 in 1989 and one in 1990. Piper built two Turbo Arrows in 1991 and none in 1992.

As for the non-turbocharged version of the Arrow, Piper delivered 10 PA-28R-201 Arrow IV airplanes in 1988, 29 in 1989, 10 in 1990 and one in 1991. Five Arrows were delivered in 1992, according to the General Aviation Manufacturers Association.

In addition to normal production Arrows built over the years, Piper built and flew experimental versions of the Arrow that were not approved for manufacture. One such design was powered by a Continental Tiara engine and was flown during 1969 and 1970, but was not produced.

In 1985 the company planned to introduce a new version of the Arrow that incorporated a one-piece windshield and a 220 hp. Teledyne Continental TSIO-360-KB2A powerplant. One airplane was flown later that year according to Roger W. Peperell and Colin M. Smith in their book titled Piper Aircraft And Their Forerunners.

Hailed by pilots and the aviation press alike as one of the most popular lightweight retractable-gear airplanes in the history of general aviation, the PA-28R Arrow exemplified Piper's tradition of selling an airplane that offered the best combination of technology, performance and value for the price.

Intended as a logical follow-on to the single-engine Arrow, a twin-engine version was developed by Piper in 1975 and later given the designation PA-44

Seminole. Featuring the fuselage and a T-tail empennage similar to that of the PA-28RT-201 Arrow IV, the Seminole incorporated Piper's semi-tapered wing as well as a larger vertical stabilizer and rudder to provide increased directional control with one-engine inoperative.

The prototype PA-44 was assigned constructor number 44-7812001, registered N998P, and was flown to develop the airplane and perform FAA certification flight tests. Instead of carrying fuel in the wings, the Seminole's bladder-type tanks were located in the aft section of the engine nacelles and each held 55 gallons of aviation fuel.

Intended primarily for use as a multi-engine trainer, the Seminole was one of three different airplanes being developed in the late 1970s for that role. Beech Aircraft Corporation had flown its PD 289 experimental aircraft in May, 1977 which developed into the Model 76 Duchess, and Grumman American's twin-engine GA-7 Cougar had been on the prowl since 1977.

Both the Duchess and Seminole were powered by two 180 hp. Textron Lycoming O-360 and left-rotation LO-360 engines, with the right propeller rotating counter-clockwise to eliminate the critical-engine issue. Grumman American's Cougar featured 160 hp. Textron Lycoming O-320 engines.

Vero Beach workers began producing the Seminole for the 1979 model year and initial deliveries commenced in July, 1978. Piper manufactured 328 PA-44-180s in the first year, followed in 1980 by 27 aircraft. In addition to the naturally aspirated PA-44s built that year, Piper produced 66 turbocharged PA-44-180T aircraft, equipped with weather radar and powered by 180 hp. Textron Lycoming TO-360-E1AD6 and left-rotation LTO-360-E1AD6 engines. Deliveries of the turbocharged Seminole began in April, 1980, for the 1981 model year.

Piper built 26 early production, turbocharged Seminoles with the original nose section that housed a landing light, but beginning in 1981 the airplanes sported a redesigned nose that protected avionic equipment and the fuel-fired cabin heater. As for the non-turbocharged Seminole, 26 airplanes also were built in the 1981 model year.

It is interesting to note that Beech flew an experimental, turbocharged version of the Duchess in January, 1979. It was unofficially known as the Model 76TC and was equipped with Textron Lycoming TO-360 engines. After a short flight test program the turbocharged Duchess project was cancelled in July, 1979.

For the 1979 model year Piper introduced the T-tail PA-28RT-201 Arrow IV and the T-tail, turbocharged PA-28RT-201T Turbo Arrow IV. A 200 hp. Teledyne Continental Motors TSIO-360 FB engine propelled the Turbo Arrow IV to a maximum speed of 178 kt. A 1980 PA-28RT-201T is illustrated in its element above the clouds. (Piper Aircraft Corporation)

Both flight schools and multi-engine flight instructors liked the Seminole, and most of the 469 airplanes produced over a four-year span earned their keep as trainers at United States and European flight training establishments. The airplane's relatively low acquisition cost and economy of operation were welcomed by customers worldwide and contributed to the Seminole's popularity.

But with three different training aircraft to choose from, the flight training market became saturated and Seminole orders declined after the first year of production. As a result, Piper ceased building the PA-44-180 in November, 1981 and terminated production of the turbocharged PA-44-180T in October, 1982. By 1989 demand existed for a limited number of new twin-engine training aircraft, prompting Piper to resume production of the non-turbocharged Seminole.

In 1989 nine airplanes were built and delivered and three Seminoles were completed and delivered to customers in 1990. No Seminoles were built in 1991, and only one aircraft was delivered in 1992. Regarding the PA-44-180's competitors, Beech built 437 Model 76 Duchess airplanes before production was halted in 1982 and Grumman American built only 115 Cougars before manufacture ended in 1979.

During the halcyon days of the 1970s when Piper was building hundreds of airplanes per month, the company had expanded to five facilities in order to meet demand. In addition to the factory locations at Lock Haven, Vero Beach and Lakeland, Piper operated a facility at Quehanna, Pennsylvania for the manufacture of prefabricated parts and components and at Renova, Pennsylvania where fiberglass parts were produced.

A sixth facility located at the municipal airport near Santa Maria, California housed production and assembly of the Piper PA-60-series Aerostar twin-

Only the Turbo Arro_ _ remained in production after the 1982 model year unti_ _0, when 10 naturally-aspirated Arrows were delivered. _ _992 only five PA-28R-201 Arrows were delivered and _ _urbocharged airplanes were produced. (Piper Aircraft _orporation)

engine business airplane, which the company had acquired from designer Ted Smith in March, 1978.

Devastated by poor sales and a growing number of product liability lawsuits in the bleak years of the 1980s, Piper's fortunes had fallen to new lows. By 1986, only the Vero Beach factory remained in operation. Lock Haven, where nearly 77,000 Piper airplanes were built in 37 years, was closed. The modern Lakeland facility was a ghost town. Quehanna and Renova were deserted, and the Santa Maria facility was padlocked.

Field inventories of unsold airplanes had swelled to alarming levels, and to reduce losses and weather the storm Lear Siegler consolidated all manufacturing operations at Vero Beach. To reduce dealer inventories, the company was forced to stop production of its small piston-powered single- and twin-engine aircraft for a period of four months in 1986. Layoffs

Three-view of PA-28RT-201 Arrow IV. (Smithsonian Institution, National Air and Space Museum Negative Number 93-2356)

Three-view of PA-28RT-201T Turbo Arrow IV. (Smithsonian Institution, National Air and Space Museum Negative Number 93-2357)

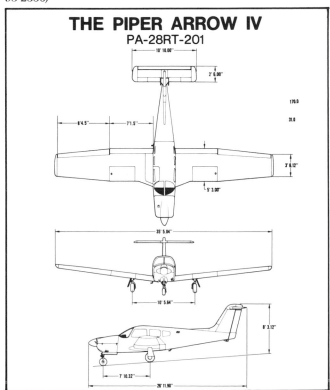

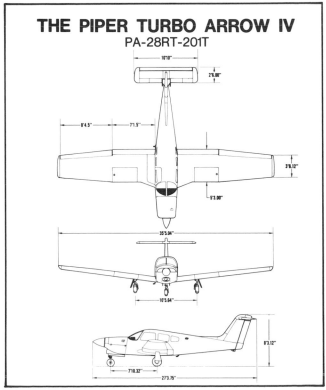

Piper's Turbo Arrow had a service ceiling of 20,000 feet and a range of 790 nautical miles at a 75% power setting. A 1990 Turbo Arrow is illustrated. (Piper Aircraft Corporation)

became commonplace and the workforce shrank to a fraction of its former size.

The highly successful Malibu and turboprop Cheyenne-series business airplanes continued to be built in limited numbers chiefly because they were more profitable than the smaller airplanes and were normally flown by professionally trained, two-pilot crews.

Therefore, Piper's exposure to lawsuits was significantly lower for the Cheyenne than it was for a Warrior II. Cessna and Beech had abandoned single-engine light aircraft in part because of such reasoning, and had shifted their core business aims to Citation business jets and the legendary King Air series respectively.

Lear Siegler was acquired in May, 1987 by the investment organization of Forstmann Little & Company, which viewed Piper's huge liability problems with disdain and quickly set about selling the company. On May 27 they sold Piper and all its assets—as well as its product liability woes—to an eager buyer and entrepreneur named Monroe Stuart Millar. He purchased Piper through his privately held company Romeo Charlie, Inc.

Millar, a World War Two fighter pilot and an active general aviation flier, was enthralled with the idea of returning a crippled and virtually impotent Piper Aircraft Corporation to its former glory. Although his intentions were genuine, Millar lacked experience in the general aviation manufacturing industry.

Caught up by Millar's enthusiasm and charisma, the aviation community hailed him as a knight on a white horse and the potential savior of the light aircraft industry in the Unites States. Indeed, Millar had grandiose plans for Piper and he acted swiftly to bring them to fruition.

Soon after taking the helm, Millar announced that Piper would resume production of its single-engine airplane product line, including the venerable PA-18 Super Cub that would be available as a production airplane or in kit form. He surprised the aviation world by introducing a two-place flight training derivative of the PA-28-161 Warrior known as the Cadet, and further stunned the industry by offering them at unheard-of low prices.

The tactic worked and Piper was soon flooded with orders for the airplane. Unfortunately, the Cadet's

base price of $45,995 for a VFR-equipped airplane did not account for any overhead costs and would prove to be a serious misstep by the company's management.

To boost sagging morale within Piper, Millar raised salaries and wages of the more than 750 workers at the Vero Beach factory, swelled the ranks of marketing and sales personnel and hired hundreds of new employees to build airplanes. By 1990 the workforce had increased to more than 1,600 people.

Millar also vowed to aggressively fight product liability cases brought against Piper and hired a group of tough, experienced lawyers he described as "meaner than junkyard dogs" to do battle in the courtroom. In the next few years, the lawyers were successful in reducing the number of cases filed against Piper as well as winning cases brought to trial.

The PA-46-350P Malibu Mirage project, already underway when Millar bought Piper, was completed and superseded the original PA-46-310P Malibu that had been in production since 1983. Within two years of Millar's arrival the Vero Beach factory was humming with activity and customers were flocking to Piper's door. Flight schools, in particular, were desperate for new two-place trainers and orders for the Cadet kept rising.

By the summer of 1989, Vero Beach workers were busy building 14 different Piper airplanes and "we will nearly triple unit production of our current Piper product line in 1989," Millar said optimistically at the time. In addition, he planned to build the two-place SwiftFury developed by Roy LoPresti at Vero Beach.

The Model LP-1 SwiftFury was a highly modified and modernized version of the post-war, two-place Globe Swift aircraft. LoPresti, a talented and highly respected aircraft engineer and designer, had joined forces with Millar in December, 1987, to form LoPresti Piper Aircraft Engineering, Inc., a subsidiary of Millars' Romeo Charlie, Inc. Millar owned 75% of the business and LoPresti owned 25%.

Unveiled in May, 1989 the sole SwiftFury prototype initially was powered by a 180 hp. Textron Lycoming engine and featured a one-piece, sliding canopy and new instrument panel as well as other modifications. During that summer LoPresti had accepted 550 customer deposits for the new aircraft. By 1990 the prototype had been fitted with a 200 hp. Textron Lycoming O-360 powerplant.

In addition to the SwiftFury program, Piper owner Monroe Stuart Millar announced in November, 1989

FLYING THE LP-1 SWIFTFURY

The LoPresti-Piper LP-1 SwiftFury was an interesting example of how advanced technology can transform an obsolete aircraft into a modern, high-performance design. In 1990, SwiftFury creator Roy LoPresti invited the author to fly the LP-1 prototype for a pilot report to be published in AVIATION WEEK & SPACE TECHNOLOGY magazine. The flight demonstrated to me how thoroughly the transformation from Globe Swift to SwiftFury had been accomplished by LoPresti and his team.

I was accompanied on the flight by Curtis R. LoPresti, senior project manager and test pilot for the SwiftFury program. During the pre-flight inspection, LoPresti said the new, one-piece windshield and sliding canopy helped the two-place aircraft attain a maximum speed of 217 mph., although the program's goal was to attain 220 mph.

In addition, he explained that the SwiftFury featured an upgraded cockpit which included a new instrument panel and a console-mounted throttle with Hands-On-Throttle-And-Stick (HOTAS) technology. The throttle's grip had switches for taxi and landing lights, wing flaps and optional speed brakes.

With the canopy open, I started the engine and taxied to Runway 11R at the Vero Beach Municipal Airport. Visibility over the nose was more than adequate because of the tall tailwheel strut, and obviated the customary S-turns necessary with many conventional-gear airplanes.

Differential braking was applied to steer the aircraft, but production SwiftFurys would have had steerable tailwheels, according to LoPresti. After engine runup, I set elevator trim for takeoff and verified that the single, large cowl flap was open fully.

LoPresti and I pulled the canopy closed and he secured the latch. Cleared for takeoff, I kept the stick full aft as I taxied into position and smoothly applied full throttle. The SwiftFury accelerated rapidly. Forward visibility during the takeoff roll was excellent.

Directional control was good as the rudder became effective above 30 mph. At 40 mph. indicated airspeed I eased the stick forward to raise the tail. At 60 mph. I moved the stick aft slightly and the airplane flew itself off the runway. The landing gear was retracted at 85 mph., and I adjusted pitch attitude to maintain a 120 mph. climb airspeed.

To reduce drag, LoPresti had designed the Swift-Fury's main and tailwheel gears to be fully enclosed when retracted. The main gear featured inner doors that were sequenced to close and cover the wheelwell when the gear was retracted or extended.

Other major changes that set the SwiftFury apart from its Globe Swift ancestor included the wing, which was moved forward 4 inches and contained two integral gasoline tanks that held 59 gallons of useable fuel. In addition to relocating the wing to reduce drag, the fuselage contour aft of the cockpit was redesigned. The aluminum alloy skin panels were flush-riveted and butt-joined to further decrease drag, according to Roy LoPresti.

During the climb, I made shallow banks to check for other aircraft. The aileron and elevator stick forces were extremely light, chiefly because of ball bearings installed throughout both control systems. After leveling off at 7,500 feet above the Atlantic Ocean

The LoPresti-Piper LP-1 SwiftFury was a highly-modified version of the postwar GC-1 Globe Swift. The prototype illustrated was powered by a 200 hp. Textron Lycoming engine. Maximum speed was 217 mph. The SwiftFury had excellent handling characteristics and was capable of performing fundamental aerobatic maneuvers. (Roy LoPresti and AVIATION WEEK & SPACE TECHNOLOGY)

east of Vero Beach, I conducted a mild aerobatic routine beginning with a loop.

At an entry airspeed of 170 mph., the SwiftFury performed the loop with ease and required no more than 3.5g to complete the maneuver. The light, pleasant elevator control force was retained throughout the loop. Following another three consecutive loops, I applied maximum power and eased the nose upward to obtain 140 mph. for an aileron roll to the left. Once again, stick force was light and the aircraft's roll response was excellent. The airplane completed the maneuver in less than 3 seconds. I found the airplane performed loops and aileron rolls easily and with little physical effort by the pilot.

The LP-1 SwiftFury, despite its 10g positive and 4g negative ultimate load factor, was not intended to perform more complex aerobatics such as outside loops. Limit load factor was 6g positive and 3g negative.

With the aerobatic routines completed, I descended to 5,500 feet, reduced throttle and slowed the aircraft to evaluate its slow-flight and stall behavior. At 80 mph. indicated airspeed, the SwiftFury responded quickly to pitch and roll inputs from the stick as I maintained altitude at bank angles up to 60 degrees.

Rolling level out of a right turn I decreased power to idle. As the airplane slowed, flight controls remained highly effective as the wing approached its critical angle of attack. At 63 mph. indicated airspeed an aerodynamic buffet occurred, followed almost immediately at 61 mph. by the stall break.

The break was positive and clean. I was able to hold the stick fully aft in the stall without aggravating the airplane. The SwiftFury simply buffeted and attempted to put its nose down and resume flying. As the landing gear and flaps were extended for an approach-to-landing stall, there was little pitch change and the electrically operated elevator trim system rapidly retrimmed the aircraft. The controls remained effective as airspeed slowly decreased to 65 mph.

The stall break occurred at 60 mph. and was preceded by a strong, although transitory, aerodynamic buffet. The break was clean but more pronounced than with gear and flaps retracted. I relaxed back pressure on the stick, added full power and the airplane immediately recovered from the stall.

To improve slow-speed and stall behavior, LoPresti

112

had mounted a stall strip on the inboard leading edge of each wing. Wing fences inboard of each aileron further improved airflow patterns and improved handling characteristics.

After completing a few additional stalls, I began an initial descent toward the Vero Beach airport at 2,000 feet per minute. The aircraft's 270 mph. Vne (Never Exceed airspeed) not only allowed for rapid descents in smooth air, but permitted the SwiftFury to easily mix with other high-speed aircraft in terminal areas. During the flight back to the airport, I paused at 3,500 feet to indulge in a few more aileron rolls before reluctantly resuming the descent.

We were cleared to land on Runway 11R. After entering base leg per the control tower's instructions, I extended the landing gear and selected 20 degrees of flaps using the throttle-mounted HOTAS switch. On final approach at 80 mph. I extended full flaps. Only minor trim changes were required to reconfigure the airplane for landing.

LoPresti suggested I make a wheel landing instead of the customary three-point procedure, chiefly because the hard rubber tailwheel tire often caused the tail to bounce. Over the runway threshold, I slowly reduced power and the main gear tires touched down gently a few hundred feet beyond the numbers. The rudder remained effective throughout the landing rollout and I had no difficulty maintaining directional control.

Complying with LoPresti's previous instruction, I held the stick forward to keep the tail flying as long as possible. Finally, the tailwheel came down with a slight thud as I turned off the runway and taxied back to Lopresti's facility.

Although I had flown the airplane for only 1.5 hours, the SwiftFury was both fun to fly and a true pilot's airplane. Its fighter-like handling was balanced by docile low-speed behavior, and the airplane made no unusual demands on the pilot from takeoff to landing. Had it been produced, the LP-1 SwiftFury would have put excitement back into general aviation flying.

that the famed Lock Haven factory would be reopened to assemble the PA-31-350 Navajo Chieftain, to be followed later by other Navajo models.

"The Piper North projects are exciting ones that I have long wanted to start," Millar told the aviation media. He expected to employ 100 people at Lock Haven by the end of 1990, and planned to have 700 workers busy building Navajos by the end of 1995. John Piper was named as president and William T. Piper, a grandson of William T. Piper, Sr., was to be vice president of Piper North.

In only two short years it appeared that Millar had delivered on his promise to resurrect Piper Aircraft Corporation from oblivion. Operating under the new motto "We Are Flying," the company was building a full array of airplanes from the Cadet to the Cheyenne 400.

LoPresti had worked wonders with the SwiftFury and production seemed assured. The immortal Super Cub was back. Piper North would soon be building the venerable Navajo. Millar had become the darling of the aviation press. Although success and glory appeared to be within his grasp, it was not to be.

Amid all the hype and a $200 million order backlog, in 1989 the castle Millar had begun to build suddenly began to crumble. There were serious problems at Vero Beach, and chief among these was a chronic lack of cash flow. In his enthusiasm to get Piper off the ground, Millar had attempted to do too much too fast.

Part of the problem centered on the Cadet. In the 1989 model year, Piper sold the airplane for $57,495 equipped for VFR flight operations. The IFR version cost only $66,495. Such prices virtually assured large orders, but Piper management knew the company would lose money on every Cadet it built.

By early 1990, Piper had buyers for more than 400 Cadets and an order backlog "that has become unmanageable," C. Raymond Johnson, president and chief executive officer for Piper, said. He explained that the Cadet "does not carry its weight in overhead" and that the price "covers only the cost of labor and materials."

There was not enough money to buy the thousands of vendor-supplied parts and key, high-dollar items such as engines, propellers and avionics needed to keep production flowing and meet delivery com-

Piper began delivering the Seminole in 1978 from its Vero Beach, Florida, factory and in 1980 unveiled the Turbo Seminole powered by two turbocharged Textron Lycoming L/TO-360 engines. (Piper Aircraft Corporation)

mitments. A few vendors were willing to supply parts on credit, but most demanded payment before conducting further business.

Reacting to the problem, in January, 1990 Millar laid off 449 workers—27% of the workforce—and furloughed more than 120 additional employees in February when Piper suspended normal operations at Vero Beach for a two-week period beginning on February 26.

In addition, the staff of LoPresti Piper Aircraft Engineering Company went on a four-day workweek to further reduce costs and the SwiftFury's future suddenly became uncertain. Manufacture of the small, single-engine product line rapidly slowed to a crawl as about 400 workers struggled to complete, and more importantly deliver $3 million Cheyenne IIIA turboprop aircraft and $370,000 Malibu Mirages in an effort to increase revenues.

The company's chief lending institution, Congress Financial Corporation, provided additional cash in March, 1990 that allowed Piper to pay some of the growing debts it owed to vendors and suppliers. About 475 employees were recalled to work that month after the two-week suspension and Piper management cancelled plans to institute a 32-hour workweek. Despite the recall, the company's woes continued to worsen and the outlook remained bleak.

To help deflect the doom and gloom that hung over Vero Beach and its many troubles, in May, 1990 Piper announced Project Phoenix—a modified Malibu Mirage featuring twin Pratt & Whitney Canada PT6B-35F turboprop engines mounted side-by-side in the nose section. The engines would drive a single propeller through a special, Soloy Dual Pac gearbox.

Hailed as a "new class of business, personal and special mission twin-engine aircraft" by Piper president C. Raymond Johnson, Project Phoenix had been initiated in 1988 as another of Millar's programs to promote Piper's future. Without funds to develop or build the airplane and with Piper slowly sinking in a sea of red ink, the ill-fated Phoenix proposal was quickly forgotten both by Piper and the aviation press.

In June, 1990 Millar and California-based Transcisco Industries, Inc., reached an agreement whereby Transcisco would make a substantial investment in the company and take over sales and distribution of generic, non-proprietary parts common to all Piper airplanes. The agreement was cancelled in July because of legal problems and unresolved business issues between the two companies, according to senior Piper officials.

In the wake of the Transcisco failure, Piper furloughed another 170 workers in July and made deep cuts into what was described as "top-heavy management and marketing staffs," a Piper official said. About 62 product support people were dismissed in addition to 108 production line employees laid off during the summer.

With hopes of reopening the Lock Haven factory rapidly evaporating, officials of Piper's parent company Romeo Charlie, Inc., terminated their November, 1989 agreement with the Commonwealth of Pennsylvania to begin operations at the Piper North facility. Millar also placed the empty Lakeland, Florida, factory on the real estate market in August in a further effort to raise cash.

Still looking for an investment partner, in the summer of 1990 Millar began talks with French light air-

The PA-44-180 Seminole essentially was a twin-engine Arrow with an extended nose section. Designed for the multi-engine trainer market of the late 1970s, the Seminole was also popular as a personal and business aircraft. (Piper Aircraft Corporation)

craft manufacturer Socata's Aerospatiale General Aviation division. Aerospatiale produced a series of attractive, four-place airplanes including the TB-9 Tampico trainer and TB-20 Trinidad.

On October 24 the two companies signed a Letter of Intent specifying that Aerospatiale would conduct due diligence and investigate the possibility of purchasing Piper Aircraft Corporation. By early 1991 Aerospatiale officials had decided to proceed with the transaction, but reluctance by senior Piper officials to accept financial terms forced Aerospatiale to withdraw its offer.

As for LoPresti Piper Aircraft Engineering, Inc., the SwiftFury project had been costing Millar about $50,000 per week and he already had spent millions of dollars to develop the prototype. LoPresti estimated it would require at least $5 million to certify the airplane and build tooling to produce the sleek monoplane.

That was additional millions of dollars Millar did not have nor would likely possess in the future. The

Three-view of PA-44-180 Seminole. (Smithsonian Institution, National Air and Space Museum Negative Number 93-2371)

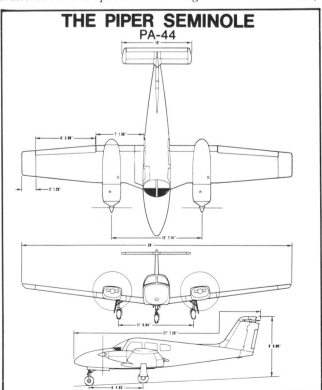

During initial development of the Saratoga SP series, Piper flew a turbocharged, T-tail Lance II fuselage equipped with semi-tapered wings that was unofficially known as the Turbo Lance III. Plans to certify the T-tail configuration were abandoned in favor of a conventional empennage. (Piper Aircraft Corporation)

SwiftFury project was suspended and LoPresti's little band of talented workers ceased operations in December, 1990.

Undaunted, LoPresti continued to search for an investor and in July, 1991 he and business associate Roy A. Henderson reached an agreement with Monroe Stuart Millar to acquire all rights to the SwiftFury design.

They formed LoPresti Flight Concepts in 1991 to continue development and pursue certification of the airplane. In concert with his three sons, LoPresti also formed LoPresti Speed Merchants to develop and market drag-reducing modifications for a wide variety of Piper single- and twin-engine airplanes.

Millar and his Piper Aircraft Corporation were on the ropes in the summer of 1991. Investors were not forthcoming chiefly because they feared the ramifications of product liability lawsuits, and nearly 1,000 vendors were refusing to supply parts and other key aircraft components to the company.

As a result, production of the lucrative Cheyenne and Malibu Mirage came to a halt. With no airplanes to build, the Vero Beach workforce was reduced to less than 40 people compared with nearly 1,800 employees early in 1990.

When yet another group of would-be investors failed to deliver promised cash to Piper's empty coffers in June, 1991, Millar was running out of money and options. With his back to the wall Millar chose the last, although difficult, recourse that remained available to him.

In West Palm Beach, Florida on July 1 he voluntarily filed a petition as debtor-in-possession for protection under Chapter 11 of the United States Bankruptcy Code. By doing so, Piper was automatically shielded from its creditors and from lawsuits.

When Millar filed the petition, Piper Aircraft Cor-

poration had assets worth $75 million and liabilities totalling $47 million and owed more than $20 million to secured creditors and about $8 million to unsecured creditors.

Chief lender Congress Financial Corporation once again came to Piper's rescue. In August, 1991 a six-month, interim finance package was arranged that would permit Piper to resume production of much-needed spare parts. About 40 workers were recalled that month to begin parts production.

An acute shortage of Piper parts in the field had driven up prices and supplies were becoming increasingly scarce. The company had a parts backlog worth $5.1 million in July and had reduced that amount by $1 million in late October, 1991.

In addition to building parts, a portion of the financing was used to complete four Malibu Mirages, four PA-28R-201 Arrows, one PA-34-220T Seneca III, one PA-42 Cheyenne IIIA and one PA-42 Cheyenne 400 that was delivered on September 13, 1991, to Korean Air Airlines for advanced pilot training. One of the Mirages also was delivered in September.

As a result of the bankruptcy proceedings, Charles M. Suma succeeded C. Raymond Johnson as president and chief operating officer of the company. Suma had held a number of managerial positions with Piper after joining the company in 1976. Johnson assumed the title of vice chairman to assist Millar in discussions with potential investors.

With Piper shielded by bankruptcy protection, a new wave of would-be investors stepped forward to make their bid. One of the first proposals received by Millar came from the Cyrus Eaton Group International, Ltd. The organization intended to form an international company with headquarters in Canada to produce and distribute the Piper product line. Plans initially called for the airplanes to be built in Eastern Europe or Russia.

Although the transaction was scheduled to be completed by January 15, 1992, problems with financing arose and the Eaton Group did not proceed with its proposal. Other investors also made their offers, but none were finalized.

After discussions with the United States Bankruptcy Court in Florida early in 1992, Piper officials were able to secure additional financing and received a time extension for filing a reorganization plan. The money was used to complete and deliver more than 60 new airplanes including 23 Cadet

The PA-32R-301 Saratoga SP series was developed in the late 1970s and featured a semi-tapered wing mated to the Lance II airframe with a conventional empennage. Deliveries began in 1980. (Piper Aircraft Corporation)

trainers, four Warrior IIs, one Dakota, six Malibu Mirages, 14 Archer IIs, one Super Cub, four Saratogas, nine Seneca IIIs and one Seminole.

Revenues from the sales of the airplanes were used to help repay Congress Financial Corporation. In addition, Piper was given until July 31, 1992, to submit its plan to reorganize the company, but the court later approved two additional extensions.

In June, 1992 the Lakeland factory was sold for $5,500,000 to Firewolf, Inc. and by September, 1992 Piper had paid in full its $12 million debt to Congress Financial Corporation. By early 1993 the backlog of spare parts orders had been reduced to less than $2.7 million from a high of $5.3 million. As limited production was slowly resumed employees were recalled to the Vero Beach factory, and the workforce had increased to more than 330 employees by February, 1993.

When he took command of Piper Aircraft Corporation in 1987, Millar had plans to return the ailing company to its former glory. Unfortunately, his good intentions were derailed by lawsuits, questionable management and fiscal practices as well as overall weak demand for new light aircraft.

In May, 1992 a frustrated and bitter Monroe Stuart Millar resigned as chairman of Piper Aircraft Corporation. He was no longer directly associated with the operation of the company on a day-to-day basis, and instead became involved in furthering discussions with potential buyers interested in acquiring Piper, according to company officials.

Perhaps justifiably, Millar was angered about what had happened and publicly lashed out at the legal system he chiefly blamed for his demise and that of Piper Aircraft Corporation. Before his departure, friend and business associate A. Stone Douglass had acquired Romeo Charlie, Inc., from Millar, but the transaction was subject to approval by the creditors and the court.

Douglass became the company's chief executive officer and Charles M. Suma was retained as president. Early in 1993 the company was struggling to emerge from bankruptcy.

Despite its problems, Piper Aircraft Corporation

The Seminole was not produced in the 1983 through 1988 calendar years, but manufacture was resumed for the 1989 model year when eight airplanes were delivered. Four were delivered in 1990, zero in 1991 and only one in 1992. (Piper Aircraft Corporation)

delivered 85 new single- and twin-engine airplanes in calendar year 1992 that generated $39 million in revenues. Piper officials remained optimistic about the future. In 1993 they planned to produce 120 new aircraft worth $56 million. "The projections (for 1993) are conservative," and the market for small aircraft "will be bigger than we are expecting," according to Suma.

Regardless of the company's repeated attempts to emerge from bankruptcy and official optimism for the future, Piper Aircraft Corporation faced serious challenges. The thousands of Piper aircraft owners and operators around the world, however, hoped that the company would survive and reestablish itself as a major force in the general aviation industry.

LoPresti Piper Aircraft Engineering Company developed the Swiftfire as a potential two-place military trainer powered by a 420 shp. Allison 250-B17-C turboprop engine. Photograph shows Roy LoPresti (left seat) and the author preparing to fly the Swiftfire in March, 1989. (Roy LoPresti)

CHAPTER NINE
FROM NAVAJO TO CHEYENNE

In 1965, Piper Aircraft Corporation was flying high. The Cherokee series of single-engine airplanes were gaining in popularity and both the Aztec and Twin Comanche had become the best-selling twin-engine airplanes in their respective classes. Despite a diverse and popular product line, Piper lacked a larger, multi-engine airplane that could do battle with the Beechcraft A65 Queen Air and Aero Commander 500-series aircraft that dominated the market in the mid-1960s.

With William T. Piper, Sr.'s approval, the engineers at Lock Haven went to work early in 1963 designing an all-new airplane that would be Piper's initial foray into the highly competitive cabin-class arena. Their efforts culminated more than one year later in the PA-31 prototype, constructor number 31-1, registered N3100E, which made its first flight in September, 1964. Larger and more powerful than its Aztec sibling, the PA-31 was powered by two Lycoming TIO-540-A1A engines each developing 310 hp.

The turbocharged powerplants maintained sea level horsepower to an altitude of 16,000 feet and delivered 75% of their rated power up to 25,000 feet. A large, two-piece airstair door installed on the left side of the fuselage provided easy entry and exit from the spacious cabin, which could be configured for six or eight seats. The interior measured 15 feet 10 inches from the forward cockpit bulkhead to the aft cabin bulkhead.

Mr. Piper took a keen interest in the PA-31 project and explained to the aviation press that the aircraft

"was in a completely new category" and would sell for less than $100,000. By autumn, 1965 the PA-31 had been officially named "Navajo," and the sole prototype N3100E had been modified with two additional cabin windows on each side of the fuselage bringing the total number of windows to 10. In addition, the engines were housed in longer, more streamlined nacelles to further reduce drag.

Two pre-production airplanes joined the original PA-31 in the FAA certification program that was completed in spring, 1966. None other than the senior William Piper himself accepted the Navajo's Type Certificate from Oscar Bakke, director of the FAA's Eastern Region. Bakke and his staff of inspectors were responsible for certifying the airplane.

Production of the Navajo began in the autumn of 1966 and initial deliveries occurred in March, 1967. With a base price of $89,500, the Navajo not only beat William Piper's price goal but was the least expensive, medium-weight piston twin available.

The airframe was corrosion-proofed at no extra cost and Piper offered the Navajo in Standard, Executive and Commuter configurations. Standard seating was for six occupants, the Executive version seated four in a club arrangement and two fold-away tables were mounted on the cabin sidewalls.

Eight passengers could be seated in the Commuter variant. Two baggage compartments, one in the nose section and another aft of the cabin, together held up to 350 lb. To broaden the airplane's market appeal the Navajo was offered with a choice of two engines: the naturally aspirated Lycoming IO-540-M rated at 300 hp. in the PA-31-300, and the turbocharged Lycoming TIO-540-A1A that developed 310 hp. in the PA-31. The PA-31 cost $97,290 and had a higher maximum gross weight of 6,500 lb.

Piper began development of the PA-31 Navajo in 1963. The prototype airplane, constructor number 31-1, registered N3100E flew in September of that year. Two 310 hp. Lycoming TIO-540 engines powered the aircraft. (Piper Aviation Museum)

Instrument panel of an early production Navajo. (Piper Aviation Museum)

Two additional cabin windows were added to the prototype during the Navajo's development program conducted at Piper's Lock Haven facility. FAA certification was granted in 1966 and production began at Lock Haven in March, 1967. The Navajo's base price was $89,500 for the 300 hp. PA-31-300 version, and $97,290 for the 310 hp., turbocharged PA-31 variant. (Piper Aviation Museum)

In terms of performance the turbocharged PA-31 had a cruise speed of 247 mph. at 75% power at an altitude of 23,500 feet and a maximum speed of 260 mph., easily qualifying it as the fastest Piper in the family tribe. To accommodate demand for the Navajo, Piper expanded the Lock Haven factory and was building one airplane per day by June, 1967. Initial production airplanes had been in the field for more than three months and company demonstrators were flying in Europe and South America as well as the United States.

Piper retained seven airplanes at the factory for additional engineering work and one of the pre-production Navajos had accumulated more than 700 hours by summer, 1967. When Lock Haven built 91 PA-31 turbocharged Navajos for the 1967 model year compared with only a few of the PA-31-300 versions, it was obvious to Piper management that the turbocharged variant would dominate production. Buyers strongly preferred the 310 hp. engines and in 1969 Piper ceased production of the naturally aspirated Navajo after building only 14 airplanes.

As the Navajo set new standards of comfort and speed in the cabin-class market, Piper was setting records for exporting its products. In 1965 the United States Commerce Department had presented Piper with the government's coveted "E" award for export activity. That year, 877 airplanes or 19.7% of Piper's sales volume were attributed to the export business. In spring, 1967 the company delivered its 10,000th export aircraft, Cherokee Six constructor number 32-40042, to Wilken Air Services in Mombasa, Nairobi, Kenya.

With domestic and international Navajo sales forging ahead, Piper improved the increasingly popular twin in 1970 by introducing the PA-31 Navajo B. Most of the changes were minor, such as a more efficient air conditioning system, optional wing nacelle lockers and utility door, a cockpit hatch for the pilot to enter the airplane if the airstair door could not be opened after cargo was loaded (the door also served as an escape hatch), and an improved electrical system. Engines were the 310 hp. Lycoming TIO-540-A/S similar to those installed in the original PA-31, driving two-blade propellers, although three-blade units were optional. Produced for the 1971 model year, 58 Navajo Bs were built followed by 110 in 1972 and 76 in 1973. Twenty airplanes were built at Lock Haven

the next year, when Piper moved Navajo production to its new facility at Lakeland, Florida where 68 additional Navajo B aircraft were manufactured in 1974.

Lakeland became home to PA-31 production beginning in the 1975 model year when the upgraded PA-31 Navajo C was introduced. No major changes were incorporated into the new variant, although the engines were changed to Textron Lycoming TIO-540-A2C versions.

A parallel development with the Navajo C was the Navajo C/R that featured counter-rotating propellers. Also introduced in the 1975 model year, the airplane featured a left-rotation Textron Lycoming LTIO-540-F2BD engine on the right side with a standard TIO-540-F2BD powerplant on the left. The engines each developed 325 hp. and were fitted with three-blade propellers. Lengthened nacelle compart-

Three-view of PA-31 Navajo. (Smithsonian Institution, National Air and Space Museum Negative Number 93-2360)

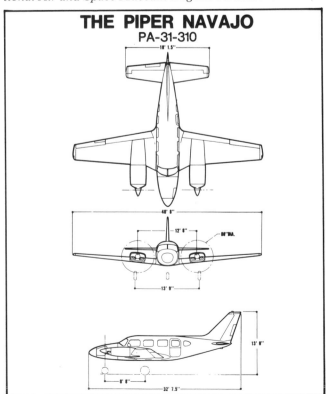

The improved PA-31 Navajo B entered production in 1971. Navajo N6796L, constructor number 31-537 was one of two pre-production airplanes used for development. (Piper Aircraft Corporation)

ments, which could house small, optional gasoline tanks to boost useable fuel capacity to 236 gallons, were installed and helped to distinguish the C/R from the standard Navajo C.

Workers at Lakeland built a total of 72 PA-31 Navajo C and PA-31-325 C/R airplanes for the 1975 model year. Navajo sales continued strong throughout the late 1970s and into the early 1980s before declining. More than 460 aircraft were built during the 1976 to 1979 model years, with production falling to 77 airplanes in 1981.

By 1983 the sluggish general aviation market in the United States forced Piper to terminate PA-31 production. Only 19 Navajos were built in that model year, with the last airplane being completed in September. The company produced 1,785 Navajos from 1967 through the 1983 model year.

Piper's rugged PA-31 had proved itself in the global marketplace and would provide the basis for a number of advanced versions of the airplane including the Chieftain, the PA-31-350 T-1020 and the Pressurized Navajo. More importantly, the PA-31 would ultimately evolve into the turboprop Cheyenne series.

The first of these advanced, derivative aircraft was the PA-31-350 Chieftain in development at Lock Haven by 1971. Using the basic Navajo airframe, Piper engineers lengthened the fuselage two feet and added a cargo door on the left side to facilitate loading.

Two additional windows were included on each side of the fuselage and the cabin floor was strengthened to accept heavier loads per square foot of area. Max-

imum gross weight was increased to 7,000 lb. To handle the extra weight, 350 hp. Textron Lycoming TIO-540-J2DB and left-rotation LTIO-540-J2DB engines were fitted, with the right propeller rotating counter-clockwise as with the PA-39 Twin Comanche and the PA-34 Seneca.

In addition to the Chieftain's role as a corporate and air taxi aircraft, Piper Aircraft Corporation was tailoring the airplane for the burgeoning commuter airline market that had experienced significant expansion in the late 1960s and early 1970s. A number of different airplanes were performing that role in 1972 when the PA-31-350 began entering service.

Beechcraft's venerable Model 18 was soldiering on in modified form and some of the aging aircraft had been equipped with Pratt & Whitney Canada PT6A-series turboprop engines. The 9-place Beechcraft Model 70 Queen Airliner was being sold in small numbers as well.

In commuter-aircraft guise the new Chieftain would compete against these two airplanes, and the turboprop Beechcraft Model 99 Airliner and the piston-powered Cessna 402 Utilitwin. Beech had introduced the 15-place Model 99 in 1967, and the eight-place 402B made its debut the same year.

Three prototype aircraft were built to develop the Chieftain, but the second was damaged in the disastrous flood that occurred in June, 1972 and was scrapped. Initial deliveries of the Chieftain began early in 1973 from factories at Lock Haven and Lakeland.

As with the PA-31 Navajo, the production schedule for 1973 was split between the two facilities and was later transferred entirely to Lakeland. Lock Haven built 121 Navajo Chieftains in 1973 and 132 in 1974. Lakeland manufactured 97 PA-31-350 Chieftains in 1974.

The PA-31 Navajo C made its debut in the 1975 model year, along with the Navajo C/R powered by 325 hp. Textron Lycoming L/TIO-540 engines with counter-rotating propellers. (Piper Aviation Museum)

The right engine's propeller of the Navajo C/R rotated counter-clockwise to reduce the effect of assymetrical thrust with one-engine inoperative. (Piper Aviation Museum)

In 1973 Piper began delivering the PA-31-350 Navajo Chieftain. Designed as a 10-seat commuter transport and business aircraft, the Chieftain featured a lengthened fuselage and additional cabin windows. Maximum gross weight increased to 7,000 lb. Two 350 hp. Textron Lycoming L/TIO-540 engines powered the aircraft. (Piper Aircraft Corporation)

Production of the PA-31-350 Chieftain was terminated in 1984 after 1,825 airplanes had been built. (Piper Aircraft Corporation) ▶

When demand for upgraded Navajo commuter airliners occurred in the late 1970s, Piper responded in 1981 with not only a new airplane but also a new organization to administer the program. Instead of selling aircraft through its network of dealers and distributors, Piper established a separate division to communicate directly with commuter and regional airline operators whose special needs and requirements demanded rapid response and unfailing product support.

To equip the regional and commuter airlines, Piper

Three-view of PA-31-325 Navajo C/R. (Smithsonian Institution, National Air and Space Museum Negative Number 93-2361)

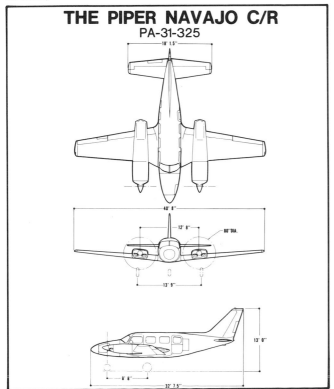

THE PIPER NAVAJO C/R
PA-31-325

introduced the PA-31-350 T-1020. Essentially an 11-place Chieftain in utilitarian dress, the aircraft was powered by Textron Lycoming TIO-540-J2B and left-rotation LTIO-540-J2B engines each rated at 350 hp. The landing gear was strengthened and the fuel system was redesigned to provide simplified operation and ease of maintenance. The lightweight transport was approved under the Chieftain's type certificate and the T-1020 entered production at Lakeland in late 1980. Deliveries began early in 1981.

That year Piper expanded the T-1000-series program by developing the PA-31T3 T-1040. Intended to compete against the upgraded Beechcraft C99 Airliner, the T-1040 was powered by Pratt & Whitney Canada PT6A-11 turboprop engines each rated at 500 shp. The T-1040's wings, empennage and nose section were borrowed from the turboprop Cheyenne I business aircraft.

Seating up to nine occupants in its Chieftain cabin, the T-1040 could be equipped with a cargo pod mounted under the fuselage. Twenty-four airplanes were built at the Lock Haven factory before production ended late in 1984. An additional 21 piston-powered T-1020 airplanes had been built when production ended at the Lakeland, Florida facility and the factory was closed in October, 1985.

A further development of the Chieftain and the T-1020 was the PA-31-353, of which Piper built one prototype known as the PA-31-353 T-1020 and one pre-production aircraft designated as the PA-31-353 Chieftain in 1982 and 1984 respectively. The engines for both versions were the 350 hp. Textron Lycoming TIO-540-X48 and LTIO-540-X48 featuring modifications to rotate the propellers counter-clockwise on the left side and clockwise on the right side.

A major change was the incorporation of wings from the PA-31P-350 Mojave and the horizontal stabilizer and elevator from the turboprop PA-31T3 T-1040. The Mojave wings increased overall span four feet compared with the Chieftain's. Maximum gross

The PA-31-350 T-1020 transport was a derivative of the Chieftain series. Designed for the regional airline market, the T-1020 could accommodate 11 passengers. (Doug Smith)

◄ *Piper introduced the PA-31P Pressurized Navajo in 1970. Designed as a fast, comfortable twin-engine business aircraft, the Pressurized Navajo competed against the Beechcraft Model 60 Duke and Cessna 421B Golden Eagle. (Piper Aircraft Corporation)*

weight was boosted by 300 lb. and the useful load was increased accordingly.

Although the new Chieftain and the improved T-1020 showed promise, Piper did not produce either aircraft primarily because of declining Navajo sales and lack of a firm market. The two PA-31-353 airplanes eventually were dismantled.

As for the standard PA-31-350 Navajo Chieftain, Piper manufactured 1,825 of the rugged airplanes from 1973 through the 1984 model year when production was terminated. Many Chieftains were flown by small commuter airlines and air taxi and charter companies, but the airplane also proved popular as a business aircraft and corporate shuttle.

Another derivative spawned by the PA-31 design was the PA-31P Pressurized Navajo. Developed in 1966 at the same time and for the same market as the sleek Beechcraft Model 60 Duke, the PA-31P featured a pressurized cabin that seated six occupants. The airplane had a maximum speed of 243 knots.

Beechcraft's mighty Duke seated four passengers in comfort and could accommodate eight in an optional configuration. The airplane had a cruise speed of 278 mph. at 25,000 feet. Both the PA-31P and the Duke were powered by turbocharged Textron Lycoming engines, with the Pressurized Navajo using 425 hp. TIGO-541-E1A6 geared powerplants. The Duke was fitted with 380 hp. TIO-541-E1A4 engines.

The Pressurized Navajo was based on the PA-31-350 but the fuselage featured fewer windows of reduced size as well as a smaller cockpit windshield because of the pressurized cabin. The prototype aircraft first flew in March, 1968 and the Lock Haven factory began production early in 1970.

Beech's Duke and Piper's Pressurized Navajo battled each other in the owner-flown, cabin-class market and both found eager buyers. The PA-31P Navajo lacked the Duke's unique appearance but cost less, although the Duke was faster and was capable of flying at higher altitudes than the heavier PA-31P.

Piper terminated production of the Pressurized

Navajo in 1977 after 259 airplanes had been built at Lock Haven. As for the flamboyant Duke, Beech ceased production in 1982 after building 596 aircraft.

In 1982-1983 Piper revived the Pressurized Navajo theme when it developed the PA-31P-350 Mojave. Borrowing from the turboprop Cheyenne series, the Mojave had the pressurized fuselage of the Cheyenne I mated to an empennage from the PA-31-350 Navajo Chieftain.

Chieftain wings were fitted, although the overall span was increased four feet and structural modifications were made for additional strength. The Mojave

Three-view of PA-31-350 Navajo Chieftain. (Smithsonian Institution, National Air and Space Museum Negative Number 93-2362)

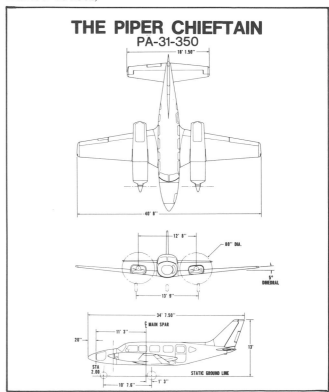

THE PIPER CHIEFTAIN
PA-31-350

The PA-31P series were powered by 425 hp. turbocharged, geared Textron Lycoming TGIO-541 engines and had a maximum speed of 243 kt. and a service ceiling of 29,000 feet. Piper built 259 Pressurized Navajos before production ended in 1977. (Piper Aircraft Corporation)

In 1984 Piper built 50 PA-31P-350 Mojave aircraft before production was terminated that year. The pressurized Mojave was powered by two Textron Lycoming L/TIO-540 engines with the right engine's propeller rotating counter-clockwise. Mojave constructor number 31P-8314002, registered N9198Y was one of two PA-31P-350 prototypes built. (Piper Aircraft Corporation)

was powered by Textron Lycoming TIO-540-V2AD and left-rotation LTIO-540-V2AD engines, each rated at 350 hp.

When Piper introduced the PA-31P-350 in 1984 the market for such an aircraft was weak, chiefly because of the dearth of general aviation sales that were beginning to seriously affect the industry's health. Only 50 of the twin-engine airplanes were built by Lock Haven workers before Mojave production was terminated in June, 1984.

It is interesting to note that when the Pressurized Navajo was developed in the mid-1960s, Piper Aircraft Corporation management already had decided to flight-test a PA-31 Navajo fitted with turboprop engines. Until that time, popular business airplanes such as Beech's Queen Air, Cessna's Model 320 Skyknight and Piper's Navajo were powered by reciprocating engines, but by the mid-1960s the turboprop engine had established itself as the powerplant of choice for medium-weight business aircraft.

In 1964 Beech Aircraft Corporation had been the first to enter the turboprop market when it introduced the Model 65-90 King Air, which quickly established Beech as the industry leader. Since May, 1963 Beech engineers had been flying a Model 87 Queen Air testbed equipped with Pratt & Whitney Canada PT6A-6 engines, and from that aircraft developed the United States Army's NU-8F lightweight transport. With military contracts in hand, company president Mrs. Olive Ann Beech approved production of a commercial version that became the legendary King Air.

Piper management was impressed by the success of the King Air program and by 1966 had similar aspirations of developing a turboprop business aircraft.

Beech had proved that there was demand for such an airplane and Piper needed a low-cost, high-performance aircraft with which to enter the market. In addition to Beech, Rockwell International had introduced the Rockwell Turbo Commander 680T in 1966, powered by Garrett AiResearch TPE-331-43 turboprop engines.

Edward J. Swearingen was employed to modify the prototype PA-31 Navajo (constructor number 31-1, registered N3100E) to accept Pratt & Whitney Canada PT6A-20 turboprop engines each rated at 550 shaft horsepower. The aircraft made its first flight in April, 1967 and subsequent tests by Swearingen and Piper demonstrated that the combination of PT6A engines and the Navajo airframe was compatible.

To create a marketable airplane, however, Piper selected the Pressurized Navajo as the basis for what would become the PA-31T Cheyenne. Two Pratt & Whitney Canada PT6A-28 engines were installed on constructor number 31-T1, registered N7500L which served as the PA-31T prototype.

First flown in October, 1969 the airplane featured wing tip tanks for additional fuel capacity. In addition, a stability augmentation system designed by Piper was installed later in the flight test program to meet FAA certification criteria for longitudinal stability, and to enhance handling characteristics for a range of aircraft weight and center of gravity loadings.

Eight years after the Beechcraft King Air had ushered in the era of turbine power for business aircraft, Piper's Cheyenne was ready to join the fray.

PA-31 Navajo prototype N3100E was modified by Edward J. Swearingen in 1967 with two Pratt & Whitney PT6A-20 turboprop engines as part of a feasibility study by Piper for a turboprop-powered business aircraft. (Edward Swearingen)

Swearingen's successful modification of Navajo N3100E led to development of the PA-31T Cheyenne. Introduced for the 1974 model year, the Cheyenne was powered by Pratt & Whitney Canada PT6A-28 turboprop engines each rated at 620 shaft horsepower (shp). The first production airplane, constructor number 31T-7400002, registered N131PT is illustrated. (Piper Aircraft Corporation)

Production began at the Lock Haven factory in 1973 with initial deliveries beginning in 1974.

In the Piper tradition, the Cheyenne offered turbine engine performance and value for the money. From a marketing standpoint the aircraft was aimed at owners and operators who flew Navajo Chieftains and Pressurized Navajos, and pilots and companies eager for transition to an entry-level turboprop aircraft.

The airplane's cabin seated eight occupants in comfort and the cockpit was similar to that of the Pressurized Navajo. With a maximum speed of 283 knots, the Cheyenne carried 382 gallons of useable fuel and could fly more than 900 nautical miles. Maximum gross weight was 9,050 lb.

Initial sales were slow, primarily because the turboprop engines were new technology for many corporate pilots who were unfamiliar with their operation. The benefits of smooth, quiet turbine power combined with pressurization and faster speeds were irresistable, however, and sales steadily increased after 1974.

Piper's 100,000th airplane was a Cheyenne, built in the spring of 1976. Cessna Aircraft Company had reached that hallowed milestone in 1975 when it delivered a Model 172 Skyhawk registered N100M. As for Beech, it delivered its 50,000th airplane, a Model C90B, in 1992.

In addition to Beech and Piper, Cessna had entered the competitive cabin-class turboprop market in 1978 with its Model 441 Conquest. Based on the company's

Equipped with Pratt & Whitney Canada PT6A-11 turboprop engines rated at 500 shp. each, the T-1040 featured a Chieftain fuselage mated to the wings, empennage and nose section of the Cheyenne 1. (Doug Smith)

Piper developed the Cheyenne 1 and Cheyenne 1A as low-cost turboprop business aircraft. The PA-31T1 had Pratt & Whitney Canada PT6A-11 engines and was introduced in 1978. The PA-31T1-1A Cheyenne 1A was an upgraded version that entered production in 1983. (Piper Aircraft Corporation)

421-series twin-engine design, the pressurized 441 was powered by two Garrett AiResearch TPE-331 turboprop engines each flat-rated to 635 shp.

The Conquest competed against Piper's Cheyenne II and Cheyenne IIXL and the Beechcraft Model 90. Cessna built 362 Conquests before production ended in 1985. In the 1983 model year, Cessna changed the name to Conquest II. The 441's base price was $1,795,000.

Like Piper with its Cheyenne I, Cessna also developed a low-cost turboprop aircraft by mating 450 shp. Pratt & Whitney Canada PT6A-112 engines to a modified Model 421C Golden Eagle airframe. Introduced in 1980, the Model 425 Corsair cost $825,000 and 236 were produced. The name was changed to Conquest I in 1983.

Despite tough competition from Cessna and Beech, Piper's Cheyenne program was well established by the late 1970s and new, improved turboprop designs were being developed. In 1978 Piper added the low-cost PA-31T1 Cheyenne I to the product line in an attempt to lure business away from its higher-priced competitors.

With the advent of the Cheyenne I, the original Cheyenne was renamed the Cheyenne II. The Cheyenne I's forte was affordability and simplicity. The airplane had optional wing tip tanks and its Pratt & Whitney Canada PT6A-11 engines were flat-rated to 500 shp.

Piper made minor improvements to the design until 1983 when the upgraded Cheyenne IA version made its debut. The PA-31T1 IA had PT6A-11 engines that provided 4% more shaft horsepower at

In 1978 the original Cheyenne was redesignated the Cheyenne II but continued to be powered by two 620 shp. Pratt & Whitney Canada PT6A-28 engines. Cruise speed was 283 kt. (Piper Aircraft Corporation)

high altitudes and boosted cruise speed to 261 knots. Other changes included an improved cabin and redesigned engine cowlings. Lock Haven workers built 215 Cheyenne I and IA aircraft before manufacture was terminated in 1983 and 1984 respectively. Production of the Cheyenne II ended early in 1983.

The next version of the Cheyenne was the PA-31T2 Cheyenne IIXL introduced in 1981. The Cheyenne IIXL essentially was a Cheyenne II with 24 inches added to the fuselage length and 620 shp. Pratt & Whitney Canada PT6A-135 powerplants. Late in the first year of IIXL production, Piper increased the airplane's zero fuel weight by 500 lb. but the maximum gross weight remained at 9,450 lb. Eighty-two aircraft were produced before production ended at Lock Haven in December, 1984, and the facility was closed.

Early in 1984 Piper had planned to upgrade the IIXL to create the PA-31T2 Cheyenne IIXLA, with improved PT6A-135 engines that provided 6% more power at high altitudes, according to Peperell and Smith in their book titled Piper Aircraft And Their Forerunners.

In addition to a new interior and system refinements, the IIXLA would have featured increased fuel capacity and nacelle lockers. Although two prototypes were constructed, Piper cancelled the program and converted both airplanes to standard Cheyenne IIXL configuration. No production aircraft were built.

Reinforcing its role as the leading manufacturer of turboprop business and military airplanes, in 1973 Beech Aircraft Corporation introduced its next generation turboprop—the Model 200 Super King Air. Sporting a large, graceful T-tail empennage, the Model 200 first flew in October, 1972. Beech received FAA certification in December, 1973 and began initial

Three-view of PA-31T II Cheyenne II. (Smithsonian Institution, National Air and Space Museum Negative Number 93-2363)

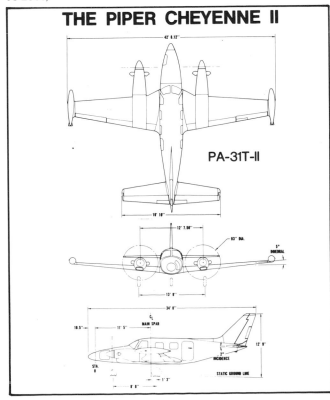

THE PIPER CHEYENNE II

PA-31T-II

Piper built 526 PA-31T II Cheyenne II aircraft before production was terminated in 1983. (Piper Aircraft Corporation)

The 1981 PA-31T II Cheyenne IIXL essentially was a Cheyenne II with a fuselage 24 inches longer than that of its predecessor. Note additional cabin window. The Cheyenne IIXL series were powered by Pratt & Whitney Canada PT6A-135 engines, each rated at 620 shp. (Mal Holcomb)

customer deliveries in February, 1974.

The Super King Air was powered by Pratt & Whitney Canada PT6A-41 engines each rated at 850 shp., carried 544 gallons of fuel and accommodated eight to 10 passengers in its large cabin. For Beech, the Model 200 was the company's crowning achievement and set new standards for turboprop business airplanes.

To meet the latest Beechcraft challenge, in 1976 Piper began development of the PA-42 Cheyenne III. Engineers modified a Chieftain airframe with Cheyenne wings, a new T-tail was installed and the fuselage lengthened by more than eight feet compared with the Cheyenne II's. Wing span was increased by four feet and two Pratt & Whitney Canada PT6A-41 engines were fitted, each rated at 680 shp.

To compete more effectively against the Super King Air, however, in 1978 Piper delayed introducing the PA-42 Cheyenne III until additional modifications were made. Chief among these were lengthening

Piper's original, experimental Cheyenne III featured 680 shp. PT6A-41 turboprop engines, Cheyenne wings and a T-tail empennage mated to an unpressurized Navajo Chieftain fuselage. Note parachute for deep stall testing mounted on tail boom. (Mal Holcomb)

Experimental, unpressurized PA-42 N7676L after painting. Production airplanes featured cabin pressurization and lengthened fuselages. (Mal Holcomb)

Aimed directly at the market dominated by the Beechcraft Model 200 Super King Air, the PA-42-720 Cheyenne III was unveiled by Piper in 1980. Powered by two, 720 shp. Pratt & Whitney Canada PT6A-41 turboprop engines, the Cheyenne III cruised at 299 kt. Constructor number 42-7801003, registered N142PC is illustrated. (Piper Aircraft Corporation)

the fuselage 3 feet, adding more powerful, 720 shp. engines and mounting the powerplants 14 inches farther forward to reduce cabin noise.

Following FAA certification, Cheyenne III production began at the Lakeland, Florida, facility in 1980 and initial deliveries had commenced by the end of the year. When the first Cheyenne III rolled off the assembly lines, Beech already had built nearly 800 Super King Airs and was about to introduce an upgraded version known as the B200 which entered production in 1981.

In terms of performance, comfort and value, both airplanes were well matched. The Super King Air was more expensive and weighed 2,000 lb. more than the Cheyenne III. In terms of sales and popularity, the Model 200 proved to be unbeatable.

Despite the Super King Air's domination of the market, Piper's Cheyenne program was a success and posed the most serious threat to Beech's tight grip on turboprop sales. In 1983 the Cheyenne III was improved to create the PA-42-720 Cheyenne IIIA, powered by 720 shp. PT6A-61 engines, a maximum gross weight of 11,285 lb. and a new interior and cabin configuration.

After building four prototype aircraft and 85 production Cheyenne IIIs, Piper began producing the Cheyenne IIIA version at the Lakeland factory late in 1983 and continued until December, 1985 when the

facility was closed. Production resumed in 1986 in new facilities built for the Cheyenne series at Piper's Vero Beach, Florida site, where 46 additional Cheyenne IIIA aircraft had been built by the end of the 1987 model year.

When Monroe Stuart Millar acquired Piper Aircraft Corporation in May, 1987 the Cheyenne IIIA remained in production. The company delivered 12 Cheyenne IIIAs in 1987, zero in 1988 and one in 1989, according to data supplied by Piper to the General Aviation Manufacturers Association.

Nine airplanes were delivered in 1990 before severe cash flow problems inhibited the company's ability to pay vendors for parts and components to complete production aircraft. To generate revenue, Piper concentrated on completing and delivering as many Cheyenne IIIAs and piston-powered Malibu Mirages as parts availability and workforce would permit. Three PA-42-720 airplanes were delivered in 1991 and one in 1992.

Before Millar took control of the company, Piper had promoted the PA-42-720's cost and performance

Three-view of PA-42 Cheyenne III. (Smithsonian Institution, National Air and Space Museum Negative Number 93-2365)

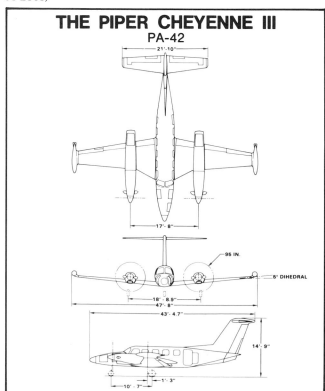

THE PIPER CHEYENNE III
PA-42

The upgraded Cheyenne IIIA incorporated a new interior and PT6A-61 turboprop engines. Introduced in 1983, the PA-42-720 IIIA became popular with major international air carriers as an advanced multi-engine trainer. (Piper Aircraft Corporation)

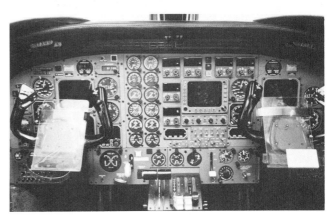

Cheyenne IIIA instrument panel. (Piper Aircraft Corporation)

virtues and was able to sell the Cheyenne IIIA as an advanced trainer for major international airlines. In October, 1990 the Civil Aviation Administration of China (CAAC) took delivery of its fourth Cheyenne IIIA, joining three others already in service at CAAC's Flying College at Guanghan City, China. One additional airplane was accepted by CAAC officials in September, 1992 and a sixth Cheyenne IIIA Airline Trainer aircraft was delivered to the Flying College early in February, 1993.

These airplanes were equipped with Collins electronic flight instrument system avionic suites and the cabins were configured to seat eight students in a special training arrangement. Piper also modified the Cheyenne IIIA to serve as a maritime patrol aircraft capable of performing surveillance missions as well as drug interdiction, airway and navigation facilities inspection and high-altitude photography roles.

Although the Cheyenne IIIA was a popular and successful design, in 1984 Piper unleashed its ultimate turboprop aircraft—the Cheyenne IV. Mounting 1,000 shp. Garrett TPE-331-14 series turboprop engines and large, four-blade propellers, the airplane could fly faster than any previous Cheyenne and was significantly faster than the Beechcraft Super King Air. Maximum gross weight was 12,135 lb.

To reflect its speed capability, the PA-42-1000

Cheyenne IV was renamed the 400LS in September, 1984. The number 400 indicated the airplane's maximum speed and the letters "LS" stood for Lear Siegler, which had acquired Piper's parent company Bangor Punta during the year.

Certified by the FAA in July, 1984 the 400LS was built at the Lakeland factory and initial customer deliveries began in December for the 1985 model year. As with the Cheyenne IIIA, 400LS production at Lakeland was terminated in December, 1985 and resumed at the Vero Beach facilities in 1986.

After Millar's acquisition of Piper in May, 1987 the airplane's name was changed to Cheyenne 400 and the letters LS were deleted. The company built three 400s in 1987 and another three in 1988, followed by two in 1989 and two in 1990. Only one Cheyenne 400 was delivered in 1991 and none were delivered in 1992. Piper had built 42 PA-42-1000 aircraft by the end of 1991.

The trend toward turboprop business aircraft that occurred in the mid-1960s had its parallel in the 1970s

Introduced in 1983 as the fastest of the Cheyenne series, the PA-42-1000 Cheyenne IV had a maximum speed of 351 kt. and set numerous speed and time-to-climb records. Piper renamed the Cheyenne IV the Cheyenne 400LS (LS for Lear Siegler) in 1984, and renamed it again in 1987 as the Cheyenne 400, after Monroe Stuart Millar acquired the company. (Mal Holcomb)

Two Garrett TPE-331-14A and -14B turboprop engines powered the PA-42-1000. Each engine was rated at 1,000 shp. (AlliedSignal)

Piper's pressurized PA-46-310P Malibu set new standards for single-engine, high performance general aviation airplanes when it was introduced in 1984. The six-place Malibu featured a high aspect ratio wing that spanned 43 feet, and was powered by a 310 hp. Teledyne Continental Motors TSIO-520-BE engine. PA-46-310P Malibu prototype, constructor number 46-8408001, registered N35646 is illustrated. (Piper Aircraft Corporation)

when bustling market activity prompted Piper, Cessna and Beech to seriously consider development of a piston-powered, single-engine airplane featuring a pressurized cabin. The benefit of pressurization would make flight at high altitudes much more comfortable for the pilot and the passengers, who normally had to wear uncomfortable oxygen masks when flying above 20,000 feet.

A thirst for more performance, coupled with the growing desire by general aviation pilots to climb above most weather systems, convinced industry officials that the time had come to develop the pressurized cabin, single-engine airplane for the general aviation market. Although Mooney's expensive and short-lived M22 Mustang built in the mid-1960s was a serious attempt to sell a such an airplane, the market failed to respond. Priced at $46,000, the M22 struggled to survive and only 39 airplanes including the prototype were produced.

Following in Mooney's footsteps, in 1978 Cessna introduced the Model P210N Pressurized Centurion. Powered by a Teledyne Continental TSIO-520-P engine rated at 310 hp. for takeoff, the P210 was capable of climbing to an altitude of 23,000 feet while maintaining a cabin altitude of 12,000 feet.

First flown in October, 1976 the P210 could be equipped with optional weather radar and had a maximum speed of 237 knots at an altitude of 17,000 feet. From 1978 until production ended in 1985, Cessna's P210N and the improved P210R were the only production pressurized, single-engine, piston-powered aircraft available to general aviation pilots.

In 1978 Beech Aircraft Corporation transformed a six-seat Bonanza A36 into the experimental Model T36TC with a T-tail empennage and 325 hp. Teledyne Continental TSIO-520 engine. Intended strictly to test the feasibility of a pressurized, T-tail Bonanza, the engineering prototype's cabin was unpressurized. Beech management cancelled the project early in 1980.

In parallel with development of a piston-powered pressurized aircraft, Beech officials decided also to develop a turbine-powered version known as the Model 38P Lightning. Only one proof-of-concept airplane was built and made its first flight in June, 1982 powered by a 550 shp. Garrett AiResearch TPE-331-9 turboprop engine.

A Pratt & Whitney Canada PT6A-40 turboprop engine flat rated to 630 shp. was fitted to the 38P test airframe and first flew in March, 1984. Although the Lightning project showed promise, escalating costs prompted Beech to terminate the program later that year.

As for Piper, it flew an experimental, pressurized, proof-of-concept six-seat airplane assigned constructor number 46-E1 and registered N35646 in November, 1979. The aircraft originally was powered by a six-cylinder, 300 hp. Textron Lycoming IO-540 engine that was replaced by a 310 hp. Teledyne Continental Motors TSIO-520 powerplant early in 1982. The experimental airplane was followed in October, 1982 by a new prototype aircraft that Piper developed into the PA-46-310P Malibu.

It should be noted that in 1988 Piper used the prototype Malibu to flight-test a turboprop derivative designated the PA-46-600PT Turbine Malibu. The airplane also was designated as the Turboprop Malibu, according to Piper documents. The constructor number was changed to 468408001 but the airplane retained its original registration number N35646.

First flown on September 26, 1988 with pilot Bill Bubb at the controls, the aircraft was powered by a Pratt & Whitney Canada PT6A-series turboprop engine. Production airplanes would have had a 600 shp. PT6A-series engine. Unfortunately, the Turbine Malibu project was cancelled when Piper's financial problems worsened in 1989-1990.

From its inception, the pressurized, piston-powered Malibu set new standards of design and performance for the single-engine, general aviation marketplace. The airplane's high aspect ratio wing spanned 43 feet and featured a single-piece spar. The pressurization system was capable of maintaining a sea-level cabin up to 12,500 feet aircraft altitude, and provided a cabin altitude of 7,900 feet at the Malibu's maximum operating height of 25,000 feet.

In addition to being a sleek, attractive airplane the PA-46-310P was fast. At mid-cruise weight flying at a high-speed cruise power setting, the airplane had a true airspeed of 225 knots and cruised at 185 knots true airspeed at a long-range cruise power setting.

After FAA certification was received in September, 1983 Piper began initial customer deliveries in December for the 1984 model year when 86 Malibus were built. The airplane, which sold for $300,000, was an instant success for Piper and 344 PA-46-310P Malibus were built through the 1987 model year.

The upgraded PA-46-350P Malibu Mirage was introduced in 1989. A 350 hp. Textron Lycoming TSIO-540 engine with dual turbochargers and dual intercoolers replaced the PA-46-310 Malibu's Continental powerplant. Piper built 90 Mirages in 1989, 26 in 1990 and one in 1991. Ten were delivered in 1992. (Piper Aircraft Corporation)

◄ *The Malibu Mirage's instrument panel featured a new power quadrant, color weather radar and an optional computerized fuel management system. (Piper Aircraft Corporation)*

When Monroe Stuart Millar took the reins at Piper in May, 1987 company engineers already had begun working on a next-generation Malibu known as the PA-46-350P Malibu Mirage. The chief change was under the cowling, where the Teledyne Continental engine was replaced by a 350 hp. Textron Lycoming TIO-540-AE2A powerplant with dual turbochargers, dual intercoolers, and dual vacuum pump systems for added redundancy and safety—particularly when operating in instrument weather conditions.

Maximum gross weight was increased to 4,300 lb. from the original Malibu's 4,000-lb. limit, giving the airplane an useful load of 1,692 lb. Like the Malibu, the Mirage featured stainless steel control cables and flush-riveting. A new, integrally heated windshield was optional and a six-position cylinder head temperature selector was made standard equipment. The instrument panel was redesigned, and the airstair door was relocated lower on the fuselage and had an automatic dampener for easier opening and closing.

Piper began deliveries of the Mirage in 1987 for the 1988 model year. The company received an order for its 200th Mirage in May, 1990 and offered the Allied Signal Aerospace, Bendix-King EHI 40 electronic flight instrument system (EFIS) in the PA-46-350P.

The single-tube EHI 40 could be integrated with the Bendix-King RDS-81 or RDS-82VP weather radar systems that were mounted in a streamlined pod under the airplane's right wing. Base price of the Malibu Mirage increased to $369,900 beginning with constructor number 4622076, although the price escalated to more than $400,000 after the bankruptcy declaration in July, 1991.

In September, 1991 the Vero Beach factory delivered the first Mirage to be completed since

Piper conducted testing of a 1/5-scale Turbine Malibu in the 8 x 12-foot wind tunnel at the University of Washington. The model was powered by a 50 hp. electric motor. (Mal Holcomb)

In 1988 Piper flew the prototype Malibu powered by a Pratt & Whitney Canada PT6A-series turboprop engine. Note unpainted sections where modifications were made to the original airframe. The photograph was taken during the airplane's first flight. Piper officials cancelled the program chiefly because of the company's financial crisis. (Mal Holcomb)

Millar's Chapter 11 filing. One PA-46-310P and 90 PA-46-350P Mirages were produced in 1989, followed by 26 in 1990 and one in 1991. Ten Mirages were delivered in 1992, and additional Mirages were scheduled to be built in 1993. Suggested list price for the 1993 PA-46-350P was $539,075.

Despite strong sales and recognition as the general aviation industry's most sophisticated single-engine airplane, the Malibu suffered a series of in-flight structural breakups that threatened to damage the airplane's reputation and add to the already heavy burden of woes faced by Piper Aircraft Corporation.

Between May, 1989 and March, 1991 seven airplanes—six PA-46-310P Malibus and one PA-46-350P Mirage, crashed killing 18 people. Five of the accidents occurred in the United States, one in Mexico and another in Japan.

Responding to the accidents, the Federal Aviation Administration (FAA) issued an emergency airworthiness directive on March 21, 1991 that prohibited Malibus from operating under instrument meteorological conditions (IMC) and recommended that pilots avoid areas of weather where moderate or severe turbulence was present or forecast.

The notice affected 518 Malibus, including the Mirage version. Specifically, the directive required placards, prohibiting flight in IMC, to be installed in full view of the pilot; use of the Bendix-King KFC 150 automatic flight control system was prohibited; pitot heat and alternate induction air had to be used at all times except for takeoff and landing; and the autopilot vertical speed and altitude select controls were removed from the instrument panel.

Although the FAA and the National Transportation Safety Board (NTSB) had been studying the crashes before the directive was issued, no apparent cause was forthcoming. "If there is a common thread for all these accidents, it is that the aircraft is breaking up in flight," an NTSB official said.

Piper officials were quick to react to the airworthiness directive. "We believe there is nothing wrong with the structural integrity of the Malibu," a senior company official said. He blamed the accidents on "operational error and weather" factors, and emphasized that the directive "in no way suggests any structural deficiency of the Malibus." In addition, he stressed that that the FAA's document did not ground the airplanes.

In an attempt to determine if the Malibu's in-flight breakups were linked with the FAA's certification procedures, the agency initiated a Special Certification Review of the PA-46 series and found nothing amiss. In conjunction with the FAA, Piper already had conducted exhaustive tests of the airframe and determined that it met or exceeded all certification requirements. For example, failure load analysis of the wing showed that about 7.7 G would be required to overload the structure, and the horizontal stabilizer withstood 239% of the required torsion limit load and 180% of the bending limit load.

The FAA also reviewed certification procedures for the Bendix-King KFC 150 system, which was the only automatic flight control system approved for the aircraft. Testing showed that the autopilot met all certification criteria.

After a hail of protest from Malibu owners and pilots, in February, 1992 the FAA rescinded the airworthiness directive and returned the aircraft to unrestricted flight status. The FAA had concluded that "there is no unsafe condition that would warrant continuation of the operational restrictions," a Piper official said.

The first Mirage to be delivered after the FAA lifted flight restrictions was constructor number 4622122 that was accepted in March, 1992 by AMR Combs based in Grand Rapids, Michigan. In the aftermath of the Malibu accidents Piper, the FAA and NTSB officials strongly urged Malibu pilots to study and understand all procedures involving use of the airplane's flight manual, systems and particularly the autopilot and its vertical speed functions.

Piper owner Millar agreed. "There is nothing wrong with the airplane, but a focus is needed on pilot training and systems familiarity," he said. The company had operated a pilot ground school for the Malibu and strengthened its curricula following the investigations.

Although the Malibu accidents caused the price of used PA-46-310P aircraft to decline, by 1992 their value was on the rise again following resolution of the airworthiness controversy. Production of the PA-46-350P Malibu Mirage continued at Vero Beach in 1993.

Piper's pressurized Malibu was a new breed of high performance airplane for the general aviation market. Its combination of speed, comfort and utility made it the logical choice for many small companies and business people.

With the Malibu and the Mirage, Piper Aircraft Corporation had successfully developed and produced an advanced-technology, single-engine, piston-powered general aviation airplane. And in the true spirit of William T. Piper, Sr., had again provided the industry with the best value for the money.

CHAPTER 10

PIPER POTPOURRI

The legendary J-3 Cub was Piper Aircraft Corporation's most famous product and has become a revered symbol of American general aviation. In contrast to the Cub and its place of honor in aviation history, Piper also built a number of interesting, although obscure, airplanes that are deserving of attention.

One such aircraft was the PA-35 Pocono. In March, 1965 Piper management planned to design and build an 18-20 passenger transport aimed at what they perceived was a growing market for small, utility and passenger transports. After engineer Fred E. Weick and his staff discussed the project with senior Piper officials, their proposal called for an aircraft with a maximum gross weight of 8,700 lb. powered by two 400 hp. Lycoming piston engines.

Cabin specifications included a width of 7 feet 4 inches, height of 5 feet 3 inches and 530 cubic feet of volume. The interior was designed with rows of two seats on one side and rows of single seats on the other side with an aisle in the center of the cabin.

The fuselage resembled that of an inflated Navajo and was circular in cross section. In addition, the fuselage was intended for pressurization primarily because the Pocono was intended to serve as a commuter airliner and a corporate shuttle aircraft. Pressurization would have been desirable for both versions.

Two baggage compartments were provided, each with a volume of 50 cubic feet. One compartment was located in the nose section and the other was in the aft cabin area. Total baggage weight was limited to 500 lb.

To develop the Pocono concept, Piper established a separate engineering group at the Vero Beach development center to design and build a prototype PA-35 airplane. In May, 1967 Pug Piper disclosed the existence of the PA-35 project and details about the prototype's specifications.

These included a wing span of 51 feet, length of 39 feet and a useful load of 4,100 lb. The PA-35's maximum gross weight was increased to 9,500 lb. from the original estimate of 8,700 lb. Both wings would carry 200 gallons of fuel and the PA-35 would cruise at more than 200 mph.

The prototype, constructor number 35-E1, registered N3535C, was completed in May, 1968 and was powered by two Lycoming TIO-720-B1A piston engines each rated at 500 hp. The airplane made its first flight on May 13 from Vero Beach, with pilots William Barnhouse and Lou Mason at the controls. Following the flight, Piper proclaimed the new airplane the Pocono.

Piper conducted flight tests with the PA-35 prototype for more than a year. As a result, the fuselage was lengthened more than three feet and the horizontal stabilizer area was enlarged. Although the PA-35 was a promising design and could fulfill its role as a commuter airliner, Piper engineers realized the airplane needed more powerful engines.

The Pratt & Whitney Canada PT6A-series of turboprop engines were the most logical candidates, but they cost much more than the Lycoming powerplants and would significantly increase the airplane's selling price. In addition, Pug Piper was hesitant to use turboprop engines because of his doubts regarding worldwide service capability.

Two turboprop versions of the Pocono were designed at Vero Beach. One version featured 680 shp. PT6A-27 engines and a maximum gross weight of 11,000 lb., and the other had 800 shp. PT6A-30 powerplants and a lengthened fuselage to accommodate two additional passengers.

The PA-35 Pocono was designed as an 18-seat commuter aircraft for the regional airline market. Only one airplane was built, constructor number 35-E1, registered N3535C. The prototype was photographed during flight tests and was covered with tufts to evaluate airflow patterns. (Grahme Gates)

Powered by two 475 hp. turbocharged Lycoming TIO-720 engines the Pocono was underpowered. More powerful piston engines could not be obtained and turboprop engines were deemed too expensive. (Piper Aviation Museum)

As a result of flight testing Piper engineers lengthened the Pocono's fuselage and installed a larger empennage. Faced with shrinking demand and costly design changes to make the Pocono competitive, Piper officials cancelled the program in 1969. (Piper Aviation Museum)

Pocono cockpit and instrument panel. (Piper Aviation Museum)

Unfortunately, a combination of events in 1969 sounded the death knell for Piper's PA-35 Pocono. First, Lycoming could not redesign the TIO-720 piston engines to deliver a minimum of 520 hp. each, which meant a low-cost Pocono could not be offered. Second, Beech Aircraft Corporation's competitive Model 99 Airliner powered by PT6A turboprop engines already was on the market. Third, the commuter airline industry had fallen on hard times and demand for new airplanes was slowly shrinking.

Piper management ceased further development of the PA-35 in the summer of 1970. In October the prototype was flown to Lakeland, Florida where Piper had built a multi-million dollar factory to produce the airplane. Stripped of its Lycoming engines, the airframe sat idle until 1976 when it was sold to the Pezetel aircraft company in Poland.

Piper's involvement with Poland, however, did not end with the Pocono. In 1976 Piper and Pezetel reached an agreement whereby the Polish manufacturer would build as many as 400 PA-34-200T Senecas from kits supplied by Piper and sell the aircraft to Eastern Bloc nations.

The airplanes were to be powered by 220 hp. Franklin engines produced by PZL in Poland, who owned design and production rights for Franklin piston powerplants. Nine kits were shipped. Pezetel completed its first Seneca in 1982.

Supplying kits to foreign manufacturers and becoming involved in co-production programs proved to be a good business decision for Piper as early as the 1940s, when a small number of airplanes were shipped as kits to Denmark. Piper supplied aircraft in various phases of completion depending upon customer requirements, and had sent about 4,000 kits to its affiliates between 1970 and 1990. The highly successful co-production program provided important business for Piper and helped generate employment for foreign workers. It also promoted or supported an aerospace industrial base in those nations.

In addition to Pezetel in Poland, Chincul, S.A., based in San Juan, Argentina, assembled hundreds of single- and twin-engine aircraft from kits including Warriors, Aztecs and Navajos, some of which received new constructor numbers assigned by Chincul.

The company served as Piper's sales representative and aircraft were sold through LaMarcarena, S.A., Piper's distributor and a co-company of Chincul, located in Buenos Aires, Argentina.

In November, 1989 Piper shipped four Phase VIII PA-28R Arrow kits to Chincul aboard an Argentine air force Lockheed C-130 transport. One additional Arrow kit was shipped in December, 1990 and two were shipped in January, 1991. The phase VIII kits required the highest level of knowledge and technical competency to complete. The Arrow kits brought the total number of aircraft shipped to Chincul to more than 900 since 1972.

Chile's Aero Salfa and Enaer aircraft companies as well as Aero Mercantile in Colombia also assembled kits shipped from Piper, and sold the airplanes within their countries to civilian and military buyers. The largest recipient of Piper kits was Brazil's Embraer that began assembling aircraft in 1974. More than 2,000 airplanes had been completed by 1987 and shipments continued after Piper was bought by Monroe Stuart Millar in May of that year. Embraer assigned new constructor numbers to the Piper aircraft it built.

In a cooperative program, Piper and Chile's Enaer developed the PA-28R-300 T-35 Pillan trainer in 1980 to replace the Chilean air force's fleet of aging Beechcraft T-34 Mentors. The T-35 was designed as a low-cost military aircraft capable of performing primary, intermediate, instrument and aerobatic training missions.

The T-35A featured a tandem, two-seat cockpit designed by Enaer, enclosed by a one-piece, side-hinged bubble canopy. To reduce development costs, the aircraft used an aft fuselage structure from the PA-32 Saratoga, the empennage, wing structure and leading edges of the Piper PA-28-236 Dakota but with

AEROBATICS AND THE T-35 PILLAN

The Piper-Enaer T-35 Pillan's forte was versatility. The aircraft was capable of performing basic, instrument and aerobatic flight training duties with equal aplomb. In 1988 the author was invited by Piper Aircraft Corporation and the Chile Air Force to fly the T-35 Pillan for a pilot report to be published in AVIATION WEEK & SPACE TECHNOLOGY magazine.

I flew the 66th production T-35 from Piper's Vero Beach, Florida facility, and was accompanied on the flight by Chile Air Force Major Mario Gonzalez. Before boarding the aircraft, Gonzalez explained how to operate the canopy's manual jettison system which was activated by a handle located in the forward and aft cockpits. When pulled, the handles activated four carbon dioxide cartridges that released the latch mechanism. An explosive cord system designed to shatter the canopy was optional.

After I started the engine, we closed the canopy, donned headsets and received clearance to taxi to Runway 11R at the Vero Beach Municipal Airport. The T-35's electro-hydraulic landing gear system was similar to that installed in the PA-32R-301 Saratoga, but the nosewheel was not interconnected with the rudder pedals. Differential braking was used to provide steering control.

After completing the pre-takeoff checklist, we were cleared by the control tower to taxi onto the active runway for departure. I activated the electric fuel boost pump and the control for pressurizing the canopy seal, which was inflated by engine manifold pressure.

Cleared for takeoff, I released the brakes and advanced the throttle to 100% RPM. In keeping with its jet-trainer theme, the T-35 was not equipped with a tachometer graduated in revolutions per minute. Instead, the instrument read in percent RPM to more accurately reflect turbine engine power settings.

The Pillan accelerated rapidly and the rudder became effective for directional control at 35 kt. I rotated the aircraft at 65 kt. and the T-35 was airborne after a takeoff roll of 900 feet.

With landing gear retracted and a normal climb airspeed of 100 kt. established, the rate of climb settled at 1,500 feet per minute. I was impressed by the excellent visibility afforded by the bubble canopy. The Pillan was equipped with an electric stabilator

The Piper-Enaer PA-28R-300 was designated the T-35 Pillan for service with the Chile Air Force as a primary and advanced trainer. The aerobatic T-35 was powered by a 300 hp. Textron Lycoming IO-540-K1K5 engine. (Piper Aircraft Corporation and AVIATION WEEK & SPACE TECHNOLOGY)

trim switch mounted on the throttle grip, and a small wheel installed in the left console was provided for manual trimming, if desired. An electric rudder trim system was standard equipment.

After leveling off and performing clearing turns to check for other aircraft in the practice area offshore, I configured the airplane for a power-off stall with the landing gear and flaps retracted. With the throttle retarded to idle power, the airspeed decreased slowly.

A strong, aerodynamic buffet preceded the stall break that occurred at 68 kt. indicated airspeed. Using full aft stick, I held the T-35 in the stall. The airplane tended to pitch down in an attempt to recover from the stall by itself. Rudder control was highly effective in raising a low wing throughout the prolonged stall. Releasing the stick brought an immediate recovery without adding power.

With landing gear and flaps still retracted, I next performed a series of stalls in turns at bank angles up to 45 degrees. As I expected, the stalls were predictable and benign. The pre-stall buffet provided more than ample warning of the impending loss of lift. An accelerated stall performed at 60 degrees of bank proved equally docile.

Because the T-35 was designed as a military trainer, I was anxious to sample the aircraft's aerobatic capabilities. During the climb to gain altitude, Gonzalez suggested I begin with spins to the left and to the right.

Level at 6,000 feet, I reduced power to idle and held the nose high above the horizon as airspeed decreased. When the stall occurred, I held full aft stick and applied full left rudder to initiate a spin in that direction. The Pillan entered the incipient spin phase smoothly as the nose pitched down and initial rotation began.

Although the first turn was lethargic, by the second turn the spin had developed fully. The T-35 spun with its nose well down. Its relatively high rotation rate of one turn each 2.5 seconds was comfortable, but not so fast as to disorient a student pilot and delay locating a recovery reference. The airplane lost about 600 feet per turn.

It was easy to maintain pro-spin controls during the maneuver, and after six complete turns I moved the stick forward to break the stall and applied full right rudder to stop rotation. Spin recovery was immediate and positive. Airspeed increased rapidly in the ensuing dive, and the energy was used to climb back to 6,000 feet where a second spin in the opposite direction proved as easy as the first.

After climbing to 5,000 feet, 98% power was set and an aileron roll to the left was executed from level flight. As the nose reached 30 degrees above the horizon I applied full left stick. Rolling through 90 degrees of bank, I pressed right rudder to hold the nose up followed by left rudder at the 270-degree point before completing the maneuver in a wings-level attitude. The roll took about 3 seconds to accomplish.

Next, Gonzalez suggested a standard loop. I eased the T-35's nose down about 20 degrees below the horizon and quickly attained the required 180-kt. entry speed. I applied 100% power and simultaneously pulled the stick smoothly aft to obtain 3g on the upside of the maneuver.

Passing through 7,000 feet at the top of the arc, I acquired the horizon in the canopy and pulled 3g on the downside of the loop. After completing the loop, I rolled the Pillan inverted and pushed forward on the stick to hold about 1.2g negative needed to maintain level flight. The airplane's fuel and oil systems were approved for unlimited inverted operation, and a T-35 was flown inverted for 40 minutes during certification testing.

To complete the aerobatic portion of the flight, Gonzalez took the controls and flew an uninterrupted aerobatic sequence to demonstrate typical maneuvers learned by fledgling cadets in Chile. He began with a loop, followed immediately by a half-roll to inverted flight for 5 seconds. He next executed a split-S followed by a full Cuban Eight, then rolled inverted for another 5 seconds before rolling to wings-level flight. Not more than 3.5g was required to complete the entire sequence.

Returning to Vero Beach, I was cleared for a straight-in approach to Runway 22. The landing gear was extended at its maximum operating limit of 138 kt. indicated airspeed, and approach flaps were selected after the Pillan had slowed below its maximum flap extension speed of 118 kt.

On final approach I trimmed the T-35 to fly at 90 kt. On short final, full flaps were deflected and I slowly reduced power as the airplane crossed the runway threshold. I initiated the flare and reduced power to idle as the main gear tires touched down at 65 kt. After turning off the runway I taxied back to Piper's facilities.

The T-35 Pillan was an impressive aircraft. It possessed docile behavior important to building a student pilot's confidence, yet it had the ability to perform advanced maneuvers essential to pilots preparing to fly jet airplanes.

In addition, the PA-28R-300 was a capable aerobatic trainer and possessed excellent overall handling characteristics. Unfortunately, the airplane was not offered to civilian buyers and would have cost more than $300,000 to acquire, according to Piper officials.

thicker aluminum alloy skins; and single-slotted flaps from the Saratoga.

To improve roll rate and structural integrity for acrobatic maneuvers, the Pillan's wingspan was reduced 6.4 feet to 29 feet, compared with 34.5 feet for the Dakota. The wing design also included a new center section, and two wing tanks held 72 gallons of useable fuel.

Powered by a 300 hp. Textron Lycoming

Cockpit of the T-35 Pillan was designed to represent a primary jet trainer aircraft. Note use of Piper parts such as fuel selector handle and fresh air vents. (Enaer and Piper Aircraft Corporation)

IO-540-K1K5 engine driving a three-blade, constant-speed propeller, the PA-28R-300 prototype first flew in March, 1981 at the Vero Beach, Florida factory and was followed by a second prototype that flew in August.

Piper shipped three pre-production kits to Enaer in 1982 and the first production T-35 Pillan assembled was completed in 1984. In 1982 the Chilean air force ordered 80 T-35A versions to screen service applicants and to perform basic and advanced flight training. The T-35B Pillan featured a more comprehensive avionic installation to teach instrument flight and instrument approach procedures.

The Chilean order was followed in 1984 by a purchase of 40 T-35C Pillans for the Spanish air force. The Spanish version was designated the E.26 Tamiz and was assembled in Spain by CASA from kits supplied by Enaer. To boost the T-35's performance, in 1985

In 1985 a 420 shp. Allison 250-B17D turboprop engine was installed in a Pillan airframe to create the T-35A Aucan. T-35A CC-PZC was the prototype airplane. (Enaer)

In the late 1950s Piper built the PA-29 Papoose using fiberglass and plastic materials for construction of the airframe. Designed as a two-place trainer, the Papoose was powered by a 108 hp. Lycoming O-235 engine. Only one airplane was built, constructor number 29-01, registered N2900M that made its first flight in April, 1962. (Piper Aviation Museum)

After Piper cancelled the Papoose development program the PA-29 was displayed in the Experimental Aircraft Association Museum, but later was returned to the Piper Aviation Museum in Lock Haven, Pennsylvania for restoration. Note sliding canopy. (Piper Aviation Museum)

Enaer developed a turboprop version designated as the T-35TX Aucan, powered by a 420 shp. General Motors Allison 250B-17D turboprop engine.

Although not intended for the military training role, early in the 1960s Piper developed the two-place PA-29 Papoose. The Papoose was a low-wing design, with fixed, tricycle landing gear, and a conventional empennage configuration with a stabilator for pitch control.

The airplane was powered by a 108 hp. Lycoming 0-235-C1B engine. Maximum gross weight was 1,500 lb. and maximum speed was 130 mph. Work on a prototype airplane began in 1959 and the ship made its first flight in April, 1962. The concept of designing a new trainer built from fiberglass and plastic composites came from Howard Piper and engineer Fred E. Weick.

Three-view of the PA-35 Pocono. (Piper Aviation Museum)

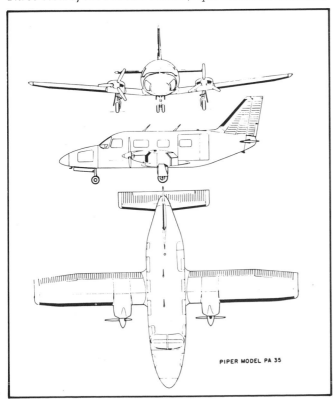

Both men realized that Piper's successful application of plastics and molded fiberglass components on the PA-25 Pawnee indicated that the materials could prove satisfactory for building a complete airplane, possibly with less weight and at a lower cost than traditional methods and materials.

The PA-29's airframe was constructed of a paper honeycomb with fiberglass layers embedded in polyester plastic, which after about six months of flight testing began to weaken from improper curing and exposure to sunlight. Although Weick knew the fabrication process could be improved to remedy these problems, analysis indicated that material costs and weight were likely to be higher than that of a comparable airplane built from aluminum alloy. The cost of building the Papoose also was predicted to be higher.

As a result, Piper cancelled the PA-29 after flying the prototype for about 80 hours. The company donated the aircraft to the Experimental Aircraft Association in Oshkosh, Wisconsin where it was placed on display in the association's museum. The aircraft later was transferred to the Piper Aviation Museum in Lock Haven, Pennsylvania and was scheduled for a complete restoration.

Not long after the development of the Papoose was terminated, Piper's success with the PA-24 Comanche series led company management to contract with Edward J. Swearingen for development of a pressurized version of the Comanche designated the PA-33.

Swearingen already had developed the PA-30 Twin Comanche for Piper in 1962, and in 1966 he designed and built a PA-33 prototype that was given constructor number 33-1 and registered N4600Y. Although the wings and empennage essentially were the same as those of a Comanche, the fuselage was new and designed to be pressurized. Two, gull-wing type cabin doors were mounted, one on each side of the fuselage, for easy entry and egress.

To support the PA-33 on the ground, Swearingen used long-length main landing gear struts similar to those he developed earlier for the Twin Comanche, and an electrically operated nosewheel steering system was installed to improve ground handling characteristics.

A 240 hp. Lycoming 0-540 engine was installed driving a two-blade, constant-speed propeller. Edward Swearingen piloted the pressurized Comanche's

134

In 1967 Edward J. Swearingen completed development of the pressurized PA-33 Comanche. Powered by a 260 hp. Lycoming O-540 engine, the airplane featured lengthened main landing gear struts designed by Swearingen for the PA-30 Twin Comanche, and two, gull-wing type cabin doors. The PA-33 project was terminated after the prototype was damaged in a takeoff accident. The only PA-33 built was constructor number 33-1, registered N4600Y. (Edward Swearingen)

The PA-40 Arapaho was designed in the early 1970s to replace the PA-39 Twin Comanche C/R. Incorporating hydraulic landing gear, a larger cabin and 160 hp. Textron Lycoming IO-320 engines with counter-rotating propellers, the Arapaho was scheduled to enter production for the 1975 model year, but lack of market demand forced Piper to terminate the program in 1974. The third prototype PA-40, constructor number 40-7400003, registered N9997P was photographed on the ramp at Lock Haven. (Roger Peperell collection)

first flight in March, 1967 but in May the airplane was damaged during a takeoff accident at the Lock Haven factory.

Instead of rebuilding the PA-33, Piper cancelled the program. Although it survived only a few months, the pressurized Comanche was the progenitor of a future Piper, namely the PA-46-310P Malibu that debuted in 1983. Typical of Swearingen's designs, the PA-33 was a sleek, fast airplane that could have set new standards for the industry if Piper had proceeded with the program.

In the early 1970s, however, Piper did plan to supersede the PA-39 Twin Comanche C/R with a new airplane designated the PA-40 Arapaho. The airplane's size and performance were similar to those of the PA-39, but it featured a hydraulic landing gear

In 1978 Piper Aircraft Corporation acquired the twin-engine Aerostar product line from designer Ted Smith. Piper continued to produce the Aerostar at Santa Maria, California before moving production to Vero Beach, Florida in 1981. (Piper Aircraft Corporation)

system, lengthened main landing gear struts, larger cabin windows and seating for six occupants.

Like the Twin Comanche, the Arapaho was powered by Textron Lycoming IO-320 and left-rotation LIO-320 engines each developing 160 hp. and driving three-blade, constant-speed propellers. A turbocharged version also would be available.

Although Piper intended to introduce the PA-40 for the 1975 model year, market studies indicated that there was insufficient demand for such an aircraft at that time and the program was cancelled. Of the three PA-40 prototypes built the first airplane, constructor number 40-7300001, registered N9999P, flew in January, 1973 but crashed during flight testing. The second aircraft and the third, which had turbocharged Textron Lycoming TIO-320 and left-rotation LTIO-320 powerplants, were test-flown and eventually dismantled.

During the same time that Piper was developing the PA-40, it was flying a pressurized prototype of the PA-23-250 Aztec known as the PA-41P. Powered by two Textron Lycoming TIO-540 engines each rated at 270 hp., the pressurized Aztec was not developed beyond the prototype stage and the project was terminated in 1974.

In 1978 Piper management decided to purchase the Aerostar, a twin-engine, unpressurized business airplane designed by Ted Smith. In production since 1968, the Aerostar had first flown in 1966 and was powered by two, 290 hp. Textron Lycoming IO-540 engines. The Aerostar had a reputation for speed, and Piper viewed the acquisition as an economical way to expand the company's high-performance product line.

Piper continued production of the Aerostar 600A, 601B and 601P at the Santa Maria, California facility used by Smith to build the aircraft. Initially, Piper did not assign a new designation to the Aerostar series. The 600A was the standard version with 290 hp. Textron Lycoming IO-540-K1J5 engines; the 601B featured increased wing span, a higher maximum gross weight and was powered by Lycoming TIO-540-S1A5 engines. The 601P essentially was a pressurized variant of the 601B.

In 1981, the general aviation industry's slow decline meant the once-strong market for small aircraft was becoming increasingly unstable. To reduce costs and consolidate, Piper's corporate parent Bangor Punta closed the Santa Maria, California factory and terminated production of the 600A and 601B in favor of the 602P Aerostar.

Production was relocated to Piper's Vero Beach, Florida facilities where manufacture resumed in February, 1982 under the new designation PA-60-602P Aerostar. In 1983 the 602P was replaced by the PA-60-700P Aerostar which incorporated a number of changes made by Piper.

Foremost among these were more powerful, counter-rotating Textron Lycoming TIO-540-U2A and LTIO-540-U2A engines. The left propeller rotated counter-clockwise and the right propeller rotated clockwise and the powerplants each developed 350 hp. To provide additional fuel for the thirsty Lycomings, Piper offered an optional 40-gallon fuel tank.

Introduced in the 1984 model year, the 700P was the right airplane at the wrong time. Despite the airplane's excellent performance, PA-60-700P sales were slow and only 25 were sold. As the industry continued its downward spiral in the mid-1980s, Piper ceased Aerostar production in 1985 after building 512 airplanes.

When Monroe Stuart Millar acquired Piper in May, 1987, he had ambitious plans to resume production of the PA-60. Millar owned and flew his own Aerostar and did not hesitate to express his fondness for the airplane. His wish did not come true. In May, 1991 Piper was on the verge of bankruptcy and Millar was trying to sell selected type certificates for out-of-production Piper airplanes in an attempt to raise revenue.

As a result, he sold the Aerostar's type certificate and Supplemental Type Certificates to Aerostar Aircraft Corporation in Spokane, Washington. The company specialized in service and support of all versions of the 600-series airplanes.

Although Piper's history centers on private and

In 1983 Piper developed the PA-60-700P Aerostar with 350 hp. Lycoming engines and counter-rotating propellers. Piper built 512 Aerostars before production ended in 1985. A 1983 PA-60-700P is illustrated. (Piper Aircraft Corporation)

business aircraft, in the 1970s the company engaged in a program to modify the North American Aviation P-51 Mustang airframe into an anti-armor, close air support aircraft known as the Enforcer.

Piper's goal was to win the United States Air Force competition for its AX anti-tank airplane. Although two prototype Enforcers were built, the competition was won by Fairchild and its twin-jet design that eventually became the A-10 Thunderbolt II.

The United States Air Force did offer Piper suggestions to improve the aircraft, although it did not have any mission requirement suitable for the Enforcer. Acting on these suggestions, in the early 1980s the company executed a major redesign of the aircraft and created the PA-48 Enforcer.

Piper engineers lengthened the fuselage 19 inches and the aft fuselage was reshaped, the empennage

Embraer EMB-711C Corisco was the Brazilian equivalent of the PA-28R-200 Arrow II. (Roger Peperell collection)

Three-view of Piper Aerostar 601P. (Smithsonian Institution, National Air and Space Museum Negative Number 93-2373)

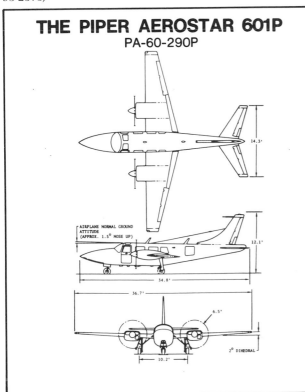

Piper's highly successful foreign affiliate program included Brazil's Embraer, Argentina's Chincul, Chile's Aero Salfa and Enaer as well as Colombia's Aero Mercantile and Poland's Pezetel company. Embraer built the EMB-710C Carioca, equivalent to the PA-28-235, from kits supplied by Piper. (Roger Peperell collection)

136

In the 1980s Piper Aircraft Corporation built two PA-48 Enforcers for evaluation by the United States Air Force. The two airplanes were each powered by a Lycoming T-55 turboprop engine rated at 2,445 shp. PA-48 constructor number 48-8301001, registered N481PE is illustrated. (Piper Aircraft Corporation)

The Embraer Nieva N821 Caraja was a Navajo Chieftain modified with Pratt & Whitney Canada PT6A-27 turboprop engines. (Roger Peperell collection)

Embraer's EMB-720C Minuano was equivalent to the PA-32-300 Cherokee Six built by Piper. (Roger Peperell collection)

Twin-engine Piper airplanes built by Embraer included the EMB-810C Seneca, equivalent to the PA-34-200T Seneca II. (Roger Peperell collection)

was redesigned with increased area for the horizontal and vertical stabilizer and the rudder, and a yaw stability augmentation system was installed.

Powered by a Lycoming T55-L-9 turboprop engine rated at 2,445 shp., the PA-48 had only a superficial resemblance to the famed P-51 Mustang of World War Two fame and the two Enforcers previously built by Piper.

In 1984 the air force agreed to evaluate two prototypes built by Piper but the airplanes were not purchased. When the tests were completed, both Enforcers were flown to Davis-Monthan Air Force Base in Arizona and placed in storage.

Whether designed for military, business or private flying, the airplanes of Piper Aircraft Corporation were esteemed by those who flew them for their value, performance and reliability. They served their country in peace and in war, distinguishing themselves not only in the skies above America, but also in hostile skies over foreign battlefields.

Under the guidance of William T. Piper, Sr., and his sons, the Piper company matured into more than an airplane manufacturer. It grew to become an integral part of America's general aviation industry, which itself evolved into an important national resource and the centerpiece of the nation's air transportation system.

To thousands of pilots, the airplanes that Piper built were the best that money could buy. They had become a part of America's aviation heritage, a symbol of the freedom of flight, and a legend aloft.

Appendix A features a variety of Piper and Taylor photographs that were not included in specific chapters, but have historical and technical value for the reader. A broad selection of airplanes have been included in an effort to further portray the history of the Taylor and Piper aircraft companies.

A duo of Piper L-4s are maneuvered into position at their makeshift base in Europe. Note that D-Day invasion stripes have been removed from the upper fuselage only. (Piper Aviation Museum)

A Lycoming-powered J-3L on floats was photographed enjoying the Florida sunshine. (Piper Aviation Museum)

Registered X20135, a Taylor J-2 Cub was modified with a streamlined fuselage and empennage of reduced size and area. (Piper Aviation Museum)

Photograph of the PT-1 trainer prototype shows open glass hatch for access to the front cockpit. (Piper Aviation Museum)

A young aviatrix smiles in approval of her mud-spattered Taylor E-2 Cub. (Piper Aviation Museum)

An L-4 based in the United States awaits its next training mission as four pilots study a map. (Piper Aviation Museum)

◄ William T. Piper, Sr., and his three sons discuss the airplane business in front of a trio of PA-22 Tri-Pacers. Tony Piper is at far left, William Piper, Jr., is wearing a hat and Pug Piper is at far right. (Piper Aviation Museum)

An L-4 dubbed "Elizabeth" takes off from the deck of the aircraft carrier U.S.S. Ranger in November, 1942 during the Allied invasion of North Africa. (Piper Aviation Museum)

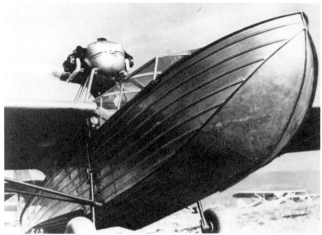

Detailed view of the Applegate Duck Amphibian's hull, landing and beaching gear. (Piper Aviation Museum)

Cabin of a pre-war J-3 Cub Sport. (Piper Aviation Museum)

Posing for a publicity photograph in 1939, two ladies prepare to depart Lock Haven in their Piper J-4B Cub Coupe powered by a 60 hp. Franklin 4AC-171 engine. (Piper Aviation Museum) ▶

During the National Air Races held in Cleveland, Ohio on September 2-4, 1939, famed air show pilot Mike Murphy flew an unusual aircraft capable of taking off and landing upside down. Known as "Cheek to Cheek" because of its two cockpits—one above and one below the wing—Murphy's ship contained parts and assemblies from Piper Cubs. Note pilot hanging inverted from lower cockpit. Registration was NX15354. (Piper Aviation Museum) ▼

A PA-25-235 Pawnee C and PA-36 Pawnee II (later designated Brave) pose nose-to-nose, illustrating the difference in size. (Piper Aviation Museum)

Cabin of a factory-fresh PA-18-125 Super Cub at Lock Haven. (Piper Aviation Museum)

Piper's director of marketing J. Willard Miller (right) congratulates Cal Jacobsen (center) as he takes delivery of the 1,000th Piper Twin Comanche in November, 1966. The aircraft was operated by Harlan Manufacturing Company, Harlan, Iowa. Piper dealer Eugene Wood is at left. (Piper Aviation Museum)

Front, oblique view of the experimental Piper Skycoupe shows fixed landing gear and generous window area. (Piper Aviation Museum)

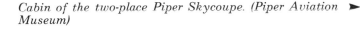

Cabin of the two-place Piper Skycoupe. (Piper Aviation Museum) ►

Engineers and technicians responsible for development of the PA-6 Sky Sedan pose for the camera in front of the first prototype, registered NX580. Standing, left to right: Charles Howenstine, Harold Kriedler, John Carlson, Paul Groves, John Bowes, Betty Miller, Malcolm Stahley, Almont Henry, Wallace Wilkie, Fred Strickland, Ray Howe, Robert Saff, George Hemphill. Kneeling, left to right: Allen Butler, Ralph Benedict, Robert Herr, Donald Hoffstedt, Ray Frank, John Crowley, Larry Keen, Sam Phillips, Charles Dale, Bill Chatley, Ralph McRae. (Piper Aviation Museum) ▼

A J-3 registered NC30641 was the 5,000th Cub trainer built by Piper. Percy Williams of the Civil Aeronautics Authority congratulates William T. Piper, Sr. (right) as company officials Gordon Curtis, J. E. Swan and John E. P. Morgan add their approval. (Piper Aviation Museum)

Instrument panel of an agricultural PA-18A Super Cub. Note emergency dump lever beneath engine tachometer. (Piper Aviation Museum)

In-flight view of a turbocharged Lance II emphasizes the airplane's rectangular wing planform. (Piper Aviation Museum)

Close-up view of a PA-12 Super Cruiser. (Rare Birds via Joseph P. Juptner) ►

Miss Kay Williams prepares to start the Skycycle's 37 hp. Continental A-40 engine. Note cowling details. (Piper Aviation Museum) ▼

Piper L4X, constructor number 5-3001, registered NX33529 landing after a demonstration flight. (Piper Aviation Museum)

Former Piper employee Captain Mike Strok (right) discusses the approaching end of World War Two in Europe with William T. Piper, Sr., in April, 1945. Note L-4s in background. (Piper Aviation Museum) ▼

Two-place Pawnee featured increased wing span and was designed to be an agricultural training aircraft. The modification was not performed by Piper Aircraft Corporation. (Piper Aviation Museum)

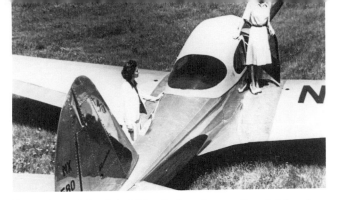

Rear view of the PA-6 Sky Sedan shows all-metal fuselage and empennage. (Piper Aviation Museum)

Piper L-14 registered NC69255 was photographed in Pennsylvania in October, 1947. (Peter M. Bowers via Joseph P. Juptner)

In-flight view of Sky Sedan registered NX580. (Piper Aviation Museum)

◄ Lineup of United States Army L-21A aircraft at Lock Haven. (Piper Aviation Museum)

J-3C-65S Cub on floats was constructor number 4272, registered N26928. (Piper Aviation Museum)

Mr. Piper, his sons and company officials (left) watch as the 45,000th Piper airplane built, a PA-23-150 Apache, emerges from the Lock Haven assembly lines. (Piper Aviation Museum)

William T. Piper, Sr., poses with a J-3P Cub powered by a three-cylinder, Lenape Papoose static radial engine. Mr. Piper was a pioneer in the United States light aircraft industry and was responsible for much of its rapid growth in the 1950s and 1960s. (Piper Aviation Museum)

Piper's 5,000th Cherokee was a PA-32 Cherokee Six sold to Houston L. McCann (center) of Bishop, Texas, in 1966. T.I. Case (right), manager of Cherokee sales and service at the Vero Beach, Florida, factory and Roger Gault, Piper dealer in Corpus Christi, Texas, made the delivery. Note special luggage designed to fit inside the airplane's forward baggage compartment. (Piper Aviation Musuem)

In 1967 Piper delivered it 10,000th export airplane, a PA-32-300 Cherokee Six constructor number 32-40042, to Wilken Air Services of Mombasa, Kenya. V.H. Hunt (left), Piper regional sales manager in Nairobi, Kenya, Arnold Meyer (center), manager of Wilken Air Services in Mombasa, and John Williams, Piper distributor for Central Africa, are shown after the airplane's arrival at Wilken facilities in Kenya. (Piper Aviation Museum)

With its 37 hp. Continental A-40 chugging confidently, a Taylor E-2 Cub and its passengers taxi for takeoff at the Bradford, Pennsylvania, factory. The airplane is constructor number 31, registered NC12626 built in 1931. (Piper Aviation Museum) ▼

1961 PA-22-108 Colt registered N5088Z was equipped with wheel fairings. (Piper Aviation Museum)

Clyde Smith, Sr., flies the prototype PT-1 trainer close to the camera ship during a photographic flight in 1944. Note deflected flaps. (Piper Aviation Museum)

A Taylor J-2 Cub registered CS-AAQ was delivered to a customer in Portugal. (Piper Aviation Museum)

The postwar PA-11 Cub Special was powered by a 65 hp. Continental A-65 engine and later by the 90 hp. Continental C-90 powerplant. Constructor number 11-893, registered

N4998H was photographed at the Lock Haven factory. (Piper Aviation Museum)

APPENDIX B

The Taylor-built airplanes carried a sequence of constructor numbers that accounted for the few airplanes and one glider that were manufactured from 1925 to 1930. When the E-2 Cub was produced, constructor numbers began with number 11 and proceeded in sequence through the F-2, G-2 and H-2 and ended with constructor number 363 in 1936. The first J-2 Cub, however, was assigned constructor number 500 and subsequent aircraft were assigned in sequence for the J-2 Cub and J-3 Cub until the United States entered World War Two in December, 1941.

In mid-1938 Piper instituted a new identification system that was first implemented for the J-4 Cub Coupe. With the new system, airplane model designations were followed by a sequential number. For example, J-4 Cub Coupe production began with constructor number 4-401, built in October, 1938 and ran consecutively to constructor number 4-1649, completed in December, 1941.

After the war Piper continued to use the sequential system. Postwar PA-18 Super Cubs were assigned constructor number 18-1 to 18-9004 and the PA-22 Tri-Pacer was given constructor number 22-1 through 22-7642. Other models followed the same procedure.

The established method worked well until Piper developed the next-generation of aircraft such as the PA-23 Aztec and PA-24 Comanche. Piper certified the Aztec under the Apache's type certificate but assigned the PA-27 designation to production airplanes. Therefore, a PA-23-250 Aztec would have a constructor number such as 27-505, not 23-505.

The 400 hp. Comanche 400 that was developed as the PA-26 also used the same system with production airplanes receiving PA-24 constructor numbers such as 24-148. When the PA-28 Cherokee series were introduced, Piper continued using the numbering process for the 150 hp., 160 hp. and 180 hp. versions. For example, Cherokee 140-series airplanes were assigned numbers beginning at 28-20000 and the Cherokee 235 was assigned numbers beginning at 28-10001.

Other single-engine aircraft that followed the procedure included the PA-28R Arrow, which received constructor numbers that began with 28R-30000, and the Cherokee Six 300 that was assigned numbers beginning at 32-40000. Starting in 1971 at the Vero Beach factory and in 1973 at the Lock Haven facility, Piper again changed the identification system. Under the new method, the model year was included in the constructor number and a four-part code identified each airplane.

An example would be constructor number 28-7205010. The number 28 denotes the aircraft type, a PA-28; the number 72 denotes 1972 model year; the number 05 was a code identifying the airplane as a PA-28-180; the number 010 denotes the tenth airplane built during the model year.

In 1975 the code numbers were again revised but applied only to airplanes produced at the Lock Haven, Pennsylvania and Lakeland, Florida factories. The new codes were assigned to each airplane type although the general constructor number sequence remained the same.

Piper changed the system again in 1986 when the model year was deleted and constructor numbers ran consecutively each year without starting a new batch of figures, such as 2816001 to 2816099, for the PA-28-161 Warrior II. The PA-38 Tomahawk used the prefix "A" as the identification code number followed by four digits. It was the only Piper airplane to use such a procedure.

The following list provides readers with the aircraft type designator and identification number used for the late-model Piper product line:

MODEL	CODE	PREFIX
PA-18-150 Super Cub	09	18
PA-28-181 Archer II	90	28
PA-28-161 Warrior II	16	28
PA-28-161 Cadet	41	28
PA-28-236 Dakota	11	28
PA-28R-201 Arrow	37	28R
PA-28R-201T Arrow IV	31	28R
PA-28R-201T Arrow	30	28R
PA-32-301 Saratoga	06	32
PA-32-R-301 Saratoga SP	13	32R
PA-32R-301T Saratoga SP	29	32R
PA-34-220T Seneca III	33	34
PA-44 Seminole	95	44
PA-46-350 Malibu Mirage	22	46
PA-42-720 Cheyenne IIIA	01	42
PA-42-1000 Cheyenne 400	27	42

PIPER AIRCRAFT SPECIFICATIONS

Specifications for production and experimental aircraft are presented in numerical sequence based on the Taylor and Piper numbering system for each model. Readers desiring additional information should consult the bibliography for references.

TAYLOR BROTHERS AIRCRAFT CORPORATION

ARROWING A-2 CHUMMY

Wing span ....34.0 feet
Length ....22.0 feet
Height ....7 feet 6 inches
Engine ....90 hp. Anzani or 96 hp. Siemens-Halske
Empty weight ....985 lb.
Maximum gross weight.................................1,485 lb.
Useful load ....500 lb.
Service ceiling...Uncertain
Maximum speed...110 mph.
Cruise speed ....100 mph.
Range ....Approximately 500 statute miles

B-2 CHUMMY

Wing span ....34.0 feet
Length ....22 feet 6 inches
Height ....7 feet 6 inches
Engine ....90 hp. Kinner K-5
Empty weight ....1,082 lb.
Maximum gross weight.................................1,643 lb.
Useful load ....561 lb.
Service ceiling...Uncertain
Maximum speed...110 mph.
Cruise speed ....90 mph.
Range ....400 statute miles

TAYLOR AIRCRAFT COMPANY

E-2 CUB, F-2 CUB, H-2 CUB

Wing span ....35 feet 3 inches
Length ....22 feet 3 inches (E-2)
                                    22 feet (F-2)
                                    22 feet 1 inch (H-2)
Height ....6 feet 6 inches
Engine..........................37 hp. Continental A-40-2 or A-40-3 (E-2)
                                    40 hp. Aeromarine AR-3-40 (F-2)
                                    35 hp. Szekely SR-3-35 (H-2)
Empty weight................532 lb. (E-2); 545 lb. (F-2); 582 lb. (H-2)
Maximum gross weight ....925 lb. (E-2); 988 lb. (F-2); 988 lb. (H-2)
Useful load.........................393 lb. (E-2); 412 lb. (F-2); 406 lb. (H-2)
Service ceiling ....12,000 feet (E-2)
                                    13,000 feet (F-2)
                                    12,000 feet (H-2)
Maximum speed..........85 mph. (E-2); 82 mph. (F-2); 80 mph. (H-2)
Cruise speed.............62 mph. (E-2); Uncertain (F-2); 70 mph. (H-2)
Range ....180 statute miles (E-2)
                                    240 statute miles (F-2)
                                    220 statute miles (H-2)

J-2 CUB

Wingspan...35 feet 3 inches
Length ....22 feet 5 inches
Height ....6 feet 8 inches
Engine...37 hp. Continental A-40-3
Empty weight ....563 lb.
Maximum gross weight ....970 lb. to 1,000 lb.
Useful load ....407 lb.
Service ceiling ....12,000 feet
Maximum speed...87 mph.
Cruise speed ....70 mph.
Range ....210 statute miles

PIPER AIRCRAFT CORPORATION

J-3 CUB   J-3C-40 CUB   J-3F CUB

Wingspan...35 feet 3 inches
Length ....22 feet 3 inches
Height ....6 feet 8 inches
Engine...............................40 hp. Continental A-40-4 (J-3)
                                    40 hp. Continental A-40-4 (J-3C)
                                    40 hp. Franklin 4AC-150 (J-3F)
Empty weight ....578 lb. (J-3) Uncertain (J-3C-40 and J-3F)
Maximum gross weight...............................1,000 lb.
Useful load ....422 lb. (J-3) Uncertain (J-3C-40 and J-3F)
Service ceiling ....10,000 feet
Maximum speed...87 mph.
Cruise speed ....72 mph.
Range...210 statute miles (J-3)

J-3C-50 CUB   J-3F-50 CUB   J-3L CUB

Wingspan...35 feet 3 inches
Length ....22 feet 3 inches (J-3C-50)
                                    22 feet 4 inches (J-3F-50 and J-3L)
Height ....6 feet 8 inches
Engine ....50 hp. Continental A50-1, -3, -5 (J-3C)
                                    50 Franklin 4AC-150 (J-3F-50)
                                    50 hp. Lycoming 0-145-A1 (J-3L)
Empty weight ....635 lb.
Maximum gross weight...............................1,100 lb.
Useful load ....465 lb.
Service ceiling ....10,000 feet
Maximum speed...90 mph.
Cruise speed ....80 mph.
Range ....250 statute miles

J-3P CUB   J-3C-65 CUB   J-3F-65 CUB   J-3L-65 CUB

Wingspan...35 feet 3 inches
Length ....22 feet 4 inches (J-3P, J-3F-65 and J-3L-65))
                                    22 feet 3 inches (J-3C-65)
Height ....6 feet 8 inches
Engine...............................50 hp. Lenape LM-3-50 (J-3P)
                                    65 hp. Continental A-65-1, -3, -7, -8 (J-3C-65)
                                    65 hp. Franklin 4AC-176-B2 or -BA2
                                    65 hp. Lycoming 0-145-B1, -B2
Empty weight...630 lb. (J-3P)
                                    640 lb. to 680 lb. (J-3C-65)
                                    640 lb. (J-3F-65, J-3L-65)
Maximum gross weight ....1,100 lb. (J-3P)
                                    1,100 lb. to 1,220 lb. (J-3C-65)
                                    1,100 lb. (J-3F-65, J-3L-65)
Useful load...470 lb. (J-3P)
                                    460 lb. to 540 lb. (J-3C-65)
                                    460 (J-3F-65, J-3L-65)
Service ceiling...12,000 feet (J-3P)
                                    11,500 feet to 12,000 feet (J-3C-65)
                                    10,000 feet (J-3F-65, J-3L-65)
Maximum speed...92 mph.
Cruise speed...81 mph. (J-3P)
                                    73 mph. to 82 mph. (J-3C-65)
                                    82 mph. (J-3F-65, J-3L-65)
Range...270 statute miles (J-3P)
                                    220 statute miles to 250 statute miles (J-3C-65)
                                    250 statute miles (J-3F-65, J-3L-65)

TG-8 TRAINING GLIDER

Wingspan	35 feet 2.5 inches
Length	23 feet 1 inch
Height	5 feet 2 inches
Engine	None
Empty weight	522 lb.
Maximum gross weight	1,060 lb.
Useful load	538 lb.
Service ceiling	Not applicable
Maximum speed	122 mph.
Cruise speed	Not applicable
Range	Not applicable

J-4 CUB COUPE   J-4A CUB COUPE   J-4B CUB COUPE

Wingspan	36 feet 2 inches
Length	22 feet 6 inches
Height	6 feet 10 inches
Engine	50 hp. Continental A-50-1, A-50-3 (J-4)
	65 hp. Continental A-65-1, -3, -8 (J-4A)
	60 hp. Franklin 4AC-171 (J-4B)
Empty weight	710 lb. (J-4)
	740 lb. (J-4A)
	730 lb. (J-4B)
Maximum gross weight	1,200 lb. (J-4)
	1,300 lb. (J-4A)
	1,250 lb. (J-4B)
Useful load	490 lb. (J-4)
	560 lb. (J-4A)
	520 lb. (J-4B)
Service ceiling	10,500 feet (J-4)
	12,000 feet (J-4A)
	11,000 feet (J-4B)
Maximum speed	93 mph. (J-4)
	100 mph. (J-4A)
	96 mph. (J-4B)
Cruise speed	83 mph. (J-4)
	92 mph. (J-4A)
	85 mph. (J-4B)
Range	325 statute miles (J-4)
	460 statute miles (J-4A)
	340 statute miles (J-4B)

J-4E CUB COUPE   J-4F CUB COUPE

Wingspan	36 feet 2 inches
Length	22 feet 6 inches
Height	6 feet 10 inches
Engine	75 hp. Continental A-75-9 (J-4E)
	65 hp. Lycoming 0-145-B2 (J-4F)
Empty weight	865 lb. (J-4E)
	740 lb. (J-4F)
Maximum gross weight	1,400 lb. (J-4E)
	1,300 lb. (J-4F)
Useful load	535 lb. (J-4E)
	560 lb. (J-4F)
Service ceiling	12,000 feet
Maximum speed	105 mph. (J-4E)
	100 mph. (J-4F)
Cruise speed	96 mph. (J-4E)
	92 mph. (J-4F)
Range	460 statute miles

J-5A CUB CRUISER   J-5B CUB CRUISER
J-5C CUB CRUISER

Wingspan	35 feet 6 inches
Length	22 feet 6 inches
Height	6 feet 10 inches (J-5A, J-5A-80, J-5B)
	6 feet 8 inches (J-5C)
Engine	75 hp. Continental A-75-A, -9
	or 80 hp. Continental A-80-8 (J-5A, J-5A-80)
	75 hp. Lycoming GO-145-C2, -C3 (J-5B)
	100 hp. Lycoming 0-235-C (J-5C)
Empty weight	760 lb. (J-5A, J-5A-80)
	830 lb. (J-5B)

Maximum gross weight	1,450 lb.
Useful load	690 lb. (J-5A, J-5A-80)
	620 lb. (J-5B)
Service ceiling	10,000 feet (J-5A, J-5A-80)
	10,200 feet (J-5B)
Maximum speed	95 mph.
Cruise speed	85 mph.
Range	300 statute miles (J-5A, J-5A-80)
	430 statute miles (J-5B)

L-14 AND HE-1

Wingspan	35 feet 6 inches (HE-1)
	35 feet 10 inches (L-14)
Length	22 feet 6 inches (HE-1)
	23 feet 5 inches
Height	6 feet 8 inches (HE-1)
	7 feet (L-14)
Engine	100 hp. Lycoming 0-235-C (HE-1)
	125 hp. Lycoming 0-290-C (L-14)
Empty weight	906 lb. (HE-1)
	1,000 lb. (L-14)
Maximum gross weight	1,550 lb. (HE-1)
	1,800 lb. (L-14)
Useful load	644 lb. (HE-1)
	800 (L-14)
Service ceiling	15,000 feet (HE-1)
	12,000 feet (L-14)
Maximum speed	110 mph. (HE-1)
	115 mph. (L-14)
Cruise speed	100 mph.
Range	385 statute miles (HE-1)
	300 statute miles (L-14)

PT-1 (Experimental)

Wingspan	34 feet
Length	22 feet 10 inches
Height	6 feet 6 inches
Engine	Franklin 6AC-298-D, 130 hp.
Empty weight	1,325 lb.
Maximum gross weight	2,000 lb.
Useful load	675 lb.
Service ceiling	12,400 feet
Maximum speed	150 mph.
Cruise speed	135 mph.
Range	700 statute miles

PWA-1 SKYCOUPE (Experimental)

Wingspan	30 feet
Engine	Franklin 4ACG-199-H3, 113 hp.
Maximum gross weight	1,597 lb.
Maximum speed	110 mph.

PWA-6 SKY SEDAN (Experimental)

Wingspan	34 feet 8 inches
Length	25 feet 5.5 inches
Height	7 feet 3 inches
Engine	Franklin 6AC series, 140 hp.
Useful load	1,050 lb.
Maximum speed	140 mph.
Cruise speed	125-130 mph.

PA-6 SKY SEDAN (Experimental)

Wingspan	34 feet 8 inches
Length	25 feet 5.5 inches
Height	7 feet 3 inches
Engine	Continental E-165, 165 hp.
Maximum gross weight	2,400 lb.
Maximum speed	160 mph.
Cruising speed	140 mph. at 60% power
Range	620 statute miles

PA-8 SKYCYCLE (Experimental)

Wingspan ....20 feet
Length ....15 feet 8 inches
Height ....5 feet
Engine....................................Continental A-40-3, 37 hp.
                                         Lycoming O-145-2, 55 hp.
Maximum gross weight..630 lb.
Maximum speed...120 mph.
Cruise speed ....95 mph.
Range ....400 statute miles

PA-11 CUB SPECIAL

Wingspan ....35 feet 2.5 inches
Length..............................22 feet 4.5 inches
Height ....6 feet 8 inches
Engine.........................65 hp. Continental A-65-8 or 90 hp. C-90-8
Empty weight ....730 lb. (65 hp.)
                                         750 lb. (90 hp.)
Maximum gross weight................................1,220 lb.
Useful load ....490 lb. (65 hp.)
                                         470 lb. (90 hp.)
Service ceiling ....14,000 feet (65 hp.)
                                         16,000 feet (90 hp.)
Maximum speed ....100 mph. (65 hp.)
                                         112 mph. (90 hp.)
Cruise speed..........................87 mph. (65 hp.)
                                         100 mph. (90 hp.)
Range ....300 statute miles (65 hp.)
                                         350 statute miles (90 hp.)

PA-12 SUPER CRUISER (Utility and Normal Category versions)

Wingspan ....35 feet 6 inches
Length ....23 feet 1 inch
Height ....6 feet 10 inches
Engine ....100 hp. Lycoming 0-235-C or 108 hp. 0-235-C1
Empty weight ....855 lb. (100 hp.)
                                         900 lb. (108 hp.)
                                         950 lb. (Normal Category)
Maximum gross weight....................1,500 lb. (100 hp.)
                                         1,550 lb. (108 hp.)
                                         1,750 lb. (Normal Category)
Useful load ....645 lb. (100 hp.)
                                         650 lb. (108 hp.)
                                         800 lb. (Normal Category)
Service ceiling...............................15,700 feet (Utility Category)
                                         12,600 feet (Normal Category)
Maximum speed.......................................115 mph.
Cruise speed ....103-105 mph.
Range ....300 statute miles

PA-14 FAMILY CRUISER

Wingspan...............................35 feet 6 inches
Length ....23 feet 2 inches
Height ....6 feet 5 inches
Engine ....115 hp. Lycoming 0-235-C1
Empty weight ....1,020 lb.
Maximum gross weight....................................1,850 lb.
Useful load ....830 lb.
Service ceiling ....12,000 feet
Maximum speed ....123 mph.
Cruise speed ....110 mph.
Range ....500 statute miles

PA-15 VAGABOND

Wingspan...............................29 feet 3 inches
Length..................................18 feet 8 inches
Height ....6 feet
Engine ....65 hp. Lycoming 0-145-B2
Empty weight ....620 lb.
Maximum gross weight.....................................1,100 lb.
Useful load ....480 lb.

Service ceiling ....12,500 feet
Maximum speed..102 mph.
Cruise speed ....92 mph.
Range ....255 statute miles

PA-16 CLIPPER

Wingspan...............................29 feet 4 inches
Length....................................20 feet
Height ....6 feet 2.5 inches
Engine ....115 hp. Lycoming 0-235-C1
Empty weight ....850 lb.
Maximum gross weight....................................1,650 lb.
Useful load ....800 lb.
Service ceiling ....11,000 feet
Maximum speed..125 mph.
Cruise speed ....112 mph.
Range ....480 statute miles

PA-17 VAGABOND TRAINER

Wingspan...............................29 feet 4 inches
Length................................18 feet 8 inches
Height.................................6 feet 1 inch
Engine ....65 hp. Continental A-65-8
Empty weight ....650 lb.
Maximum gross weight....................................1,150 lb.
Useful load ....500 lb.
Service ceiling ....10,500 feet
Maximum speed..102 mph.
Cruise speed ....90 mph.
Range ....250 statute miles

PA-18 SUPER CUB   PA-18-105 SUPER CUB
PA-18-125 SUPER CUB

Wingspan...............................35 feet 4 inches
Length....................................22 feet 5 inches
Height ....6 feet 8 inches
Engine ....90 hp. Continental C-90-12F (PA-18)
                                         100 hp. Lycoming 0-235-C1 (PA-18-105)
                                         125 hp. Lycoming 0-290-D (PA-18-125)
Empty weight.................................800 lb. (PA-18)
                                         825 lb. (PA-18-105)
                                         845 lb. (PA-18-125)
Maximum gross weight.....................................1,500 lb.
Useful load ....700 lb. (PA-18)
                                         675 lb. (PA-18-105)
                                         655 lb. (PA-18-125)
Service ceiling ....15,750 feet (PA-18 and PA-18-105)
                                         17,100 feet (PA-18-125)
Maximum speed ....112 mph. (PA-18)
                                         115 mph. (PA-18-105)
                                         123 mph. (PA-18-125)
Cruise speed................................100 mph. (PA-18)
                                         105 mph. (PA-18-105)
                                         108 mph. (PA-18-125)
Range..........................360 statute miles (PA-18)
                                         270 statute miles (PA-18-105 and PA-18-125)

PA-18-135 SUPER CUB   PA-18-150 SUPER CUB
PA-18A-150 SUPER CUB

Wingspan ....35 feet 2.5 inches (PA-18)
                                         35 feet 3 inches (PA-18-150 and PA-18A-150)
Length ....22 feet 5 iches (PA-18)
                                         22 feet 6 inches (PA-18-150 and PA-18A-150)
Height.................................6 feet 7.5 inches (PA-18)
                                         6 feet 8 inches (PA-18-150 and PA-18A-150)
Engine ....135 hp. Lycoming 0-290-D (PA-18)
                                         150 hp. Lycoming 0-320-A2A or -A2B
                                         (PA-18-150 and PA-18A-150)
Empty weight.....................................895 lb. (PA-18)
                                         930 lb. (PA-18-150)
                                         1,060 lb. (PA-18A-150)
Maximum gross weight ....1,500 lb. (PA-18)
                                         1,750 lb. (PA-18-150)
                                         2.070 lb. (PA-18A-150)

Useful load ....605 lb. (PA-18)
820 lb. (PA-18-150)
1,010 lb. (PA-18A-150)
Service ceiling...................................19,000 feet (PA-18-150)
17,000 feet (PA-1A-150)
Maximum speed ....127 mph. (PA-18)
130 mph. (PA-18-150)
105 mph. PA-18A-150)
Cruise speed..112 mph. (PA-18)
115 mph. (PA-18-150)
105 mph. (PA-18A-150)
Range..500 statute miles (PA-18)
460 statute miles (PA-18-150)
360 statute miles (PA-18A-150)

L-21A AND L-18C MILITARY VERSIONS OF PA-18 SUPER CUB

Wingspan ....35 feet 3 inches (L-21A)
35 feet 2.5 inches (L-18C)
Length ....22 feet 5 inches (L-21A)
22 feet 4.5 inches (L-18C)
Height...6 feet 7.5 inches (L-21A)
Engine ....125 hp. Lycoming 0-290-D-11 (L-21A)
95 hp. Continental 0-205-1 (L-18C)
Empty weight ....895 lb. (L-21A)
800 lb. (L-18C)
Maximum gross weight ....1,500 lb.
Useful load ....605 lb. (L-21A)
700 lb. (L-18C)
Service ceiling ....Uncertain for L-21A and L-18C
Maximum speed ....127 mph. (L-21A)
110 mph. (L-18C)
Cruise speed...112 mph. (L-21A)
100 mph. (L-18C)
Range ....500 statute miles

PA-19 SUPER CUB

The PA-19 military designation was applied to three airplanes. The PA-19 essentially were identical to the PA-18 series aircraft in terms of performance and dimensions.

PA-20-115 PACER AND PA-20-125 PACER

Wingspan...29 feet 4 inches
Length ....20 feet 5 inches
Height ....6 feet 2.5 inches
Engine.............................115 hp. Lycoming 0-235-C1 (PA-20-115)
125 hp. Lycoming 0-290-D (PA-20-125)
Empty weight..920 lb. (PA-20-115)
970 lb. (PA-20-125)
Maximum gross weight ....1,750 lb. (PA-20-115)
1,800 lb. (PA-20-125)
Useful load ....830 lb.
Service ceiling...11,000 feet (PA-20-115)
14,250 feet (PA-20-125)
Maximum speed ....125 mph. (PA-201-115)
135 mph. (PA-20-125)
Cruise speed..112 mph. (PA-20-115)
125 mph. (PA-20-125)
Range...580 statute miles

PA-20-135 PACER

Wingspan...29 feet 4 inches
Length ....20 feet 5 inches
Height ....6 feet 2.5 inches
Engine...135 hp. Lycoming 0-290-D2
Empty weight...975 lb.
Maximum gross weight ....1,950 lb.
Useful load ....975 lb.
Service ceiling 15,500
Maximum speed ....139 mph.
Cruise speed ....134 mph.
Range...530 statute miles

PA-22-135 TRI-PACER

Wingspan...29 feet 4 inches
Length ....20 feet 5 inches
Height ....8 feet 2.5 inches
Engine.....................................135 hp. Lycoming 0-290-D2
Empty weight...1,005 lb.
Maximum gross weight ....1,950 lb.
Useful load ....945 lb.
Service ceiling ....15,000 feet
Maximum speed ....137 mph.
Cruise speed ....123 mph.
Range...550 statute miles

PA-22-150 TRI-PACER

Wingspan...29 feet 4 inches
Length ....20 feet 6 inches
Height ....8 feet 4 inches
Engine.....................................150 hp. Lycoming 0-320-A2B
Empty weight ....1,100 lb.
Maximum gross weight................................2,000 lb.
Useful load ....900 lb.
Service ceiling ....15,000 feet
Maximum speed ....139 mph.
Cruise speed ....128 mph.
Range...528 statute miles

PA-22-160 TRI-PACER

Wingspan...29 feet 4 iches
Length ....20 feet 6 inches
Height ....8 feet 4 inches
Engine.....................................160 hp. Lycoming 0-320-B
Empty weight ....1,110 lb.
Maximum gross weight................................2,000 lb.
Useful load ....890 lb.
Service ceiling ....16,500 feet
Maximum speed ....141 mph.
Cruise speed ....134 mph.
Range...536 statute miles

PA-22-108 COLT

Wingspan...29 feet 3 inches
Length ....20 feet 2 inches
Height ....8 feet 3 inches
Engine ....108 hp. Lycoming 0-235-C1B
Empty weight ....940 lb.
Maximum gross weight................................1,650 lb.
Useful load ....710 lb.
Service ceiling ....12,000 feet
Maximum speed ....120 mph.
Cruise speed ....108 mph.
Range...648 statute miles

PA-23-150 APACHE

Wingspan...37 feet
Length...27 feet 1.5 inches
Height ....9 feet 6 inches
Engines....................................Two Lycoming 0-320-A, 150 hp.
Empty weight ....2,180 lb. (varied with optional equipment)
Maximum gross weight................................3,500 lb.
Useful load ....1,342 lb. (varied with optional equipment)
Service ceiling ....18,500 feet
Maximum speed ....180 mph.
Cruise speed ....150-170 mph.
Range...660-720 statute miles

PA-23-160 APACHE

Wingspan ....37 feet
Length...27 feet 1.5 inches
Height ....9 feet 6 inches

Engines ....Two Lycoming 0-320-B, -B1A, -B1B, -B3B, 160 hp.
Empty weight ....2,320 lb. (varied with optional equipment)
Maximum gross weight..3,800 lb.
Useful load ....1,520 lb. (varied with optional equipment)
Service ceiling ....17,000 feet
Maximum speed...183 mph.
Cruise speed ....173 mph.
Range ....840 statute miles

PA-23-235 APACHE

Wingspan ....37 feet
Length ....27 feet 7 inches
Height ....10 feet 3.5 inches
Engines ....Two Lycoming 0-540-B1A5, 235 hp.
Empty weight ....2,735 lb.
Maximum gross weight..4,800 lb.
Useful load ....2,065 lb.
Service ceiling ....17,200 feet
Maximum speed...202 mph.
Cruise speed ....191 mph.
Range ....1,185 statute miles

PA-23-250 AZTEC

Wingspan ....37 feet
Length ....27 feet 7 inches
Height ....10 feet 3.5 inches
Engines ....Two Lycoming 0-540-A1DS, 250 hp.
Empty weight ....2,775 lb.
Maximum gross weight..4,800 lb.
Useful load ....2,025 lb.
Service ceiling ....22,500 feet
Maximum speed...215 mph.
Cruise speed ....205 mph.
Range ....1,200 statute miles

PA-23-250 AZTEC C AND AZTEC D

Wingspan ....37 feet 2 inches
Length ....30 feet 3 inches
Height ....10 feet 4 inches
Engines ....Two Lycoming IO-540-C4B5, 250 hp.
Empty weight ....2,933 lb.
Maximum gross weight...............4,400 lb. to 4,800 lb. to 5,200 lb.
depending upon model year
Useful load ....1,427 lb., 1,867 lb, and 2,267 lb.
depending upon model year/gross weight
Service ceiling.........................22,400 feet, 21,000 feet, 19,800 feet
depending upon model year/gross weight
Maximum speed.........................220 mph., 218 mph. and 216 mph.
depending upon model year/gross weight
Cruise speed ....205 mph. to 210 mph.
Range...........................1,055 statute miles to 1,075 statute miles

PA-23 TURBO AZTEC C AND TURBO AZTEC D

Wingspan...37 feet 2 inches
Length...30 feet 3 inches
Height...10 feet 4 inches
Engines ....Two Lycoming TIO-540-C1A, 250 hp.
Empty weight ....3,123 lb.
Maximum gross weight..5,200 lb.
Useful load ....2,077 lb.
Service ceiling ....30,000 feet
Maximum speed...256 mph.
Cruise speed ....224 mph. to 236 mph.
Range...........................1,215 statute miles to 1,265 statute miles

PA-23 AZTEC E AND TURBO AZTEC E

Wingspan...37 feet 2 inches
Length...31 feet 3 inches
Height ....10 feet 4 inches
Engines................Two Textron Lycoming IO-540-C4B5, 250 hp.
Empty weight..3,042 lb. (Aztec E)
3,226 LB. (Turbo E)
Maximum gross weight...5,200 lb.
Useful load ....2,158 lb. (Aztec E)
1,974 lb. (Turbo E)
Service ceiling...............................21,100 feet (Aztec E)
30,000 feet (Turbo E)
Maximum speed ....216 mph. (Aztec E)
253 mph. (Turbo E)
Cruise speed ....204 mph. to 210 mph. (Aztec E)
200 mph. to 226 mph. (Turbo E)
Range ....946 to 1,265 statute miles (Aztec E)
1,105 to 1,225 statute miles (Turbo E)

PA-23-250 AZTEC F AND TURBO AZTEC F

Wingspan...37 feet 4 inches
Length...31 feet 3 inches
Height...10 feet 1 inch
Engines...............Two Textron Lycoming IO-540-C4B5 (Aztec F)
Two Textron Lycoming TIO-540-C1A (Turbo F)
Empty weight....................3,049 lb. to 3,221 lb. (Aztec F)
3,188 lb to 3,358 lb. (Turbo F)
Maximum gross weight...5,200 lb.
Useful load ....1,979 lb. to 2,151 lb. (Aztec F)
1,842 lb. to 2,012 lb. (Turbo F)
Service ceiling ....17,600 feet (Aztec F)
24,000 feet (Turbo F)
Maximum speed ....204 mph. (Aztec F)
248 mph. (Turbo F)
Cruise speed ....204 mph. (Aztec F)
248 mph. (Turbo F)
Range...............................1,122 statute miles (Aztec F)
952 statute miles (Turbo F)

PA-24-180 COMANCHE

Wingspan ....36 feet
Length ....24 feet 8 inches
Height ....7 feet 4 inches
Engine...180 hp. Lycoming 0-360-A1A
Empty weight...1,455 lb. to 1,475 lb.
Maximum gross weight...2,550 lb.
Useful load ....1,075 lb. to 1,095 lb.
Service ceiling ....18,500 feet
Maximum speed...167 mph.
Cruise speed ....134 to 160 mph.
Range ....1,050 statute miles

PA-24-250 COMANCHE

Wingspan ....36 feet
Length...24 feet 11 inches
Height ....7 feet 4 inches
Engine...........................250 hp. Lycoming 0-540-A1A5, IO-540-C
Empty weight ....1,600 lb.
Maximum gross weight...2,800 lb.
Useful load ....1,200 lb.
Service ceiling ....20,000 feet
Maximum speed...190 mph.
Cruise speed ....161 to 181 mph.
Range ....1,100 statute miles

PA-24-260 COMANCHE

Wingspan ....36 feet
Length...25 feet 3.5 inches
Height ....7 feet 4 inches
Engine..260 hp. Lycoming 0-540-E4A5
Empty weight ....1,628 lb.
Maximum gross weight...2,900 lb.
Useful load ....1,172 lb.
Service ceiling ....20,000 feet
Maximum speed...194 mph.
Cruise speed ....163 to 182 mph.
Range ....800 statute miles

PA-24-260B COMANCHE

Wingspan ....36 feet
Length ....25 feet 3.5 inches
Height ....7 feet 4 inches
Engine ....260 hp. Lycoming 0-540-E4A5
Empty weight ....1,728 lb.
Maximum gross weight............................3,100 lb.
Useful load ....1,372 lb.
Service ceiling ....20,000 feet
Maximum speed..194 mph.
Cruise speed......................................163 to 182 mph.
Range ....775 statute miles

PA-24-260C COMANCHE

Wingspan ....36 feet
Length ....25 feet 8 inches
Height ....7 feet 4 inches
Engine ....260 hp. Lycoming IO-540-E4A5
Empty weight ....1,773 lb.
Maximum gross weight............................3,200 lb.
Useful load ....1,427 lb.
Service ceiling ....19,500 feet
Maximum speed..195 mph.
Cruise speed......................................166 to 185 mph.
Range ....800 statute miles

PA-24-260C TURBO COMANCHE

Wingspan ....36 feet
Length ....25 feet 8 inches
Height ....7 feet 4 inches
Engine..................260 hp. turbocharged Lycoming IO-540-R1A5
Empty weight ....1,810 lb.
Maximum gross weight............................3,200 lb.
Useful load ....1,390 lb.
Service ceiling ....25,000 feet
Maximum speed..242 mph.
Cruise speed ....227 mph.
Range ....750 statute miles

PA-24-400 COMANCHE

Wingspan ....36 feet
Length ....25 feet 8 inches
Height ....7 feet 10 inches
Engine ....400 hp. Lycoming IO-720-A1A
Empty weight ....2,110 lb.
Maximum gross weight............................3,600 lb.
Useful load ....1,590 lb.
Service ceiling ....19,500 feet
Maximum speed..223 mph.
Cruise speed......................................195 to 213 mph.
Range ....958 statute miles to 1,700 statute miles

PA-25-150 PAWNEE

Wingspan ....36 feet 2.5 inches
Length ....24 feet
Height ....6 feet 9.5 inches
Engine..............................150 hp. Lycoming 0-320-A1A
Empty weight ....1,220 lb.
Maximum gross weight............................2,300 lb.
Useful load ....1,080 lb.
Hopper load ....800 lb.
Service ceiling ....10,000 feet
Maximum speed..113 mph.
Cruise speed ....95 mph.
Range ....440 statute miles

PA-25-235 AND PA-25-235B PAWNEE

Wingspan ....36 feet 3 inches
Length ....24 feet 8 inches

Height ....7 feet 3 inches
Engine..........................235 hp. Lycoming 0-540-B2B5
Empty weight ....1,420 lb. (without attachments)
Maximum gross weight............................2,900 lb.
Useful load ....1,480 lb. (without attachments)
Hopper load ....1,200 lb.
Service ceiling ....13,000 feet
Maximum speed ....117 mph. (with spray equipment)
Cruise speed............................105 mph. (with spray equipment)
Range..........................300 statute miles (with spray equipment)

PA-25-235C PAWNEE AND PA-25-235D PAWNEE

Wingspan ....36 feet 3 inches
Length ....24 feet 8 inches
Height ....7 feet 3 inches
Engine..........................235 hp. Lycoming 0-540-B2B5
Empty weight ....1,420 (without equipment)
Maximum gross weight............................2,900 lb.
Useful load ....1,480 lb. (without equipment)
Hopper load ....1,200 lb.
Service ceiling................10,000 feet to 13,000 feet
Maximum speed ....117 mph. (with spray equipment)
Cruise speed............................105 mph. (with spray equipment)
Range..........................270 statute miles (with spray equipment)

PA-25-260C AND PA-25-260D PAWNEE

Wingspan ....36 feet 3 inches
Length ....24 feet 8 inches
Height ....7 feet 3 inches
Engine ....260 hp. Lycoming 0-540-E
Empty weight..................1,472 lb. (without equipment)
Maximum gross weight............................2,900 lb.
Useful load..................1,360 lb. (with spray equipment)
Hopper load ....1,200 lb.
Service ceiling................10,000 feet to 13,000 feet
Maximum speed ....120 mph. (with spray equipment)
Cruise speed............................106 mph. (with spray equipment)
Range..........................265 statute miles (with spray equipment)

PA-28-140B, 140C, 140D, 140E, 140F CHEROKEE

Wingspan ....30 feet
Length ....23 feet 4 inches
Height ....7 feet 4 inches
Engine..............................150 hp. Lycoming 0-320-A2A or -A2B
Empty weight ....1,180 to 1,245 lb.
Maximum gross weight............................2,150 lb.
Useful load ....905 to 970 lb.
Service ceiling ....14,300 feet
Maximum speed..142 mph.
Cruise speed ....135 mph.
Range ....950 statute miles

PA-28-140 FLITE LINER

Wingspan ....30 feet
Length ....23 feet 4 inches
Height ....7 feet 4 inches
Engine..............................150 hp. Lycoming 0-320-E3D
Empty weight ....1,305 lb.
Maximum gross weight............................2,150 lb.
Useful load ....845 lb.
Service ceiling ....10,950 feet
Maximum speed..139 mph.
Cruise speed ....132 mph.
Range ....705 statute miles

PA-28-140 CRUISER

Wingspan ....30 feet
Length ....23 feet 4 inches
Height ....7 feet 4 inches
Engine..............................150 hp. Lycoming 0-320-E3D

Empty weight ....1,283 lb.
Maximum gross weight...2,150 lb.
Useful load ....876 lb.
Service ceiling ....10,950 feet
Maximum speed...142 mph.
Cruise speed ....135 mph.
Range ....780 statute miles

PA-28-150 CHEROKEE

Wingspan ....30 feet
Length...23 feet 3.5 inches
Height ....7 feet 3.5 inches
Engine...150 hp. Lycoming 0-320-A2B
Empty weight ....1,205 lb.
Maximum gross weight...2,150 lb.
Useful load ....945 lb.
Service ceiling ....14,300 feet
Maximum speed...136 mph.
Cruise speed ....105 to 123 mph.
Range ....839 statute miles

PA-28-150C CHEROKEE

Wingspan ....30 feet
Length..23 feet 6 inches
Height ....7 feet 3.5 inches
Engine...150 hp. Lycoming 0-320-E2A
Empty weight ....1,250 lb.
Maximum gross weight...2,150 lb.
Useful load ....900 lb.
Service ceiling ....14,900 feet
Maximum speed...144 mph.
Cruise speed ....132 to 135 mph.
Range ....800 statute miles

PA-28-151 WARRIOR

Wingspan ....35 feet
Length..23 feet 10 inches
Height ....7 feet 4 inches
Engine ....150 hp. Textron Lycoming 0-320-E3D
Empty weight ....1,315 lb.
Maximum gross weight..2,325 lb.
Useful load ....1,024 lb.
Service ceiling ....12,700 feet
Maximum speed ....118 kt.
Cruise speed ....117 kt.
Range...632 nautical miles

PA-28-161 WARRIOR II

Wingspan ....35 feet
Length..23 feet 10 inches
Height ....7 feet 4 inches
Engine ....160 hp. Textron Lycoming 0-320-D3G
Empty weight ....1,348 lb.
Maximum gross weight ....2,325 lb. to 2,447 lb.
Useful load ....972 to 1,099 lb.
Service ceiling...11,000 to 14,000 feet
Maximum speed ....127 kt.
Cruise speed ....127 kt.
Range...640 nautical miles

PA-28-160B CHEROKEE

Wingspan ....30 feet
Length...23 feet 3.5 inches
Height ....7 feet 3.5 inches
Engine...160 hp. Lycoming 0-320-B2B
Empty weight ....1,215 lb.
Maximum gross weight...2,200 lb.
Useful load ....985 lb.
Service ceiling ....15,000 feet
Maximum speed...138 mph.
Cruise speed ....115 to 125 mph.
Range ....810 statute miles

PA-28S-160B CHEROKEE

Wingspan ....30 feet
Length...23 feet 3.5 inches
Height...11 feet 1 inch
Engine...160 hp. Lycoming 0-320-B2B
Empty weight ....1,370 lb.
Maximum gross weight...2,140 lb.
Useful load ....780 lb.
Service ceiling ....10,000 feet
Maximum speed...126 mph.
Cruise speed ....117 mph.
Range ....706 statute miles
Floats...EDO 2000 series

PA-28-160C CHEROKEE

Wingspan ....30 feet
Length..23 feet 6 inches
Height ....7 feet 3.5 inches
Engine...160 hp. Lycoming 0-320-D2A
Empty weight ....1,255 lb.
Maximum gross weight...2,200 lb.
Useful load ....945 lb.
Service ceiling ....15,800 feet
Maximum speed...146 mph.
Cruise speed ....137 mph.
Range ....815 statute miles

PA-28-180B CHEROKEE

Wingspan ....30 feet
Length...23 feet 3.5 inches
Height ....7 feet 3.5 inches
Engine...180 hp. Lycoming 0-360-A2A
Empty weight ....1,225 lb.
Maximum gross weight...2,400 lb.
Useful load ....1,135 lb.
Service ceiling ....15,700 feet
Maximum speed...150 mph.
Cruise speed ....141 mph.
Range ....750 statute miles

PA-28-180C CHEROKEE

Wingspan ....30 feet
Length..23 feet 6 inches
Height ....7 feet 3.5 inches
Engine...180 hp. Lycoming 0-360-A3A
Empty weight ....1,270 lb.
Maximum gross weight...2,400 lb.
Useful load ....1,130 lb.
Service ceiling ....16,400 feet
Maximum speed...152 mph.
Cruise speed ....143 mph.
Range ....760 statute miles

PA-28-180D CHEROKEE

Wingspan ....30 feet
Length..23 feet 6 inches
Height ....7 feet 3.5 inches
Engine...180 hp. Lycoming 0-360-A3A
Empty weight ....1,300 lb.
Maximum gross weight...2,400 lb.
Useful load ....1,100 lb.
Service ceiling ....16,400 feet
Maximum speed...152 mph.
Cruise speed ....126 to 143 mph.
Range ....760 statute miles

PA-28-180 CHALLENGER

Wingspan ....32 feet
Length...24 feet

Height ....7 feet 10 inches
Engine ....180 hp. Lycoming 0-360-A3A
Empty weight ....1,386 lb.
Maximum gross weight ....2,450 lb.
Useful load ....1,064 lb.
Service ceiling ....14,150 feet
Maximum speed...148 mph.
Cruise speed ....141 mph.
Range ....686 statute miles

PA-28-180 ARCHER

Wingspan ....32 feet
Length ....24 feet
Height ....7 feet 10 inches
Engine ....180 hp. Lycoming 0-360-A4A
Empty weight ....1,395 lb.
Maximum gross weight ....2,450 lb.
Useful load ....1,060 lb.
Service ceiling ....14,150 feet
Maximum speed...148 mph.
Cruise speed ....141 mph.
Range ....750 statute miles

PA-28-181 ARCHER II

Wingspan ....35 feet
Length ....24 feet
Height ....7 feet 4 inches
Engine.........................180 hp. Textron Lycoming 0-360-A4M
Empty weight...............................1,390 to 1,421 lb.
Maximum gross weight ....2,558 lb.
Useful load ....1,160 lb.
Service ceiling ....13,650 feet
Maximum speed...151 mph.
Cruise speed ....147 mph.
Range ....905 statute miles

PA-28-235 AND PA-28-235B CHEROKEE

Wingspan ....32 feet
Length..23 feet 8.5 inches
Height ....7 feet 1 inch
Engine ....235 hp. Lycoming 0-540-B2B5
Empty weight..................1,410 lb. (235); 1,435 lb. (235B)
Maximum gross weight ....2,900 lb.
Useful load...................1,490 lb. (235); 1,465 lb. (235B)
Service ceiling ....14,500 feet
Maximum speed ....146 kt.
Cruise speed ....137 kt.
Range...991 nautical miles

PA-28-235C, 235D, 235E, 235F CHEROKEE

Wingspan ....32 feet
Length..23 feet 8.5 inches
Height ....7 feet 1 inch (235C, 235D)
7 feet 4 inches (235E, 235F)
Engine ....235 hp. Lycoming 0-540-B4B5
Empty weight........................1,467 lb. (fixed-pitch propeller)
1,491 lb. (constant-speed propeller)
Maximum gross weight ....2,900 lb.
Useful load..............................1,433 lb. (fixed-pitch propeller)
1,409 lb. (constant-speed propeller)
Service ceiling..................14,500 feet (fixed-pitch propeller)
16,500 feet (constant-speed propeller)
Maximum speed ....143 to 144 kt.
Cruise speed...134 to 135 kt.
Range ....800 to 812 nautical miles

PA-28-235 CHARGER

Wingspan ....32 feet
Length ....24 feet 1 inch
Height ....7 feet 10 inches
Engine ....235 hp. Lycoming 0-540-B4B5

Empty weight ....1,550 lb.
Maximum gross weight ....3,000 lb.
Useful load ....1,450 lb.
Service ceiling ....12,000 feet
Maximum speed ....141 kt.
Cruise speed ....133 kt.
Range...912 nautical miles

PA-28-235 PATHFINDER

Wingspan ....32 feet
Length ....24 feet 1 inch
Height ....7 feet 10 inches
Engine ....235 hp. Lycoming 0-540-B4B5
Empty weight ....1,550 to 1,565 lb.
Maximum gross weight ....3,000 lb.
Useful load ....1,450 lb.
Service ceiling ....13,550 feet
Maximum speed ....141 kt.
Cruise speed ....134 kt.
Range...974 nautical miles

PA-28-236 DAKOTA

Wingspan ....35 feet 5 inches
Length ....24 feet 8.5 inches
Height ....7 feet 2 inches
Engine ....235 hp. Textron Lycoming 0-540-J3A5D
Empty weight ....1,582 to 1,610 lb.
Maximum gross weight ....3,011 lb.
Useful load ....1,390 to 1,419 lb.
Service ceiling ....17,000 to 20,000 feet
Maximum speed ....148 kt.
Cruise speed ....144 kt.
Range...810 nautical miles

PA-28-201T TURBO DAKOTA

Wingspan ....35 feet
Length ....25 feet
Height ....7 feet 7 inches
Engine ....200 hp. Teledyne Continental TSIO-360-FB
Empty weight ....1,563 lb.
Maximum gross weight ....2,900 lb.
Useful load ....1,337 lb.
Service ceiling ....20,000 feet
Maximum speed ....162 kt.
Cruise speed ....156 kt.
Range...795 nautical miles

PA-28R-180 AND PA-28R-180B CHEROKEE ARROW

Wingspan ....30 feet
Length..24 feet 2.5 inches
Height ....8 feet
Engine ....180 hp. Lycoming IO-360-B1E
Empty weight ....1,380 to 1,431 lb.
Maximum gross weight ....2,500 lb.
Useful load ....1,069 to 1,120 lb.
Service ceiling ....15,000 feet
Maximum speed ....149 kt.
Cruise speed ....141 kt.
Range...864 nautical miles

PA-28R-200 AND PA-28R-200B CHEROKEE ARROW

Wingspan ....30 feet
Length..24 feet 2.5 inches
Height ....8 feet
Engine ....200 hp. Lycoming IO-360-C1C
Empty weight ....1,459 to 1,470 lb.
Maximum gross weight ....2,600 lb.
Useful load ....1,130 to 1,141 lb.
Service ceiling ....16,000 feet
Maximum speed ....154 kt.

Cruise speed...146 kt.
Range.......................................833 nautical miles

PA-28R-200 ARROW II

Wingspan ....32 feet
Length.......................................24 feet 7 inches
Height...8 feet
Engine ....200 hp. Lycoming IO-360-C1C
Empty weight ....1,508 to 1,531 lb.
Maximum gross weight...........................2,650 lb.
Useful load ....1,119 to 1,142 lb.
Service ceiling ....15,000 feet
Maximum speed ....153 kt.
Cruise speed ....148 kt.
Range.......................................850 nautical miles

PA-28R-201 ARROW III

Wingspan ....35 feet
Length...25 feet
Height...8 feet
Engine ....200 hp. Lycoming IO-360-C1C6
Empty weight ....1,601 lb.
Maximum gross weight...........................2,750 lb.
Useful load ....1,149 lb.
Service ceiling ....16,200 feet
Maximum speed ....152 kt.
Cruise speed ....143 kt.
Range.......................................980 nautical miles

PA-28R-201T TURBO ARROW III

Wingspan ....35 feet
Length...25 feet
Height...8 feet
Engine ....200 hp. Teledyne Continental TSIO-360-F
Empty weight ....1,663 lb.
Maximum gross weight...........................2,900 lb.
Useful load ....1,237 lb.
Service ceiling ....20,000 feet
Maximum speed ....178 kt.
Cruise speed.........................154 to 172 kt.
Range.......................................860 nautical miles

PA-28RT-201 ARROW IV

Wingspan ....35 feet 5 inches
Length...27 feet
Height ....8 feet 3 inches
Engine ....200 hp. Lycoming IO-360-C1C6
Empty weight ....1,592 to 1,641 lb.
Maximum gross weight...........................2,750 lb.
Useful load ....1,109 to 1,157 lb.
Service ceiling ....17,000 feet
Maximum speed ....152 kt.
Cruise speed ....143 kt.
Range.......................................810 nautical miles

PA-28RT-201T ARROW IV

Wingspan ....35 feet 5 inches
Length...............................27 feet 3.5 inches
Height ....8 feet 3 inches
Engine ....200 hp. Teledyne Continental TSIO-360-FB
Empty weight ....1,638 to 1,704 lb.
Maximum gross weight...........................2,912 lb.
Useful load ....1,208 to 1,262 lb.
Service ceiling ....20,000 feet
Maximum speed ....178 kt.
Cruise speed ....172 kt.
Range.......................................790 nautical miles

PA-28R-300 PILLAN

Wingspan................................28 feet 11 inches
Length...................................26 feet 2 inches
Height.......................................7 feet 8 inches
Engine ....300 hp. Lycoming IO-540-K1K5
Empty weight ....2,050 lb.
Maximum gross weight...........................2,900 lb.
Useful load ....850 lb.
Service ceiling ....19,100 feet
Maximum speed ....168 kt.
Cruise speed ....138 kt.
Range.......................................590 nautical miles

PA-29 PAPOOSE

Wingspan...25 feet
Length...................................20 feet 8 inches
Height...7 feet
Engine.........................108 Lycoming 0-235-C1B
Empty weight ....803.5 lb.
Maximum gross weight...........................1,500 lb.
Useful load ....696.5 lb.
Maximum speed ....130 mph.

PA-30 AND PA-30B TWIN COMANCHE

Wingspan ....36 feet
Length...................................25 feet 2 inches
Height.......................................8 feet 2 inches
Engines ....Two Lycoming IO-360-B, 160 hp.
Empty weight ....2,160 lb.
Maximum gross weight...........................3,600 lb.
Useful load ....1,440 lb.
Service ceiling ....18,600 feet
Maximum speed ....205 mph.
Cruise speed ....194 mph.
Range.......................................948 statute miles

PA-30B TURBO TWIN COMANCHE

Wingspan................................36 feet 9 inches
Length...................................25 feet 2 inches
Height ....8 feet 2 inches
Engines ....Two Lycoming TIO-320-C1A, 160 hp.
Empty weight ....2,408 lb.
Maximum gross weight...........................3,725 lb.
Useful load ....1,317 lb.
Service ceiling ....30,000 feet
Maximum speed ....240 mph.
Cruise speed ....223 mph.
Range.......................................1,465 statute miles

PA-30C TWIN COMANCHE

Wingspan ....36 feet
Length...................................25 feet 2 inches
Height.......................................8 feet 2 inches
Engines ....Two Lycoming IO-320-B, 160 hp.
Empty weight ....2,238 lb.
Maximum gross weight...........................3,600 lb.
Useful load ....1,362 lb.
Service ceiling ....20,000 feet
Maximum speed...................................205 mph.
Cruise speed ....198 mph.
Range.......................................830 statute miles

PA-30C TURBO TWIN COMANCHE

Wingspan................................36 feet 9 inches
Length...................................25 feet 2 inches
Height.......................................8 feet 2 inches
Engines ....Two Lycoming TIO-320-C1A, 160 hp.
Empty weight ....2,384 lb.
Maximum gross weight...........................3,725 lb.

Useful load ....1,341 lb.
Service ceiling ....24,000 feet
Maximum speed ....246 mph.
Cruise speed ....221 mph.
Range ....1,270 statute miles

PA-31-300 NAVAJO

Wingspan ....40 feet 8 inches
Length ....32 feet 8 inches
Height ....13 feet
Engines...........................Two Lycoming IO-540-M, 300 hp.
Empty weight ....3,603 lb.
Maximum gross weight..............................6,200 lb.
Useful load ....2,597 lb.
Service ceiling ....20,500 feet
Maximum speed ....196 kt.
Cruise speed ....184 kt.
Range...1,193 nautical miles

PA-31-310 AND PA-31-310B NAVAJO

Wingspan......................................40 feet 8 inches
Length ....32 feet 8 inches
Height ....13 feet
Engines.....................Two Lycoming TIO-540-A1A, 310 hp. (310)
Two Lycoming TIO-540-A, 310 hp. (310B)
Empty weight ....3,759 lb. (310)
3,849 lb. (310B)
Maximum gross weight....................................6,500 lb.
Useful load....................................2,741 lb. (310)
2,651 lb. (310B)
Service ceiling ....26,300 feet
Maximum speed ....228 kt.
Cruise speed...................................217 to 220 kt.
Range ....982 to 1,491 nautical miles

PA-31-310C NAVAJO

Wingspan......................................40 feet 8 inches
Length..32 feet 8 inches
Height..13 feet
Engines.....................Two Lycoming TIO-540-A2C, 310 hp.
Empty weight...............................3,930 to 4,003 lb.
Maximum gross weight..................................6,536 lb.
Useful load ....2,533 to 2,570 lb.
Service ceiling...............................24,000 to 26,300 feet
Maximum speed ....228 kt.
Cruise speed ....217 kt.
Range ....935 to 1,065 nautical miles

PA-31-325 NAVAJO C/R

Wingspan......................................40 feet 8 inches
Length..32 feet 8 inches
Height..13 feet
Engines.......................................Two Lycoming TIO-540-F2BD
and LTIO-540-F2BD, 325 hp.
Empty weight...............................4,000 to 4,099 lb.
Maximum gross weight..................6,500 to 6,540 lb.
Useful load ....2,441 to 2,500 lb.
Service ceiling ....26,400 feet
Maximum speed ....228 to 232 kt.
Cruise speed ....221 kt.
Range.................................940 to 1,040 nautical miles

PA-31-350 CHIEFTAIN

Wingspan......................................40 feet 8 inches
Length...34 feet 7.5 inches
Height..13 feet
Engines.............................Two Lycoming TIO-540-J2BD and
LTIO-540-J2BD, 350 hp.
Empty weight...............................3,991 to 4,319 lb.
Maximum gross weight....................7,000 to 7,0445 lb.

Useful load ....2,726 to 3,009 lb.
Service ceiling.........................24,000 to 27,200 feet
Maximum speed ....231 to 236 kt.
Cruise speed......................................210 to 228 kt.
Range...950 nautical miles

PA-31-350 T-1020

Wingspan......................................40 feet 8 inches
Length...34 feet 7.5 inches
Height..13 feet
Engines...........................Two Textron Lycoming TIO-540-J2B
and LTIO-540-J2B, 350 hp.
Empty weight...4,450 lb.
Maximum gross weight..............................7,045 lb.
Useful load...2,595 lb.
Service ceiling ....24,000 feet
Maximum speed ....235 kt.
Cruise speed ....212 kt.
Range...695 nautical miles

PA-31P PRESSURIZED NAVAJO

Wingspan......................................40 feet 8 inches
Length...34 feet 6 inches
Height..13 feet 3 inches
Engines.............Two Textron Lycoming TIGO-541-E1A, 425 hp.
Empty weight...4,842 lb.
Maximum gross weight..............................7,800 lb.
Useful load...2,958 lb.
Service ceiling ....29,000 feet
Maximum speed ....243 kt.
Cruise speed ....233 kt.
Range ....925 to 1,260 nautical miles

PA-31P-350 MOJAVE

Wingspan......................................44 feet 6 inches
Length...34 feet 6 inches
Height..13 feet
Engines..........................Two Textron Lycoming TIO-540-V2AD
and LTIO-540-V2AD, 350 hp.
Empty weight...5,070 lb.
Maximum gross weight..............................7,245 lb.
Useful load...2,175 lb.
Service ceiling ....30,400 feet
Maximum speed ....242 kt.
Cruise speed ....235 kt.
Range ....1,113 to 1,221 nautical miles

PA-31T CHEYENNE I

Wingspan......................................40 feet 8 inches
Length...34 feet 8 inches
Height..12 feet 9 inches
Engines............Two Pratt & Whitney Canada PT6A-11, 500 shp.
Empty weight...4,900 lb.
Maximum gross weight..............................8,750 lb.
Useful load...3,850 lb.
Service ceiling ....27,000 to 29,000 feet
Maximum speed ....249 kt.
Cruise speed......................................249 to 252 kt.
Range ....1,400 nautical miles (with wing tip tanks)

PA-31T CHEYENNE 1A

Wingspan......................................42 feet 8 inches
Length...34 feet 8 inches
Height..12 feet 9 inches
Engines............Two Pratt & Whitney Canada PT6A-11, 500 shp.
Empty weight...5,110 lb.
Maximum gross weight..............................8,750 lb.
Useful load...3,640 lb.
Service ceiling ....28,200 feet
Maximum speed ....261 kt.

Cruise speed..247 to 261 kt.
Range ....935 to 1,255 nautical miles

PA-31T CHEYENNE II

Wingspan..42 feet 8 inches
Length..34 feet 8 inches
Height..12 feet 9 inches
Engines ....Two Pratt & Whitney Canada PT6A-28, 620 shp.
Empty weight..4,870 to 4,976 lb.
Maximum gross weight..9,050 lb.
Useful load..4,074 to 4,180 lb.
Service ceiling ....31,600 feet
Cruise speed..283 kt.
Range ....905 to 1,510 nautical miles

PA-31T2 CHEYENNE IIXL

Wingspan..42 feet 8 inches
Length..36 feet 8 inches
Height..12 feet 9 inches
Engines ....Two Pratt & Whitney Canada PT6A-135, 620 shp.
Empty weight..5,164 to 5,487 lb.
Maximum gross weight..9,540 lb.
Useful load..4,053 to 4,376 lb.
Service ceiling ....32,400 feet
Cruise speed..255 to 275 kt.
Range ....775 to 1,336 nautical miles

PA-31T3 T-1040

Wingspan..41 feet 1 inch
Length..36 feet 8 inches
Height..12 feet 9 inches
Engines ....Two Pratt & Whitney Canada PT6A-11, 500 shp.
Empty weight..4,800 lb.
Maximum gross weight..9,050 lb.
Useful load..4,250 lb.
Service ceiling ....24,000 feet
Maximum speed..244 kt.
Cruise speed..238 kt.
Range......................................624 nautical miles

PA-32-260B, 260C, 260D CHEROKEE SIX

Wingspan..32 feet 9 inches
Length..27 feet 8.5 inches
Height..7 feet 11 inches
Engine................................260 hp. Lycoming 0-540-E
and constant-speed propeller
Empty weight..1,680 to 1,724 lb.
Maximum gross weight..3,400 lb.
Useful load..1,676 to 1,720 lb.
Service ceiling ....14,500 feet
Maximum speed..166 mph.
Cruise speed..160 mph.
Range................................950 to 1,170 statute miles

PA-32-300B, 300C, 300D CHEROKEE SIX

Wingspan..32 feet 9 inches
Length..27 feet 8.5 iinches
Height..7 feet 11 inches
Engine................................300 hp. Lycoming IO-540K
Empty weight..1,738 to 1,799 lb.
Maximum gross weight..3,400 lb.
Useful load..1,601 to 1,602 lb.
Service ceiling ....16,250 feet
Maximum speed..174 mph.
Cruise speed..168 mph.
Range......................................1,060 statute miles

PA-32-300 CHEROKEE SIX AND PA-32-300 SIX 300

Wingspan..32 feet 9 inches

Length..27 feet 8.5 inches
Height...8 feet 2.5 inches
Engine........................300 hp. Textron Lycoming IO-540-K1G5D
Empty weight..1,837 to 1,846 lb.
Maximum gross weight..3,400 lb.
Useful load..1,554 to 1,563 lb.
Service ceiling ....16,250 to 17,100 feet
Maximum speed..178 mph.
Cruise speed..174 mph.
Range......................................952 statute miles

PA-32-301 SARATOGA

Wingspan..36 feet 5 inches
Length..27 feet 8 inches
Height..8 feet 3 inches
Engine........................300 hp. Textron Lycoming IO-540-K1G5
Empty weight..1,935 lb.
Maximum gross weight..3,615 lb.
Useful load..1,680 lb.
Service ceiling ....14,100 to 16,000 feet
Maximum speed..173 mph.
Cruise speed..166 to 171 mph.
Range......................................849 to 1,215 statute miles

PA-32-301T TURBO SARATOGA

Wingspan..36 feet 5 inches
Length..28 feet 6 inches
Height..8 feet 3 inches
Engine........................300 hp. Textron Lycoming TIO-540-S1AD
Empty weight..2,000 lb.
Maximum gross weight..3,617 lb.
Useful load..1,617 lb.
Service ceiling ....20,000 feet
Maximum speed..207 mph.
Cruise speed..188 mph.
Range......................................980 statute miles

PA-32R-300 LANCE

Wingspan..32 feet 11 inches
Length..27 feet 8 inches
Height..8 feet 3 inches
Engine........................300 hp. Textron Lycoming IO-540-K1A5
Empty weight..1,910 lb.
Maximum gross weight..3,600 lb.
Useful load..1,690 lb.
Service ceiling ....14,600 feet
Maximum speed..167 kt.
Cruise speed..160 kt.
Range......................................1,105 nautical miles

PA-32RT-300 LANCE II

Wingspan..32 feet 11 inches
Length..28 feet 1 inch
Height..9 feet 6 inches
Engine........................300 hp. Textron Lycoming IO-540-K1G5
Empty weight..1,968 to 2,011 lb.
Maximum gross weight..3,600 lb.
Useful load..1,589 to 1,632 lb.
Service ceiling ....14,600 feet
Maximum speed..165 kt.
Cruise speed..158 kt.
Range......................................864 nautical miles

PA-32RT-300T TURBO LANCE II

Wingspan..32 feet 11 inches
Length..28 feet 11 inches
Height..9 feet 6 inches
Engine........................300 hp. Textron Lycoming TIO-540-S1AD
Empty weight..2,065 to 2,071 lb.
Maximum gross weight..3,600 lb.
Useful load..1,529 to 1,535 lb.
Service ceiling ....20,000 feet

Maximum speed ....193 kt.
Cruise speed..172 to 183 kt.
Range..815 nautical miles

PA-32R-301 SARATOGA SP

Wingspan ....36 feet 5 inches
Length...27 feet 8 inches
Height ....8 feet 6 inches
Engine ....300 hp. Textron Lycoming IO-540-L1G5D
Empty weight ....1,999 lb.
Maximum gross weight.......................................3,615 lb.
Useful load ....1,616 lb.
Service ceiling ....16,700 feet
Maximum speed ....164 kt.
Cruise speed..159 kt.
Range ....784 to 963 nautical miles

PA-32R-301T TURBO SARATOGA SP

Wingspan..36 feet 5 inches
Length...28 feet 6 inches
Height ....8 feet 6 inches
Engine ....300 hp. Textron Lycoming TIO-540-S1AD
Empty weight ....2,078 lb.
Maximum gross weight.......................................3,617 lb.
Useful load ....1,539 lb.
Service ceiling ....20,000 feet
Maximum speed ....195 kt.
Cruise speed..145 to 177 kt.
Range ....730 to 950 nautical miles

PA-34-200 SENECA

Wingspan..38 feet 11 inches
Length...28 feet 6 inches
Height ....9 feet 11 inches
Engines...............................Two Textron Lycoming IO-360-A1A
                                    and LIO-360-A1A, 200 hp.
Empty weight ....2,479 to 2,623 lb.
Maximum gross weight.......................4,000 to 4,200 lb.
Useful load ....1,521 to 1,601 lb.
Service ceiling ....20,000 feet
Maximum speed ....171 kt.
Cruise speed..158 to 163 kt.
Range ....723 to 939 nautical miles

PA-34-200T SENECA II

Wingspan..38 feet 11 inches
Length...28 feet 6 inches
Height ....9 feet 11 inches
Engines...........................Two Teledyne Continental TSIO-360-E
                                    and LTIO-360-E, 200 hp.
Empty weight ....2,770 to 2,848 lb.
Maximum gross weight.......................................4,570 lb.
Useful load ....1,722 to 1,800 lb.
Service ceiling ....25,000 feet
Maximum speed ....198 kt.
Cruise speed..164 to 191 kt.
Range...................................578 nautical miles

PA-34-220T SENECA III

Wingspan..38 feet 11 inches
Length...28 feet 7 inches
Height ....9 feet 11 inches
Engines...................Two Teledyne Continental TSIO-360-KB2A
                                    and LTIO-360-KB2A, 220 hp.
Empty weight ....2,852 to 2,875 lb.
Maximum gross weight.......................................4,773 lb.
Useful load ....1,898 to 1,921 lb.
Service ceiling ....25,000 feet
Maximum speed ....196 kt.
Cruise speed..180 to 193 kt.
Range ....462 to 630 nautical miles

PA-35 POCONO (Experimental)

Wingspan ....51 feet
Length...42 feet 4 inches
Height ....17 feet 5 inches
Engines............................Two Lycoming TIO-720-B1A, 475 hp.
Empty weight ....5,572 lb.
Maximum gross weight.......................................9,750 lb.
Useful load ....4,178 lb.
Service ceiling ....29,000 feet
Maximum speed ....260 mph.
Cruise speed..235 mph.
Range ....700 statute miles

PA-36-285 BRAVE

Wingspan..39 feet
Length...27 feet 4 inches
Height ....7 feet 6 inches
Engine.........................285 hp. Teledyne Continental 6-285 Tiara
Empty weight ....2,203 lb.
Maximum gross weight.......................................4,400 lb.
Useful load ....2,197 lb.
Service ceiling ....5,900 feet
Maximum speed ....121 mph.
Cruise speed..96 mph.
Range ....466 statute miles

PA-36-300 BRAVE

Wingspan..38 feet 9.5 inches
Length...26 feet 10 inches
Height ....7 feet 6 inches
Engine.........................300 hp. Textron Lycoming IO-540-K1G5
Empty weight ....2,198 to 2,200 lb.
Maximum gross weight ....4,400 lb. (Restricted Category)
Useful load ....2,202 lb.
Service ceiling ....12,000 feet
Maximum speed ....148 mph.
Cruise speed..142 mph.
Range ....456 statute miles

PA-36-375 BRAVE 375

Wingspan..38 feet 9.5 inches
Length...27 feet 6 inches
Height ....7 feet 6 inches
Engine ....375 hp. Textron Lycoming IO-720-D1CD
Empty weight ....2,434 to 2,465 lb.
Maximum gross weight ....4,800 lb. (Restricted Category)
Useful load ....2,366 lb.
Service ceiling ....15,000 feet
Maximum speed...160 mph.
Cruise speed..149 mph.
Range ....455 statute miles

PA-38-112 TOMAHAWK

Wingspan ....34 feet
Length ....23 feet 1 inch
Height ....8 feet 8 inches
Engine ....112 hp. Textron Lycoming 0-235-L2C
Empty weight ....1,088 lb.
Maximum gross weight.......................................1,670 lb.
Useful load ....606 lb.
Service ceiling ....12,850 feet
Maximum speed ....113 kt.
Cruise speed..109 kt.
Range ....402 nautical miles

PA-38-112 TOMAHAWK II

Wingspan..34 feet
Length ....23 feet 1 inch
Height ....9 feet 1 inch

Engine ....112 hp. Textron Lycoming 0-235-L2C
Empty weight ....1,128 lb.
Maximum gross weight................................1,670 lb.
Useful load ....561 lb.
Service ceiling ....13,000 feet
Maximum speed ....109 kt.
Cruise speed...108 kt.
Range ....452 nautical miles

PA-39 TWIN COMANCHE C/R

Wingspan ....36 feet 9.5 inches (with wing tip tanks)
Length...25 feet 3 inches
Height ....8 feet 3 inches
Engines..............................Two Lycoming IO-320-B1A
LIO-320-B1A, 160 hp.
Empty weight ....2,270 lb.
Maximum gross weight................................3,600 lb.
Useful load ....1,330 lb.
Service ceiling ....20,000 feet
Maximum speed..205 mph.
Cruising speed ....198 mph.
Range...830 statute miles

PA-39 TURBO TWIN COMANCHE C/R

Wingspan..36 feet 9.5 inches
Length...25 feet 3 inches
Height ....8 feet 3 inches
Engines ....Two Lycoming TIO-320-C1A and
LTIO-320-C1A, 160 hp.
Empty weight ....2,416 lb.
Maximum gross weight................................3,725 lb.
Useful load ....1,309 lb.
Service ceiling ....25,000 feet
Maximum speed..246 mph.
Cruising speed ....221 mph.
Range...1,270 statute miles

PA-42-680 CHEYENNE III

Wingspan..47 feet 6 inches
Length...39 feet 3 inches
Height ....12 feet 4 inches
Engines ....Two Pratt & Whitney Canada PT6A-41, 680 shp.
Empty weight ....5,750 lb.
Maximum gross weight................................10,500 lb.
Useful load ....4,750 lb.
Service ceiling ....33,000 feet
Cruise speed...301 kt.
Range...1,145 nautical miles

PA-42-720 CHEYENNE III

Wingspan..47 feet 8 inches
Length...43 feet 4 inches
Height ....14 feet 9 inches
Engines ....Two Pratt & Whitney Canada PT6A-41, 720 shp.
Empty weight ....6,389 to 6,630 lb.
Maximum gross weight................11,080 to 11,285 lb.
Useful load ....4,450 to 4,896 lb.
Service ceiling ....32,000 feet
Maximum speed...299 kt.
Cruise speed...................................265 to 290 kt.
Range.......................................1,400 to 2,240 nautical miles

PA-42-720 CHEYENNE IIIA

Wingspan..47 feet 8 inches
Length...43 feet 4 inches
Height ....14 feet 9 inches
Engines ....Two Pratt & Whitney Canada PT6A-61, 720 shp.
Empty weight ....6,837 lb.
Maximum gross weight................................11,285 lb.
Useful load ....4,448 lb.

Service ceiling ....35,840 feet
Cruise speed..................................282 to 305 kt.
Range ....1,372 to 2,270 nautical miles

PA-42-1000 CHEYENNE 400

Wingspan..47 feet 8 inches
Length...43 feet 5 inches
Height...17 feet
Engines.........Two Garrett TPE331-14A/-14B engines, 1,000 shp.
Empty weight ....7,565 lb.
Maximum gross weight................................12,135 lb.
Useful load ....4,570 lb.
Service ceiling ....41,000 feet
Maximum speed...351 kt.
Cruise speed..................................294 to 351 kt.
Range..............................1,234 to 2,176 nautical miles

PA-44-180 SEMINOLE

Wingspan..38 feet 7 inches
Length...27 feet 7 inches
Height ....8 feet 6 inches
Engines............................Two Textron Lycoming O-360-E1A6D
and LO-360-E1A6D, 180 hp.
Empty weight ....2,316 to 2,422 lb.
Maximum gross weight................................3,816 lb.
Useful load ....1,394 to 1,500 lb.
Service ceiling ....17,100 feet
Maximum speed...168 kt.
Cruise speed...166 kt.
Range ....690 to 915 nautical miles

PA-44-180T TURBO SEMINOLE

Wingspan..38 feet 7 inches
Length...27 feet 7 inches
Height ....8 feet 6 inches
Engines ....Two Textron Lycoming TO-360-E1A6D
and LTO-360-E1A6D, 180 hp.
Empty weight ....2,430 to 2,461 lb.
Maximum gross weight................................3,943 lb.
Useful load ....1,482 to 1,513 lb.
Service ceiling ....20,000 feet
Maximum speed...195 kt.
Cruise speed...183 kt.
Range ....710 to 820 nautical miles

PA-46-310P MALIBU

Wingspan...43 feet
Length...28 feet 5 inches
Height ....11 feet 4 inches
Engine......................310 hp. Teledyne Continental TSIO-520-BE
Empty weight ....2,466 lb.
Maximum gross weight................................4,118 lb.
Useful load ....1,658 lb.
Service ceiling ....25,000 feet
Maximum speed...234 kt.
Cruise speed...................................196 to 215 kt.
Range..............................1,330 to 1,555 nautical miles

PA-46-350P MALIBU MIRAGE

Wingspan...43 feet
Length...28 feet 5 inches
Height ....11 feet 4 inches
Engine.....................350 hp. Textron Lycoming TIO-540-AE2A
Empty weight ....2,626 lb.
Maximum gross weight................................4,300 lb.
Useful load ....1,692 lb.
Service ceiling ....25,000 feet
Maximum speed...237 kt.
Cruise speed...225 kt.
Range ....1,018 to 1,260 nautical miles

PA-48 ENFORCER

Wingspan...41 feet 4 inches
Length..34 feet 2 inches
Height...13 feet 1 inch
Engine.............................2,455 shp. Lycoming T55-L9
Maximum gross weight.................................14,000 lb.
Useful load ....5,680 lb.
Service ceiling..37,600 feet
Maximum speed ....350 kt.
Cruise speed..315 kt.
Range......................................400 nautical miles

PA-60-602P AEROSTAR

Wingspan...36 feet 8 inches
Length..34 feet 10 inches
Height ....12 feet 2 inches
Engines ....Two Textron Lycoming TIO-540-AA1A5, 290 hp.
Empty weight ....4,075 to 4,125 lb.
Maximum gross weight ....6,029 lb.

Useful load ....1,904 to 1,954 lb.
Service ceiling ....28,000 feet
Maximum speed ....262 kt.
Cruise speed..228 to 247 kt.
Range ....1,094 to 1,143 nautical miles

PA-60-700P AEROSTAR

Wingspan...36 feet 8 inches
Length..34 feet 10 inches
Height ....12 feet 2 inches
Engines....................................Textron Lycoming TIO-540-U2A
and LTIO-540-U2A, 350 hp.
Empty weight ....4,275 lb.
Maximum gross weight....................................6,356 lb.
Useful load ....2,081 lb.
Service ceiling ....25,000 feet
Maximum speed ....266 kt.
Cruise speed...230 to 261 kt.
Range...868 nautical miles

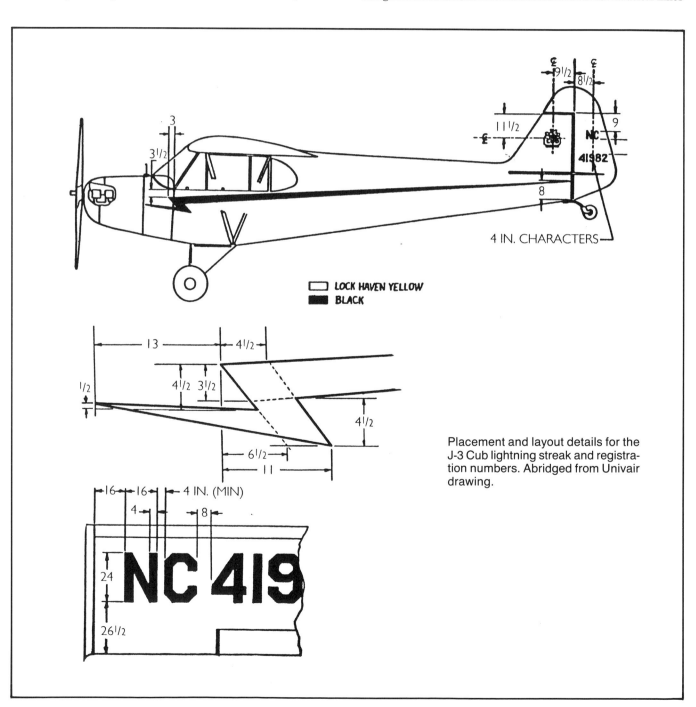

LOCK HAVEN YELLOW
BLACK

4 IN. CHARACTERS

Placement and layout details for the J-3 Cub lightning streak and registration numbers. Abridged from Univair drawing.

Your CUB is waiting... Flyaway, Lock Haven!

"Flock of J-3 Cubs await delivery outside of the Lock Haven factory in 1941." Smithsonian Institution, National Air and Space Museum negative number 93-2386.

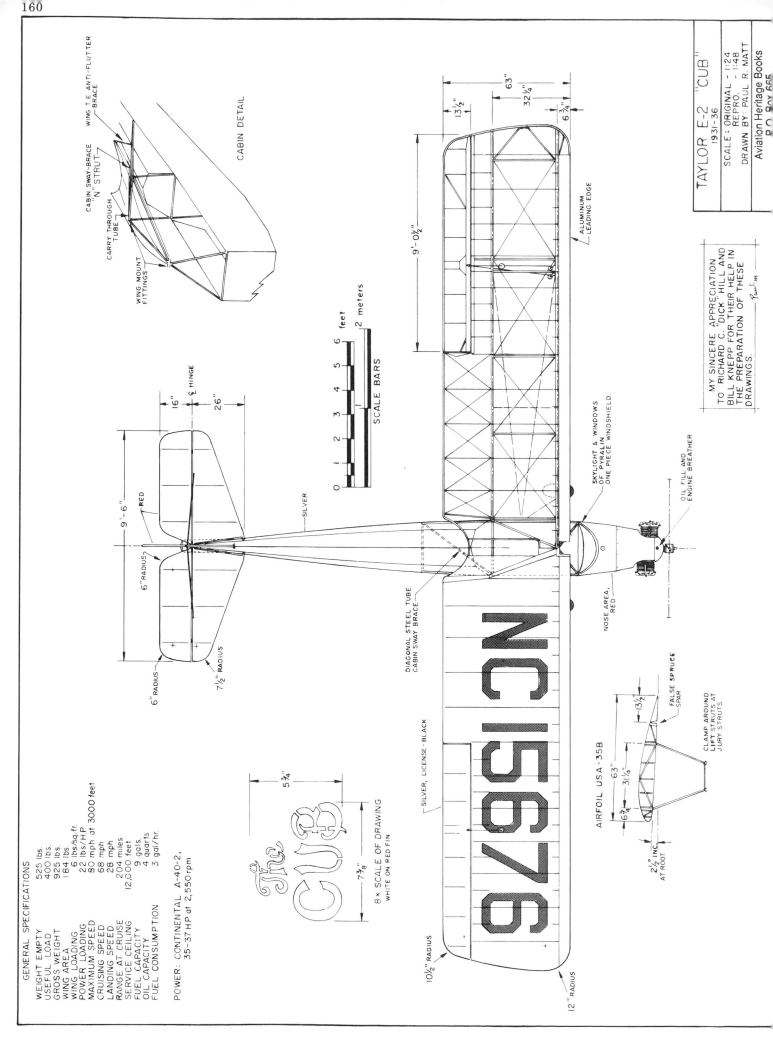

TAYLOR E-2 "CUB"
1931-36

SCALE: ORIGINAL - 1:24
REPRO. - 1:48
DRAWN BY: PAUL R. MATT

Aviation Heritage Books
P.O. Box 665

MY SINCERE APPRECIATION
TO RICHARD C. "DICK" HILL AND
BILL KNEPP FOR THEIR HELP IN
THE PREPARATION OF THESE
DRAWINGS.

CABIN DETAIL

WING T.E. ANTI-FLUTTER
BRACE

CABIN SWAY-BRACE
"N" STRUT

CARRY THROUGH
TUBE

WING MOUNT
FITTINGS

63"

13½"

32¼"

6¾"

9'-0½"

ALUMINUM
LEADING EDGE

SKYLIGHT & WINDOWS
OF PYRALIN
ONE PIECE WINDSHIELD

OIL FILL AND
ENGINE BREATHER

NOSE AREA,
RED

DIAGONAL STEEL TUBE
CABIN SWAY BRACE

SILVER, LICENSE-BLACK

NC15676

SILVER, LICENSE ON RED FIN

10½" RADIUS

12" RADIUS

SCALE BARS

0 1 2 3 4 5 6 feet
2 meters

₵ HINGE

16"

26"

9'-6"

RED

6" RADIUS

6" RADIUS

7½" RADIUS

SILVER

The
CUB

5¾"

7⅜"

8 × SCALE OF DRAWING
WHITE ON RED FIN

AIRFOIL USA-35B

63"

31¼"

6¾"

13½"

FALSE SPRUCE
SPAR

CLAMP AROUND
LIFT STRUTS AT
JURY STRUTS

2½° INC.
AT ROOT

GENERAL SPECIFICATIONS

WEIGHT EMPTY   525 lbs.
USEFUL LOAD   400 lbs.
GROSS WEIGHT   925 lbs.
WING AREA   184 lbs.
WING LOADING   6 lbs/sq.ft.
POWER LOADING   22 lbs/HP
MAXIMUM SPEED   80 mph at 3000 feet
CRUISING SPEED   68 mph
LANDING SPEED   28 mph
RANGE AT CRUISE   204 miles
SERVICE CEILING   12,000 feet
FUEL CAPACITY   9 gals.
OIL CAPACITY   4 quarts
FUEL CONSUMPTION   3 gal/hr.

POWER: CONTINENTAL A-40-2,
       35-37 HP at 2,550 rpm

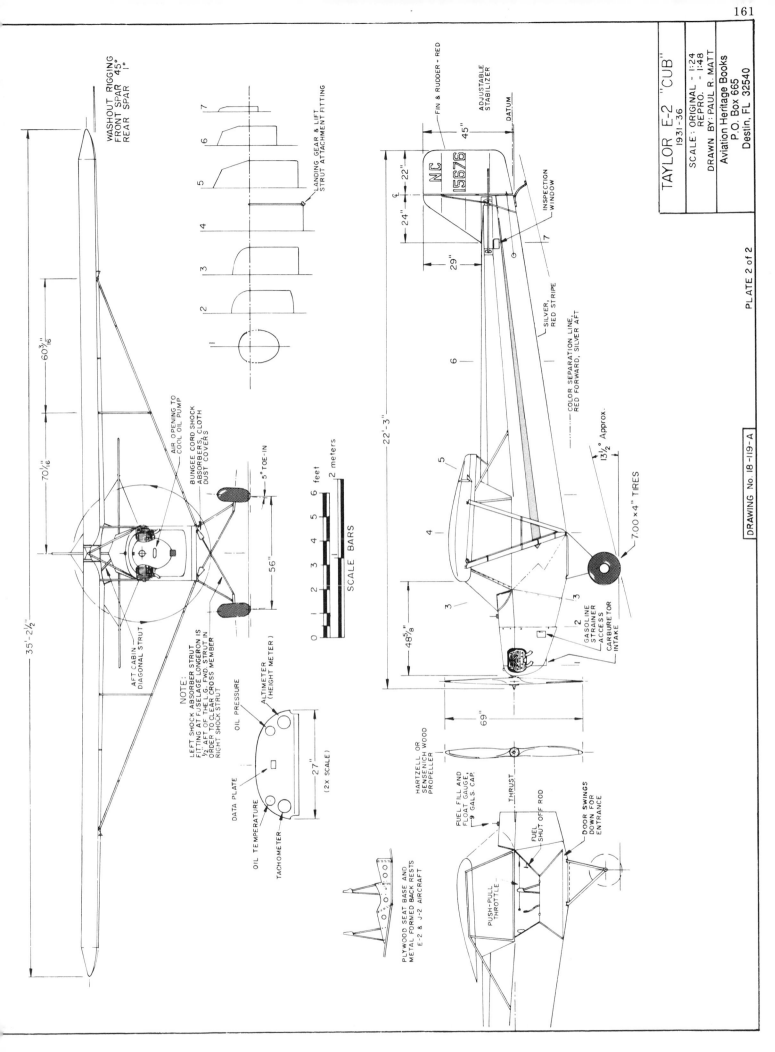

WASHOUT RIGGING
FRONT SPAR 45°
REAR SPAR 1°

AIR OPENING TO
COOL OIL PUMP

BUNGEE CORD SHOCK
ABSORBERS, CLOTH
DUST COVERS

LANDING GEAR & LIFT
STRUT ATTACHMENT FITTING

5° TOE-IN

56"

AFT CABIN DIAGONAL STRUT

NOTE:
LEFT SHOCK ABSORBER STRUT
FITTING AT FUSELAGE LONGERON IS
½" AFT OF THE L.G. FWD. STRUT IN
ORDER TO CLEAR CROSS MEMBER
RIGHT SHOCK STRUT

60³⁄₁₆"

70¹⁄₁₆"

35'-2½"

ALTIMETER
(HEIGHT METER)

OIL PRESSURE

DATA PLATE

OIL TEMPERATURE

TACHOMETER

27"

(2X SCALE)

6 feet
2 meters
SCALE BARS

PLYWOOD SEAT BASE AND
METAL FORMED BACK RESTS
E-2 & J-2 AIRCRAFT

FIN & RUDDER - RED

ADJUSTABLE
STABILIZER

DATUM

45"

22"

24"

29"

NC
15576

INSPECTION
WINDOW

SILVER,
RED STRIPE

COLOR SEPARATION LINE,
RED FORWARD, SILVER AFT

13½° Approx.

7.00 × 4" TIRES

GASOLINE
STRAINER
ACCESS

CARBURETOR
INTAKE

22'-3"

48⁵⁄₈"

HARTZELL OR
SENSENICH WOOD
PROPELLER

69"

THRUST

FUEL FILL AND
FLOAT GAUGE,
9 GALS. CAP.

FUEL
SHUT OFF ROD

DOOR SWINGS
DOWN FOR
ENTRANCE

PUSH-PULL
THROTTLE

TAYLOR E-2 "CUB"
1931-36
SCALE: ORIGINAL - 1:24
REPRO. - 1:48
DRAWN BY: PAUL R. MATT
Aviation Heritage Books
P.O. Box 665
Destin, FL 32540

PLATE 2 of 2

DRAWING No. 18-119-A

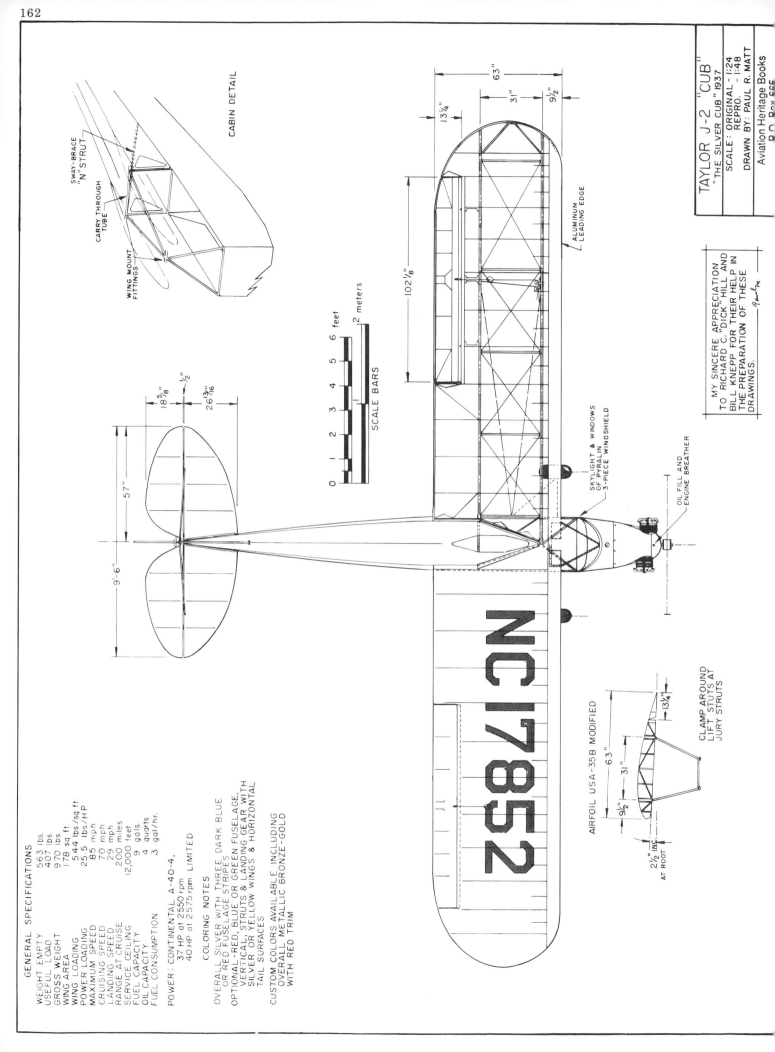

CABIN DETAIL

SWAY-BRACE
"N" STRUT

CARRY THROUGH TUBE

WING MOUNT FITTINGS

63"

31"

9½"

13¾"

102⅛"

ALUMINUM LEADING EDGE

SKYLIGHT & WINDOWS OF PYRALIN
3-PIECE WINDSHIELD

OIL FILL AND ENGINE BREATHER

18⅝"

½"

26¹³⁄₁₆

57"

9'-6"

0 1 2 3 4 5 6 feet
2 meters
SCALE BARS

NC17852

AIRFOIL USA-35B MODIFIED

63"

31"

9½"

13¾"

CLAMP AROUND LIFT STUTS AT JURY STRUTS

2½° INC.
AT ROOT

TAYLOR J-2 "CUB"
"THE SILVER CUB" 1937
SCALE: ORIGINAL - 1:24
REPRO. - 1:48
DRAWN BY: PAUL R. MATT

Aviation Heritage Books
P.O. Box 555

MY SINCERE APPRECIATION TO RICHARD C. "DICK" HILL AND BILL KNEPP FOR THEIR HELP IN THE PREPARATION OF THESE DRAWINGS.

GENERAL SPECIFICATIONS

WEIGHT EMPTY	563 lbs.
USEFUL LOAD	407 lbs
GROSS WEIGHT	970 lbs
WING AREA	178 sq ft.
WING LOADING	5.44 lbs/sq.ft.
POWER LOADING	25.5 lbs/HP
MAXIMUM SPEED	85 mph
CRUISING SPEED	70 mph
LANDING SPEED	29 mph
RANGE AT CRUISE	200 miles
SERVICE CEILING	12,000 feet
FUEL CAPACITY	9 gals
OIL CAPACITY	4 quarts
FUEL CONSUMPTION	3 gal/hr.

POWER: CONTINENTAL A-40-4,
37 HP at 2550 rpm
40 HP at 2575 rpm LIMITED

COLORING NOTES

OVERALL SILVER WITH THREE DARK BLUE OR RED FUSELAGE STRIPES

OPTIONAL-RED, BLUE OR GREEN FUSELAGE, VERTICAL, STRUTS & LANDING GEAR WITH SILVER OR YELLOW WINGS & HORIZONTAL TAIL SURFACES

CUSTOM COLORS AVAILABLE INCLUDING OVERALL METALLIC BRONZE-GOLD WITH RED TRIM

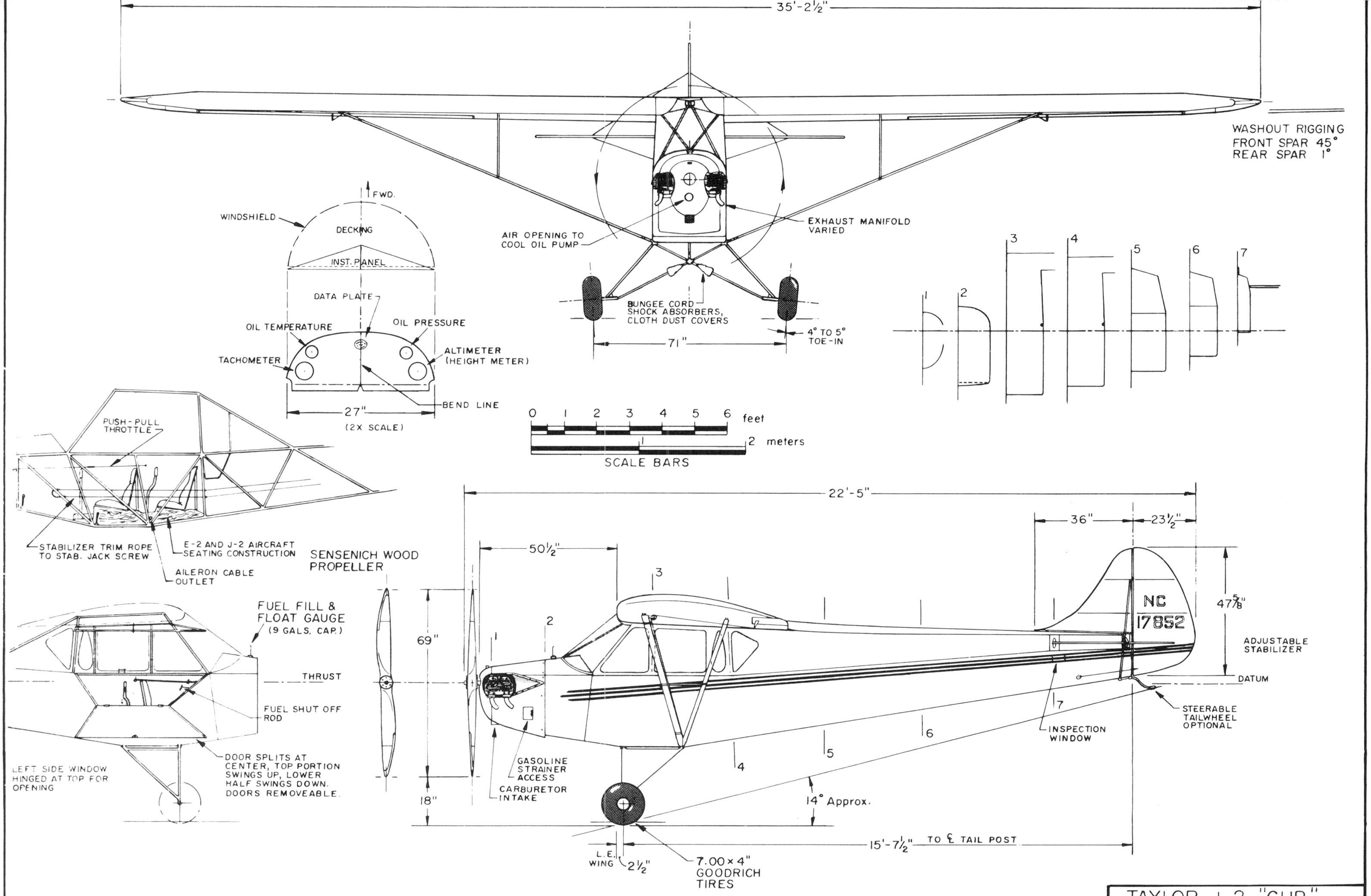

WASHOUT RIGGING
FRONT SPAR 45°
REAR SPAR 1°

35'-2½"

EXHAUST MANIFOLD VARIED

4° TO 5° TOE-IN

BUNGEE CORD SHOCK ABSORBERS, CLOTH DUST COVERS

71"

AIR OPENING TO COOL OIL PUMP

6 feet

5

4

3

2

1 meters

0

2

SCALE BARS

FWD.

WINDSHIELD

DECKING

INST. PANEL

DATA PLATE

OIL TEMPERATURE

TACHOMETER

OIL PRESSURE

ALTIMETER (HEIGHT METER)

BEND LINE

27"

(2X SCALE)

PUSH-PULL THROTTLE

STABILIZER TRIM ROPE TO STAB. JACK SCREW

AILERON CABLE OUTLET

E-2 AND J-2 AIRCRAFT SEATING CONSTRUCTION

SENSENICH WOOD PROPELLER

FUEL FILL & FLOAT GAUGE (9 GALS. CAP.)

FUEL SHUT OFF ROD

THRUST

DOOR SPLITS AT CENTER, TOP PORTION SWINGS UP, LOWER HALF SWINGS DOWN. DOORS REMOVEABLE.

LEFT SIDE WINDOW HINGED AT TOP FOR OPENING

ADJUSTABLE STABILIZER

DATUM

STEERABLE TAILWHEEL OPTIONAL

NC 17852

47⅞"

36"

23½"

22'-5"

INSPECTION WINDOW

7

6

5

4

3

2

14° Approx.

15'-7½" TO ₵ TAIL POST

7.00 × 4" GOODRICH TIRES

2½"

L.E. WING

50½"

GASOLINE STRAINER ACCESS

CARBURETOR INTAKE

69"

18"

TAYLOR J-2 "CUB"
"THE SILVER CUB" 1937
SCALE: ORIGINAL - 1:24
REPRO. - 1:48
DRAWN BY: PAUL R. MATT

Aviation Heritage Books
P.O. Box 665
Destin, FL 32540

PLATE 2 of 2

DRAWING No. 18-120-A

GENERAL SPECIFICATION

WEIGHT EMPTY .... 680 lbs
USEFUL LOAD .... 540 lbs
GROSS WEIGHT .... 1100 lbs
WING AREA .... 178.5 sq.ft.
WING LOADING .... 6.16 lbs/sq.ft.
POWER LOADING .... 22.0 lbs/HP
TOP SPEED .... 87 mph
CRUISING SPEED .... 73 mph
LANDING SPEED .... 38 mph
RANGE AT CRUISE .... 220 miles
MAXIMUM CEILING .... 12,000 feet
FUEL CAPACITY .... 12 gals.
OIL CAPACITY .... 1 gal.
FUEL CONSUMPTION .... 4.46 gals/hr

POWER: CONTINENTAL A-65-8
       LYCOMING O-145
       FRANKLIN 4AC-65

       ALL 65 HP AT 2500/2550 rpm

COLORING NOTES
STANDARD FACTORY ISSUE - OVERALL CUB YELLOW
(DEEP RED-YELLOW), BLACK TRIM
OTHER COLORS AT CUSTOMERS REQUEST

OIL TEMPERATURE
OIL PRESSURE
CABIN HEAT
ALTIMETER
PRIMER
COMPASS
CARBURETOR HEAT
TACHOMETER
AIR SPEED
26"
(2X SCALE)

SPRUCE WOOD SPARS, NICRAL METAL 1946-47 MODELS

63"
3"
9½"

ALUMINUM LEADING EDGE

102⅛"

18⅝"
26¹³⁄₁₆"

57"

9'-6"

SCALE BARS
feet
meters
0 1 2 3 4 5 6

LOGO CENTERED ON FIN
FIGURE APPROX 10" HIGH

COLORING
CUB - LIGHT BROWN
EYES & MUZZLE - WHITE
TONGUE - RED
DETAILING IN BLACK
SIGN - MAROON-RED, "PIPER CUB"
WHITE, OUTLINED IN BLACK.
LETTERING - BLACK

PIPER
CUB
PIPER AIRCRAFT CORP.
LOCK HAVEN, PA, U.S.A.

OIL FILL AND
ENGINE BREATHER

NC 26170

LICENSE NUMBERS - BLACK

AIRFOIL USA-35B MODIFIED

FRIEZE TYPE AILERON

12"
13¼"
63"
31"
9½"

JURY STRUTS CLAMP TO LIFT STRUTS

2½" INC. AT ROOT

PIPER J-3 "CUB"
1937-47

SCALE: ORIGINAL - 1:24
       REPRO. - 1:48
DRAWN BY: PAUL R. MATT

Aviation Heritage Books

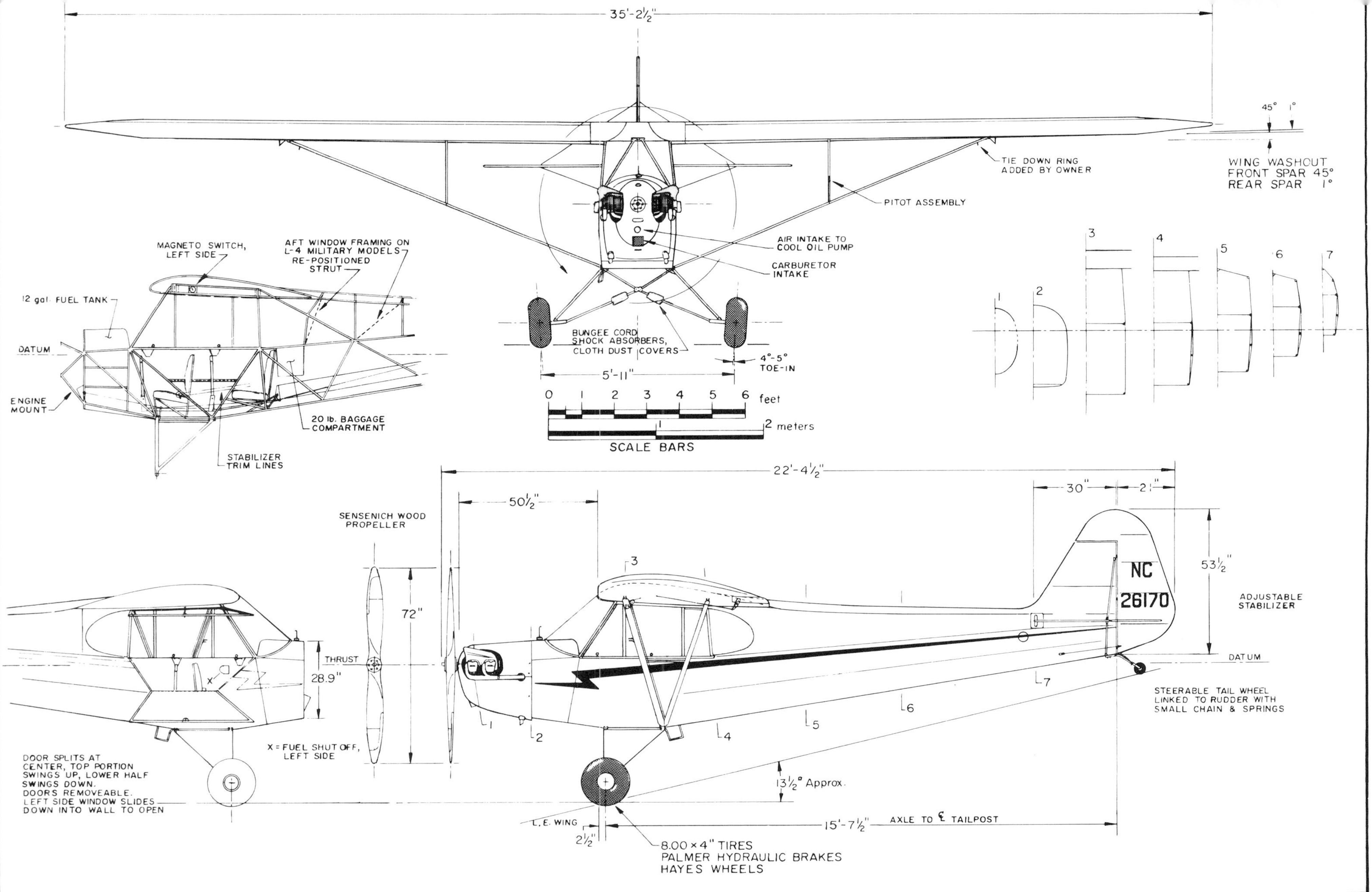

WING WASHOUT
FRONT SPAR 4½°
REAR SPAR 1°

45° 1°

7
6
5
4
3
2
1

TIE DOWN RING
ADDED BY OWNER

PITOT ASSEMBLY

AIR INTAKE TO
COOL OIL PUMP

CARBURETOR
INTAKE

4°-5° TOE-IN

BUNGEE CORD
SHOCK ABSORBERS,
CLOTH DUST COVERS

35'-2½"

2 meters

6 feet

5'-11"

SCALE BARS

ADJUSTABLE
STABILIZER

DATUM

STEERABLE TAIL WHEEL
LINKED TO RUDDER WITH
SMALL CHAIN & SPRINGS

NC
26170

53½"

2'-1"

30"

22'-4½"

7
6
5
4
3
2
1

13½° Approx.

8.00 x 4" TIRES
PALMER HYDRAULIC BRAKES
HAYES WHEELS

15'-7½" AXLE TO ℄ TAILPOST

L.E. WING

2½"

50½"

SENSENICH WOOD
PROPELLER

72"

THRUST

28.9"

X = FUEL SHUT OFF,
LEFT SIDE

AFT WINDOW FRAMING ON
L-4 MILITARY MODELS
RE-POSITIONED STRUT

20 lb. BAGGAGE
COMPARTMENT

STABILIZER
TRIM LINES

MAGNETO SWITCH,
LEFT SIDE

12 gal FUEL TANK

DATUM

ENGINE
MOUNT

DOOR SPLITS AT
CENTER, TOP PORTION
SWINGS UP, LOWER HALF
SWINGS DOWN.
DOORS REMOVEABLE.
LEFT SIDE WINDOW SLIDES
DOWN INTO WALL TO OPEN

PIPER J-3 "CUB"
1937-47
SCALE: ORIGINAL - 1:24
REPRO. - 1:48
DRAWN BY: PAUL R. MATT
Aviation Heritage Books
P.O. Box 665
Destin, FL 32540

PLATE 2 of 2

DRAWING No. 18-121-A

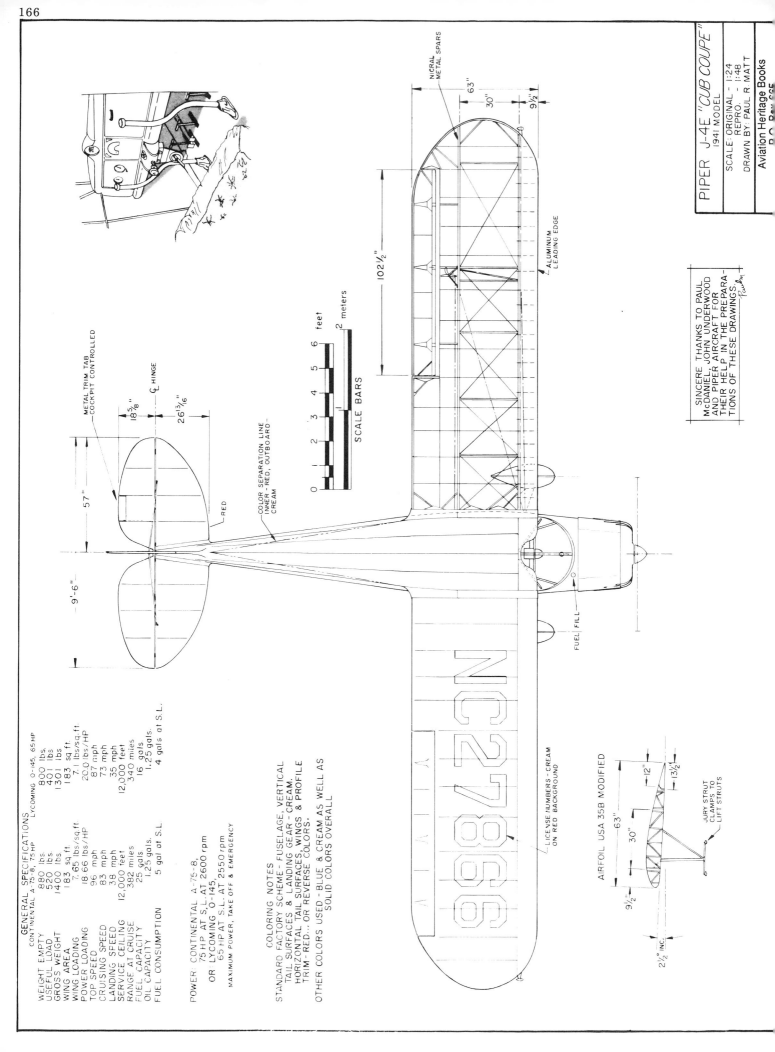

PIPER J-4E "CUB COUPE"
1941 MODEL
SCALE: ORIGINAL - 1:24
REPRO. - 1:48
DRAWN BY: PAUL R MATT

Aviation Heritage Books

SINCERE THANKS TO PAUL
McDANIEL, JOHN UNDERWOOD
AND PIPER AIRCRAFT FOR
THEIR HELP IN THE PREPARA-
TIONS OF THESE DRAWINGS.

NICRAL METAL SPARS

63"
30"
9½"

102½"

ALUMINUM LEADING EDGE

2 meters
6 feet
5
4
3
2
1
0
SCALE BARS

METAL TRIM TAB
COCKPIT CONTROLLED

18⅝"
26¹³⁄₁₆"

₵ HINGE

57"

RED

COLOR SEPARATION LINE
INNER - RED, OUTBOARD -
CREAM

9'-6"

NC27866

LICENSE NUMBERS - CREAM
ON RED BACKGROUND

FUEL FILL

AIRFOIL USA 35B MODIFIED

63"
30"
12"
13½"
9½"
2½ INC.

JURY STRUT
CLAMPS TO
LIFT STRUTS

GENERAL SPECIFICATIONS
CONTINENTAL A-75-8, 75 HP   LYCOMING O-145, 65 HP

WEIGHT EMPTY   880 lbs.   800 lbs.
USEFUL LOAD   520 lbs.   401 lbs.
GROSS WEIGHT   1400 lbs.   1301 lbs.
WING AREA   183 sq ft.   183 sq.ft.
WING LOADING   7.65 lbs/sq.ft   7.1 lbs/sq.ft.
POWER LOADING   18.66 lbs/HP   20.0 lbs/HP
TOP SPEED   96 mph   87 mph
CRUISING SPEED   83 mph   73 mph
LANDING SPEED   38 mph   35 mph
SERVICE CEILING   12,000 feet   12,000 feet
RANGE AT CRUISE   382 miles   340 miles
FUEL CAPACITY   25 gals.   16 gals.
OIL CAPACITY   1.25 gals.   1.25 gals.
FUEL CONSUMPTION   5 gal at S.L.   4 gals at S.L.

POWER: CONTINENTAL A-75-8,
       75 HP AT S.L. AT 2600 rpm
   OR LYCOMING O-145,
       65 HP AT S.L. AT 2550 rpm
   MAXIMUM POWER, TAKE OFF & EMERGENCY

COLORING NOTES
STANDARD FACTORY SCHEME - FUSELAGE, VERTICAL
TAIL SURFACES & LANDING GEAR - CREAM.
HORIZONTAL TAIL SURFACES, WINGS & PROFILE
TRIM - RED... OR REVERSE COLORS.

OTHER COLORS USED - BLUE & CREAM AS WELL AS
SOLID COLORS OVERALL

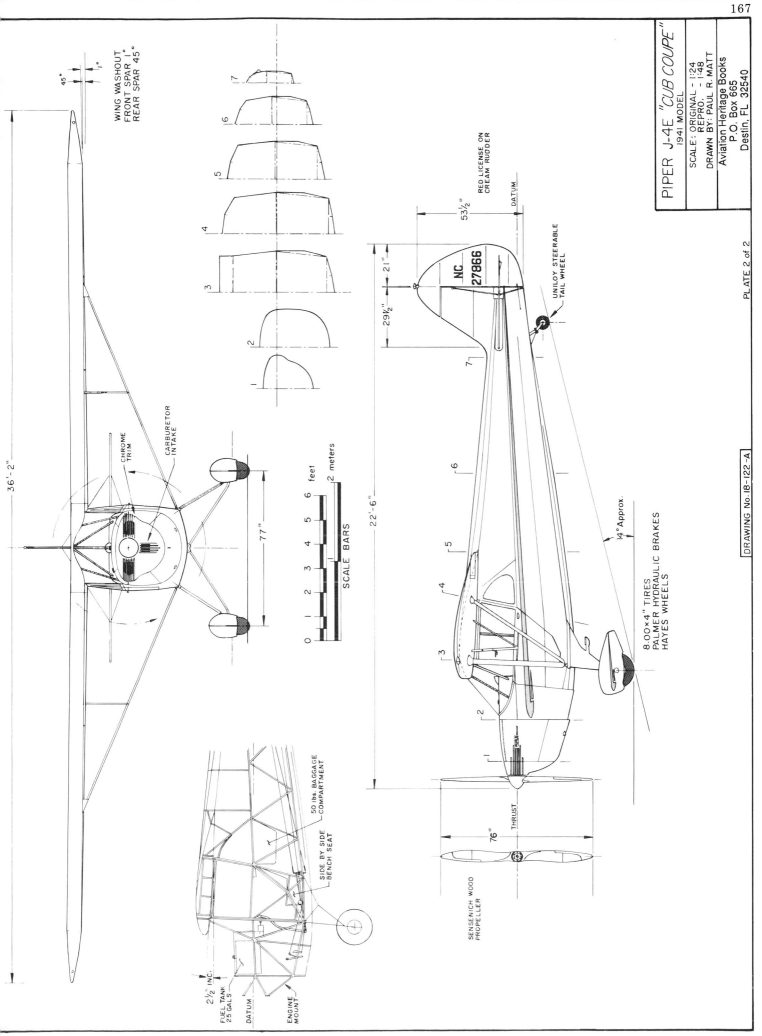

WING WASHOUT
FRONT SPAR 1°
REAR SPAR 45°

45°

CHROME TRIM

CARBURETOR INTAKE

36'-2"

77"

feet
6 5 4 3 2 1 0
SCALE BARS
2 meters

RED LICENSE ON CREAM RUDDER

PIPER J-4E "CUB COUPE"
1941 MODEL

SCALE: ORIGINAL - 1:24
REPRO. - 1:48
DRAWN BY: PAUL R. MATT

Aviation Heritage Books
P.O. Box 665
Destin, FL 32540

PLATE 2 of 2

DRAWING No. 18-122-A

53½"
DATUM
29½"
21"

NC 27866

UNILOY STEERABLE TAIL WHEEL

7

6

5

4

3

2

1

14° Approx.

8.00×4" TIRES
PALMER HYDRAULIC BRAKES
HAYES WHEELS

22'-6"

THRUST

76"

SENSENICH WOOD PROPELLER

2½" INC.
FUEL TANK 25 GALS
DATUM
ENGINE MOUNT

50 lbs. BAGGAGE COMPARTMENT

SIDE BY SIDE BENCH SEAT

7
6
5
4
3
2
1

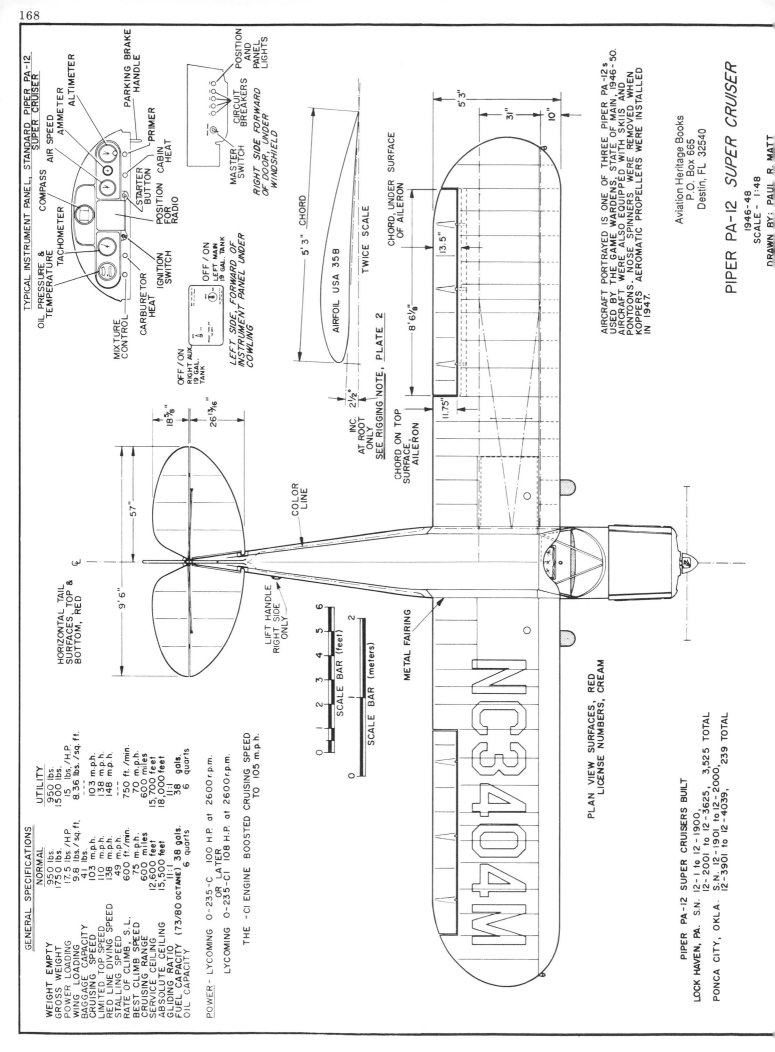

168

PIPER PA-12 *SUPER CRUISER*
1946-48
SCALE - 1:48
DRAWN BY: PAUL R. MATT

Aviation Heritage Books
P.O. Box 665
Destin, FL 32540

TYPICAL INSTRUMENT PANEL, STANDARD PIPER PA-12 SUPER CRUISER

ALTIMETER
AIR SPEED
AMMETER
COMPASS
PARKING BRAKE HANDLE
PRIMER
CABIN HEAT
POSITION FOR RADIO
IGNITION SWITCH
CARBURETOR HEAT
MIXTURE CONTROL
TACHOMETER
OIL PRESSURE & TEMPERATURE
STARTER BUTTON

POSITION AND PANEL LIGHTS
CIRCUIT BREAKERS
MASTER SWITCH
RIGHT SIDE FORWARD OF DOOR, UNDER WINDSHIELD

OFF / ON
LEFT MAIN
19 GAL. TANK
OFF / ON
LEFT AUX.
19 GAL. TANK
OFF / ON
RIGHT AUX.
19 GAL. TANK
LEFT SIDE, FORWARD OF INSTRUMENT PANEL UNDER COWLING.

5' 3" CHORD
AIRFOIL USA 35B
TWICE SCALE
INC. 2½° AT ROOT ONLY
SEE RIGGING NOTE, PLATE 2

5' 3"
3"
10"
13.5"
8' 6⅛"
11.75"
CHORD, UNDER SURFACE OF AILERON
CHORD ON TOP SURFACE AILERON

AIRCRAFT PORTRAYED IS ONE OF THREE PIPER PA-12s USED BY THE GAME WARDENS, STATE OF MAINE, 1946-50. AIRCRAFT WERE ALSO EQUIPPED WITH SKIIS AND PONTOONS. NOSE SPINNERS WERE REMOVED WHEN KOPPERS AEROMATIC PROPELLERS WERE INSTALLED IN 1947.

18⅝"
26¹³/₁₆"
57"
9' 6"

HORIZONTAL TAIL SURFACES, TOP & BOTTOM, RED
COLOR LINE
LIFT HANDLE RIGHT SIDE ONLY
METAL FAIRING

NC404M

SCALE BAR (feet)
SCALE BAR (meters)

PLAN VIEW SURFACES, RED
LICENSE NUMBERS, CREAM

GENERAL SPECIFICATIONS

	NORMAL	UTILITY
WEIGHT EMPTY	950 lbs.	950 lbs.
GROSS WEIGHT	1750 lbs.	1500 lbs.
POWER LOADING	17.5 lbs./H.P.	15 lbs./H.P.
WING LOADING	9.8 lbs./sq. ft.	8.36 lbs./sq. ft.
BAGGAGE CAPACITY	41 lbs.	
CRUISING SPEED	103 m.p.h.	103 m.p.h.
LIMITED TOP SPEED	110 m.p.h.	138 m.p.h.
RED LINE DIVING SPEED	138 m.p.h.	148 m.p.h.
STALLING SPEED	49 m.p.h.	
RATE OF CLIMB, S.L.	600 ft./min.	750 ft./min.
BEST CLIMB SPEED	75 m.p.h.	70 m.p.h.
CRUISING RANGE	600 miles	600 miles
SERVICE CEILING	12,600 feet	15,700 feet
ABSOLUTE CEILING	15,500 feet	18,000 feet
GLIDING RATIO	11:1	11:1
FUEL CAPACITY (73/80 octane)	38 gals.	38 gals.
OIL CAPACITY	6 quarts	6 quarts

POWER- LYCOMING O-235-C 100 H.P. at 2600 r.p.m.
OR LATER
LYCOMING O-235-CI 108 H.P. at 2600 r.p.m.

THE -CI ENGINE BOOSTED CRUISING SPEED TO 105 m.p.h.

PIPER PA-12 SUPER CRUISERS BUILT
LOCK HAVEN, PA. S.N. 12-1 to 12-1900, 12-2001 to 12-3625, 3,525 TOTAL
PONCA CITY, OKLA. S.N. 12-1901 to 12-2000, 12-3901 to 12-4039, 239 TOTAL

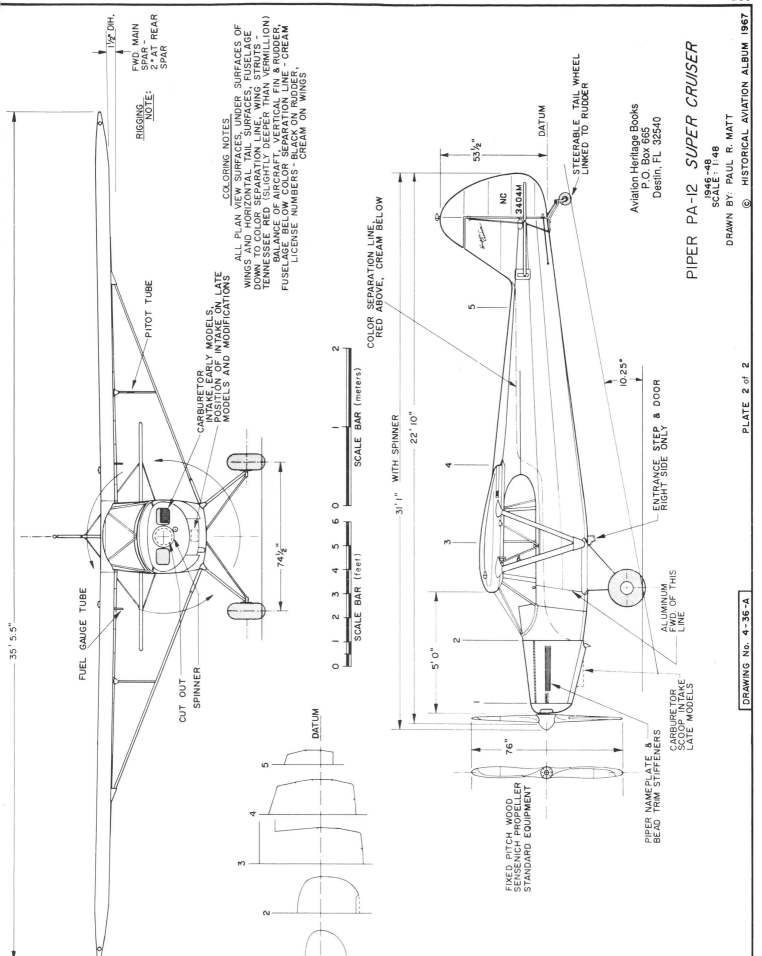

RIGGING
NOTE:

FWD. MAIN SPAR - 2° AT REAR SPAR

1½° DIH.

COLORING NOTES

ALL PLAN VIEW SURFACES, UNDER SURFACES OF WINGS AND HORIZONTAL TAIL SURFACES, FUSELAGE DOWN TO COLOR SEPARATION LINE, WING STRUTS - TENNESSEE RED (SLIGHTLY DEEPER THAN VERMILLION) BALANCE OF AIRCRAFT, VERTICAL FIN & RUDDER, FUSELAGE BELOW COLOR SEPARATION LINE - CREAM LICENSE NUMBERS - BLACK ON RUDDER, CREAM ON WINGS

PITOT TUBE

CARBURETOR INTAKE, EARLY MODELS, POSITION OF INTAKE ON LATE MODELS AND MODIFICATIONS

FUEL GAUGE TUBE

CUT OUT SPINNER

35' 5.5"

74½"

SCALE BAR (meters)
SCALE BAR (feet)

DATUM

COLOR SEPARATION LINE, RED ABOVE, CREAM BELOW

STEERABLE TAIL WHEEL LINKED TO RUDDER

DATUM

NC
3404M

53½"

5

10·25°

31' 1" WITH SPINNER

22' 10"

5' 0"

76"

4

3

2

1

ENTRANCE STEP & DOOR RIGHT SIDE ONLY

ALUMINUM FWD. OF THIS LINE

CARBURETOR SCOOP INTAKE LATE MODELS

PIPER NAMEPLATE & BEAD TRIM STIFFENERS

FIXED PITCH WOOD SENSENICH PROPELLER STANDARD EQUIPMENT

PIPER PA-12 *SUPER CRUISER*

1946-48
SCALE : 1:48

DRAWN BY: PAUL R. MATT

Aviation Heritage Books
P.O. Box 665
Destin, FL 32540

© HISTORICAL AVIATION ALBUM 1967

PLATE 2 of 2

DRAWING No. 4-36-A

"Appreciation is extended to Aviation Heritage Books for permission to reprint the internationally acclaimed Paul Matt Scale Drawings."

BIBLIOGRAPHY

BOOKS

1. Bowers, Peter M.: Piper Cubs
   Tab Books, Inc., 1993

2. Clarke, Bill: The Piper Indians
   Tab Books Inc., Blue Ridge Summit, Pennsylvania, 1988.

3. Francis, Devon: Mr. Piper and His Cubs
   The Iowa State University Press, 1973.

4. Juptner, Joseph P.: United States Civil Aircraft series;
   Aero Publishers, Inc., 1964 through 1980.

5. Peperell, Roger W. and Smith, Colin M.: Piper Aircraft and Their
   Forerunners; Air-Britain Limited, 1987.

6. Phillips, Edward H.: Beechcraft - Pursuit of Perfection;
   Flying Books
   Eagan, Minnesota, 1992.

7. Phillips, Edward H.: Wings of Cessna; Flying Books
   Eagan, Minnesota, 1986.

8. Simpson, R.W.: Airlife's General Aviation;
   Airlife Publishing Limited, 1991.

9. Weick, Fred E. and Hansen, James R.: From the Ground Up
   Smithsonian Institute Press, Washington and London, 1988.

NEWSPAPERS AND MAGAZINES

1. The Bradford Era: Years 1928 through 1931; Bradford Area
   Public Library, Bradford, Pennsylvania.

2. Piper Pilot: Years 1960 through 1970; Piper Aircraft Corporation,
   Lock Haven, Pennsylvania.

3. Piper Aircraft Corporation sales brochures for single- and twin-
   engine airplanes.

MUSEUMS

1. National Air and Space Museum, Smithsonian Institution,
   Washington, D.C.

2. Piper Aviation Museum, Clinton County Historical Society,
   Lock Haven. Pennsylvania.

PERSONAL INTERVIEWS

1. Smith, Clyde Sr.: World War Two and postwar Piper airplanes.

2. Peperell, Roger W.: Taylor and Piper aircraft constructor numbers
   and information regarding prototype and production airplanes.

3. Piper, John: Piper family and Piper Aircraft Corporation history.

In addition to PIPER - A LEGEND ALOFT, Edward H. Phillips has researched and written four additional books on United States light aircraft manufacturers including "Travel Air - Wings Over The Prairie," "Cessna - A Master's Expression," "Wings Of Cessna" and "Beechcraft - Pursuit of Perfection." Phillips also has written historical and technical articles on aviation topics as a free-lance writer, and worked five years for AVIATION WEEK & SPACE TECHNOLOGY magazine. As Business Flying Editor for Aviation Week, he wrote general aviation and aeronautical engineering articles and conducted pilot reports on a wide range of commercial aircraft, including the Piper PA-46-350 Malibu Mirage. He is a member of the Aircraft Owners and Pilots Assocation, the Wichita Aeronautical and Historical Association, the Antique Airplane Association and the Staggerwing Museum Foundation. Phillips is an active general aviation pilot, flight instructor and a licensed airframe and powerplant technician.

Author Edward H. Phillips poses with J-3L-55 NC23420, constructor number 3149, built June 14, 1939, at Lock Haven. The airplane is owned by John J. Reed and is based at Laurel, Delaware.

INDEX